The **Puzzle** of
Ethiopian Politics

The **Puzzle** of **Ethiopian Politics**

Terrence Lyons

LYNNE
RIENNER
PUBLISHERS

BOULDER
LONDON

Published in the United States of America in 2019 by
Lynne Rienner Publishers, Inc.
1800 30th Street, Boulder, Colorado 80301
www.rienner.com

and in the United Kingdom by
Lynne Rienner Publishers, Inc.
Gray's Inn House, 127 Clerkenwell Road, London EC1 5DB

Library of Congress Cataloging-in-Publication Data
Names: Lyons, Terrence, author.
Title: The puzzle of Ethiopian politics / Terrence Lyons.
Description: Boulder, Colorado : Lynne Rienner Publishers, Inc., 2019. |
  Includes bibliographical references and index.
Identifiers: LCCN 2019009433 (print) | LCCN 2019019981 (ebook) | ISBN
  9781626378339 (e-book) | ISBN 9781626377981 (hardcover : alk. paper)
Subjects: LCSH: Ya.Ityorpyea hezboic .abeyoteawi dbemokreasiyeawi genbear.
  [Ethiopian People's Revolutionary Democratic Front] |
  Democratization—Ethiopia. | Ethiopia—Politics and government—1991–
Classification: LCC JQ3769.A586 (ebook) | LCC JQ3769.A586 L96 2019 (print) |
  DDC 320.963—dc23
LC record available at https://lccn.loc.gov/2019009433

British Cataloguing in Publication Data
A Cataloguing in Publication record for this book
is available from the British Library.

Printed and bound in the United States of America

The paper used in this publication meets the requirements
of the American National Standard for Permanence of
Paper for Printed Library Materials Z39.48-1992.

5 4 3 2 1

Contents

Tables and Figures

Tables

Figures

Acknowledgments

As with all books that are years—decades—in the making, I owe many people my sincere thanks for helping me along the way. I first went to Ethiopia in 1986 and have been back dozens of times since then. It sometimes seems as if I have had an ongoing conversation about Ethiopian politics, whether during my fieldwork in the country, talking with Ethiopian students and others living in the diaspora, or meeting colleagues at academic conferences. In this book I try to summarize that conversation at a particular point in time and reflect what I have learned from hundreds of people over the decades.

I would like to thank Leonardo R. Arriola, Mark Bradbury, Christopher Clapham, Dereje Feyissa, Frew Yirgalem, Brian Gilchrest, Hallelujah Lulie, Laura Hammond, John Harbeson, Sally Healy, Edmond J. Keller, Lealem Mersha, Lulsegged Abebe, Harold Marcus, Jim McCann, Ken Menkhaus, Christopher Mitchell, Marina Ottaway, Angela Raven-Roberts, John Ryle, David H. Shinn, Lahra Smith, Kjetil Tronvoll, Steve Tucker, Solomon Dersso, Michael Woldemariam, Josef Woldense, and Terje Østebø. Awetu Simmeso, who passed away before I could share this book with him, was the first person I always sought out whenever I was in Addis Ababa and is greatly missed. In particular I want to recognize the years of discussions and invaluable research assistance of Seife Asfaw.

I have benefited from my students and colleagues at Addis Ababa University and Bahir Dar University, and thank the Fulbright program for sponsoring my time at those two universities. The Rift Valley Institute has provided me opportunities to engage with a wide range of scholars and policy analysts studying the Horn of Africa. At the School for Conflict Analysis and Resolution, George Mason University, I would like to thank Dean Kevin Avruch and the students in my graduate seminars on civil wars. My colleagues Thomas Flores, Agnieszka Paczyńska, Seife Asfaw, and Felegebirhan Belesti read the full draft manuscript and made many suggestions that I know improved the book.

Lynne Rienner encouraged me to write (and finally finish) this book for many years, and I could not ask for a kinder publisher.

I wrote the first draft of the book before the 2018 political changes in Ethiopia and the heartening opening of political space. Because most of my interviews took place when anonymity was necessary for frank discussions, I do not name any of those who agreed to be interviewed or with whom I have spent many hours discussing Ethiopian politics.

I thank all of these people and others for helping me make fewer mistakes in my quest to understand Ethiopian politics. All remaining errors are my own.

I dedicate this book with love to Agnieszka and Nell for all their support over the years. None of this would have happened without them.

1

The Puzzle of
Ethiopian Politics

*The TPLF started in February 1975 as a small guerrilla band in the
northern region of Ethiopia and eventually grew to provide the core
of the Ethiopian government.*
        —*Aregawi Berhe, TPLF founding member[1]*

Down! Down! Woyane!
        —*Protesters at Irreecha celebrations in Bishoftu, October 2016[2]*

The coming time in Ethiopia will be a time of love and forgiveness.
        —*Prime Minister Abiy Ahmed's Inaugural Address, April 2018[3]*

On April 2, 2018, Abiy Ahmed, gave his inaugural speech as
only the third prime minister since the ruling Ethiopian People's Revolutionary Democratic Front (EPRDF) took power in 1991. Abiy came
from the Oromo wing of the ruling party rather than the long-dominant
Tigray leadership. He rose to power at a tumultuous time. The EPRDF
and its affiliated parties won 100 percent of the seats in the 2015 elections and put in place development policies that created a period of
sustained economic growth. By 2016, however, ongoing and sometimes violent protests resulted in tens of thousands of arrests and tensions that did not end with the proclamation of a state of emergency.
In contrast to past patterns of mass arrests and condemnation of dissidents as "antipeace" elements working in league with ruling party
enemies, the new prime minister emphasized the opposite in 2018:
"The coming time in Ethiopia will be a time of love and forgiveness.
We desire our country to be one of justice, peace and freedom and
where its citizens are interconnected with the unbreakable chord of
humanity and brotherhood."[4]

1

Figure 1.1   Political Map of Ethiopia

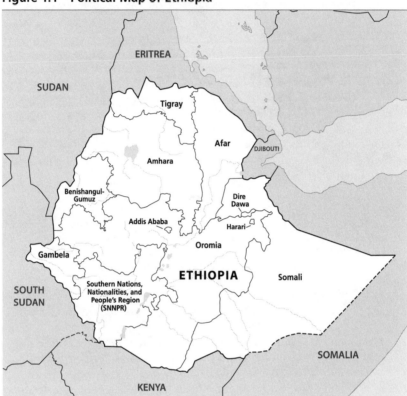

On May 28, 1991, nearly thirty years before Prime Minister Abiy Ahmed's inauguration, rebel soldiers from the northern Ethiopian region of Tigray entered Addis Ababa from four sides and, after a brief fight around the presidential palace, occupied the capital.[5] Mengistu Haile Mariam, leader of the brutal military junta that had ruled since it deposed Emperor Haile Selassie in 1974, had fled to Zimbabwe a week earlier, and his army had collapsed. As described by a Reuters correspondent who traveled with the rebels, the "piles of uniforms and boots dumped along the road" told the story of the breakdown of Mengistu's army and the rapid march of the insurgents.[6] While negotiations with the rump government took place with US mediation in London, the insurgent force moved into the capital, waving the movement's red flag emblazoned with an AK-47 rifle. What had started as a small group of Tigrayan nationalist students in 1974 transformed into the EPRDF, a battle-hardened, Marxist-Leninist, rebel movement that defeated one of Africa's largest militaries. But the EPRDF now faced the daunting challenges of ruling a war-torn country of extraordinary diversity.

In this book I connect these two moments in Ethiopian political history. I argue that the structures and contradictions within the EPRDF are key to understanding the puzzle of Ethiopian politics. This party—actually a coalition of four different parties, as we will see—operates and is structured in ways that reflect the legacies of the armed struggle and the imperatives of the war-to-peace transition. The institutions created in response to the challenges of the late 1980s and early 1990s continue to shape Ethiopian politics today; thus, understanding the EPRDF helps us to comprehend both the stability of the regime and the ways in which it faced crisis and rebalanced itself in 2018.

In the chapters that follow, I trace how the legacies of the protracted armed struggle and the exigencies of the war-to-peace transition shaped the postwar political order in Ethiopia. The militarily victorious EPRDF put in place a political system based upon two contradictory logics. On the one hand, the ruling party exemplified a disciplined, authoritarian, vanguard party organized around the principles of democratic centralism. At the same time, to expand beyond their Tigray base, the winning rebels built a ruling coalition from four diverse, ethnically based parties and wrote a constitution that emphasized ethno-federalism and consequently generated centrifugal force. From 1991 to 2016, this system remained steady because the center was sufficiently strong and the new regional states sufficiently weak to balance the ethno-federal institutions. The demonstrations in 2016 disrupted this balance and provided the opportunity for new leadership to emerge. The EPRDF as a powerful party, however, persisted and continued to dominate politics.

Ethiopia in a Comparative Context: The Importance of Institutions

The literature on Ethiopian politics is abundant, although perhaps less prolific than might be expected given the country's size and regional importance. Scholarship has often emphasized the importance of political culture and the historical process of state building in highland Ethiopia.[7] Smith and others emphasize how citizenship, gender, and other categories contribute to hierarchical social structures that go beyond formal political organizations.[8] Ethnicity and Ethiopian identity have an extensive scholarship and are key parts of contemporary Ethiopian politics, as I will explore in this book.[9] Scholarship assessing the quality of democracy and advocacy work on human rights has received considerable attention.[10]

The historical role of longtime prime minister Meles Zenawi, leader of the Tigray People's Liberation Front (TPLF) insurgency and founder of the EPRDF, has led some to emphasize his personal influence and worldview.[11] The borderlands and center-periphery relationships are another key theme in the literature.[12]

In this book I build on these insights but argue that Ethiopian politics is shaped by a fundamental tension at the core of the EPRDF. On the one hand, drawing from the party's origins as a Marxist insurgency, the EPRDF built a new order based on hierarchy, discipline, and top-down control. On the other hand, driven by the need to transform the Tigrayan rebel movement into a larger coalition to administer the entire state, the EPRDF created new institutions that emphasized ethno-federalism and institutionalized ethnically defined regional states and political parties. The contradictions between these two logics of governing remained in check until 2016, as a strong center checked the initially weak regions and ethnic parties.

In addition to arguments that help explain the puzzle of Ethiopian politics, in this book I contribute to a number of debates within the more general comparative politics and conflict resolution literatures. The scholarship by Staniland, Mampilly, and Arjona on rebel organizations and governance provide useful frames through which to understand the legacies of the Ethiopian civil wars.[13] The Ethiopian regime is in many ways the epitome of an authoritarian system with a strong political party, as suggested by Levitsky and Way, along with electoral authoritarianism, as analyzed by Schedler.[14] The ruling party has been in power since 1991, suggesting resilience and mechanisms to manage intraparty competition, as studied by Svolik.[15] It also provides an important case on the specific characteristics of war-to-peace transitions following rebel victory, as suggested by Lyons.[16] The transformation of the TPLF rebel group into the EPRDF political party, which included constituencies not involved in the armed struggle, demonstrates an important mechanism in the war-to-peace transition that links the insurgency to the strong authoritarian party.

The Legacies of the War and Dynamics of Transition

Ethiopian politics for nearly thirty years have been shaped by how the TPLF won the protracted civil war in 1991 and how the legacies of that war were linked to the mechanisms through which the EPRDF ruled.[17] Civil wars that end in rebel victory generally follow distinct war-to-peace transitions. The transition in Ethiopia, as well as in cases such as Uganda and Rwanda, emphasized power consolidation rather than power sharing and focused on transforming the armed insurgent group into an authoritarian political party.[18] In Ethiopia, the EPRDF used the war-to-peace transition to transform its armed insurgent movement into such a party and to consolidate power. These legacies continue to shape reform efforts in 2018.

The transition in Ethiopia began with military victory, not a negotiated peace settlement. The EPRDF, along with the insurgent Eritrean People's Liberation Front and the Oromo Liberation Front (OLF), met with the remnants of the old regime in London in May 1991, but military facts on the ground rather than negotiations or external powers determined the outcome. Instead of building the conditions for more democratic regimes, this kind of path dependency leads victorious insurgents to build on the successful models that contributed to their victory and to seize opportunities during the war-to-peace transition to consolidate power.[19]

In Ethiopia the legacies of war included high levels of solidarity and leadership coherence forged during the protracted armed struggle along with the precedents and organizational structures developed by the rebels to administer liberated territory. The mechanisms by which the TPLF as an insurgent movement organized and administered areas it occupied during the war were linked to how the TPLF-led EPRDF organized and governed as a ruling party. In addition, the imperative to broaden its political base and incorporate constituencies that had not participated in the armed struggle led the TPLF to create a multiethnic coalition and construct a series of ethnically defined regional states. Finally, transitional processes such as postconflict elections, transitional justice, and demobilization served as effective instruments of power consolidation.

During the protracted civil war, the TPLF developed a cohesive leadership and a disciplined, hierarchical organization that practiced decisionmaking through strict democratic centralism.[20] As I will explore in more detail in Chapter 2, the TPLF emerged out of the Ethiopian student movement in the early 1970s, and, according to its founding story, began with fewer than a hundred fighters.[21] Meles and a small group in the leadership formed the Marxist-Leninist League of Tigray (MLLT) in the mid-1980s, a tightly integrated vanguard within the TPLF, and this coterie led the movement to victory. For much of the armed struggle, the TPLF fought in a relatively confined area in the highlands of Tigray, with relatively limited external support, which reinforced the consolidation of its leadership. The challenges of the protracted struggle resulted in a cohesive leadership, hierarchical lines of decisionmaking, and a disciplined core within the organization.

Although the insurgents developed connections in the countryside in northern Ethiopia, the war did not come to areas inhabited by Oromos and others in southern Ethiopia until the final months of the struggle.

The Oromo People's Democratic Organization (OPDO) and the Southern Ethiopian People's Democratic Movement (SEPDM), two other member parties in the ruling coalition, lacked coherence and experience comparable to those of the TPLF.[22] The EPRDF therefore transitioned from a largely Tigrayan insurgency into a strong multiethnic coalition with a strong and coherent core but dissimilar constituent parties.

Victorious rebels are more likely to have experience in administering liberated territory. Therefore they develop trained, effective, and disciplined cadres with the capacity to govern civilians and with relationships with civilian constituencies and international actors.[23] In Ethiopia, this governance of liberated territory during the armed struggle often created nondemocratic norms and precedents that shaped how the party subsequently operated during peacetime. Wartime administration emphasized discipline and building connections so that the civilian population could support the military strategy. Civilians were not constituents to whom the military leadership must answer but rather auxiliaries who must be indoctrinated and mobilized by the insurgents to meet the goals of the rebellion. Relationship models developed during the civil war between rebel leadership and the population are sustained in postconflict authoritarian systems.

In northern Ethiopia, the TPLF saw itself as a classic, Maoist-style guerrilla army that would win by forging relationships with the peasants of Tigray. The rebels deployed political cadres with their military units and created local *baitos* (people's councils) to assist the TPLF in administering liberated zones. The movement had its own impressive humanitarian wing, the Relief Society of Tigray (REST), which coordinated large-scale operations with international assistance, and the Tigray Development Association (TDA), which raised significant money in the diaspora. The insurgent army played other state-like diplomatic roles, including having extensive (and often contentious) relationships with neighboring insurgents in Eritrea along with international actors and organizations.[24] The TPLF therefore had extensive local administrative structures and foreign relations in place prior to gaining power, and these models developed during wartime shaped the design of postwar institutions. The rebels began the transition in 1991 with not only a large and battle-hardened military but also cadres in nearly every village in Tigray, well integrated into a regionwide political network experienced in managing top-down relationships with the peasants.

Alongside the wartime legacies of organizational coherence and models of military administration, the imperatives of war-to-peace transitions following rebel victory help explain the Ethiopian transition. Victorious rebels are more likely to derive significant legitimacy from the costs endured in defeating the old order and ending the violence—"We rule because we sacrificed!" Rebel tanks on the streets of Addis Ababa provided ample evidence of the effective transfer of power. The war-to-peace transition provides processes such as elections, transitional justice, and demobilization used by the rebel movement to strengthen its authoritarian power. However, victory often allows the winners to break with the past and launch a new vision. They take power with an extraordinary mandate and can use the fear of a return to the old order as a rationale to renounce or abnegate opposition. The EPRDF quickly established a transitional charter, helped establish new political parties in southern Ethiopia, challenged preexisting conceptions of Ethiopian nationalism, and redrew the political map of Ethiopia to create new ethnically defined regions.

In addition to the rebels' specific claims of legitimacy born of sacrifice and victory, the process of transition from war to peace offered many opportunities to consolidate their power. The EPRDF quickly demobilized the Derg's military and reorganized its own armed forces. As the insurgent army transformed itself into the postwar Ethiopian National Defense Forces, it sought to decrease the number of soldiers from Tigray, the core of the rebel movement, and recruit more soldiers from southern Ethiopia so that the national army more closely reflected the country's diversity and looked less like an army of occupation. Although expanding membership among the rank and file, the TPLF's experienced military leaders retained top positions and dominated the officer corps. Transitional justice mechanisms remained under the control of the victorious rebels as well, who organized special prosecutor trials that convicted many high officials of the old regime of war crimes and sentenced Mengistu, the defeated leader of the Derg, to death in absentia.[25]

The legitimacy that comes from winning the war and the experiences of wartime governance are particularly powerful in the immediate aftermath of war termination. Over time, however, these claims and capacities begin to fade. Nearly thirty years after the transition, the majority of the population has no direct memories of the grim years under the Derg, the sacrifices and martyrs of the armed struggle, or the dramatic events of 1991. The ruling party, of course, takes measures to remind the population of its role as liberator. "Derg Downfall Day" is a national holiday celebrated every May 28.[26] But it is not surprising that over time the resonance of these events fades, and different forms of legitimacy are necessary. The protests of 2016 and the new leadership of 2018 are in part the outcome of this decline in the legitimacy earned through military victory.

War-to-Peace Transition: Creating a Ruling Coalition

Despite its military accomplishments, the EPRDF faced a significant challenge upon seizing power. Large national constituencies played little or no role in the armed struggle. The civil war was fought in the north, and numerous communities in the south knew little about the insurgents prior to the regime change in 1991. Some Amhara had direct experience in the armed struggle, but many of them prioritized a pan-Ethiopian identity. The OLF mobilized the key Oromo constituency, but the OLF and TPLF had generally contentious relations. Others in rural provinces in southern Ethiopia such as southern Omo, or Gamo-Gofa (today the Southern Nations, Nationalities, and People's Region, or SNNPR) were subject to the Derg's compulsory recruitment into military service but otherwise had limited roles in the civil war and never experienced living in liberated territory. Most Ethiopians had little contact with the rebel movement during the war. Because of this, the leadership of the EPRDF rapidly created local affiliates in these areas to serve as its interlocutors with populations outside of its wartime networks. These affiliated parties often emerged virtually overnight, and many had only tenuous links to the often quite isolated communities in question.

For the EPRDF, creating a national political party on the basis of an ethnoregional rebel group that could make appeals across Ethiopia's many diverse communities was a fundamental challenge and an essential step to consolidating its power. In 1991, the organization was overwhelmingly Tigrayan, with some Amhara and few Oromo members. As the TPLF created the EPRDF, it formed a coalition of ethnonational parties so that, in the same way the TPLF ruled Tigray, the OPDO would rule Oromia, and similar parties would rule each group in the SNNPR. The insurgent national liberation organizational model was replicated in other regions regardless of whether they had the historical sense of identity or experience of wartime solidarity that characterized Tigray.

The EPRDF organized elections and in other ways used political processes to consolidate and sustain its rule. Political parties in authoritarian states can serve a bargaining function in that they broker relationships among elites and create systems for distributing power and authority across both individuals and constituencies. In Ethiopia, for example, intraparty processes rather than public campaigns or violence determined who would occupy the key decisionmaking positions in the EPRDF's Executive Committee, Council of Ministers, and regional state offices. The party used elections not to provide opportunities for meaningful competition but rather to demonstrate power, reshuffle leadership, sometimes co-opt rivals, and, perhaps most importantly, create incentives for party loyalty, thus consolidating power.

Elections following rebel victory in Ethiopia therefore had little to do with determining who would rule but played key functions in power consolidation and the creation of the strong, authoritarian EPRDF party. These polls are typically noncompetitive, as was the case in Ethiopia's elections of 1995, 2000, 2010, and 2015. The exception, as I discuss in Chapter 6, was the contentious 2005 election. In the 2010 and 2015 national elections, however, the EPRDF and its affiliates won 99.6 and 100 percent of the seats, respectively. These overwhelming victories sent a message that the authoritarian party remained dominant and was not about to surrender power and that acquiescence to it was necessary for political survival. The question of whether the 2020 elections can provide an opportunity for Ethiopians to meaningfully participate in the selection of their leaders remains a matter of contention among key Ethiopian actors and analysts.

The successful transition from rebel victory to a postwar authoritarian political party was therefore related to the nature of the victorious insurgent group—its leadership cohesion and the legacies of its wartime administration—along with the imperatives of war-to-peace transitions. The exigencies of transforming an insurgent group based in a particular small community into a larger, multiethnic political party able to govern all of Ethiopia led to a coalition of diverse constituent members acting in coordination.

In this book I explain Ethiopian politics from 1991 to 2018 by tracing the legacies of the armed struggle and the war-to-peace transition of political institutions and the ruling party in particular. I argue that these two forces created a strong and centralized ruling party that held together a clamorous coalition built upon ethnically defined parties and autonomous regional states. These two contradictory logics balanced centrifugal forces with a strong center. In 2018, however, after a period of sustained protests indicated that the old balance had been disrupted, a new leader, Prime Minister Abiy Ahmed, seeks to realign power among the political elites and reconsolidate the EPRDF's power. Although the consequences of the leadership change are difficult to predict, the EPRDF remains the dominant party at this writing and seems likely to remain so.

A Note on Sources
This book builds on research that I have conducted since my first trip to Ethiopia in 1986 to carry out doctoral dissertation research. In the ensuing thirty-three years I have been back several dozen times for varying

lengths of time and in a variety of roles. In this book I draw on my experiences in observing elections in 1992, serving as the leader of the Donor Election Unit (DEU) in 1995, and serving as a senior adviser to the Carter Center's election observation mission in 2005.[27] I have also consulted with a range of international nongovernmental organizations regarding their programs in Ethiopia.[28] These occasions allowed me to travel throughout the country and to conduct hundreds of interviews with the diplomatic community, government officials, opposition party activists, civil society leaders, and Ethiopians in numerous small towns and rural villages in virtually every region.[29] I have engaged in hundreds of interviews and less formal conversations with a wide variety of Ethiopians over the decades, both in Ethiopia and in the diaspora.[30] I have participated in dozens of discussions and briefings convened by various research institutes.[31] I have taught at Addis Ababa University and Bahir Dar University.

In this book I build on this prior research and on the work of many scholars and colleagues who have helped me gain a better understanding of Ethiopia and to make fewer mistakes. I cite secondary and primary sources throughout this book. Given uncertain conditions within Ethiopia, I cite only year and location to identify interviews.

Outline of the Book

In this book I explain the puzzle of contemporary postwar Ethiopian politics by highlighting the institutional legacies of the civil war and the mechanisms of transitioning from a regionally based national liberation movement into a diverse ruling party. In Chapter 1 I frame the mechanisms that link insurgent victory and strong authoritarian political party and the process of war-to-peace transition. In Chapter 2 I focus on the period of violent conflict and how the different actors engaged in contemporary Ethiopian politics experienced and were transformed by that period of struggle. In Chapter 3 I emphasize the logic behind a postconflict dispensation that organized politics around ethnically defined regions and noncompetitive elections. These two aspects of these new rules highlight the central contradiction of a political system with significant levels of federalism and a party simultaneously centralized and hierarchical.

In Chapter 4 I examine the EPRDF and the significant differences among the member parties that compose the ruling coalition. The legacies of the civil war in battle-scared Tigray bear little resemblance to large areas of Oromia and the South in general, and the TPLF is not like the OPDO or the SEPDM. This variation is significant and helps explain many intraparty dynamics. In this chapter I also look at the degree to which these four parties have put in place four distinct political systems in their respective regions. In Chapter 5 I shift the focus to the Ethiopian opposition. Understanding the limitations on political opposition is essential to comprehending how the ruling party operates as a strong authoritarian party. In Chapter 6 I trace political developments from the 2005 electoral crisis and subsequent crackdown to the 2015 election, in which the EPRDF and its affiliates won 100 percent of the seats, and I demonstrate how intraparty dynamics shaped Ethiopian politics. In that chapter I also analyze the different patterns of central committee appointments across the four member parties of the EPRDF to understand both the early dominance of the TPLF and the leadership change within the party in 2018. In Chapter 7 I emphasize the political implications of the regime's economic policies and its commitment to a "developmental state" model. In Chapter 8 I look at the 2016 demonstrations and how they challenged parts of the EPRDF's legitimacy but, at the same time, provided space for Oromo and Amhara reformers to align with the demands of the populace while seeking to consolidate power within the party. In Chapter 9 I examine patterns of behavior visible within the EPRDF over decades to explain how new leadership took power in 2018. In Chapter 10 I draw together the implications of the argument both for our understanding of Ethiopia and for the comparative literatures on authoritarian parties and war-to-peace transitions.

Notes

1. Aregawi Berhe, "The Origins of the Tigray People's Liberation Front," *African Affairs* 103, no. 413 (2004): 569.
2. *Woyane* is a reference to the TPLF guerrilla forces. The Irreecha celebration led to a deadly stampede following security forces' efforts to disperse a crowd of Oromos.
3. Hassen Hussein, "Full [*sic*] English Transcript of Ethiopian Prime Minister Abiy Ahmed's Inaugural Address," Opride.com, April 3, 2018, https://www.opride.com/2018/04/03/english-partial-transcript-of-ethiopian-prime-minister-abiy-ahmeds-inaugural-address/.
4. Hussein, "Full [*sic*] English Transcript of Abiy Ahmed's Inaugural Address."
5. Peter Biles, "Addis Ababa Falls to Dawn Onslaught," *Guardian,* May 29, 1991.
6. Aidan Hartley, "Ethiopian Rebels Swept Past Demoralized Government Forces," Reuters, May 27, 1991. Hartley describes this scene in his memoir, *The Zanzibar Chest: The Story of Life, Love, and Death in Foreign Lands* (New York: Grove, 2004).
7. Christopher Clapham, *Haile Selassie's Government* (London: Longman, 1969); Clapham, *Transformation and Continuity in Revolutionary Ethiopia* (Cambridge, UK: Cambridge University Press, 1988); René Lefort, "Powers—Mengist—and Peasants in Rural Ethiopia: The May 2005 Elections," *Journal of*

Modern African Studies 45, no. 2 (2007): 253–276; Lefort, "Power—Mengist—and Peasants in Rural Ethiopia: The Post 2005 Interlude," *Journal of Modern African Studies* 48, no. 3 (2010): 435–460; Kjetil Tronvoll, "Ambiguous Elections: The Influence of Non-electoral Politics in Ethiopian Democratisation," *Journal of Modern African Studies* 47, no. 3 (September 2009): 449–474.

8. Lahra Smith, *Making Citizens in Africa: Ethnicity, Gender, and National Identity in Ethiopia* (Cambridge, UK: Cambridge University Press, 2013).

9. Lovise Aalen, *The Politics of Ethnicity in Ethiopia: Actors, Power, and Mobilisation Under Ethnic Federalism* (Leiden: Brill, 2011); Sarah Vaughan and Kjetil Tronvoll, *The Culture of Power in Contemporary Ethiopian Political Life,* SIDA Studies No. 10 (Stockholm: Swedish International Development Cooperation Agency, 2003); Asnake Kefale, *Federalism and Ethnic Conflict in Ethiopia: A Comparative Regional Study* (London: Routledge, 2013); Leonardo R. Arriola, "Protesting and Policing in a Multiethnic Authoritarian State," *Comparative Politics* 45, no. 2 (January 2013).

10. Kjetil Tronvoll and Tobias Hagmann, eds., *Contested Power in Ethiopia: Traditional Authorities and Multi-party Elections* (Leiden: Brill, 2012); Siegfried Pausewang, Kjetil Tronvoll, and Lovise Aalen, eds., *Ethiopia Since the Derg: A Decade of Democratic Pretension and Performance* (London: Zed, 2002); Leonardo R. Arriola and Terrence Lyons, "Ethiopia's 100% Election," *Journal of Democracy* 27, no. 1 (January 2016): 76–88. On human rights, see the documentation by the Ethiopian Human Rights Council and Human Rights Watch.

11. Gérard Prunier, "The Meles Zenawi Era: From Revolutionary Marxism to State Developmentalism," in Gérard Prunier and Éloi Ficquet, eds., *Understanding Contemporary Ethiopia: Monarchy, Revolution, and the Legacy of Meles Zenawi* (London: Hurst, 2015); Alex de Waal, "The Theory and Practice of Meles Zenawi," *African Affairs* 112, no. 446 (January 2013): 148–155.

12. Dereje Feyissa and Markus Virgil Hoehn, eds., *Borders and Borderlands as Resources in the Horn of Africa* (London: James Currey, 2010); Dereje Feyissa, *Playing Different Games: The Paradox of Anywaa and Nuer Identification in the Gambella Region, Ethiopia* (New York: Berghahn, 2011); Tobias Hagmann, "Punishing the Periphery: Legacies of State Repression in the Ethiopian Ogaden," *Journal of Eastern African Studies* 8, no. 4 (2014): 725–739; John Markakis, *Ethiopia: The Last Two Frontiers* (Oxford, UK: James Currey, 2011).

13. Zachariah Cherian Mampilly, *Rebel Rulers: Insurgent Governance and Civilian Life During War* (Ithaca, NY: Cornell University Press, 2011); Paul Staniland, *Networks of Rebellion: Explaining Insurgent Cohesion and Collapse* (Ithaca, NY: Cornell University Press, 2014); Ana Arjona, *Rebelocracy: Social Order in the Colombian Civil War* (Cambridge, UK: Cambridge University Press, 2016). See also Ana Arjona, Nelson Kasfir, and Zachariah Cherian Mampilly, eds., *Rebel Governance in Civil Wars* (Cambridge, UK: Cambridge University Press, 2015).

14. Steven R. Levitsky and Lucan A. Way, *Competitive Authoritarianism: Hybrid Regimes After the Cold War* (Cambridge, UK: Cambridge University Press, 2010); Levitsky and Way, "Beyond Patronage: Violent Struggle, Ruling Party Cohesion, and Authoritarian Durability," *Perspectives on Politics* 10, no. 4 (December 2012): 869–889; Andreas Schedler, ed., *Electoral Authoritarianism: The Dynamics of Unfree Competition* (Boulder, CO: Lynne Rienner, 2006).

15. Milan W. Svolik, *The Politics of Authoritarian Rule* (Cambridge, UK: Cambridge University Press, 2012). See also Jennifer Gandhi, *Political Institutions Under Dictatorship* (Cambridge, UK: Cambridge University Press, 2008).

16. Terrence Lyons, "The Importance of Winning: Victorious Insurgent Groups and Authoritarian Politics," *Comparative Politics* 48, no. 2 (January 2016): 167–184.

17. For war-to-peace transitions in general, see Stephen John Stedman, Donald Rothchild, and Elizabeth M. Cousens, eds., *Ending Civil Wars: The Implementation of Peace Agreements* (Boulder, CO: Lynne Rienner, 2002); Philip G. Roeder and Donald Rothchild, eds., *Sustainable Peace: Power and Democracy After Civil Wars* (Ithaca, NY: Cornell University Press, 2005); Anna K. Jarstad and Timothy D. Sisk, eds., *From War to Democracy: Dilemmas of Peacebuilding* (Cambridge, UK: Cambridge University Press, 2008); Charles T. Call, *Why Peace Fails: The Causes and Prevention of Civil War Recurrence* (Washington, DC: Georgetown University Press, 2012); Christoph Zürcher, Carrie Manning, Kristie D. Evenson, Rachel Hayman, Sarah Riese, and Nora Roehner, *Costly Democracy: Peacebuilding and Democratization After War* (Palo Alto, CA: Stanford University Press, 2013).

18. For a comparative examination of this process, see Terrence Lyons, "Victorious Rebels and Postwar Politics," *Civil Wars* 18, no. 2 (2016): 160–174. Côte d'Ivoire serves as another similar case, although with much more substantial international peacebuilding engagement. See Giulia Piccolino, "Peacebuilding and Statebuilding in Post-2011 Côte d'Ivoire: A Victor's Peace?" *African Affairs* 117, no. 468 (July 2018): 485–508.

19. Levitsky and Way, *Competitive Authoritarianism*; Beatriz Magaloni, *Voting for Autocracy: Hegemonic Party Survival and Its Demise in Mexico* (Cambridge, UK: Cambridge University Press, 2006); Gandhi, *Political Institutions Under Dictatorship*; Jason Brownlee, *Authoritarianism in an Age of Democratization* (Cambridge, UK: Cambridge University Press, 2007). For a review of the literature see Beatriz Magaloni and Ruth Krischeli, "Political Order and One-party Rule," *Annual Review of Political Science* 3 (2010): 123–143.

20. John Young, *Peasant Revolution in Ethiopia: The Tigray People's Liberation Front, 1975–1991* (Cambridge, UK: Cambridge University Press, 1997); Jenny Hammond, *Fire from the Ashes: A Chronicle of the Revolution in Tigray, Ethiopia* (Lawrenceville, NJ: Red Sea, 1999). For a general discussion of democratic centralism, see Michael Waller, *Democratic Centralism: An Historical Commentary* (Manchester, UK: Manchester University Press, 1981).

21. Aregawi Berhe, *A Political History of the Tigray People's Liberation Front (1975–1991): Revolt, Ideology, and Mobilisation in Ethiopia* (Los Angeles: Teshai, 2009).

22. Vaughan, "Revolutionary Democratic State-Building." The SEPDM evolved out of the Southern Ethiopian People's Democratic Front (SEPDF), formed by the EPRDF in 1992 after the war ended.

23. Mampilly, *Rebel Rulers*; Staniland, *Networks of Rebellion*.

24. Barbara Hendrie, "The Politics of Repatriation: The Tigrayan Refugee Repatriation, 1985–1987," *Journal of Refugee Studies* 4, no. 2 (June 1991): 200–218; John Prendergast and Mark Duffield, *Without Troops and Tanks: The Emergency Relief Desk and the Cross Border Operation in Eritrea and Tigray* (Trenton, NJ: Red Sea, 1994).

25. Kjetil Tronvoll, Charles Schaefer, and Girmachew Alemu Aneme, eds., *The Ethiopian Red Terror Trials: Transitional Justice Challenged* (Oxford, UK: James Currey, 2009); John Ryle, "Letter from Ethiopia: An African Nuremberg," *New Yorker* (October 29, 1995).

26. On the twenty-fifth anniversary, in 2016, however, the young crowd that attended these celebrations in the Amhara regional capital of Bahir Dar was generally uninterested in the political speeches but happy about the dance music played between the testimonial speeches. Author's field notes, Bahir Dar, 2016.

27. See "The Transition Toward Democracy in Ethiopia: Observations on the Elections in Welega, June 1992," testimony before the US House of Representatives Foreign Affairs Subcommittee on Africa, September 17, 1992; "The Donor Election Unit's Leaked Report," *Ethiopian Register* 2, no. 5 (July 1995): 41–53; Carter Center, *Observing the 2005 Ethiopian National Elections: Carter Center Final Report* (Atlanta, GA: Carter Center, December 2009).

28. This report has not been released by the US Agency for International Development (USAID).

29. Given the nature of my research, most of my interviews have taken place in Addis Ababa, but I have also had the chance to conduct interviews in the Oromia, Amhara, SNNPR, Somali, Benishangul-Gumuz, Gambela, Harar, and Tigray National Regional States over the years.

30. For an account of one set of dialogues, see Terrence Lyons, Christopher Mitchell, Tamra Pearson d'Estrée, and Lulsegged Abebe, *The Ethiopian Extended Dialogue: An Analytical Report, 2000–2003,* Report No. 4 (Fairfax, VA: Institute for Conflict Analysis and Resolution, 2004), http://activity.scar.gmu.edu/sites/default/files/ICAR%20Report%204-%20Lyons.pdf.

31. US Congress, House Subcommittee on Africa, Global Health, Global Human Rights, and International Organizations, "Democracy Under Threat in Ethiopia," March 9, 2017, http://docs.house.gov/meetings/FA/FA16/20170309/105673/HHRG-115-FA16-Wstate-LyonsT-20170309.pdf. Policy papers include "The Political Economy of Ethiopia," Rift Valley Institute for UNICEF, March 2016, https://www.unicef.org/esaro/UNICEF_Ethiopia_--_2016_--_The_Political_Economy_of_Ethiopia.pdf; "Ethiopia: Assessing Risks to Stability," Washington, DC: Center for Strategic and International Studies, June 2011, http://csis.org/publication/ethiopia; *Avoiding Conflict in the Horn of Africa: U.S. Policy Toward Ethiopia and Eritrea,* Special Report no. 21 (New York: Council on Foreign Relations, December 2006), http://www.cfr.org/publication/12192/; Terrence Lyons, "Ethiopia in 2005: The Beginning of a Transition?" *Africa Notes* No. 25 (Washington, DC: Center for Strategic and International Studies, January 2006), 1–8, http://csis.org/files/media/csis/pubs/anotes_0601.pdf; "The Transition in Ethiopia." *Africa Notes* No. 127 (Washington, DC: Center for Strategic and International Studies, August 1991), https://www.csis.org/analysis/africa-notes-transition-ethiopia-august-1991.

2

Legacies of War

To understand the contemporary nature of the Ethiopian People's Revolutionary Democratic Front (EPRDF), the ruling party in Ethiopia since 1991, it is necessary to trace its origins back to the political and military struggles of the 1970s and 1980s. The strong, multiethnic ruling party that dominates Ethiopia today began as a small group of Tigrayan nationalists/Marxist rebels, under attack from multiple sides and struggling to remain alive in the rugged terrain of northern Ethiopia. In this chapter I analyze how the period of armed struggle helped create the rebel party that at the time of the transition was cohesive and disciplined, had experience in administering liberated territory, and had an initial measure of legitimacy because of its wartime sacrifices. Other key political actors, including the other constituent parties in the EPRDF as well as opposition parties, had different legacies coming out of the civil war. I begin by providing some background on the Haile Selassie (1930–1974) and Derg (1974–1991) regimes and then focus on how organizations forged during the civil war shaped the postwar political order.

The Historical Origins of an Authoritarian Political Order

The Imperial State, 1930–1974

Ethiopia traces its origins as an independent political entity to the ancient kingdom of Axum, which emerged in the highland plateaus of Tigray around 500 BC. After 330 AD, when the royalty converted to Christianity, the Ethiopian Orthodox Church provided an important element of continuity and unity. As Ethiopia's rulers' authority and power waxed and waned over the ensuing centuries, its territory expanded and

15

contracted. During the Zemene Mesafint (Era of the Princes, 1769–1855), the emperor was reduced to a figurehead, and different warlords fought among themselves for territorial control and resources. In the late 1800s, under Emperors Tewodros and Menelik II, the empire reconsolidated and expanded southward to incorporate new communities beyond the original Amhara and Tigrayan inhabitants of the northern highlands. In 1890 Italy created the coastal colony of Eritrea. Emperor Menelik II defeated Rome's attempt to conquer the rest of Ethiopia in the 1896 battle of Adwa, a major event still memorialized in Ethiopia.[1]

While Ethiopia rebuffed Italian imperialism in the north, it practiced its own form of imperial rule in the south.[2] To oversimplify a complex history, northern, highland, Orthodox Christian, Amhara speakers dominated southern, lowland, Muslim agriculturalist and pastoralist people. The Ethiopian empire, however, incorporated these different groups in specific ways, and there are a multitude of microhistories about particular communities and regions. In what Markakis labels the "highland periphery," the imperial regime integrated groups such as the Oromo, Gurage, Sidama, Hadiya, and Kambata. Some local elites were "Amharaized," or assimilated into the dominant ruling group. Oromo rulers such as Abba Jifar in Jimma and Ras Gobana in the Gibe states in Wellega accommodated the new imperial order and retained considerable autonomy in exchange for tribute and loyalty.[3] Others, such as the leaders in Wolayita and Kaffa in southern Ethiopia, resisted and suffered defeat and brutal occupation.

In the lowland periphery, which included many Oromo pastoral groups (Borana, Guji), Somali, Afar, the many small groups in the southern Omo region (Aari, Maale, Dassanech, Hamar), and the border regions (Anuak, Berta, Gumuz, and Nuer) the imperial state had little presence, and local leaders and traditions retained considerable authority.[4] The legacies of the different processes of incorporation among communities remain part of the contemporary Ethiopian political landscape. The authenticity of the *indigene* (the group with a legitimate claim to authority and resources) remains contentious. The mobilization against the imperial regime of Haile Selassie and the insurgencies against the Derg drew in part upon the historical grievances and sense of marginalization these populations experienced.

Haile Selassie was crowned emperor in 1930 (after serving as regent from 1916 to 1930 during the reign of Empress Zewditu). The Italians invaded in late 1935 and successfully occupied all of Ethiopia, despite an emotional appeal for collective security by the emperor at the League of Nations. Local forces known as the Black Lions, who operated from within Ethiopia while Haile Selassie spent the war in exile, provided a new model for Ethiopian resistance that moved beyond the historical patterns of *shifta* (banditry).[5] In 1941, a British-led force working alongside Ethiopian guerrillas liberated the country.[6] One outcome of World War II in East Africa was that the former Italian colony of Eritrea was federated with the Ethiopian empire. The consequent Eritrean struggle for self-determination resulted in the civil war fought from 1962 until the Eritrean People's Liberation Front (EPLF) victory in 1991.[7]

In the post–World War II era, Haile Selassie began to adopt aspects of "modernization," notably in the areas of higher education and a professional military, but the empire remained dominated by the "classic trinity of noble, priest, and peasant," distinguished by their "relationship to the only means of production, that is, land."[8] Haile Selassie was an autocrat who sought to modernize but not transform his empire.[9] Marcus credits Haile Selassie with "fostering unity through the development of national institutions, and building a national economy, modern communications, and an official culture whose main feature was the use of Amharic language in government and education."[10] This nation-building project struggled to overcome the cultural hierarchy under which an elite composed largely of Amhara-speaking, Orthodox Christian highlanders failed to integrate people from the periphery, particularly Muslim pastoral groups.[11] In broad terms, this resulted in a country stratified along ethnic lines, from northern agricultural elites to marginalized populations in the south. The emperor's modernization efforts did not touch land reform—the key source of imperial power—and Ethiopia remained in an essentially feudal state into the 1970s.

By the late 1960s, leftist students, some of whom had been educated in Europe and North America, mobilized against the imperial order. This generation of student activists transformed political thinking in Ethiopia and provided much of the political leadership both in government and opposition for the next fifty years. The student movement firmly endorsed Marxism-Leninism and resisted the subjugation of the peasants with the slogan "Land to the Tiller!" Radicals within the student movement debated the issue of Ethiopian identity, or the "national question."[12] This framework emphasized the oppression of marginalized national communities rather than an exclusively class-conflict focus. The student movement split into those who argued that popular mobilization must be based on class solidarity and those who argued that the national question must be resolved first through a liberation struggle for the marginalized nationals. Debates on these issues divided the students into bitter rivalries that soon became deadly.

The Ethiopian Revolution

With Marxist study groups came student agitation and circulation of ideological pamphlets, the empire's legitimacy began to crack. The regime's failure to respond to famine in northern Ethiopia undermined it as well. Soldiers stationed in remote Negele, near the Kenyan border, mutinied over bad food and delays in salary payment. When the emperor faltered in his response, mutinies quickly spread to Debre Zeit, Addis Ababa, and Asmara. A "creeping coup" undermined the imperial order. A military committee, known as the Derg, eventually deposed Haile Selassie. The junta killed the emperor, other leading members of the royal family, and government officials. The Derg nationalized land and replaced relations with the United States with close ties to the Soviet Union. Some have characterized the revolution as being hijacked or "betrayed" by the military.[13] The Ethiopian revolution, however, was far more than a military coup and, along with those in Russia and China, is one of the great revolutions of the twentieth century.[14]

The student movement broke into several factions, divided by ideological differences and personal rivalries that appear minor today.[15] The Marxist-Leninist Ethiopian People's Revolutionary Party (EPRP) and the All-Ethiopia Socialist Movement (known by its Amharic acronym Meison) were ardent supporters of the revolution, and each believed it should be the vanguard party through which the military would rule. This rivalry broke down into violent street battles and assassinations, with the Derg providing weapons and support to Meison in a period known as the Red Terror (1976–1977). The violence was not limited to Addis Ababa but erupted in daylight assassinations in smaller provincial towns in the north as well.[16] Both groups were shattered, with remnants fleeing to the countryside or into exile.

The destruction of the EPRP and Meison in the cities shifted the focus of resistance from urban uprising to rural insurgency. The surviving militants of the EPRP fled to Mount Asimba (on what is now the Ethiopian-Eritrean border), where they eventually fought and lost to their rivals in the Tigray People's Liberation Front (TPLF). Some EPRP members formed the Ethiopian People's Democratic Movement, which eventually formed an alliance with the TPLF, while others went into exile, where they remained highly politicized and key players in Ethiopia's transnational politics (see discussion in Chapter 5). Many of the political movements active in Ethiopia in the 1990s and 2000s trace their lineages back to their resistance to the Derg and, for some, their violent rivalry with the TPLF.

The Derg: 1974–1991

The Derg put in place several policies and institutions that shaped the subsequent period under the EPRDF. These included instituting land reform, creating neighborhood associations designed to control and collect information, and changing the role of the military in politics. Perhaps the most revolutionary act of the Derg was land reform. As Markakis noted, "The 1975 Land Reform was an authentic revolutionary act, a landmark in the country's history symbolizing a clear rupture with the past by wiping out the economic foundations of the *ancien régime*."[17] The nationalization of land ended an imperial order based on northern *neftenya* ("men with guns," or feudal lords) dominating southern peasants. Church lands were also nationalized, transforming the relationship of the Orthodox establishment and the Ethiopian government.

By 1977 Mengistu Haile Mariam consolidated his power in the Derg by assassinating a number of rivals. His rule lasted until 1991 and caused constant warfare that made economic development impossible, put in place an intricate system of control of the population, and dramatically shifted resources to the armed forces.[18] The Soviet Union, the Eastern bloc, and Cuba provided considerable military assistance, and East Germany provided capacity building training to the police and intelligence services.[19]

Clapham argues that the Derg rapidly and effectively put in place policies of "encadrement" that incorporated local communities into structures of central control. "It sought to intensify the long-standing trajectory of centralized state formation by removing the perceived sources of peripheral discontent and espousing an ideal of nation-statehood in which citizens would equally be associated with, and subjected to, an omnipotent state."[20] The Derg's resettlement and villagization campaigns were the most dramatic manifestation of its desire to reengineer the underdeveloped society. Between 1984 and 1986, during the height of famine, the regime moved an estimated 600,000 people from the cool, dry highland areas in northern Ethiopia, where insurgents operated, to the hot, wet lowlands, where the land was portrayed as "unoccupied" but where highlanders often faced unfamiliar diseases and farming methods and hostility from displaced indigenous populations.[21] The Derg's Agricultural Marketing Corporation assessed quotas and paid little for the grain small farmers were compelled to sell, allowing the Derg to monopolize resources. This led to "agricultural involution," the withdrawal of crops from the market, and a return to subsistence farming in some areas.[22] The Derg regime created a centralized garrison state that sought to control its population and attacked its enemies with brutal military force.[23]

The revolutionary regime faced the sustained threat of rebellion from Eritrean liberation movements in the North, Somalia and Somali-speaking Ethiopians in the East, the Oromo Liberation Front in the populous Oromo zone, Tigray nationalists in the North, and a range of rebellions led by national liberation fronts in different regions along the marginalized borderlands. In response, the Derg expanded the size of Ethiopia's armed forces from 46,000 to nearly 500,000 between 1974 and 1991. This required conscription and enormous quantities of military equipment, largely supplied by the Soviet Union. In several instances, the Derg used poorly trained, lightly armed, peasant militias as shock troops. Mengistu placed political commissars within each military unit, creating a divided command that contributed to key military defeats and low morale. An attempted coup in May 1989 led to the execution of many of the military's most capable officers, further accelerating the collapse of the army and hence the regime.[24]

The most important insurgent force was the EPLF, which had defeated its rival, the Eritrean Liberation Front, in the 1970s and fought a bloody and sustained struggle for independence of the former Italian colony.[25] The Derg launched multiple, costly military campaigns to defeat the Eritreans without success. The TPLF also fought the Derg in northern Ethiopia and sometimes coordinated its actions with the EPLF.[26] The Ethiopian army suffered major military reversals in battles against the EPLF at Afabet (March 1988) and Massawa (February 1990) and the TPLF in Shire (February 1989) and Guna (February 1990).[27] In May 1991, with the EPLF in control of almost all of Eritrea and the TPLF-led EPRDF surrounding Addis Ababa, Mengistu fled into exile in Zimbabwe, and the war effectively ended.

The Derg regime brought war, repression, and economic hardship to Ethiopia and Eritrea. The legacies of the Derg and of the rebellion against its rule continue to shape politics in postwar Ethiopia. In particular the Derg's 1974 land reform remains in place, and the *kebele* system of neighborhood associations remains a ubiquitous feature of Ethiopian life today. The Derg's violent policies to centralize power and repress liberation movements spawned insurgencies based on nationality. The TPLF, OLF, and national liberation movements mobilized among the Somali and the Afar have their origins in resistance to the Derg's efforts to impose national unity and a strong central state through force. These legacies played crucial roles in the postwar, ethnofederal constitutional order.

The Ethiopian Civil Wars, 1977–1991

The story of the civil war against the Derg includes a set of distinct, if interlinked, conflicts. Marxist parties that developed out of the student movement fought a brutal political campaign from 1977 to 1978, largely in urban areas. The struggle for national liberation in Eritrea, led by the Eritrean Liberation Front and later the EPLF, originated during Haile Selassie's regime and had as its goal the creation of an independent state. The TPLF at first focused on liberating Tigray but then later in the war shifted its aim to forming the multiethnic EPRDF coalition to defeat the Derg and create a new national government. The OLF fought for national liberation of the Oromo people. Other liberation groups pursued their own agendas among the Afar, Somali, Sidama, and so on. These different fronts had a common goal in defeating the Derg but otherwise had different histories, agendas, constituencies, and tactics to mobilize and organize resources for warfare.[28] The EPLF and TPLF had significant and often contentious relations with each other and, to a more limited extent, with the OLF.

Large areas of the country, particularly in the South, remained outside of the principal war zones, and their populations experienced the conflict in different ways than those in Eritrea, Tigray, and other areas of armed combat and liberated zones did. The civil war included internecine violence among a variety of anti-Derg insurgents. The TPLF, for example, at times clashed with the Ethiopian People's Revolutionary Army and the Ethiopian Democratic Union and had difficult and often hostile relations with the EPLF, OLF, and the Afar Liberation Front. Not surprisingly, postwar institutions were shaped by the diverse legacies of the prolonged conflict—in particular, the significantly different ones of northern communities and parties that directly experienced the war and southern communities with less salient, indirect involvement.

In this book I focus on Ethiopian politics after the civil war. I will say little about the liberation war and its consequences in Eritrea because the legacies of that war have their own dynamics, felt most strongly in Eritrea. Issues relating to Eritrea that remained unresolved despite the political dispensation of 1991, which shaped the subsequent border war of 1998–2000 with important consequences for Ethiopian politics, will be part of my analysis. My argument here largely focuses on the politics in the four regional states of Tigray, Amhara, Oromo, and the Southern Nations, Nationalities, and People's Region, governed by the four member parties of the EPRDF. These four, along with the capital, Addis Ababa, represent more than 90 percent of Ethiopia's population and are the central core of the state. This, of course, is not to say that politics in the four developing regions—Somali, Afar, Gambela, and Benishangul-Gumuz—are not important and worthy of study. In fact, the EPRDF made claims to legitimacy based on liberating and empowering these previously marginalized communities. It is rather to argue that focusing on the EPRDF and how it relates to the four main regions best explains the fundamental dynamics of postwar, statewide politics.[29]

Political Life During Wartime: Insurgents as Proto–Political Parties

To survive the harsh environment of protracted civil war, rebel groups simultaneously must operate as military organizations, have the ability to mobilize resources, and function in ways similar to peacetime political parties. As Collier and his colleagues note, a successful insurgency is simultaneously a political party, a military organization, and a business organization, and this "triple feature" is essential to understanding protracted armed conflict.[30] In this formulation, civil war is a form of contentious politics that requires a particular type of organization: the insurgent group. Political life during wartime, therefore, is shaped in significant ways by how rebel movements engage with civilians and operate as proto–political parties.

Southall emphasizes how violence shapes politics during armed struggle. "War is violent, and the use of violence in politics comes at the expense of the gentler virtues which make for a good society."[31] In particular, an armed struggle reinforces hierarchy at the expense of internal democracy. Rival organizations are treated as backstabbing traitors rather than legitimate competitors in a marketplace of ideas. Organizations operating in the context of civil war must respond successfully to specific incentives and opportunities of war or collapse under the pressures. The presence of protracted violence leads to modes of governance in the form of norms, expectations, and patterns of behavior. These expectations shape perceptions of what is politically feasible and thereby create the political context in which strategies are considered and adopted. The sustained violence of civil war is clear evidence of the failure of one system of governance. But the patterns of violence and consequent expectations are themselves reflections of another type of order, not a sign of collapse or ungoverned population. For example, Menkhaus argues that in Somalia an informal mosaic of business groups, traditional authorities, and civic groups created "governance without government" and "functional failed states."[32] War destroys many types of political institutions but provides the setting for others to thrive.[33] As Clapham suggests, "Warfare exposes organizations to the supreme test of prolonged conflict, often accompanied by heavy casualties, and the ultimate indicator of their effectiveness is the way in which they develop or decay over time."[34]

Other types of violence—communal conflicts, pogroms, urban riots— might not require a high level of institutionalization and indeed reflect a relatively unorganized, spontaneous outpouring of grievance-driven frustration or anger. Protracted civil wars such as in Ethiopia, however, require institutions with highly developed capacities and structures to mobilize supporters and provision armed forces. Civil wars might be initiated by grievance, frustration, greed, but to be sustained for decades require institutions that respond to the incentives and opportunities of violence, successfully mobilize and coordinate large numbers of fighters and supporters, and overcome collective action problems in extremely difficult circumstances.[35]

Insurgent groups generally are studied as military organizations and more recently as greedy mafia-style business enterprises motivated by profits from illicit diamond mining or narcotics trafficking.[36] New research investigates different forms of what Staniland calls "wartime political orders" and what Arjona labels "rebelocracy," or phenomena in which insurgents and states develop both cooperative and conflictual relationships during protracted armed struggle.[37] The internal dynamics of alliance formation and fragmentation of rebel movements is another way of understanding political processes during violent conflict.[38]

A relatively new and growing literature considers how insurgent groups may be studied as proto–political parties and how they must overcome some of the same challenges any other political party does.[39] In other words, although they differ with regard to the use of violence, insurgent groups and political parties play similar roles in relation to mobilization in pursuit of political power. A rebel group differs from the classic definition of a political party as "a team seeking to control the governing apparatus by gaining office in a duly constituted election" but primarily in the tactics it uses to gain power.[40] Wartime organizations use selective incentives (such as land or jobs that benefit only those who participate), collective incentives (solidarity on the basis of an ethnic or other identity), or a combination of both to overcome collective action problems.[41]

Della Porta's work on clandestine political violence emphasizes the specific nature of solidarity that arises from underground politics.[42] The founders of rebel groups often come with a long history of political engagement and know each other as comrades with overlapping political, ethnic, and friendship ties. Leadership coherence is therefore in part a function of sustained struggle and relationships that often predate the origin of the liberation movement. Clandestine organizations are particularly centralized, hierarchical, and compartmentalized and become more so as repression and violence escalate.

In Ethiopia, members of rebel groups did not begin their political activism as insurgents but often participated in the more general student movement and other clandestine opposition networks in the 1960s and 1970s. The leaders of the TPLF, for example, first engaged in contentious politics as members of the underground student movement that advanced the Ethiopian revolution in the cities in the early 1970s and only later took up the armed struggle in the rural areas. In other words, the EPRDF as a ruling party has its roots in the TPLF armed insurgent movement that in turn traces its ancestry back to earlier clandestine political activists within the Ethiopian student movement. Other political parties, affiliated both with the EPRDF and with the political opposition such as the EPRP and OLF, also had their origins in the underground, radical student politics of the 1970s. Solidarity—and memories of perceived betrayal—from clandestine politics tend to endure.

Different types of civil wars tend to generate variation in wartime organizations, and these organizations, in turn, are likely to remain powerful beyond the war and consequently shape postwar political order.[43] These organizations are not necessarily formal and can be in the form of different types of "social processes," as Wood puts it, in which "social actors, structures, norms, and practices" change during war.[44] In particular, a rebel movement's degree of leadership cohesion and experience in wartime governance shapes whether the insurgency can transform into an effective party that can consolidate its power after the war ends. A coterie of linked leaders and high levels of solidarity forged in wartime facilitate the transition from a rebel movement to a strong authoritarian political party. To understand the EPRDF from 1991 to 2018, therefore, we must start by examining its origins in the period of protracted armed struggle.

War in Tigray

Origins

Tigray is the northernmost region of Ethiopia, bordering Eritrea. It was the center of the ancient Axumite kingdom, marked by the dramatic twenty-three-meter obelisks in the city of Axum. The region is high plateau, 95 percent ethnic Tigray, and 95 percent Orthodox Christian. The kingdom controlled key trading routes until it lost the Red Sea coast to the Ottoman Empire in the sixteenth century and thereafter lost its status, with the exception of the reign of Yohannes IV in the late nineteenth century.[45] Although part of the core of the Orthodox, highland region, Tigray was also poor, long characterized by the out-migration of labor. In the aftermath of World War II and Italy's occupation, Haile Selassie returned to the throne and sought to increase central power at the expense of regional nobles. In eastern Tigray, the Woyane rebellion mobilized local elites and residents aggrieved by government corruption and threatened the emperor's rule. He responded by collaborating with the British Royal Air Force to destroy the rebellion with aerial bombardment. The Woyane rebellion was a "typical agrarian protest," according to Gebru Tareke, and failed in part because of its diverse goals and lack of coordination.[46] Although the student movement that became the TPLF emerged from a different social background, it recognized its link with the rebellion of 1943 by identifying as the "Second Woyane."

The TPLF grew out of the Tigray University Student Association and the Tigray National Organization (TNO), which had mobilized students and teachers in the Tigrayan countryside in the early 1970s. The initial group was small. The origin story recalls that the first meeting of the TNO took place in a café in the Piazza neighborhood in Addis Ababa and included just seven members.[47] The TPLF faced enormous challenges from the start: "With no previous military knowledge, hardly any experience in popular mobilization, and without clearly defined objectives, the organization was apparently ill equipped to deal with the adverse conditions it soon confronted."[48] An important source of grievance was the perception that Tigrayans had too little representation in the central government. Although Tigrayans share many cultural traits with the highland Amhara, rivalry between Tigray and Amhara over national leadership has a deep history. Nationality, more than class, framed the sense of deprivation. At first the TPLF advocated for an independent Tigray on the basis of national oppression but later changed its charter to advocate for autonomy within the Ethiopian state.

The TPLF was not cohesive at birth but became so over time as a vanguard within the party consolidated its hold and purged the movement of dissent. The TPLF had to eliminate several competing rebel movements before it could become the hegemonic national resistance movement of Tigray. Between 1976 and 1978, the TPLF militarily defeated the Tigray Liberation Front, the Ethiopian Democratic Union (a monarchist group led by the old elite), and the Ethiopian People's Revolutionary Army (the military wing of the EPRP). As is common in civil wars, successful insurgents fight other insurgent groups while simultaneously struggling against the incumbent regime. These deadly battles within the larger anti-Derg constellation of forces set the precedent for how future rivals would be treated. Unilateral victory rather than power sharing characterized competition among insurgent groups. After defeating its rivals in Tigray, the TPLF consolidated its position and began to focus on the Derg army. Leadership coherence developed through a process of conflict with rivals in the Tigray region and within the movement itself.

In the late 1970s the TPLF faced fissuring in a period known as *hin-fishfish* (chaos). This struggle represented the competition between two factions within the organization—characterized by differences between whether the goal should be secession or autonomy, although other issues mattered as well. The faction that included Meles Zenawi (future prime minister) and Abay Tsehaye (future minister of federal affairs and top adviser to Meles) came under attack as overly dominated by individuals from Adwa, Shire, and Axum, in northern Tigray. The dissident group was reportedly executed. TPLF founder Aregawi Berhe was clear on the importance of loyalty and argued that the insurgent group's success was "dependent on the front's ability to maintain its corporate identity and internal cohesion: and not always by democratic means."[49]

In July 1985, key leaders including Meles, Abay, and Sebhat Nega formed the Marxist-Leninist League of Tigray (MLLT).[50] This tightly integrated vanguard party within the front served to reinforce the kind of leadership coherence and clear strategic thinking its leaders believed was necessary to win the war. The MLLT followed the interpretation of Marx presented in Lenin's *What Is to Be Done?* (1902).[51] Lenin argued that a party of enlightened elites could lead the masses to revolution and that revolutionary democracy could serve as a bridge between precapitalist and socialist societies.[52]

The TPLF and the MLLT operated according to the precepts of democratic centralism. As Paulos notes, under the democratic centralism of the TPLF, "once policies were adopted, power was intended to flow only downward."[53] Decisionmaking within top leadership circles often involved lengthy debates. Members outside of the central committee, however, were not encouraged to challenge policies but rather to implement orders from above. The TPLF was a highly disciplined organization with strict rules of conduct and deployed political cadres with its military units to ensure discipline. As Mulugeta Gebrehiwot, a high-level military official during the armed struggle, puts it: "The insurgent army was a politico-military hybrid; commanders in the army were also members of the political leadership of the party."[54]

The insurgency, following Maoist precepts, organized regular self-criticism sessions known as *gimgema,* "an instrument used to reprimand defects and mistakes in members," as the party defined it.[55] Top leaders referred to dissidents as "gangrene . . . an infected limb [that] must be amputated."[56] During the armed struggle, loyalty to the movement could not be questioned, and there was no method for fighters to leave the TPLF except through injury.[57] Recruitment was rarely a problem because many prisoners of war chose to join the TPLF/EPRDF rather than return home, where they risked being reconscripted into the collapsing Derg army.

Wartime Governance

From 1975 to 1984 the TPLF remained a relatively small insurgent force of 1,000 soldiers.[58] The Derg military at the time numbered 65,000.[59] Under the leadership of the vanguard MLLT, the front followed classic principles of guerrilla warfare and Maoist models of mobilization, where the political and the military are unified.[60] In the beginning of the civil war, leaders from the cities needed the local knowledge of peasants to survive.[61] Over time the TPLF negotiated working relationships with small farmers and remained a fundamentally rural movement. The rebels did not occupy significant cities until late in the war. The guerrillas gained support during the mid-1980s and by 1988 were estimated to have 25,000 soldiers in the field.[62] By 1989 the TPLF was able to liberate Mekele, the Tigray regional capital, and to move southward into Wollo and Shewa, provinces inhabited by Amhara rather than predominantly Tigrayan peasants.

The TPLF began its armed struggle in western Tigray but moved to the northeast and began to set up liberated zones. The Derg's military responded with aerial bombardment, including brutal attacks on market towns and ground offenses from garrison towns.[63] From 1980, the rebels established the foundations of rural administration in support of the rebellion. During the famine of the mid-1980s, the TPLF organized complex humanitarian operations. Hendrie argues that the TPLF gained the support of the Tigrayan peasants by emphasizing Tigrayan nationalism, sharing wartime deprivations, and providing some measure of law and order.[64] By the early 1980s, the TPLF's small core of student activists now led an army largely composed of peasant fighters.[65]

The TPLF described itself as "a people's democratic front fighting for the national self-determination of the Tigrean people and waging a people's democratic revolution."[66] This suggested that warmaking and a "people's democratic revolution" went hand in hand. The TPLF was a political army that emphasized indoctrination and the military being under the control of the political party. A senior general stated, "All armies are political. All armies serve as protectors of a certain political system. An apolitical army is an illusion. What differentiates armies is the political system they serve."[67]

Land reform undertaken by the TPLF during the war, for example, sought not only to provide land to poor peasants but also to create the base of popular support necessary for the success of the armed struggle.

The interests of "the people" and "the front" were the same. Local elites, however, often resisted the TPLF's efforts to redistribute land, creating conflicts between the front and local "big men" the front identified as "feudals." To mobilize the peasants, the TPLF used "cultural symbols, propaganda, and coercion," according to one of its founders.[68]

To administer land reform and to gain support for the insurgency, the TPLF made use of popularly elected *baitos* (people's councils). Many observers supportive of the TPLF, such as Firebrace and Smith and Hendrie, emphasize the democratic and participatory nature of these councils. Others, such as TPLF founder Aregawi, emphasize their role as support structures that worked under TPLF military guidance to administer liberated zones. The *baitos* provided a mechanism for top-down wartime governance. *Kifli hizbis* (specially trained cadres) had the responsibility to "agitate, organize and arm the people" in order to "generate the maximum contribution to the movement's project."[69] The *baito* members were selected by the population but under strict TPLF supervision to ensure loyalty. The party also created mass organizations, notably the peasant associations all adults had to join, as instruments of popular mobilization and indoctrination. Again, Aregawi is clear on the purpose of these institutions: "With the growth of the TPLF, the consolidation of the mass associations and the subsequent *baitos* (people's councils), persuasion was gradually replaced by orders and coercion."[70] Clapham argued that the TPLF replicated the *encadrement* (the process of penetrating and controlling local communities) of the Derg.[71]

The *baitos* were not institutions of local self-governance but were organized by the insurgent group to advance their key military goals.[72] A leader in the TPLF's Department of Health noted the close relationship between *baitos* as institutions to resist the Derg and as the administrative structure to provide social support to those affected by war, drought, and famine.[73] Health workers and local administrators in liberated zones were regarded as "fighters" in the "people's struggle."[74] Meles is clear that the overriding objective during the armed struggle was "to win the war" rather than to provide services for the peasants. Gill cites Meles as saying,

> Obviously we wanted to keep our people alive because if they died the objective of the cause died at the same time. But we felt that in keeping them alive we had to transform their circumstances, and in order to transform their circumstances we had to remove the Mengistu regime. So we felt we had an even higher objective than just keeping people alive.[75]

The great Ethiopian famine of 1984–1985 provided the context for the TPLF to solidify its administrative reach into Tigray. The rebel movement had the capacity and local legitimacy to organize a massive movement of the population from Tigray to rebel-controlled camps in Sudan.[76] The movement had its own impressive humanitarian wing, the Relief Society of Tigray (REST). It raised money from supporters in the diaspora through the Tigray Development Association (TDA) and formed relationships with neighboring insurgents in Eritrea, government authorities in Sudan, and a range of international actors and organizations.[77]

The necessity to administer liberated territory provided incentives to develop cadres with skills to mobilize civilians under the difficult circumstances of violence and insecurity with the goal of supporting a military strategy. Not surprisingly, these precedents shaped postwar governance because successful military administrators were converted (at least formally) into peacetime governors. Chinigò and Fantini state,

> During the fourteen-years-long armed struggle, the TPLF successfully tested strategies of peasant mobilization inspired by Leninist and Maoist doctrines. The TPLF acted as vanguard of the rural masses, matching military and political encadrement with the provision of basic social services in the liberated areas of Tigray, thus guaranteeing the political legitimacy and the material support to its struggle.[78]

Wartime Diplomacy and Regional Relations

Although the TPLF appropriately emphasized its self-reliance during the struggle, the rebels also benefited from refugee camps in and supply lines through Sudan, diplomatic support from Somalia, and fundraising among diaspora populations. The TPLF's relationships with insurgents in neighboring Eritrea and its ability to operate through Sudan were fundamental to the dynamics of the war and the legacies that shaped Ethiopian politics after 1991. During the period of armed struggle, the Soviet Union became the most important supporter of the Derg regime. Washington, DC, developed military relations with Somalia but remained skeptical of the TPLF and the EPLF, regarding them as Marxists with problematic positions on secessionism. The TPLF had quasidiplomatic offices in the United States, where it mobilized among the diaspora and shared information with think tanks, advocacy networks, and government officials to shape international perceptions of the insurgents. The TPLF therefore not only governed liberated territory but it also operated as a quasistate with regard to relations with its neighbors and global powers.[79]

By far the TPLF's most important relationship was with the EPLF.[80] The two rebel movements shared the overarching goal of defeating the Mengistu regime but differed on a range of critical issues of strategy and ideology. The EPLF was established before the TPLF, and in the early years the Tigrayans sought and received assistance from the more experienced and well-connected Eritrean movement. A number of key TPLF leaders received training in EPLF camps.[81] Young, a longtime observer of both movements, argues that despite these similarities the relationship during wartime was "problematic and beset with tensions."[82]

Cooperation depended on the TPLF accepting the EPLF's position on the right of the multinational Eritrean people to self-determination rather than the right of each nationality for self-determination. The TPLF held a different view and argued, "If the future Eritrea is to be truly democratic, it will have to respect the right of nations and nationalities to self-determination up to, and including, secession."[83] The EPLF favored a military strategy that included defending key bases, whereas the TPLF emphasized a more classic guerrilla strategy of giving up territory and retreating in order to attack at a time and place of its choosing.

In the early 1980s some TPLF soldiers were trained at the EPLF's Sahel military base, and these soldiers played an important role in stopping the Derg's Red Star offensive in 1982. From 1985 to 1988, however, the two groups broke off relations. Not only did it end military cooperation but also the EPLF refused to allow the Relief Society of Tigray to use the main supply link from Kassala, Sudan, that ran through Eritrea. The two liberation fronts negotiated a new agreement to cooperate in 1988, in part because TPLF victories at that time made the two rebel movements more equal in power.

The Final Military Offensive

The TPLF did not return to its military offensive until 1987, after the worst of the famine abated. In 1988, the insurgents had a string of victories against a collapsing Ethiopian military. As the TPLF moved beyond its goal of liberating Tigray, it began to articulate a strategy to continue the war beyond its home province. Because resistance outside of Tigray was weak and ineffective, the TPLF argued, it had to play a role in leading the struggle in the rest of the country. "The level of development of the struggles waged in different parts of Ethiopia is . . . uneven" and therefore required the movement to turn its sights to larger goals across multinational Ethiopia.[84] In 1989, the TPLF wrote,

---

> This is a year when the TPLF, as an important part of the Ethiopian Revolution, has made it possible for the Tigrayan people to increase their consciousness, and has armed and organized them. More than ever before it is recognized that TPLF has a positive contribution to make towards the rest of Ethiopia. This revolutionary supportive message and TPLF's ability and responsibility to the masses in Ethiopia is rapidly gaining wider recognition.[85]

The TPLF began to deemphasize its earlier appeals to Tigray nationalism and to transform its ethnic appeals to serve less parochial goals in order to mobilize broad support to defeat the Derg. This shift in war aims created another period of internal factionalism within the TPLF. Some fighters returned to their villages rather than remain in the front as it moved through non-Tigrayan areas toward Addis Ababa.[86]

The TPLF therefore had extensive local political structures prior to gaining national power, and the models that developed during wartime shaped the design of postwar institutions. The rebels began the transition in 1991 with not only a large and battle-hardened military but also cadres in every village in Tigray, well integrated into a regionwide political network and with experience in administering liberated territory and managing top-down relationships with the peasants. In response to military necessities, the insurgents moved outside of Tigray and built the multiethnic EPRDF. The TPLF effectively administered a ministate governed by a proto–political party before it seized power and took control over all of Ethiopia. The war-to-peace transition therefore included considerable elements of organizational continuity.

Oromo Resistance, 1977–1991

The Oromo people inhabit territory that traverses central and southern Ethiopia and almost bisects the country from Somalia in the East to Sudan in the West. As noted above, the history of the region with regard to the imperial regime was complex, with some areas such as Jimma relatively autonomous and others occupied by northern landlords in feudal arrangements. Resistance to central government took place in Bale (southeastern Ethiopia) from 1963 to 1968, and a sense of Oromo distinctiveness and marginalization developed among Oromo intellectuals and students.[87] The Mecha and Tulama Self-Help Association provided an early focal point for growing Oromo identity until it was banned by the emperor and its leaders arrested in 1966. The upheavals of the Ethiopian revolution provided the context to reexamine Oromo history and to articulate a sense of nationalism that contrasted the marginalized Oromo with the Amhara elites.[88] Clandestine Oromo newspapers such as *Kana Bekta?* (*Did You Know?*), established in 1969, circulated among Oromo students and intellectuals.

Some Oromo political leaders concluded that self-determination required an independent Oromia, whereas others sought greater autonomy and a political role commensurate with Oromia's demographic size. Many in the Oromo leadership framed the conflict in terms of "Abyssinian colonial rule." The imperial government restricted the use of the indigenous language and tried to forcefully assimilate the Oromo into the dominant Amhara culture. Some saw this assimilation as a form of colonial conquest through which the Oromo would lose their identity.[89] How the Oromo would relate to the Ethiopian state was and has remained a key political issue. As Baxter put it frankly before the revolution, "If the Oromo people only obtain a portion of the freedoms which they seek, then the balance of political power in Ethiopia will be completely altered."[90]

In June 1976 a group of some thirty Oromo, mostly students, organized the OLF's first congress and endorsed a program that called for the "total liberation of the Oromo nation from Ethiopian colonialism."[91] As with other clandestine organizations of the era, it developed out of the student movement and the debates around class and nationality of the 1970s. According to Assefa, the founding fathers were fewer than ten.[92] The 1975 land reform and the removal of imperial landlords led many Oromos initially to perceive significant benefits from the revolution.[93] Brigadier General Teferi Bante, an Oromo, led the Derg for a period of time, and an Oromo-led Marxist-Leninist party known as Meison and another known as the Ethiopian Oppressed People's Revolutionary Struggle (ECHA'AT) initially had close relationships with the military junta.

By 1978, however, Teferi Bante had been killed and Meison and ECHA'AT crushed. The renewed political marginalization and conscription of Oromos to die in the Derg's wars alienated many. The Red Terror led key Oromo nationalists to flee into the countryside and moved the OLF in a more radical direction. A small group of fighters retreated to the Chercher Mountains (in Hararghe, east of Addis Ababa) to reorganize. They fought the Derg but also the Somali-sponsored Western Somali Liberation Front. In the late 1970s, the OLF had opened an office in Khartoum, where it had contact with the EPLF and TPLF.

In 1979 the first OLF unit went to EPLF-controlled Eritrea for training. Lencho Letta, the longtime OLF leader, states that cooperation with the EPLF was easier than with the TPLF because "our claim [that the independence of Oromia was a colonial issue] was parallel to that of the EPLF in Eritrea."[94] In the mid-1980s, however, the OLF and TPLF cooperated, at least tactically, and a TPLF unit joined the OLF in its operational zone around Asosa on the Sudanese border. The TPLF criticized the OLF for remaining in the non-Oromo areas along the Sudanese border rather than engaging in a Maoist-style mobilization in the Oromo heartland. The OLF, in the eyes of the TPLF, was not an "action-oriented organization."[95] The OLF was unwilling to adopt the kind of ideological positions the TPLF promoted, making it impossible for anything more than a short-term tactical alliance.

In 1982–1983 the OLF moved its operations into Wellega and Illubabor in western Oromia, and analysts estimated at that time that it had some 2,000–3,000 fighters.[96] The rebels began to have success in mobilizing the population and at this time represented a more formidable threat to the Derg than did the TPLF. From the beginning the OLF, like other liberation movements, faced divisions and factionalism. Rival organizations such as the Islamic Front for the Liberation of Oromia and the Somali Abo Liberation Front competed for control of Oromo territory and made claims for the peasants' loyalty.

Oromo nationalism is diffuse, and the Oromo people occupy a large and varied territory. Unlike the TPLF, which could articulate the idea of historical Tigray nationalism in a relatively homogenous, compact region, the OLF had a more difficult job of appealing to a broader and more diverse constituency. Western Oromo in the Wellega area included many Protestants, northern Oromo in Shewa had been more Amharaized, and Bale was home to Oromo pastoralists or agriculturalists who were generally Muslim. The degree of assimilation into the dominant Amhara culture varied considerably, and key symbols of unity such as the *gada* system of governance were practices predominantly in the Borana area.[97] Asafa Jalata explains:

> It was not easy to transform qualitatively the spontaneous and scattered struggle into a politically conscious and centrally organized armed struggle. . . . Because of regional and religious divisions among the Oromo people, which a century of colonialism had intensified, and because of other differences in social and political backgrounds of participants, it was difficult to build a centralized national political institution.[98]

The OLF administered limited territories during the war but ruled using traditional Oromo *gada* principles of governance, according to OLF sympathizers. An OLF official stated: "In our liberated areas the politicization and organization of the masses have reached such a stage as to allow us to enable the people to elect village and district committees. . . . We are accumulating experience in creating a healthy, literate and politically conscious society. The foundation of a new and democratic society is being laid."[99] The OLF created the Oromo Relief Association (ORA), following on the model of the Eritrean Relief Association and REST to help coordinate humanitarian assistance and the care of refugees. Damazin, Sudan, became a hub for the OLF/ORA in the 1980s.[100]

In the late 1970s and early 1980s, the OLF controlled territory in southeastern Ethiopia and in 1981 expanded into areas around Asosa and Dembidolo, operating from bases in Sudan. In 1984 and 1985, the Derg's policies of villagization, which moved peasants from famine zones in Wollo into Oromo lands in western Ethiopia, created significant grievances and sparked increased mobilization in support of the OLF.[101] The Derg increased repression in Wellega, targeting the Mekane Yesus Church among other institutions that had high levels of Oromo support.[102]

The OLF liberated limited territories along the Sudanese border (and some of these areas were not in fact inhabited by Oromos). In April 1991, as TPLF troops, along with their recently established Oromo People's Democratic Organization (OPDO) affiliate, moved into Oromo-inhabited lands in Wellega, the OLF advanced east from Dembidolo and reached Nejo in western Wellega by the time the EPRDF seized power in Addis Ababa in May. After the Derg fell, the OLF rapidly grew its military force by recruiting demobilized Oromo soldiers from the old army sent home without jobs or other means of livelihood. Although a relatively minor military actor in the defeat of the Derg, the OLF remained politically important because of its large potential constituency and its history as a national resistance movement.

With a sense of itself as the only legitimate representative of Oromo nationalist aspirations, the OLF was inherently in conflict with the TPLF-created OPDO. As one Oromo nationalist puts it, "The OPDO is led by Tigrayan cadres, elements of Oromo-speaking colonial settlers, and opportunist Oromos who do anything in exchange for luxurious lifestyles."[103] The OLF leadership resented the effort to challenge its authority and recalled the history of Oromo traitors who had worked with northern imperial forces to subjugate the Oromo people.

Compared with the TPLF, the OLF had different experiences, operating in a substantially different context as it fought the Derg. The Oromo people are spread across a much more dispersed territory and include significant numbers of Muslims, Orthodox Christians, and Protestants. Ideologically, the OLF could reach agreement on a general sense of historical marginalization and the importance of self-determination, but few other policy positions went beyond amorphous support for democracy and development. Tigrayans had a different relationship with the imperial state and the Derg and did not have the same experiences that led many Oromo to perceive a colonial relationship with the center. During the civil war, the TPLF controlled significant liberated zones, whereas the OLF's area of operation was much smaller. Creating a hierarchical, cohesive organization and fighting in Tigray posed different challenges than the OLF faced, and, as a result, the TPLF and OLF reached 1991 with different legacies from the struggle.

The OPDO emerged from the civil war with its own specific legacies from the armed struggle and from Oromo nationalist sentiments. The OPDO was part of the TPLF-created EPRDF coalition but lacked a history of struggle to liberate the Oromo people comparable with that of the OLF. This placed the OPDO from its very origins in a difficult position to mobilize Oromo nationalists. Many Oromos perceived the OPDO as an agent of the TPLF, or more generally of northern political interests, and therefore treated the party with suspicion if not hostility. As I discuss below, the OPDO established itself as the most powerful political actor across Oromia following the 1992 regional elections, but generally it was a less coherent party than the TPLF. The demonstrations in Oromia in 2016 and the change of leadership in the EPRDF that brought OPDO officials into top positions in 2018 represented a significant change both in how the OPDO was perceived by Oromos and in its position with regard to other parties within the coalition.

Southern Ethiopia During the War Years

Many southerners applauded the Derg's land reform and the removal of highland feudal landlords and imperial administrators. In Sidamo, residents recalled the revolution "relief from Amhara oppression."[104] The *zemecha*, a campaign to send university students to the countryside, along with the Derg's early literacy campaign, created materials in local languages, providing symbolic recognition to groups long subservient to Amhara overlords.[105] Despite these openings to the South, many still regarded the Derg as centrist, with commitments to "Abyssinian" values. Villagization in 1984 was widely disliked and was particularly disastrous in areas where the people depended on *enset* (false banana), a staple typically grown around scattered homesteads so that it can be intensively cultivated. Southern Ethiopia's diversity, however, resulted in a wide variety of experiences with the Derg regime.

In Konso, the transition from the emperor to the Derg led to the arrest of many who had served the empire as intermediaries. The Derg pursued policies against local traditions regarded as "backward" or as an alternative form of organization that could challenge the Derg's peasant associations.[106] Among the Maale, the revolutionary state pushed aside traditional kings in bringing what the Marxist regime regarded as "modern" administration, and that served to strengthen the power of the state over peripheral peoples.[107] The Derg banned and executed many of the local authorities in Surma communities (a small area near the border with Sudan), ordered that the pastoralists "start wearing clothes" and incorporated them through state-controlled peasant associations.[108]

The Sidama Liberation Movement (SLM) was founded in 1977 and demanded self-determination for the Sidama people. As with other ethnonationalist movements in the 1970s, the SLM developed out of the student movement and was organized by members of the small Sidama intelligentsia. The SLM fought a low-level insurgency against the Derg, with some military assistance from Somalia, as part of the mutual-intervention-by-proxy policies pursued by both Addis Ababa and Mogadishu in the early 1980s. The rebellion collapsed in 1984 as the leadership fractured.[109] Although militarily ineffective, this resistance provided a focal point for Sidama nationality as a distinct political identity.

The SLM-led rebellion, however, was the exception. The southern region generally was not directly involved in the civil war. The TPLF and OLF fought in different zones, and although many in southern Ethiopia objected to the Derg, few participated in organized rebellion. Thousands, of course, participated as drafted soldiers in the Derg military, and some became engaged with the TPLF or its affiliated organizations after being captured or deserting.

In the late 1980s, the Derg began to back away from its policies of villagization and control of agricultural marketing. Many small farmers in the South correctly interpreted this as a sign of the center's growing weakness and spontaneously began to expel cadres and disassemble the agricultural marketing corporations. As a consequence, by May 1991, when the transition began, large parts of southern Ethiopia were autonomous.[110] In sum, the political communities of southern Ethiopia had few organized ties to or participation in the armed struggle. Therefore, they experienced yet another distinct set of wartime legacies that shaped postwar politics.

The Creation of the EPRDF

In January 1989, the TPLF and Ethiopian People's Democratic Movement (EPDM) joined forces and created the EPRDF.[111] The first congress ratified what had been a de facto alliance since 1981. The EPDM developed out of the so-called Belessa Group of the EPRP. This group had moved into TPLF-controlled territory and decided to work alongside the

TPLF. Other EPRP factions chose to move into exile in Sudan.[112] The TPLF regarded the EPDM as a "strategic ally" and hence formed a broad "united front" to "facilitate the downfall of the fascist regime in Addis Ababa and shorten the dark days and plight of the Ethiopian people."[113] The organization that began as a Tigray nationalist movement in the mid-1970s saw that it had an essential role to play—a "responsibility to the masses"—in the larger Ethiopian transformation. In the late 1980s the TPLF moved into the Amhara region, and the tension between Tigray nationalism and the imperative to overthrow the Derg by mobilizing a multiethnic movement required an insurgency that positioned itself as a liberation front that could welcome diverse supporters.

The EPRDF political party positioned itself to represent all of Ethiopia, moving beyond the more regionally focused TPLF insurgent force. The OLF did not join the EPRDF coalition. Talks between the OLF and the TPLF broke down in 1988 on the question of ideology, and there was deep distrust and suspicion between the two rebel groups.[114] Vaughan suggests that the TPLF's creation of the rival OPDO was a "last resort" after concluding that cooperation with the OLF was impossible.[115] The EPRDF recruited the original membership of the OPDO from Derg soldiers who had been captured or defected over the years.[116] The OPDO joined the TPLF and EPDM in the EPRDF in January 1990. The EPRDF was from its origins a broad front of TPLF affiliates rather than a united democratic front of preexisting organizations. The TPLF and to a significant extent the EPDM had leaders honed by decades of armed struggle and military administration, whereas the OPDO was a new party with largely untested and untrained leaders. These different origins generated a hierarchy among the constituent parties in the coalition, a source of resentment that resurfaced in the intraparty conflicts in 2016–2018.

After the massive defeats of the Derg's military by the EPLF at the Eritrean towns of Nakfa and Afabet, the TPLF moved into Enda Selassie (Tigray) in March 1988. It captured significant amounts of weaponry and ammunition, including T-55 tanks and artillery. In collaboration with the EPDM, the TPLF briefly occupied Maychew (southern Tigray) and captured more war materiel. In 1989, after signing a peace agreement with Somalia that allowed Addis Ababa to shift troops to the north, the Derg launched a counteroffensive and forced the TPLF-EPDM troops back to Dejene in northern Gondar. By February 1989, the insurgents, reinforced by Eritrean units with heavy armor and artillery, retook Enda Selassie. By fall 1989, the EPRDF was moving to capture the road that linked Addis Ababa to Gondar and moved on

Dessie, in Wollo province. Amharas were the majority in these areas, making the alliance with the EPDM strategically important. The final phase of the war included complex coordination among the TPLF, EPDM, and EPLF in pursuit of their common goal of defeating the Derg. Some TPLF troops reportedly resisted moving farther south, feeling that they had already liberated their homeland and had no reason to die in someone else's war.[117] But the top TPLF leadership concluded that their aims required taking the war beyond Tigray, so they created a multiethnic coalition to achieve this.

The Border Regions

Armed opposition to the Derg took place in other parts of Ethiopia as well. The border regions were historically the location of instability, violence, and rebellion. During the Derg period, the Western Somali Liberation Front (WSLF) remained active in the Somali-speaking areas of Ethiopia such as the Ogaden. The WSLF played a major role in the Ogaden war of 1977–1978, when it served as the local wing of the invasion by the Somali army. The WSLF supported another Ethiopian rebel movement, the Somali Abo Liberation Front, which operated in areas where Somali and Oromo communities historically had intermixed.[118] The defeat of the Somali army by Ethiopian and Cuban troops in 1978 led the WSLF to retreat into Somalia. In the 1980s Ethiopia and Somali supported each other's opposition movements, and there were skirmishes between the Ethiopian-supported Somali Salvation Democratic Front and the Somali-supported WSLF.[119] Mogadishu provided diplomatic support for the EPLF and TPLF, and insurgent leaders traveled on Somali passports. TPLF leader Meles and EPLF leader Isaias Afewerki both lived in Mogadishu for a period of time in the 1980s. Some key WSLF leaders joined the Somali National Army and, in 1989, the WSLF was disbanded, although a faction reemerged as the Ogaden National Liberation Front.[120] The Somali threat required the Derg to keep a significant military force on its eastern frontier, reducing the number of soldiers available to fight in Eritrea and Tigray. The internal dimensions of the war and the ability of the WSLF to play an important role during the 1980s and early 1990s, however, were less significant than the war in the north.

Similarly, instability and nonstate armed actors had long been a feature in the Afar region. The Afar Liberation Front (ALF) developed following an effort by the Derg to arrest Sultan Alimirah Hanfadhe, a powerful traditional leader.[121] The border with Sudan had large populations of Sudanese refugees, and Khartoum periodically provided support to

Ethiopian nonstate actors in response to the Derg's support to the Sudan People's Liberation Movement (SPLM). For example, the Anuak formed the Gambela People's Liberation Movement (GPLM) in 1985 and received support from Sudan and cooperated with the OLF. The GPLM's rhetoric against "highlanders" interfering in Gambela made relations with the TPLF difficult.[122]

All of these nonstate armed actors, whether they represented liberation movements, proxy forces, locals fighting for control over their resources, or all of the above, played a part in the overarching patterns of violence and conflict in Ethiopia during the Derg period. The need to deploy troops along the Somali and Sudanese borders and the ability of the ALF to periodically attack the road leading to the port of Assab, for example, contributed to overstretching the Derg's military capacity, leading to its eventual disintegration. Most of the fighting, however, took place in Eritrea and Tigray. As I discuss in Chapter 3, some of these insurgent groups participated in the transitional government following the 1991 EPRDF victory, but none joined the EPRDF coalition. Politics in the border regions generally did not play a major role at the national level. I can therefore focus my argument on how the EPRDF operated in Tigray, Amhara, Oromo, and the Southern Nations, Nationalities, and People's Region (SNNPR) as a way to put together the Ethiopian political puzzle.

War Termination

The Derg begrudgingly entered peace talks following major military defeats at the hands of the EPLF and TPLF and clear messages from the Soviet Union that its interest in providing more military assistance to Addis Ababa was waning. The government met with EPLF officials in Atlanta (September 1989), Nairobi (November 1989), and Washington, DC (October 1990 and February 1991) in talks mediated by former US president Jimmy Carter.[123] The Derg's military was collapsing rapidly, however, and the EPLF saw no reason to negotiate the end of a war it was on the verge of winning. Talks with the TPLF in Rome in late 1989 and early 1990 similarly produced little.[124] The EPRDF quickly occupied the Amhara-inhabited provinces of Gojjam and Gondar, moved through the Oromo areas of Wellega to the west of Addis Ababa, captured the provincial capital Nekemte in April 1991, and halted around the town of Ambo. The rapid advance by the insurgent forces allowed military dynamics on the ground rather than negotiations in foreign capitals to settle the outcome of the protracted war.[125]

As the EPRDF approached the outskirts of Addis Ababa, Mengistu fled into exile in Zimbabwe, and the United States convened negotiations in London.[126] By the time the talks commenced, the military facts on the ground determined the outcome. US Assistant Secretary of State Herman Cohen, hoping to prevent the sort of chaos that recently had devastated the Liberian capital of Monrovia and Somalia's Mogadishu under similar circumstances, publicly "recommended" that the EPRDF enter Addis Ababa "as soon as possible to help stabilize the situation."[127] EPRDF troops moved into Addis Ababa during the night of May 27–28, and the change of government effectively took place. Washington played a small role in the final formalization of the war's outcome, but the victory had been determined by the EPRDF's ability to encircle Addis Ababa as the Derg's army collapsed.

On May 21, 1991, the EPRDF issued this dispatch from the front: "The forces that he [Mengistu] had amassed on the Ambo front to defend the capital—the 3rd 'Revolutionary' Army, of which he had great confidence—evaporated like dew under a hot sun as a result of EPRDF's assault."[128] The war was over.

Conclusion

Ethiopia entered postwar politics with a complex set of political actors seeking to play roles in creating the new political order. Diverse legacies of the armed struggle and different experiences in relation to the Ethiopian state generated varied perceptions, goals, and patterns of behavior. As I argued above, the period of the civil war and the many microdynamics of multiple conflicts influenced how different political organizations evolved. In May 1991, the TPLF was a cohesive, battle-hardened actor that had established the EPRDF to bring in non-Tigrayan constituencies. The EPDM built upon a certain stream of Amhara resistance, and the OPDO, although formed only recently, made claims to advance Oromo national interests. The parties in southern Ethiopia were either inchoate or not yet created in May 1991. The EPRDF coalition set the rules for political competition and consolidated its power from 1991 to 1995, as I discuss in Chapter 3. But internally, the postwar scenario was from the start a coalition of different and unequal political parties.

Notes

1. Harold G. Marcus, *A History of Ethiopia* (Berkeley: University of California Press, 2002); Bahru Zewde, *A History of Modern Ethiopia, 1855–1974* (Addis Ababa: Addis Ababa University Press, 1992).
2. Haggai Erlich, *Ethiopia and the Challenge of Independence* (Boulder, CO: Lynne Rienner, 1986), 4; Harold G. Marcus, *Life and Times of Menelik II of Ethiopia, 1844–1913* (Oxford, UK: Oxford University Press, 1975). For a view from the periphery, see Donald L. Donham and Wendy James, eds., *The*

Southern Marches of Imperial Ethiopia: Essays in History and Social Anthropology (Athens: Ohio University Press, 2002).

3. Herbert S. Lewis, *Jimma Abba Jifar: An Oromo Monarchy—Ethiopia, 1830–1932* (Lawrenceville, NJ: Red Sea, 2001).

4. John Markakis, *Ethiopia: The Last Two Frontiers* (Oxford, UK: James Currey, 2011).

5. Donald Crummey, "Banditry and Resistance: Noble and Peasant in Nineteenth-century Ethiopia," in *Banditry, Rebellion, and Social Protest in Africa,* ed. Donald Crummey (Oxford, UK: James Currey, 1986).

6. Aregawi Berhe, "Revisiting Resistance in Italian-occupied Ethiopia: The Patriots' Movement (1936–1941) and the Redefinition of Post-war Ethiopia," in Jon Abbink, Klaas van Walraven, and Mirjam de Bruijn, eds., *Rethinking Resistance: Revolt and Violence in African History* (Leiden: Brill, 2003), 88–113. See also Charles Schaefer, "Serendipitous Resistance in Fascist-occupied Ethiopia, 1936–1941," *Northeast African Studies* 3, no. 1 (1996): 87–115.

7. The story of the civil war between the Eritrean national liberation movements and the Ethiopian state is complex and largely beyond this book's aims. For an introduction to the Eritrean case, see David Pool, *From Guerrillas to Government: Eritrea People's Liberation Front* (Athens: Ohio University Press, 2001); Richard J. Reid, *Frontiers of Violence in North-east Africa* (Oxford, UK: Oxford University Press, 2011); Michael Woldemariam, *Insurgent Fragmentation in the Horn of Africa: Rebellion and Its Discontents* (Cambridge, UK: Cambridge University Press, 2017); Bereket Habte Selassie, *Conflict and Intervention in the Horn of Africa* (New York: Monthly Review, 1980).

8. John Markakis, *Ethiopia: Anatomy of a Traditional Polity* (London: Clarendon, 1974), 73.

9. The best introduction to politics under the emperor is Christopher Clapham, *Haile Selassie's Government* (London: Longman, 1969). See also Margery Perham, *The Government of Ethiopia* (London: Faber and Faber, 1948); Patrick Gilkes, *The Dying Lion: Feudalism and Modernization in Ethiopia* (London: Julian Friedmann, 1975); and Markakis, *Ethiopia: Anatomy of a Traditional Polity.*

10. Harold G. Marcus, "Does the Past Have Any Authority in Ethiopia?" *Ethiopian Review,* April 18, 1992. Generally, see Harold G. Marcus, *A History of Ethiopia* (Berkeley: University of California Press, 2002).

11. John Markakis, *Ethiopia: The Last Two Frontiers* (Oxford, UK: James Currey, 2011).

12. Student leader Wallelign Makonnen wrote the influential article "On the Question of Nationalities in Ethiopia" in the underground journal *Struggle* in 1969. There were sharp—even murderous—divisions within the student movement around positions on both land and nationality. See Marina Ottaway, "Social Classes and Corporate Interests in the Ethiopian Revolution," *Journal of Modern African Studies* 14, no. 3 (September 1976): 469–486, and Ottaway, "Democracy and New Democracy: The Ideological Debate in the Ethiopian Revolution," *African Studies Review* 21, no. 1 (April 1978): 19–31.

13. Michael Chege, "The Revolution Betrayed: Ethiopia, 1974–1979," *Journal of Modern African Studies* 17, no. 3 (September 1979): 359–380.

14. Andargachew Tiruneh, *The Ethiopian Revolution: 1974–1987—a Transformation from an Aristocratic to a Totalitarian Autocracy* (Cambridge, UK:

Cambridge University Press, 1993); Fred Halliday and Maxine Molyneux, *The Ethiopian Revolution* (London: Verso, 1982); René Lefort, *Ethiopia: A Heretical Revolution* (London: Zed, 1983); John Markakis and Nega Ayele, *Class and Revolution in Ethiopia* (Nottingham, UK: Spokesman, 1978); Marina Ottaway and David Ottaway, *Ethiopia: Empire in Revolution* (London: Africana, 1978); Gebru Tareke, *The Ethiopian Revolution: War in the Horn of Africa* (New Haven, CT: Yale University Press, 2009); Messay Kebede, *Ideology and Elite Conflicts: Autopsy of the Ethiopian Revolution* (Lanham, MD: Lexington, 2011).

15. For a personal view see Hiwot Teffera, *Tower in the Sky* (Addis Ababa: Addis Ababa University Press, 2012).

16. For an account from northern Shewa, see Ahmed Hassan Omer, "Close Yet Far: Northern Shewa Under the Derg," in *Remapping Ethiopia: Socialism and After,* ed. Wendy James, Donald L. Donham, Eisei Kurimoto, and Alessandro Triulzi (Oxford, UK: James Currey, 2002), 74–89.

17. Markakis, *Ethiopia: The Last Two Frontiers*, 170.

18. Christopher Clapham, *Transformation and Continuity in Revolutionary Ethiopia* (Cambridge, UK: Cambridge University Press, 1988).

19. Gareth M. Winrow, *The Foreign Policy of GDR in Africa* (Cambridge, UK: Cambridge University Press, 2009).

20. Christopher Clapham, "Controlling Space in Ethiopia," in *Remapping Ethiopia: Socialism and After,* ed. Wendy James, Donald L. Donham, Eisei Kurimoto, and Alessandro Triulzi (Oxford, UK: James Currey, 2002), 14.

21. Alula Pankhurst, *Resettlement and Famine in Ethiopia: The Villagers' Experience* (Manchester, UK: Manchester University Press, 1992), 56; Getachew Woldemeskel, "The Consequences of Resettlement in Ethiopia," *African Affairs* 88, no. 352 (July 1989): 359; Taddesse Berisso, "Modernist Dreams and Human Suffering: Villagization Among the Guji Oromo," in *Remapping Ethiopia: Socialism and After*, ed. Wendy James, Donald L. Donham, Eisei Kurimoto, and Alessandro Triulzi (Oxford, UK: James Currey, 2002). For context see Dawit Wolde Giorgis, *Red Tears: War, Famine, and Revolution in Ethiopia* (Trenton, NJ: Red Sea, 1988).

22. Dessalegn Rahmato, *Agrarian Reform in Ethiopia* (Trenton, NJ: Red Sea, 1985), 61–62.

23. John Markakis, "Garrison Socialism: The Case of Ethiopia," *MERIP Reports* 79 (June 1979): 3–17.

24. Jane Perlez, "Ethiopia Coup Attempt Reported: Authorities Say Revolt Is Crushed," *New York Times,* May 17, 1989, http://www.nytimes.com/1989/05/17/world/ethiopia-coup-attempt-reported-authorities-say-revolt-is-crushed.html.

25. Woldemariam, *Insurgent Fragmentation in the Horn of Africa.*

26. John Young, "The Tigray and Eritrean People's Liberation Fronts: A History of Tensions and Pragmatism," *Journal of Modern African Studies* 34, no. 1 (March 1996): 105–120; Awet T. Weldemichael, "Formative Alliances of Northeast African Insurgents: Eritrean Liberation Strategy and Ethiopian Armed Opposition, 1970s–1990s," *Northeast African Studies* 14, no. 1 (2014): 83–122.

27. Fantahun Ayele, *The Ethiopian Military: From Victory to Collapse, 1977–1991* (Evanston, IL: Northwestern University Press, 2014), chap. 2.

28. Stathis Kalyvas, *The Logic of Violence in Civil War* (Cambridge, UK: Cambridge University Press, 2007), argues that civil wars are generally agglomerations of distinct subconflicts, each with its own sources, actors, and dynamics.

29. On the Somali National Regional State, see Tobias Hagmann, "Punishing the Periphery: Legacies of State Repression in the Ethiopian Ogaden," *Journal of Eastern African Studies* 8, no. 4 (2014): 725–739; and Tobias Hagmann and Mohamud Hussein Khalif, "State and Politics in Ethiopia's Somali Region Since 1991," *Bildhaan: An International Journal of Somali Studies* 6, no. 6 (2008), http://digitalcommons.macalester.edu/bildhaan/vol6/iss1/6. On Benishangul-Gumuz, see John Young, "Along Ethiopia's Western Frontier: Gambella and Benishangul in Transition," *Journal of Modern Africa Studies* 37, no. 2 (1999): 321–436. On Gambela, see Dereje Feyissa, *Playing Different Games: The Paradox of Anywaa and Nuer Identification in the Gambella Region, Ethiopia* (New York: Berghahn, 2011). On Afar, see John Markakis, "Anatomy of a Conflict: Afar and Ise Ethiopia," *Review of African Political Economy* 30, no. 97 (2003): 445–453.

30. Paul Collier et al., *Breaking the Conflict Trap: Civil War and Development Policy* (Oxford, UK: Oxford University Press/World Bank, 2003), 56.

31. Roger Southall, *Liberation Movements in Power: Party and State in Southern Africa* (Oxford, UK: James Currey, 2013), 56–57.

32. Ken Menkhaus, "Governance Without Government in Somalia: Spoilers, State Building, and the Politics of Coping," *International Security* 31, no. 3 (2006–2007): 74–106.

33. David Keen, "Incentives and Disincentives for Violence," in *Greed and Grievance: Economic Agendas in Civil Wars,* ed. Mats Berdal and David Malone (Boulder, CO: Lynne Rienner, 2000); Mark Duffield, *Global Governance and the New Wars: The Merging of Development and Security* (London: Zed, 2001).

34. Christopher Clapham, "Introduction: Analysing African Insurgencies," in *African Guerrillas,* ed. Christopher Clapham (Oxford, UK: James Currey, 1998), 9.

35. Georg Elwert, "Markets of Violence," in *Dynamics of Collective Violence: Processes of Escalation and De-escalation in Violent Group Conflicts,* ed. Georg Elwert, Stephan Feuchtwant, and Dieter Neubert (Berlin: Duncker and Humblot, 1999), 90.

36. Paul Collier, Anke Hoeffler, and Dominic Rohner, "Beyond Greed and Grievance: Feasibility and Civil War," *Oxford Economic Papers* 61 (2009): 1–27.

37. Ana Arjona, *Rebelocracy: Social Order in the Colombian Civil War* (Cambridge, UK: Cambridge University Press, 2016); Paul Staniland, *Networks of Rebellion: Explaining Insurgent Cohesion and Collapse* (Ithaca, NY: Cornell University Press, 2014); Zachariah Cherian Mampilly, *Rebel Rulers: Insurgent Governance and Civilian Life During War* (Ithaca, NY: Cornell University Press, 2011).

38. Fortini Christia, *Alliance Formation in Civil Wars* (Cambridge, UK: Cambridge University Press, 2012); Woldemariam, *Insurgent Fragmentation in the Horn of Africa.*

39. Alia M . Matanock, *Electing Peace: From Civil Conflict to Political Participation* (Cambridge, UK: Cambridge University Press, 2017). See also John Ishiyama, "From Bullets to Ballots: The Transformation of Rebel Groups into Political Parties," *Democratization* 23, no. 6 (2016): 969–971; and Gyda Marås Sindre and Johanna Söderström, "Understanding Armed Groups and Party Politics," *Civil Wars* 18, no. 2 (2016): 109–117.

40. Anthony Downs, *An Economic Theory of Democracy* (Boston: Addison Wesley, 1957), 25.

41. Elisabeth Jean Wood, *Insurgent Collective Action and Civil War in El Salvador* (Cambridge, UK: Cambridge University Press, 2003).

42. Donatella della Porta, *Clandestine Political Violence* (Cambridge, UK: Cambridge University Press, 2013).

43. Arjona, *Rebelocracy*; Patricia Justino, Tilman Brück, and Philip Verwimp, eds., *A Micro-level Perspective on the Dynamics of Conflict, Violence, and Development* (Oxford, UK: Oxford University Press, 2013).

44. Elisabeth Jean Wood, "The Social Processes of Civil War: The Wartime Transformation of Social Networks," *Annual Review of Political Science* 11, no. 1 (2008): 539.

45. Bahru Zewde, *A History of Modern Ethiopia, 1855–1974* (Addis Ababa: Addis Ababa University Press, 1992).

46. Gebru Tareke, *Ethiopia: Protest and Power—Peasant Revolts in the Twentieth Century* (Lawrenceville, NJ: Red Sea, 1996), 116.

47. John Young, *Peasant Revolution in Ethiopia: The Tigray People's Liberation Front, 1975–1991* (Cambridge, UK: Cambridge University Press, 1997), 101–103.

48. Gebru Tareke, *Ethiopia: Protest and Power—Peasant Revolts in the Twentieth Century* (Lawrenceville, NJ: Red Sea, 1996), 208.

49. Cited in Gebru, *Ethiopia*, 217.

50. Aregawi Berhe, *A Political History of the Tigray People's Liberation Front (1975-1991): Revolt, Ideology, and Mobilisation in Ethiopia* (Los Angeles: Tsehai, 2009), 156.

51. Vladimir Lenin, *Revolution, Democracy, Socialism: Selected Writings of Lenin*, ed. Paul Le Blanc (London: Pluto, 2008), 143.

52. Jean-Nicolas Bach, "*Abyotawi* Democracy: Neither Revolutionary nor Democratic—a Critical View of EPRDF's Conception of Revolutionary Democracy in Post-1991 Ethiopia," *Journal of Eastern African Studies* 5, no. 4 (2011): 641–663.

53. Paulos Milkias, "Ethiopia, the TPLF, and the Roots of the 2001 Political Tremor," *Northeast African Studies* 10, no. 2 (2003): 13.

54. Mulugeta Gebrehiwot Berhe, "The Ethiopian Post-transition Security Sector Reform Experience: Building a National Army from a Revolutionary Democratic Army," *African Security Review* 26, no. 2 (2017): 168.

55. Ethiopian People's Revolutionary Democratic Front (EPRDF), *The Development Lines of Revolutionary Democracy* (Addis Ababa EPRDF, 2000). See also Paulos, "Ethiopia, the TPLF, and the Roots of the 2001 Political Tremor"; Medhane Tadesse and John Young, "TPLF: Reform or Decline?" *Review of African Political Economy* 97 (2003): 389–403; Lovise Aalen, *Ethnic Federalism in a Dominant Party State: The Ethiopian Experience, 1991–2000* (Bergen: Chr. Michelsen Institute, 2002); Young, *Peasant Revolution in Ethiopia*.

56. Kahsay Berhe, *Ethiopia: Democratization and Unity—the Role of the Tigray People's Liberation Front* (Munich: Verlagshaus Monsenstein and Vannerdat, 2005), 84. Kahsay was an early member of the TPLF who broke with the top leadership.

57. According to Alex de Waal, the TPLF recruited fighters with little difficulty—if anything, the problem was that more volunteered than the movement had the capacity to absorb. De Waal, *Evil Days: 30 Years of War and Famine in Ethiopia* (New York: Africa Watch, September 1991), 313.

58. Young, *Peasant Revolution in Ethiopia*; Jenny Hammond, *Fire from the Ashes: A Chronicle of the Revolution in Tigray, Ethiopia* (Lawrenceville, NJ: Red Sea, 1999).

59. *Ethiopia: A Country Study* (Washington, DC: Federal Research Division, Library of Congress, 1993).

60. Mulugeta, "The Ethiopian Post-transition Security Sector Reform Experience."

61. Jenny Hammond, "Garrison Towns and the Control of Space in Revolutionary Tigray," in *Remapping Ethiopia: Socialism and After,* ed. Wendy James, Donald L. Donham, Eisei Kurimoto, and Alessandro Triulzi, (Oxford, UK: James Currey, 2002), 92–93.

62. "Ethiopia: A Battle Lost and a War in Stalemate," *Africa Confidential* 29, no. 9 (April 29, 1988).

63. An estimated 1,800–2,000 died in the daylong aerial bombardment of the market town of Hawzen in June 1988. See de Waal, *Evil Days*, 261. This attack was particularly brutal because the town was not under the control of the TPLF, indicating that terrorizing civilians was perceived as an effective and justified means to defeat the insurgents. There is now a memorial to the massacre in the center of town. Author's field notes, Tigray, 2018.

64. Barbara Hendrie, "'Now the People Are Like a Lord': Local Effects of Revolutionary Reform in a Tigray Village, Northern Ethiopia," PhD diss., University College London, 1999.

65. James Firebrace and Gayle Smith, *The Hidden Revolution: An Analysis of Social Change in Tigray (Northern Ethiopia) Based on Eyewitness Accounts* (London: War on Want, 1982).

66. Tigray People's Liberation Front, "Memorandum, Presented by the Tigray People's Liberation Front (TPLF) to the 36th Session of the United Nations General Assembly" 1981, 2, cited in Hendrie, "'Now the People Are Like a Lord,'" 72.

67. Quoted in anonymous document.

68. Aregawi, *Political History of the Tigray People's Liberation Front*, 251.

69. Aregawi, *Political History of the Tigray People's Liberation Front,* 252, 281.

70. Aregawi, *Political History of the Tigray People's Liberation Front*, 282. Aregawi further states, "Nobody was left behind, whether one liked it or not, yet no association was in a position to defend or articulate its members' interest as much as it was required to defend the interest of the Front, i.e., 'the struggle.' The pervasive thinking was that the interest of the associations and the society at large would be best served *after* the war against the oppressive system came to an end" (310–311).

71. Clapham, "Controlling Space in Ethiopia," 23.

72. For a view that emphasizes solidarity between the TPLF and the peasants, see Alex de Waal, "Ethiopia's Transition to What?" *World Policy Journal* 9, no. 4 (Fall–Winter 1992): 719–737.

73. Gebre ab Barnabas and Anthony Zwi, "Health Policy Development in Wartime: Establishing the Baito Health Care System in Tigray, Ethiopia," *Health Policy and Planning* 12, no. 1 (1997): 42.

74. De Waal, *Evil Days*, 314.

75. Meles Zenawi quoted in Peter Gill, *Famine and Foreigners: Ethiopia Since Live Aid* (Oxford, UK: Oxford University Press, 2010), 70.

76. Barbara Hendrie, "The Politics of Repatriation: The Tigrayan Refugee Repatriation, 1985–1987," *Journal of Refugee Studies* 4, no. 2 (June 1991): 200–218.

77. John Prendergast and Mark Duffield, *Without Troops and Tanks: The Emergency Relief Desk and the Cross Border Operation in Eritrea and Tigray* (Trenton, NJ: Red Sea, 1994); Gayle Smith, "Ethiopia and the Politics of Famine Relief," *MERIP Reports* 17, no. 145 (March–April 1987); John Young, "Development and Change in Post-revolutionary Tigray," *Journal of Modern African Studies* 35, no. 1 (March 1997): 81–99. For a sense of the organization's self-presentation, see Tigray Development Association, "1989–2014: 25th Anniversary," http://www.tdaint.org/Docs/TDA%2025%20Anniversary.pdf.

78. Davide Chinigò and Emanuele Fantini, "Thermidor in Ethiopia? Agrarian Transformations Between Economic Liberalization and the Developmental State," *EchoGéo* 31 (2015): 4.

79. This was not unique to the TPLF. The EPLF had particularly active international offices. In general, see Bridget L. Coggins, "Rebel Diplomacy: Theorizing Violent Non-state Actors' Use of Talk," in *Rebel Governance in Civil War,* ed. Ana Arjona, Nelson Kasfir, and Zachariah Mampilly (Cambridge, UK: Cambridge University Press, 2015); Reyko Huang, "Rebel Diplomacy in Civil War," *International Security* 40, no. 4 (2016): 89–126.

80. Young, "Tigray and Eritrean People's Liberation Fronts." See also Richard Reid, "Old Problems in New Conflicts: Some Observations on Eritrea and Its Relations with Tigray, from Liberation Struggle to Inter-state War," *Africa* 73, no. 3 (2003): 369–401; Ruth Iyob, "The Ethiopian-Eritrean Conflict: Diasporic vs. Hegemonic States in the Horn of Africa, 1991–2000," *Journal of Modern African Studies* 38, no. 4 (2000): 659–682.

81. Siye Abraha (later minister of defense), Yemane "Jamaica" Kidane, and Mahari "Mussie" Haile received training in EPLF camps. See Andebrhan Welde Giorgis, *Eritrea at a Crossroads: A Narrative of Betrayal and Hope* (Houston, TX: Strategic, 2014), 145–146.

82. Young, "Tigray and Eritrean People's Liberation Fronts," 105.

83. "On Our Difference with the EPLF," *People's Voice: Publication of the Tigray People's Liberation Front,* Special Issue (1986): 7, cited in Young, "Tigray and Eritrean People's Liberation Fronts," 112.

84. "Formation of the Ethiopian People's Revolutionary Democratic Front," *People's Voice: Publication of the Tigray People's Liberation Front* Special Issue 11, no. 1 (1989): 9.

85. "The Tigray People's Liberation Front: 14 Years of Struggle," *People's Voice: Publication of the Tigray People's Liberation Front* Special Issue 11, no. 1 (1989): 1.

86. Kjetil Tronvoll, *War and the Politics of Identity in Ethiopia: The Making of Enemies and Allies in the Horn of Africa* (Oxford, UK: James Currey, 2009), 49, 56.

87. P. T. W. Baxter, "Ethiopia's Unacknowledged Problem: The Oromo," *African Affairs,* 77, no. 308 (July 1978): 283–296; Edmond J. Keller, "The Ethnogenesis of the Oromo Nation and Its Implications for Politics in Ethiopia," *Journal of Modern Africa Studies* 33, no. 4 (1995): 621–634.

88. This process of self-consciousness as a nation is well developed in P. T. W. Baxter, Jan Hultin, and Alessandro Triulzi, eds., *Being and Becoming Oromo: Historical and Anthropological Enquiries* (Lawrenceville, NJ: Red Sea, 1996).

89. Mekuria Bulcha, "Survival and Reconstruction of National Identity," in *Being and Becoming Oromo: Historical and Anthropological Enquiries,* ed. P. T. W. Baxter, Jan Hultin, and Alessandro Triulzi (Lawrenceville, NJ: Red Sea, 1996).

90. Baxter, "Ethiopia's Unacknowledged Problem."

91. For the OLF's official history, see "The Birth of the Oromo Liberation Front," http://www.gadaa.com/OromoLiberationFront.html and Gadaa Melbaa, *Oromia: A Brief Introduction* (Finfine: Oromia, 1980).

92. Asafa Jalata, *Oromia and Ethiopia: State Formation and Ethnonational Conflict, 1868–1992* (Boulder, CO: Lynne Rienner, 1993), 165.

93. de Waal, *Evil Days*, 69. For some analysis emphasizing Oromos in western Ethiopia, see Øyvind M. Eide, *Revolution and Religion in Ethiopia: The Growth and Persecution of the Mekane Yesus Church, 1974–1985* (Oxford, UK: James Currey, 2000).

94. Lencho Letta, quoted in Sarah Vaughan, *The Addis Ababa Transitional Conference of July 1991: Its Origins, History, and Significance* (Edinburgh: Edinburgh University, Centre for African Studies, 1994), 17.

95. Mesfin Seyoum, quoted in Vaughan, *Addis Ababa Transitional Conference of July 1991*, 18.

96. *Africa Confidential* 27, no. 16 (July 30, 1986): 6.

97. Martin Plaut, "The Oromo Liberation Front," *Review of African Political Economy* 33, no. 109 (September 2006): 587–593; John Markakis, *National and Class Conflict in the Horn of Africa* (Cambridge, UK: Cambridge University Press, 1987), 263; Clapham, *Transformation and Continuity in Revolutionary Ethiopia*, 218–219.

98. Asafa, *Oromia and Ethiopia*, 167.

99. "Ethiopia's Hidden War: The Oromo Liberation Struggle," *Horn of Africa* 5, no. 1 (1983).

100. Thomas Zittlemann, "Toward Acquisition of Conflict Knowledge: Fieldwork Among the Oromo Liberation Front and Oromo Refugees During the 1980s," in *Fieldwork: Social Realities in Anthropological Perspectives,* ed. Peter Berger et al. (Berlin: WeiBensee Verlag, 2009).

101. Andargachew Tiruneh, *Ethiopian Revolution, 1974–199*, 366.

102. Eide, *Revolution and Religion in Ethiopia*, 204.

103. Asafa Jalata, *Contending Nationalisms of Oromia and Ethiopia: Struggling for Statehood, Sovereignty, and Multinational Democracy* (Binghamton, NY: Global Academic Press, 2010), 105.

104. Interview cited in Kifle Wansamo, "Towards Building Stability in a Multinational/Ethnic Society: Conflicts in Sidamaland, Ethiopia," PhD diss., Lancaster University, 2007, 156.

105. Paulos Milkias, "*Zemecha:* An Assessment of the Political and Social Foundations of Mass Education in Ethiopia," *Northeast African Studies* 2, no. 1 (1980): 19–30.

106. Elizabeth E. Watson, "Making a Living in the Postsocialist Periphery: Struggles Between Farmers and Traders in Konso, Ethiopia," *Africa* 76, no. 1 (February 2006): 79.

107. Donald L. Donham, *Marxist Modern: An Ethnographic History of the Ethiopian Revolution* (Berkeley: University of California Press, 1999).

108. Jon Abbink, "Authority and Leadership in Surma Society (Ethiopia)," *Africa* 52, no. 3 (1997): 324, 330–331.

109. Kifle Wansamo, *Towards Building Stability in a Multinational/Ethnic Society*.

110. Dessalegn Rahmato, "The Unquiet Countryside: The Collapse of 'Socialism' and Rural Agitation," in *Ethiopia in Change: Peasantry, Nationalism, and*

Democracy, ed. Abebe Zegeye and Siegfried Pausewang (London: British Academic Press, 1994), 242–279.

111. Another organization, the Ethiopian Democratic Officers Revolutionary Movement, was also an original member of the EPRDF but soon disappeared, with its members absorbed into the ethnically defined constituent units.

112. Many of the EPRP fighters who went into exile later became leaders of the opposition in the diaspora.

113. "Formation of the Ethiopian People's Revolutionary Democratic Front," *People's Voice: Publication of the Tigray People's Liberation Front,* Special Issue 11, no. 1 (1989): 10.

114. Patrick Gilkes, *Ethiopia: Perspectives of Conflict, 1991–1999* (Bern: Swisspeace Foundation, 1999), 23.

115. Vaughan, *Addis Ababa Transitional Conference of July 1991,* 6.

116. According to the EPRDF, the OPDO had its foundational conference in Adet, an area in Tigray under the control of the TPLF. See http://www.eprdf.org .et/web/opdo/about-opdo.

117. MOND, Intelligence 022-24, Yä Soasä Wätadärawi Märäja Amätawi Report (TRA's Military Intelligence Annual Report), 1982 E.C., 52–56. Cited in Fantahun, *Ethiopian Military,* 195.

118. For context see Fekadu Adugna, "Overlapping Nationalist Projects and Contested Spaces: The Oromo-Somali Borderlands in Southern Ethiopia," *Journal of Eastern African Studies* 5, no. 4 (2011): 773–787.

119. Maria Bongartz, *The Civil War in Somalia: Its Genesis and Dynamics* (Uppsala: Nordiska Afrikainstitutet, 1991).

120. The ONLF joined the transitional government after the fall of the Derg and participated in the 1992 elections, as I discuss in Chapter 3.

121. Members of the ALF participated in local government following the 1991 transition.

122. Dereje, *Playing Different Games,* 137.

123. For context, see Terrence Lyons, "Great Powers and Conflict Reduction in the Horn of Africa," in *Cooperative Security: Reducing Third World Wars,* ed. I. William Zartman and Victor A. Kremenyuk (Syracuse, NY: Syracuse University Press, 1995).

124. Marina Ottaway, "Eritrea and Ethiopia: Negotiations in a Transitional Conflict," in *Elusive Peace: Negotiating an End to Civil Wars,* ed. I. William Zartman (Washington, DC: Brookings Institution, 1995).

125. de Waal, "Ethiopia's Transition to What?"

126. Terrence Lyons, "The Transition in Ethiopia," *Africa Notes* No. 127 (Washington, DC: Center for Strategic and International Studies, August 27, 1991), https://www.csis.org/analysis/africa-notes-transition-ethiopia-august-1991.

127. "'Cohen's Coup' in Ethiopia," *Newsweek,* June 9, 1991, http://www .newsweek.com/cohens-coup-ethiopia-204144.

128. Statement by the Supreme Council of the EPRDF, May 21, 1991, cited in Vaughan, *Addis Ababa Transitional Conference of July 1991,* 1.

3

New Rules of the Game

The Ethiopian People's Revolutionary Democratic Front (EPRDF) faced enormous hurdles when it took power in May 1991. The country was in ruins, surrounded by neighbors in turmoil, and the population was bone tired of fighting. Politically the alliance was newly formed; some constituent parties such as the Tigray People's Liberation Front (TPLF) were strong and battle hardened, whereas others such as the Oromo People's Democratic Organization (OPDO) were still inchoate. The alliance did not yet include representation from the large and diverse southern region or the border regions such as Somali, Afar, Benishangul-Gumuz, and Gambela. The question of Eritrea's independence had been settled on the battlefield, but significant constituencies objected to losing what they regarded as a historical part of Ethiopia and, more instrumentally, access to the sea. Ethiopians had suffered from years of famine and agricultural policies that stifled growth. The TPLF's ideology during the time of the armed struggle, with its emphasis on Marxism-Leninism and revolution, seemed unlikely to receive significant international support in a time of neoliberal triumphalism. The victorious rebel movement's position on national self-determination was anathema to many Ethiopian nationalists, especially among urban professionals and the diaspora. Demobilization of both insurgent forces and the collapsing Derg military, writing and enacting a new constitution, and creating a system of accountability for war crimes added to the already formidable challenges.

The war-to-peace transition following the EPRDF's victory provided opportunities to scrap dysfunctional institutions, address contentious issues, and put in place new rules that remained nearly three decades later. First, both in terms of priority and sequence, the EPRDF needed to transform itself from a largely Tigrayan-led insurgent army

49

into a civilian ruling party that could govern the enormously diverse country. Second, the historical sociopolitical order based on a hierarchy in which the highlands dominated the lowland periphery had to be overturned and required a new conception of state-society relations and a new national narrative. Third, the war-torn economy, with its failed state farms and villagization schemes, had to be reorganized dramatically to support the rapidly growing population. Finally, the new regime had to manage a difficult set of regional relationships with Sudan, Somalia, and newly independent Eritrea as well as a shift from external support from the Soviet Union to the new neoliberal "Washington consensus" of donors and international financial institutions.

Although the Derg regime and its military had collapsed, the state in the form of an administrative structure remained in place. There is a particular conception of the state in Ethiopia that builds upon the hierarchical and authoritarian notions of governance associated with the cultures and societies of the northern Ethiopian highlands.[1] In 1991, most civil servants except high-level political officials remained at work, managing the complex bureaucracy with its seemingly insatiable appetite for red tape, official stamps, and requirements for approvals from higher offices. Even the removal of the Lenin statue from its prominent position in Addis Ababa was not an act of popular spontaneity but was conducted by civil servants working for the Ethiopian Building and Construction Authority. Michael Hiltzik, a *Los Angeles Times* reporter, spoke with the civil servant who removed the statue and found that he was the same engineer who had supervised its erection. "'They ordered me to put it up,' he said. 'Now they've told me to take it down.'"[2] The *mengist* (state), in the form of power and authority, was never absent.

In contrast with war-to-peace transitions in places such as El Salvador, Mozambique, Liberia, Cambodia, or Bosnia-Herzegovina that also took place in the 1990s, the Ethiopian transition was not the result of a negotiated settlement. Consequently, the international community played a decidedly secondary role. In many cases of war-to-peace transitions, the central challenges relate to power sharing between the regime and the rebels.[3] In Ethiopia, however, the test was to incorporate a broader and more diverse set of constituencies than had been part of the wartime coalition. The EPRDF victory, not a third-party brokered settlement involving a UN peacekeeping operation and internationally verified postconflict elections, determined the transition's outcome. The transition in Ethiopia, as in Uganda and Rwanda, where the rebels also won their respective civil wars, was an endogenous process of which the outcome was determined by the victors.[4] The old Derg regime was largely irrelevant to the postwar political dispensation because its leadership fled, the Worker's Party of Ethiopia collapsed, and its army rapidly dissipated. Although the transition included many key processes and institutions of liberal peace building, such as elections, demobilization, and new transitional justice mechanisms, in Ethiopia the victorious EPRDF created these to promote its consolidation of power.

The Rebels in Control

> This was a new model dictated partly by necessity—how could an ethnoregional minority from Tigray suddenly rule a large, diverse country without secure 'ethnic allies'?—and partly by an ideological programme aimed at reversing 'ethnic' hierarchies, ousting the perceived elites in place, and impose a new political dispensation.[5]

After Mengistu Haile Mariam fled in 1991, the EPRDF seized power in Addis Ababa without resistance beyond a brief skirmish with remnants of the old regime's army near the presidential palace.[6] Some observers suggested, "Overjoyed with the coming of peace, Ethiopians took heart . . . and the change of regime from the Dergue to the EPRDF went through unopposed."[7] This was true in the sense that there was no significant armed resistance to the EPRDF's entry into Addis Ababa, but many urban professionals perceived the EPRDF rebels as uncultured *balagars* (hicks) from the countryside, not legitimate rulers. Some residents and professionals suffered culture shock as they watched the peasant soldiers, men with wild hair and women in trousers, enter the city. Anti-EPRDF protests in late May turned violent as marchers defied the ban on demonstrations.[8]

Several legacies of the Ethiopian revolution and the Derg regime shaped postwar developments. The nationalization of land in 1974 meant that the government had enormous influence over the most fundamental day-to-day requirements of the overwhelmingly rural society. In addition, the structures of the *kebele* (neighborhood associations) established by the Derg remained in place, a potent mechanism for distributing patronage, collecting information, and controlling the population. The state institutions the EPRDF seized in 1991 had been brutal but also effective, notably in their capacity to monitor and discipline the population. The postwar state built upon these legacies, not on the assumed blank slate of a failed state.

Perhaps the most difficult challenge the EPRDF faced in 1991 was how to address relations among Ethiopia's ethnic groups. Although the seventeen-year, multiple-front armed struggle had many origins, insurgent groups mobilized around diverse identities dominated the struggle and ultimately won the war. The Eritrean People's Liberation Front (EPLF) mobilized around an Eritrean identity. The TPLF, Oromo Liberation Front (OLF), and the smaller liberation fronts in Sidamo, Afar, Somali, and Benishangul-Gumuz all organized on the basis of national liberation and narratives of historical marginalization by an Amhara-dominated state. As Clapham put it, the new regime faced the fundamental challenge of "the relationship between a Christian-dominated and Amharic-speaking center and the various peripheral peoples and regions."[9] A new political order rooted in a new set of relationships among ethnic groups was needed to consolidate the EPRDF's power.

Previous regimes had sought to hold the state together by emphasizing Ethiopian nationalism and unity, even though many of the people beyond the Orthodox Christian, highland core saw this as a system of government that treated them as second-class citizens at best.[10] The EPRDF, in a dramatic reversal, emphasized group rights and shifted focus away from Ethiopian nationalism. Meles Zenawi, longtime TPLF and EPRDF leader, reportedly said, "The Tigreans had Axum, but what could that mean to the Guragie? The Agew had Lalibela, but what could that mean to the Oromo? The Gonderes had castles, but what could that mean to the Wolaita?"[11] The change of national narrative was dramatic. Markakis said, "All in all, it seemed a reversal of direction followed in the century-old process of Ethiopian state building."[12] This radical redirection, however, was driven by a pragmatic sense of what was needed to govern a country already mobilized around ethnicity and to marginalize some of the new regime's pan-Ethiopian critics rather than by an ideological position hostile to Ethiopian nationalism.[13]

Meles suggested that the key to the war was the issue of the right of all nationalities to self-administration and to use their own language and maintain their own culture. This might well have been true after fifteen years of armed struggle in Tigray and to an extent in Oromia. But it was far less true in the Amhara region, where ideas of pan-Ethiopian nationalism remained powerful, or in southern Ethiopia, which had a diffuse sense of identity before 1991. Being a Kambata or Wolayita as a primary political identification became much more salient after the 1991 transition. When it became clear that leading a "nationality" that had its own people's democratic organization (PDO) was the only way to gain access to power and resources, it is not surprising that nationality became the most important criterion for mobilization. After political institutions defined around identity became powerful, nonethnic parties had little opportunity to gain power.

Ethnofederalism and the New Political Dispensation

Following its military victory in 1991, the EPRDF restructured the Ethiopian state as a federation of ethnically defined regions. The adoption of ethnofederalism drew upon a long tradition of Marxist-Leninist thought and fierce debates within the 1970s Ethiopian student movement on the "national question." The EPRDF deemphasized Ethiopian nationalism and argued that the state could only survive if group rights were made the central organizing principle. Meles argued in 1991, for example, "A feudal monarchy and a repressive dictator couldn't hold Ethiopia together. Now we are trying another way. If Ethiopia breaks apart, then it wasn't meant to be."[14] Meles further argued, "We cannot ignore that Ethiopia is a diverse country. Previous attempts to do that have led to wars, to fueling nationalistic tendencies."[15] Rather than emphasizing national unity and linking the contemporary state to the glorious past as symbolized by the historical treasures of Axum, Lalibela, and Gondar, the EPRDF boldly—some say recklessly—chose to construct a political system that reflected the aspirations of many in the historically marginalized south.[16] Meles stated that a new Ethiopian identity would emerge from below after the "first" and "real" identities of the Ethiopian people had an opportunity to flourish. "People should be proud of their identity and ethnic identity. . . . What incites disintegration is the view that we are all one."[17]

The impact of this new dispensation was profound and transformed the old social hierarchy.[18] In many parts of southern Ethiopia, populations such as the Konso had felt as if they "passed their time as slaves" under the emperor and the Derg.[19] After 1991, however, Konso people staffed local government offices in their own special *woredas,* and their local language was accepted for conducting official business. Many historically marginalized groups perceived this new political order as their first real opportunity to have any say in their own political lives.

The EPRDF recognized the challenge of developing non-Tigray affiliates during the civil war and, in response, recruited leaders from among prisoners of war to form ethnic vanguards that could move quickly into southern areas after victory. These cadres established peace and stability committees within days of the regime change and transformed these committees into PDOs throughout southern Ethiopia in time to dominate local elections in 1992. This proved crucial and facilitated the EPRDF penetration of these areas unknown to the top leadership because they had remained outside the areas where the civil war was fought. Many of the new parties from southern Ethiopia were created on the spot. Senior TPLF official Sebhat Nega explained:

"We picked organizations from all over—two from here, two from there. One day Hayelom telephoned from Awassa to say that he had just come across another one."[20] Many of these had minimal connections with the notional "nationality" they each represented.[21] The OPDO had evolved into a sizeable organization by the time of the EPRDF's victory, but many others were very much works in progress in the early transition period. In some cases, EPRDF cadres came into conflict with local elites or traditional structures of authority.

The first steps taken by the new EPRDF-led Transitional Government of Ethiopia (TGE), however, suggested a surprisingly inclusive transition that welcomed a variety of actors into politics. The TPLF had decided at its third congress (1989) that it would establish a provisional government "constituted from all political organizations" following the defeat of the Derg. In July 1991, just five weeks after seizing power, the EPRDF convened a national conference, to which it invited representatives from more than twenty political movements. Some of these were small ethnic parties, newly organized under EPRDF tutelage, led by urban elites with weak ties to the countryside. A few had participated in the struggle against the Derg and had autonomous bases of support, most importantly the OLF, a potentially powerful political force to the extent that it could mobilize Oromo nationalism. Some organizations were not invited: the discredited Workers' Party of Ethiopia (WPE) and several nonethnic parties with their origins in the student movement of the 1970s, including archrivals EPRP and Meison, which had united in exile to form the Coalition of Ethiopian Democratic Forces (COEDF).[22] The absence of these multiethnic organizations reinforced the leadership roles played by ethnic parties and shaped the ethnofederal transitional charter adopted.

The EPRDF dominated the national conference and kept participation, the agenda, and therefore the eventual outcome firmly under its careful control. As de Waal correctly puts it, "The EPRDF, despite its rhetoric to the contrary, is both the brains and the muscle of the Transitional Government."[23] The new rulers asserted that the transitional charter represented the "common political issues" of all parties that participated in the conference.[24] The OLF played a key role, acting in tactical alliance with the EPRDF in developing the charter, and welcomed the charter's promises of self-determination and the empowerment of traditionally marginalized peoples. Lencho Letta, the OLF leader, perceived an important shift in the relationships between the OLF and the EPRDF as they moved to create a "covenant" that would be a "departure from the past."[25]

The transition commenced, it seemed, with a working coalition of multiple parties around a broad-based pact that most of these major social groups supported.[26] But the OLF maintained that it alone had the right to represent the Oromo people and saw the OPDO, the EPRDF's Oromo wing, as an affront to its historical struggle. The Amhara were not represented explicitly. What later became the Amhara National Democratic Movement (a constituent part of the EPRDF) was organized at the time of the transitional government as the multiethnic Ethiopian People's Democratic Movement (EPDM). Although the initial national conference was diverse, it already raised questions about how Oromo and Amhara outside the EPRDF would participate and whether the newly founded southern PDOs could develop into viable parties.

The EPRDF intended to build new political and administrative structures on the basis of ethnicity. The transitional charter accepted the rights of all Ethiopia's nationalities to self-determination, including secession, and established "local and regional councils defined on the basis of nationality" (Article XIII). The decision to favor ethnically defined regions shaped the subsequent patterns of representation and political competition. In January 1992 the Transitional Council of Representatives reorganized the country into thirteen regions, gerrymandered to be as ethnically homogenous as possible (I discuss the map more extensively later).[27]

Not surprisingly, the history of migration and intermarriage in Ethiopia and the overlapping, fluid, and contextual nature of identity created a much more complicated social reality on the ground than suggested by these regions, and the boundaries became the subject of controversy and strife, not least because they institutionalized ethnicity as the dominant consideration in determining who had legitimate claims to power and resources. In an electoral environment in which the constituencies were defined ethnically, political parties and leaders had few options but to campaign on the basis of ethnic appeals that often threatened to incite chauvinism, discrimination against minority enclaves, and intercommunal violence. In a largely ethnically homogeneous constituency, parties had incentive to claim they would advance the interests of their people (sometimes at the expense of the "other" and minority enclaves) better than competing parties would. This kind of ethnic outbidding often polarized populations and required a strong center to constrain centrifugal forces.

The role of the Oromo—the largest single ethnic group in Ethiopia— in the new state was contentious from the start. As the Derg regime collapsed, the OLF had expanded its military capacity by rapidly recruiting demobilized Oromo soldiers. The OLF sought to fill the vacuum created by the disintegration of the Derg by rapidly establishing its presence across Oromia. At the London talks the EPRDF and the OLF agreed to continue to administer the areas they controlled at the time the Derg was defeated. The EPRDF, however, claimed that the OLF moved into new areas in the southeast, trying to create military facts on the ground before new government institutions could be established.

The transition process nearly broke down in late 1991 and early 1992, when tensions between the EPRDF and the OLF escalated from bickering within the Transitional Government to military clashes that threatened to return the country to full-scale civil war.[28] The OLF and the OPDO competed for political control over the same strategic areas and maneuvered for position in anticipation of elections and the establishment of regional administrations. In April 1992, talks cochaired by the provisional government of Eritrea and the United States resulted in a cease-fire and an encampment of OLF forces monitored by the Eritreans, thereby allowing the transition to continue.[29] This tense and tenuous peace allowed the Transitional Government to schedule local and regional elections in June 1992.

Beyond its establishment of the OPDO, the EPRDF worked rapidly to recruit, train, and deploy political operatives to the areas of the South where it had no presence during the armed struggle. The rebel movement specifically identified prisoners of war from southern Ethiopia and trained them to become the first wave of administrators and local party candidates. In the countryside the EPRDF sought to recruit the rural petty intelligentsia—elementary school teachers, nurses, agricultural extension agents, and so forth. The party feared that the more educated and prominent members of the local elite—engineers, doctors, and civil servants—might "vacillate" and "could align itself with enemy forces."[30] Politicization of ethnicity, however, did not lead to increased respect for traditional rulers and institutions. Tronvoll and Hagmann argue, "The EPRDF's philosophy of ethnic politics has been markedly modernist and provides no space for customary powers within the representative institutions of the country."[31] This follows the pattern of the TPLF during the civil war when it systematically sought to abolish traditional hierarchies and cultural institutions it saw as contributing to the backwardness of the peasantry. The EPRDF therefore had aspirations not only to replace the old political order but also to transform and modernize Ethiopian social relations at the grassroots.

Creating a New National Armed Force

The process of demobilization and the creation of a new national army provided additional opportunities to broaden the postwar EPRDF and incorporate constituencies from areas outside the northern highlands.[32] Conscripts from the shattered military of the vanquished regime desperately wanted to return to their homes, and the new regime perceived threats from ex-combatants without livelihoods or community ties. Demobilization was not a matter of a negotiated agreement with external monitoring, as with many civil war settlements, but rather related to domestic concerns of security, financial resources, and the welfare of ex-combatants.[33] Reintegrating them into communities, therefore, was imperative for the stability of the postwar regime. The new regime set up the Commission for the Rehabilitation of Members of the Former Army and Disabled War Veterans to manage the process. The commission's goal was to contribute to security and stability by restricting the movement of ex-combatants rather than to manage the dilemmas characteristic of security sector reform after a negotiated settlement. In the end, much of the army, estimated to be 300,000–350,000, simply returned home with modest stipends.

In January 1992, the TGE assigned the EPRDF to oversee security affairs of the new state. The insurgent army formally became the post-transition national army.[34] The postwar Ethiopian National Defense Force (ENDF) sought to decrease the number of soldiers from Tigray and recruit more soldiers from southern Ethiopia so that the national army more closely reflected national diversity.[35] Observers estimated that the TPLF represented 80 percent of the fighters in the military during the 1989–1991 campaign.[36] The demobilization of some longtime TPLF fighters was difficult, as solidarity built up over the course of protracted struggle had created deep bonds. One senior Ethiopian military leader recalled demobilization "was one of the saddest moments; seeing off comrades was difficult."[37]

The first steps of the war-to-peace transition, therefore, immediately put in place key structures of governance and new rules that continued to shape Ethiopian politics from 1991 to 2018. Politics would be organized around ethnically defined regions and parties. The EPRDF, as the victorious party, would control the transition and the subsequent regime. Reconstruction of the state's security forces would provide a means to integrate populations that had not participated in the civil war but would come under the leadership of the EPRDF. The new rules, in other words, served to allow the TPLF insurgent force to broaden its base and transform itself into a national political party and national military force.

The New Map and Ethnofederalism

The TGE restructured regional borders from the generally multiethnic pre-1991 regions that sometimes served as a source of local identity. The emperor had created a new set of internal boundaries following the

Italian occupation, and many of the provinces reflected even earlier historical focal points (see Figure 3.1). Gojjam was its own kingdom, for example, before the late nineteenth century, and many there self-identified as Gojjami rather than Amhara. The emperor's map had the further quality of bringing lowland and highland areas together in many provinces. Gondar and Begemder included both Amhara-inhabited highlands but also lowland populations along the border with Sudan, whereas Wollo included highlands and the Afar depression. Wellega, Illubabor, and Kaffa included a majority of Oromos but also non-Oromos in the far west and south as well as multiethnic cities that had their origins as garrison towns, such as Jimma, Nekemte, and Goba.[38] This map shows ethnicity was not the only viable basis for forming local political structures.

In 1987, the Derg created a new map designed to regroup the population into regions in a way that divided opposition movements and

Figure 3.1   Ethiopia's Provinces Under Haile Selassie

provided incentives for some ethnic groups to remain within the state.[39] The state was demarcated into twenty-five administrative regions and five autonomous regions. Eritrea was split into two, Tigray lost territory, and the Somali region was split into several distinct states. This map moved toward ethnic regions but stopped many steps short of the EPRDF's 1991 map.

The post-1991 map developed by the EPRDF (see Figure 1.1 on p. 2) divided the population into regions explicitly defined by their ethnicity, along with multiethnic chartered cities in Addis Ababa and later Dire Dawa.[40] The Oromo, for example, who had lived in the imperial regions of Wellega, Shewa, Sidamo, Illubabor, Kaffa, Arsi, Bale, and Hararghe before 1991, were clustered into a single, large Oromia regional state. These new boundaries often set off local conflicts because the Oromo and Somali populations, for example, fought over claims of which ethnic group "belonged" in an area and which group controlled resources on one or the other side of the new border.[41] In what became the Southern Nations, Nationalities, and People's Region (SNNPR), the question of whether to create special zones designed to be dominated by a particular group became contentious. These intraregional border questions escalated into significant violence in 2016–2017.

As Table 3.1 shows, the regional states in Ethiopia differ dramatically. The Oromo regional state has a population almost seven times larger than that of the Tigray state. The complex ethnic conglomeration of the SNNPR is quite different from the historic sense of identity among the Amhara.

For the purposes of this new ethnofederalist order, Ethiopia adopted a static, almost primordial concept of ethnicity. Language was regarded as the main marker for identity despite considerable variation across groups. Politically, an individual was treated as if she or he had a single ethnic identity. Those with parents from different ethnic groups had to choose one, and "Ethiopian" was not an option.[42] Political rights were associated with the idea that communities based upon descent were the most salient basis for identity and that this identity was the most appropriate unit for political representation. Reconstituting the country as an ethnic federation brought into the politicolegal arena the question of who belonged to which ethnic group and which group was entitled to govern which territory. As a result, the boundaries between ethnic groups became a source of endless contention. Each regional state or, in the multiethnic SNNPR, each ethnically defined zone or *woreda*, had a titular ethnic group that had the right to claim legitimate authority to govern and administer territory. As long

Table 3.1   Area and Population of Regional States

Region	Area (km²)	Population (2017 est.)	Percentage of Total
Oromia	284,538	35,467,001	37.6
Amhara	154,709	21,134,988	22.4
SNNPR	105,476	19,170,007	20.3
Somali	279,252	5,748,998	6.9
Tigray	53,638	5,247,005	5.6
Addis Ababa	527	3,433,999	3.6
Afar	72,053	1,812,002	1.9
Benishangul-Gumuz	50,699	1,066,001	1.1
Gambela	29,783	435,999	0.5
Dire Dawa	1,213	466,000	0.3
Harar	334	246,000	0.3
Total	1,032,222	94,228,000	100

Note: Population figures are estimates provided by the Central Statistical Agency, *Population Projection of Ethiopia for All Regions at Woreda Level from 2014–2017* (Addis Ababa: Central Statistical Agency, August 2013). The planned 2019 census was postponed in March 2019. Country totals include estimated population from eight rural kebeles in Elidar wereda, Afar Regional State, and additional populations in Special Enumeration Areas.

recognized by scholars of ethnic identity formation, the construction of an "other" is key to creating a distinct identity.[43] The conflation of ethnicity and territorial boundaries heightened the importance of and therefore conflict over how identities were created and consolidated.

The constitutions of the regional states made the link between a people and the regional government clear. The constitution of Oromia, for example, provided that "sovereign power in the region resides in the people of the Oromo nation."[44] Non-Oromo living in Oromia therefore were not part of the body politic and had different status. The Benishangul-Gumuz regional state constitution said, "Notwithstanding the recognition of other peoples living in the Region, the indigenous nationalities of the Region are Berta, Gumuz, Shinasha, Mao, and Como."[45] The SNNPR had its Council of Nationalities, the only regional state with a bicameral legislature, in recognition of the more than fifty ethnic groups who shared the region and the need for an institution to manage interethnic competition. The relationships between language and identity and hence power in Ethiopia were clear; hence, the adoption of official languages—and thus the languages of schools and government—was contentious.[46] Although ethnofederalism served as an overarching principle and group rights the dominant legal framework, the specificities of each region required different institutional arrangements.

Elections Under Authoritarian Rule

Ethiopia, like many other authoritarian regimes, held elections regularly. However, "electoral authoritarian" regimes such as in Ethiopia, Schedler argues, are neither democratic nor democratizing but are essentially authoritarian.[47] Leaders in these regimes typically create the full panoply of institutions of liberal democracy, such as written constitutions, elections, parliaments, and courts.[48] Electoral authoritarian regimes hold regular elections but do so without the kinds of political rights and freedoms necessary for them to be a tool for advancing democracy. Citizens generally are not empowered to choose their political leaders fairly. Incumbents can limit their risks of losing by fragmenting opposition parties, denying the opposition fair access to public media and space to campaign, or using the power of the state to manipulate voter preferences through patronage and/or threats.[49] Participation by opposition parties is allowed, and the principle, if not the practice, of political pluralism is accepted. Well-run elections are possible, and decisions are framed with regard to the rule of law, but the authoritarian context does not allow for competition to threaten the power of the incumbent leadership.

Elections, however, can be consequential without being democratic or competitive. They often serve as one of the central arenas for struggle and help define the rules, actors, resources, and strategies of politics. Participation in elections can serve as a mechanism to recruit those who will be successful in attracting votes and to retire those who are incompetent or corrupt.[50] As suggested by Gandhi, institutions in authoritarian contexts help promote stability by providing a mechanism to co-opt opposition.[51]

In addition to competing for votes, the authoritarian incumbent in an election seeks to control key institutions to determine substantive outcomes, whereas the opposition tries to challenge and reform those institutions. In these circumstances opposition parties are often ambivalent about electoral contests. On the one hand, noncompetitive elections legitimate the system they regard as unfair, but on the other they provide opportunities to reach out to voters and dramatize the authoritarian nature of the regime. Before an election, the key strategic decision for opposition parties is whether to boycott or participate and, after results are announced, whether to protest or accept them. The key challenge for an authoritarian ruling party in holding an election is how to gain the benefits of the process to distribute patronage, demonstrate power, and thereby consolidate its rule while minimizing the risks of allowing dissent to mobilize.[52]

Ethiopian elections (with the exception of 2005) have been non-competitive but have played fundamental roles in shaping the rules, resources, and actors engaged in the political process. The EPRDF used a series of elections to build a powerful, dominant party and to marginalize political opposition. It controlled the key institutions, which shaped the conditions of political competition, and used harassment and politically motivated arrests to marginalize opposition candidates. The opposition used the opportunities afforded by the elections to protest electoral procedures and patterns of political intimidation as well as to challenge the regime's legitimacy and authority. Some parties, notably the OLF, the Ogaden National Liberation Front (ONLF), and, after 2005, Ginbot 7, abandoned electoral strategies and claimed to be engaged in armed struggle. Others sought to create alternative institutions based on all-party conventions, boycotted elections they regarded as unfair, and appealed to the international community for support. In this chapter I consider the 1992 regional elections, the first postconflict elections in Ethiopia, and the national elections of 1995, the first polls under the new constitution. In Chapter 6 I further analyze electoral competition, and in particular the 2005 electoral crisis—to better understand the nature of the EPRDF and how elections helped it consolidate its authority.

1992: Elections to Consolidate Power

The transformation of the EPRDF from a Tigray-dominated insurgent movement into a powerful political party can be traced in part through elections. Noncompetitive elections provided the EPRDF a mechanism to consolidate its power, expand and deepen its reach to the most remote corners of the vast country, maneuver opposition movements into self-defeating acts of boycott, and create incentives to reward the loyalty and discipline of its midlevel leaders.

The first in a series of elections was held for local and regional offices in 1992, a little more than a year into the transition.[53] Many argue that elections shortly after civil war termination risk stability and can put in place nondemocratic political actors.[54] In Ethiopia, however, the EPRDF correctly noted the need for local councils to manage security and the massive tasks of reconstruction. The country could not wait three or four years to reconstitute local administrative structures.

The EPRDF had two roles during these elections. On the one hand, as the de facto transitional government with control over national security services, it had a responsibility to act as a neutral umpire in the electoral process. On the other, it was also a political contender, seeking victory for its affiliated parties and willing to restrict opposition participation as necessary. When these two roles conflicted, the EPRDF emphasized its partisan role and used its power to restrict political competition.

The OLF was the most important challenger to the EPRDF in 1992. The OLF participated in the Transitional Council of Representatives, had a putative base of support in the largest single ethnic group in Ethiopia, and could refer to its own history of resistance against Mengistu to highlight its independence from either the old order or the EPRDF. The transitional charter's emphasis on ethnic self-determination and the creation of ethnically defined regions seemed to favor the OLF. The OPDO, however, was part of the EPRDF, the most powerful political actor in postwar Ethiopia.

In 1992 Wellega (western Ethiopia) represented a key area of competition between the OLF and OPDO. The OLF had no public presence in Ambo, both the OLF and OPDO were present in Gimbi and Nekemte, and the OPDO had no office in Mendi or Dembidolo.[55] OLF campaign rallies in places under its control focused on Oromo nationalist themes and featured videos of Oromo music and prominent displays of flags and other signs promoting Oromo culture. In symbolically important defiance of the old policies of Amharaization, business signs and billboards written in Oromo used the Latin script rather than the *fidel* system used for Amharic. Little was said about policy, but the freedom to identify publicly as Oromo was crucial and empowering for many participants. Not surprisingly, fears of violence remained pervasive in the immediate aftermath of war and brutal period of state repression. Both the OPDO and the OLF remained military organizations with armed wings. OLF activists who had fled areas in Jarso and Nejo (western Wellega) to the relative safety of Nekemte told election observers they had heard that their names were on lists and that people were knocking on doors at night, so they fled.[56]

The EPRDF pushed hard on behalf of its member party, the OPDO. OLF officials and supporters faced harassment and intimidation.[57] The Transitional Council of Representatives rejected a petition from the OLF and seventeen other parties requesting a postponement of the election, and OLF officials subsequently announced that their party would boycott. Other non-EPRDF affiliated parties soon followed. The lack of choice made formalities of voting largely irrelevant and the outcome foreordained. In the end, the EPRDF won 1,108 of 1,147 regional assembly seats (96.6 percent).[58] A few non-EPRDF but closely affiliated parties won their respective regions in places such as the Somali and Afar regional states.

After withdrawing from the elections, the OLF left the TGE and pulled its 15,000 troops out of the camps, where they were vulnerable; a short civil war ensued. The main OLF leaders fled into exile. The EPRDF quickly destroyed the OLF's military capacity and detained 19,000 Oromo, many rounded up as suspected sympathizers rather than combatants.[59] This brief conflict demonstrated that behind the EPRDF's political strategy of ethnic affiliates and regional elections was an experienced and battle-hardened military that could act effectively and decisively when necessary.

International observers reached critical conclusions about the elections. The US observer group concluded,

> The June 21 elections represented a sterile, surreal, and wholly formalistic affair . . . [that] did not contribute directly to Ethiopia's development as a democratic state. At best, the elections were premature, especially for the southern half of Ethiopia. Less kindly judged, the elections were ill-conceived, dubious, and counterproductive in their contribution to the democratization of Ethiopia. The elections, moreover, exacerbated existing tensions, reinforced the hegemonic power of the EPRDF while marginalizing other fledgling parties, and were a central factor in the withdrawal of the OLF from the TGE and the return to war in the Oromo region.[60]

The Ethiopian government, however, suggested, "While the elections process was flawed in many ways and suffered the effects of administrative and logistical difficulties, budgetary problems, and the withdrawal of some organizations from the process, the Transitional Government views the elections as an important first step towards establishing a democratic political process in Ethiopia."[61]

Several developments took place in the context of the 1992 elections that shaped politics in the decades that followed. The new regions rewarded ethnically defined political parties, which then created vested interests and facts on the ground that determined subsequent political competition. The OLF's withdrawal left the TGE without a party that could even partially balance the power of the EPRDF. The 1992 elections also brought other patterns that would endure, including harassment and intimidation of the opposition, especially in remote, rural areas. The legacy of mistrust among the parties and the experiences of the 1992 elections have been dominant factors in determining opposition party perceptions of the possibility of meaningful electoral competition.[62] The opposition's boycotting strategy also remained central to Ethiopian electoral competition in subsequent years. The EPRDF's use of incumbency and state resources to strengthen its candidates was evident by 1992, and those strategies have been strengthened in subsequent elections.

The new ethnically based regions established in 1991 and the 1992 local and regional elections settled many of the most fundamental rules in postwar Ethiopian politics. Ethnofederalism had been institutionalized, and the elections put in place leaders of ethnically defined parties within or affiliated with the EPRDF coalition. The elections marginalized the OLF and several potential Amhara and multiethnic opposition movements. The EPRDF's determination to forge ahead with elections rather than engage with political organizations that had dropped out of the process increased the ruling party's domination and made meaningful democratization less likely.

The Hierarchy of Government Structures

The next step to advance the transition and instantiate new rules entailed elections on June 5, 1994, for a constituent assembly charged with considering, modifying, and ratifying a draft constitution.[63] The EPRDF's commitment to group rights and its dramatic move away from the ideas of national unity and Ethiopian nationalism were clear in the constitution's opening phrase: "We, the Nations, Nationalities, and Peoples of Ethiopia." The constitution states, "Every nation, nationality, and people in Ethiopia has an unconditional right to self-determination, including the right to secession" (art. 39). This provision was particularly controversial among many groups who saw Ethiopia as a unified state, not a loose federation from which groups could secede.

The 1995 Ethiopian Federal Constitution established a four-tier system of government. The nine regional states were divided into approximately 650 woredas.[64] At times woredas were grouped together into zones. Special zones were set up to represent pockets of minority populations, such as the Agaw in the Amhara region. Woredas had populations of approximately 115,000, although there was considerable variation. Woredas were subdivided further into kebeles, with an average population of 5,000 and, after 2005, into a dense network of "one-to-five" cells, in which every individual is part of a five-person unit. Urban areas have their own forms of administration and are organized in "urban woredas."

The regional states differ from each other in many ways. Each has its own flag, anthem, and sports teams. Whereas some (Tigray, Amhara, Oromo, Somali, and Afar) are composed of a dominant, titular, ethnic group, others (notably the SNNPR and Addis Ababa) are clearly multiethnic.[65] The largest in terms of area and population is Oromia, with a population of some 35.5 million, whereas Harar is a small city-state with

246,000 inhabitants.[66] Regional states serve as the fundamental building block of the federal structure, but the constituent units differ vastly.

The SNNPR is a multiethnic state but also contains more-or-less monoethnic woredas and in some places zones. The TGE initially set up five regions in the South: Gurage-Hadiya-Kambata, Wolayita, Omo, Sidamo, and Kaffa along with five "special districts" for small ethnic groups (Yem, Amaro, Burji, Konso, and Dirashe). In 1992 key ethnic elites from these groups recognized that the victorious EPRDF planned to divide power and set up new administrations on the basis of identity. Not surprisingly, a process of inventing or reinventing group identities along the lines of perceived "natural" ethnic units took place to gain more effective access to state and federal resources.[67] In 1992, these diverse regions merged into the larger, multinational SNNPR.

The Amhara national regional state also had special zones inhabited by Agaw, Awi Himra, and Oromo—that is, non-Amhara—who had their own elected councils and executive committees.[68] The Benishangul-Gumuz and Gambela regions seemed to be geographical and hence political expressions for groups that did not belong in other regions. Finally, Addis Ababa and the key trading center of Dire Dawa were governed as charter cities. The city of Harar is its own regional state for historical reasons. The map left millions of people, especially Amhara, Oromo, and Gurage, living outside of their respective, notional home regions, particularly in urban areas. The logic of the 1995 constitution reflected a perceived social structure based on distinct cultural groups tied to the land that more closely resembled some places in Ethiopia, particularly Tigray, than others. This logic, however, remained static as Ethiopia became more mobile, more educated, and more urban in the 2010s.

Not much checked the authority of the administrators in the regional and woreda offices because the executive members were simultaneously members of the council and the ruling party. For many years Abadula Gemeda, for example, served as both the president of Oromia and the chair of the OPDO, making party oversight of Abadula's performance as regional president difficult. Similarly, Ayalew Gobeze was regional president of the Amhara regional state from 2005 to 2013 while at the same time a member of the Amhara National Democratic Movement (ANDM) Executive Committee. It was unrealistic for a regional council composed entirely of OPDO or ANDM members to constrain the executive who was the chair of their party. As a result, regional parliaments have not played important roles in regional state governance.

There is a contradiction between the logic of autonomous regional states and the strong centralizing dynamic of the ruling party, with its commitment to democratic centralism and origins in the disciplined, hierarchical, rebel movement. As Aalen argues, "The constitutional rights for the regions to formulate and implement plans and policies are severely diminished by the fact that the regional governments, which are all under the EPRDF's hegemony, follow the centrally designed policies and five-year plans."[69] Based on party rules, policy decisions reached by the Executive Committee are passed down to the regional states, woredas, and kebeles for implementation. This creates a system for the lower levels to be accountable to the top but does not facilitate accountability of the top to the citizens.

Regional states have their own capacity to raise revenues and to collect payroll and other taxes, but over the period from 1997–1998 to 2011–2012, the federal government's share of total revenue exceeded 80 percent.[70] After 2002–2003, these resources were transferred largely through block grants to the woreda administrations.[71] This bypassed the executives and legislatures of the regional states on key resource allocation decisions and served to strengthen the center relative to the regional states. Although the woredas received significant resources from the center, most of the funds only covered the recurrent budget needs of the local civil service, leaving local officials with little scope regarding discretionary spending.[72] Federal block grants were allocated based on a formula that included the size of population, degree of development, and revenue-raising capacity of the region.[73] The so-called emerging regions (Somali, Afar, Benishangul-Gumuz, and Gambela) received an additional allotment of 1 percent.[74]

The kebeles were the key unit that most directly touched every Ethiopian on a regular basis. Kebeles had elected councils that ranged in size from 100–300 members, an executive committee, a "social court," a local militia, and a development staff.[75] Kebeles controlled the most essential services for average citizens. An Ethiopian noted, "The house belongs to the kebele. If I need to repair it, I need to get the approval from the kebele. If I get sick, I have to pass through the kebele to the hospital. If my sons and daughters are looking for a job, they have to go to the kebele first. Unless and otherwise we follow the orders of the kebele we have no services."[76] Rather than serving as mechanisms of social empowerment and local control, the kebeles served primarily as arms of central authority and functioned to monitor and control the population.

Local government did not act to provide information on grassroots concerns to higher administrative levels. The flow of information was almost always downward.[77] Locally based development agents, therefore, replicated centrally designed programs despite important local contextual differences. The World Bank, for example, found that in the Amhara region, "agricultural development agents were intent on promoting packages of seeds, fertilizer, and credit on half-acre teff [a staple grain] demonstration plots in a manner identical to what could simultaneously be observed in teff-producing areas in Oromia or [the] Southern Nations Region."[78] Officials who showed greater concern for local needs rather than the directives of the central party leadership risked losing their positions.

Local officials were always members of the EPRDF or its affiliated parties, at least formally. As a consequence, decentralizing the power to allocate resources strengthened local party elites and patronage networks. Caeyers and Dercon conclude: "In practice, targeting in food aid distribution in Ethiopia depends on local political leaders, within the Kebele administration, in principle elected but in practice typically close [*sic*] linked to those in power regionally and nationally."[79] These dynamics encouraged vulnerable, small-scale farmers and the millions who were chronically poor to seek good relations with local representatives of the ruling party in order to secure needed resources.

As part of the rapid expansion of EPRDF membership after the 2005 elections, the party put in place a "one-to-five" network. This system created microstructures in which one party member was responsible for monitoring five others. These small groups existed everywhere—workplaces, rural communities, college campuses, and government ministries. They met periodically to discuss the latest principles articulated by the EPRDF and to share information on health and development, but their most important function was to collect information and mobilize the group, particularly in the context of elections or progovernment rallies.[80]

Conclusion

The transitional period that began with a noisy diversity of views among a broad array of political organizations ended quietly with the clear hegemony of the EPRDF. The victorious insurgent group dominated the transition and consolidated power as a multiethnic coalition. The EPRDF put in place rules that championed group rights and ethnically defined institutions, creating concerns among many who favored a pan-Ethiopian national unity agenda. Local elections in 1992 provided an early opportunity for the EPRDF to consolidate its power, marginalize its rivals in the OLF and in multinational opposition parties, and to move forward with its specific program to rebuild the institutions of government.

As I argued in Chapter 2, the EPRDF came to power in 1991 with a legacy of cohesion and hierarchical discipline shaped by the demands of protracted war and the consequences of victory. The EPRDF's origin in the liberation struggle created path-dependent dynamics that supported the ability of Addis Ababa and the EPRDF Executive Committee to dominate the state. In this chapter I have emphasized the importance of the transition from war to peace and the exigencies that led the EPRDF to put in place new rules that structured politics around ethnically defined parties and regions. I have also noted the different characteristics of the regional states in terms of their size and the historical development of the relevant ethnic communities they govern. This dynamic created the potential for the constituent parties within the EPRDF coalition to develop autonomous interests and for the main regional states to become focal points less dependent on the center. These two contradictory logics of the war-to-peace transition in Ethiopia characterized the first nearly three decades of EPRDF rule.

Notes

1. Christopher Clapham, "Post-war Ethiopia: The Trajectories of Crisis," *Review of African Political Economy* 36, no. 120 (2009): 181–192. There is a well-developed literature on political culture in Ethiopia. See Allan Hoben, *Land Tenure Among the Amhara of Ethiopia* (Chicago: University of Chicago Press, 1973); Donald Levine, *Greater Ethiopia: The Evolution of a Multiethnic Society* (Chicago: University of Chicago Press, 1974); and Levine, *Wax and Gold: Tradition and Innovation in Ethiopian Culture* (Chicago: University of Chicago Press, 1965). For a political scientist's interpretation with an emphasis on gender, see Lahra Smith, *Making Citizens in Africa: Ethnicity, Gender, and National Identity in Ethiopia* (Cambridge, UK: Cambridge University Press, 2013). Oromo scholars have often positioned Oromo culture as the opposite. For an example see Asafa Jalata, "The Struggle for Knowledge: The Case of Emergent Oromo Studies," *African Studies Review* 39, no. 2 (September 1996): 95–123.

2. Michael A. Hiltzik, "Lenin Statue Takes a Tumble After Dictator's Ouster," *Los Angeles Times,* May 24, 1991, http://articles.latimes.com/1991-05-24/news/mn-2356_1_rebel-advance.

3. The literature here is extensive. For a good starting point, see Caroline A. Hartzell and Matthew Hoddie, *Crafting Peace: Power-sharing Institutions and the Negotiated Settlement of Civil Wars* (University Park: Pennsylvania State University Press, 2007).

4. Terrence Lyons, "The Importance of Winning: Victorious Insurgent Groups and Authoritarian Politics," *Comparative Politics* 48, no. 2 (January 2016): 167–184.

5. Jon Abbink, "Ethnic-based Federalism and Ethnicity in Ethiopia: Reassessing the Experiment After 20 Years," *Journal of Eastern African Studies* 5, no. 4 (2011): 597.

6. Peter Biles, "Addis Ababa Falls to Dawn Onslaught," *Guardian,* May 29, 1991.

7. John Markakis, *Ethiopia: The Last Two Frontiers* (Oxford, UK: James Currey, 2011): "There was great popular relief that the civil war [was] over, and great hopes were pinned on the anticipated 'peace dividend'" (230).

8. Associated Press, "Two Ethiopian Protesters Are Killed as Rebels Fire on Anti-U.S. Rally," *New York Times,* May 31, 1991, http://www.nytimes.com/1991 /05/31/world/2-ethiopian-protesters-are-killed-as-rebels-fire-on-anti-us-rally.html. The protesters were angry with Washington for facilitating the EPRDF's entry into Addis Ababa, and some called the transition "Cohen's Coup," after Assistant Secretary of State for African Affairs Herman Cohen, who chaired the London talks.

9. Christopher Clapham, "Ethiopia and Eritrea: The Politics of Post-insurgency," in *Democracy and Political Change in Sub-Saharan Africa,* ed. John A. Wiseman (London: Routledge, 1995), 117.

10. In fact, many lowlanders were referred to as *barias* (slaves), a word also used to connote dark skin. It was only in 1942 that Haile Selassie issued a proclamation banning slavery.

11. Donald Levine, "Greater Ethiopia Reconsidered," *Ethiopian Review* 2, no. 6 (1992).

12. Markakis, *Ethiopia: The Last Two Frontiers,* 237.

13. See Jean-Nicolas Bach, "*Abyotawi* Democracy: Neither Revolutionary nor Democratic—a Critical View of EPRDF's Conception of Revolutionary Democracy in Post-1991 Ethiopia," *Journal of Eastern African Studies* 5, no. 4 (2011): 641–663.

14. *Time Magazine,* November 4, 1991, 3. For further analysis, see Sarah Vaughan, "Responses to Ethnic Federalism in Ethiopia's Southern Region," in *Ethnic Federalism: The Ethiopian Experience in Comparative Perspective*, ed. David Turton (Oxford, UK: James Currey, 2006).

15. Cameron McWirter and Gur Melamede, "Ethiopia: The Ethnicity Factor," *Africa Report* 3, no. 7 (September–October 1992): 33. See also Michaela Wrong, "Ethiopia Buries the African 'Nation State,'" *Financial Times*, May 5, 1995.

16. David Turton, *Ethnic Federalism: The Ethiopian Experience in Comparative Perspective,* (Oxford, UK: James Currey, 2006), called it "radical and pioneering" (1).

17. Quoted in Jean-Nicolas Bach, "Compromising with Ethiopianness After 1991: The Ethiopian Festival of the Millennium (September 2007–September 2008), *Northeast African Studies* 13, no. 2 (2013).

18. The question of identity in Ethiopia has an extensive literature. Key works include Levine, *Greater Ethiopia*; Donald Donham and Wendy James, eds., *The Southern Marches of Imperial Ethiopia: Essays in History and Social Anthropology* (Athens: Ohio University Press, 2002); and P. T. W. Baxter, Jan Hultin, and Alessandro Triuliz, eds., *Being and Becoming Oromo: Historical and Anthropological Enquiries* (Lawrenceville, NJ: Red Sea, 1996).

19. Elizabeth E. Watson, "Making a Living in the Postsocialist Periphery: Struggles Between Farmers and Traders in Konso, Ethiopia," *Africa* 76, no. 1 (February 2006): 79.

20. Cited in Sarah Vaughan, *The Addis Ababa Transitional Conference of July 1991: Its Origins, History, and Significance* (Edinburgh: Edinburgh University, Centre for African Studies, 1994), 38. Hayelom was the nom de guerre of TPLF commander Hadush Araya.

21. For the example of the Omotic People's Organization, see Markakis, *Ethiopia: The Last Two Frontiers,* 337.

22. "Ethiopia: From Rebels to Rulers," *Africa Confidential* 32, no. 11 (May 31, 1991): 1–3 and "Ethiopia: Majorities and Minorities," *Africa Confidential* 32, no. 14 (July 12, 1991): 1–2; Walle Engedayehu, "Ethiopia Democracy and the Politics of Ethnicity," *Africa Today* 40, no. 2 (1993): 29–52.

23. Alex de Waal, "Ethiopia's Transition to What?" *World Policy Journal* 9, no. 4 (Fall–Winter 1992): 724.

24. Transitional Government of Ethiopia (TGE), *Ethiopia's Economic Policy During the Transitional Period* (Addis Ababa: TGE, November 1991), 15.

25. Cited in Vaughan, *Addis Ababa Transitional Conference of July 1991*, 35.

26. J. Stephen Morrison, "Ethiopia Charts a New Course," *Journal of Democracy* (Summer 1992): 1. Beyene Petros, then leader of the Hadiya National Democratic Organization (HNDO), said the initial negotiations about the establishment of the transitional government represented a "magnanimous and positive gesture" by the EPRDF. Cited in Vaughan, *Addis Ababa Transitional Conference of July 1991*, 36.

27. Proclamation No. 7 of 1992. See also "Ethiopia: New Government, New Map," *Africa Confidential* 32, no. 22 (November 8, 1991): 7.

28. Michael A. Hiltzik, "Ethiopia Fears New Civil War, Loss of Its Aid," *Los Angeles Times,* April 15, 1992, A1; Jennifer Parmelee, "Skirmishes Put Ethiopia 'Between War and Peace,'" *Washington Post,* April 4, 1992, A19.

29. "EPRDF-OLF Communique on U.S. Brokered Agreement," *Voice of Ethiopia,* April 15, 1992, trans. Foreign Broadcast Information Service, April 16, 1992, 5. See also "Ethiopia: Power Struggles and the Ethnic Weapon," *Africa Confidential* 33, no. 9 (May 8, 1992): 6–7.

30. The quote is from the EPRDF document "On the Revolutionary Democratic Goals and the Next Steps," cited in Markakis, *Ethiopia: The Last Two Frontiers,* 233.

31. Kjetil Tronvoll and Tobias Hagmann, "Traditional Authorities and Multi-party Elections in Ethiopia," in *Contested Power in Ethiopia: Traditional Authorities and Multi-party Elections,* ed. Kjetil Tronvoll and Tobias Hagmann (Leiden: Brill, 2012), 10.

32. Mulugeta Gebrehiwot Berhe, "The Ethiopian Post-transition Security Sector Reform Experience: Building a National Army from a Revolutionary Democratic Army," *African Security Review* 26, no. 2 (2017): 161–179. See also Mulugeta Gebrehiwot Berhe, "Transition from War to Peace: The Ethiopian DDR Experience," World Peace Foundation paper no. 16, *African Politics, African Peace* (June 2016), https://sites.tufts.edu/wpf/files/2017/07/16.-Transitions-from-War-to-Peace-DDR.pdf. Mulugeta was the chair of the Disarmament, Demobilization, and Reintegration Commission in Ethiopia.

33. Hartmut Quehl, ed. *Living in Wartimes—Living in Post-wartimes,* proceedings of an international workshop on the Horn of Africa held in Melsungen, Germany (2002).

34. Transitional Government of Ethiopia (TGE), *A Proclamation to Provide for the Development of the Central Transitional Government and for the Establishment of the Police Force,* Proclamation no. 8/1992, January 1992; Robin Luckham, "Radical Soldiers, New Model Armies, and the Nation State in Ethiopia and Eritrea," in *Political Armies: The Military and Nation Building in the Age of Democracy,* ed. Kees Koonings and Dirk Krujt (London: Zed, 2002), 259.

35. Nat Colletta, Markus Kostner, and Ingo Wiederhofer, *The Transition from War to Peace in Sub-Saharan Africa* (Washington, DC: World Bank, 1996). Although integration was relatively successful, ex-soldiers faced the same levels of poverty as the larger communities they joined. See Stefan Dercon and Daniel Ayalew, "Where Have All the Soldiers Gone? Demobilization and Reintegration in Ethiopia," *World Development* 26, no. 9 (1998): 1661–1675.

36. Patrick Gilkes, *Ethnic and Political Movements in Ethiopia and Somalia* (Fairfield, CT: Save the Children, May 1992), 6.

37. Interview, Addis Ababa, 2011.

38. Akalou Wolde-Michael, "Urban Development in Ethiopia (1889–1925)," *Journal of Ethiopian Studies* 11, no. 1 (January 1973): 1–16.

39. For example, the Afar region was expanded to break up the Eritrean region, and the Ogaden region became separated from the majority of Ethiopian Somalis. A version of the map can be found at https://en.wikipedia.org/wiki/Provinces_of_Ethiopia.

40. In 1991, Dire Dawa was included in Oromia. However, both Somali and Oromos claimed the strategic trading town, resulting in a series of clashes early in the transitional period. In 1993 Addis Ababa removed Dire Dawa from the Oromia National Regional State and made it a chartered city with an extraconstitutional consociational power-sharing arrangement. See Milkessa Midega, "Ethiopian Federalism and the Ethnic Politics of Divided Cities: Consociationalism Without Competitive Multiparty Politics in Dire Dawa," *Ethnopolitics* 16, no. 3 (2017): 279–294.

41. Asnake Kefale, "Federal Restructuring in Ethiopia: Renegotiating Identity and Borders Along the Oromo-Somali Ethnic Frontiers," *Development and Change* 41, no. 4 (July 2010): 615–635.

42. Jon G. Abbink, "New Configurations of Ethiopian Ethnicity: The Challenge of the South," *Northeast African Studies* 5, no. 1 (1998): 59–81.

43. Fredrik Barth, *Ethnic Groups and Boundaries: The Social Organization of Cultural Difference* (Boston: Little, Brown, 1969).

44. Article 8, Constitution of the Regional State of Oromia, Proclamation No 46/2001.

45. Article 2, Constitution of the Benishangul-Gumuz National Regional State. For a translation, see http://ehrc.org.et/documents/10184/29876/Benishangul_Gumuz _Constitution_English.pdf/41054950-bc46-491c-b384-e11316021f35?version=1.0.

46. Lahra Smith, "The Politics of Contemporary Language Policy in Ethiopia," *Journal of Developing Societies* 24, no. 2 (2008): 207–243.

47. Andreas Schedler, ed., *Electoral Authoritarianism: The Dynamics of Unfree Competition* (Boulder, CO: Lynne Rienner, 2006).

48. Andreas Schedler, "Authoritarianism's Last Line of Defense," *Journal of Democracy* 21, no. 1 (January 2010): 69–80.

49. Barbara Geddes, "Why Parties and Elections in Authoritarian Regimes?," paper presented at the annual meeting of the American Political Science Association, Washington, DC, 2005; Andreas Schedler, "Elections Without Democracy: The Menu of Manipulation," *Journal of Democracy* 13, no. 2 (April 2002): 36–50.

50. For a comparative case, see Ora John Reuter and Graeme B. Roberton, "Subnational Appointments in Authoritarian Regimes: Evidence from Russian Gubernatorial Appointments," *Journal of Politics* 74, no. 4 (October 2012). For an argument that emphasizes relations between the elite and the base in authoritarian party recruitment, see Dimitar D. Guerorguiev and Paul J. Schuler, "Keeping Your Head Down: Public Profiles and Promotion Under Autocracy," *Journal of East Asian Studies* 16, no. 1 (March 2016): 87–116.

51. Jennifer Gandhi, *Political Institutions Under Dictatorship* (Cambridge, UK: Cambridge University Press, 2008).

52. Andreas Schedler, "The Logic of Electoral Authoritarianism," in *Electoral Authoritarianism: The Dynamics of Unfree Competition,* ed. Andreas Schedler (Boulder, CO: Lynne Rienner, 2006).

53. The author served as an election observer in Wellega (Oromia National Regional State), and this section draws on my field notes from that time.

54. Thomas Flores and Irfan Nooruddin, *Elections in Hard Times: Building Stronger Democracies in the 21st Century* (Cambridge, UK: Cambridge University Press, 2016).

55. Author's field notes, June 1992.

56. Author's field notes, June 1992.

57. OLF prisoners' interviews with author, Gimbi, June 1992.

58. National Democratic Institute, *An Evaluation of the June 21, 1992, Elections in Ethiopia* (Washington, DC: National Democratic Institute, 1992).

59. US Department of State, *Country Reports on Human Rights Practices for 1992* (Washington DC: US Department of State, 1993).

60. National Democratic Institute, *Evaluation of the June 21, 1992, Elections in Ethiopia*, 6–7.

61. Embassy of Ethiopia, "A Significant Step Toward Democracy," *News from Ethiopia,* July 14, 1992, 1–2.

62. Stevens Tucker, *Ethiopia in Transition, 1991–1998* (Geneva: UNHCR Writenet, 1998).

63. Kassahun Berhanu, "Ethiopia Elects a Constituent Assembly," *Review of African Political Economy* 22, no. 63 (March 1995): 129–135.

64. One of the key drivers of local politics and conflict is the creation of new woredas and zones, so these numbers are fluid over time. These figures are from World Bank, *Ethiopia: Enhancing Human Development Outcomes Through Decentralized Service Delivery,* Report No. 32675-ET (Washington, DC: World Bank, May 2007).

65. Although the Oromia, Somali, and Afar regions are notionally monoethnic, important clan and religious differences make mobilizing behind these identities challenging.

66. Central Statistical Agency, *Population Projection of Ethiopia for All Regions at Wereda Level from 2014–2017* (Addis Ababa: Central Statistical Agency, August 2013).

67. David Turton, ed., *Ethnic Federalism: The Ethiopian Experience in Comparative Perspective* (Oxford, UK: James Currey, 2006); Abbink, "New Configurations of Ethiopian Ethnicity."

68. Solomon Negussie, *Fiscal Federalism in the Ethiopian Ethnic-based Federal System* (Ottawa: Forum of Federations, 2008), 87.

69. Lovise Aalen, *Ethnic Federalism in a Dominant Party State: The Ethiopian Experience, 1991–2000* (Bergen: Chr. Michelsen Institute, 2002), 80.

70. Tegegne Gebre-Egziabher, "Decentralization and Regional and Local Development: Trends and Policy Implications," in *Reflections on Development in Ethiopia: New Trends, Sustainability, and Challenges,* ed. Dessalegn Rahmato and Meheret Ayenew (Addis Ababa: Forum for Social Studies, 2014), 137.

71. According to the World Bank, woredas managed 45 percent of regional public expenditures. See World Bank, *Ethiopia*, 8.

72. World Bank, *Ethiopia.*

73. The formula was modified a number of times since the mid-1990s. Solomon, *Fiscal Federalism in the Ethiopian Ethnic-based Federal System*, 218–219.

74. Tegegne, "Decentralization and Regional and Local Development," 149. See also Qaiser M. Khan, Jean-Paul Faguet, Christopher Gaukler, and Wendmsyamregne Mekasha, *Improving Basic Services for the Bottom Forty Percent: Lessons from Ethiopia* (Washington, DC: World Bank, 2014).

75. After the 2005 elections, the size of the *kebele* councils increased to 300 members.

76. Cited in Siegfried Pausewang, Kjetil Tronvoll, and Lovise Aalen, eds., *Ethiopia Since the Derg: A Decade of Democratic Pretension and Performance* (London: Zed, 2002).

77. Serdar Yilmaz and Varsha Venugopal, "Local Government Discretion and Accountability in Ethiopia," International Studies Program Working Paper 08-38 (Atlanta: George State University, December 2008), 10–11.

78. World Bank, Ethiopia Woreda Studies, 2001, cited in Yilmaz and Venugopal, "Local Government Discretion and Accountability in Ethiopia," 14.

79. Bet Caeyers and Stefan Dercon, *Political Connections and Social Networks in Targeted Transfer Programmes: Evidence from Rural Ethiopia,* CSAE WPS /2008-33 (September 2008): 24, https://www.academia.edu/people/search?utf8=%E2 %9C%93&q=Political+Connections+and+Social+Networks.

80. Kimiko de Freytas-Tamura, "'We Are Everywhere': How Ethiopia Became a Land of Prying Eyes," *New York Times,* November 5, 2017.

4

The EPRDF in Power

It was like having a football team, a really good football team, suddenly transform into a basketball team. It did not go smoothly.
—*Mulugeta Gebrehiwot,*
TPLF Central Committee Member[1]

During the transitional period between the Ethiopian People's Revolutionary Democratic Front (EPRDF) seizing power in 1991, its adoption of a new constitution in 1994, and its winning virtually every seat in the 1995 national elections, the victorious party created an ethnofederal state and transformed its insurgent force with its origins in the Tigray People's Liberation Front (TPLF) into a national army and powerful political party with broad membership. The EPRDF controlled the appointed Transitional Council of Representatives, dominated the local administrative councils established in 1992, transformed its regional rebel army into the Ethiopian National Defense Force (ENDF), and had a near monopoly over representation in the 1994 Constitutional Convention. It began 1995 with its favored rules firmly in place, an integrated party infrastructure, and close relationships with affiliated parties in control of the Somali, Afar, Gambela, and Benishangul-Gumuz regions. Opposition to the EPRDF was weak, disorganized, externally focused, and divided. As I detail in this chapter, elections held in 1995 and 2000 were not competitive but were important as mechanisms to consolidate the EPRDF's power and marginalize its opposition.

I begin this chapter by explaining the logics, or rationales, that shaped the transformation of the EPRDF from a parochial, Tigray-based insurgency into a multiethnic coalition that dominated the diverse

Ethiopian state. Two dynamics explain this process. The first is the legacy of the armed struggle, in the form of a highly centralized hierarchical organization with a cohesive military-political leadership, particularly within the TPLF. The second involves the imperatives of the war-to-peace transition, which required transforming the Tigray-based insurgent group into a national political party that incorporated membership from multiple regions and ethnic groups. The EPRDF, although on the one hand a hierarchical, battle-hardened, disciplined party, was simultaneously a coalition of disparate parties with different relationships to their respective peoples. The TPLF, Amhara National Democratic Movement (ANDM), Oromo People's Democratic Organization (OPDO), and Southern Ethiopian People's Democratic Movement (SEPDM) each had different historical bases, carried different legacies from the period of armed struggle, and had distinct records as administrators in their specific regional states. The constitutional emphasis on ethnofederalism generated centrifugal forces that required some kind of equilibrium, or the regime risked fragmenting. The extremely centralized, hierarchical, and powerful ruling party provided that balance. As I discuss in Chapters 8 and 9, a disruption of this balance in the mid-2010s created a period of turmoil, and in 2018 a new set of party leaders came to power. But the central contradiction remained.

In this chapter I elaborate on the logics of the EPRDF to uncover how hierarchical, central control operated alongside regional and ethnically defined institutions. The coalition's internal dynamics in general, and relationships among its member parties in particular, help explain the regime's stability based on a powerful authoritarian order, the creation of the party-state, and its structural divisions. My analysis of the elections in 1995 and 2000 emphasizes both the centrifugal and centripetal dynamics of the core institutional structure in Ethiopia since the end of the civil war. Regional and international relationships created both threats and opportunities for the ruling party to govern, and the war with Eritrea (1998–2000) developed in part from the legacies of the armed struggle and had important consequences for the EPRDF and the TPLF in particular. In this chapter I consider the four regional states ruled by the EPRDF constituent parties—in Tigray, Amhara, Oromia, and the Southern Nations, Nationalities, and People's Region (SNNPR). I examine key episodes to dig deeper into intrinsic political dynamics and to demonstrate variation across regional states. I then briefly outline how the EPRDF relates to the Afar, Somali, Gambela, and Benishangul-Gumuz border regions, governed by EPRDF affiliates rather than the coalition itself.

Logics of the EPRDF

The political system designed, implemented, and maintained by the EPRDF has at its core a tension between centralizing tendencies and subnational identity-based autonomous institutions. This contradiction derives from two fundamental characteristics of the war-to-peace transition. First, the legacies of the armed struggle brought to power an organization that had won the war as a highly centralized, hierarchical, and disciplined rebel movement. The EPRDF in general, and the TPLF at its core in particular, began the transition with cohesive leadership and strong institutions. They had the experience in governing liberated territory and civilian populations through administrative structures subservient to the military leadership and the priority of winning the war. Policy deliberations and decisions were made at the top and then, in orthodox democratic centralist manner, communicated down to the lowest levels.

Second, the exigencies of a movement that emanated from the highlands of Tigray, with its ideological origins in Tigray nationalism, to govern a state that consisted of Oromo, Amhara, Somali, Sidama, Wolayita, Gurage, and dozens of other groups compelled the insurgents to transform from an overwhelmingly Tigray rebel movement into a political movement that brought in the many non-Tigrayan constituencies. This process of developing the Oromo, Amhara, and other large non-Tigrayan wings of the EPRDF began during the final stages of the civil war but accelerated when the transitional process required representatives from across the country to administer areas of southern Ethiopia not occupied by the rebel movement to participate in the Transitional Council of Representatives, the Constitutional Convention, and the national Parliament. These two processes and contradictory logics—the first integrative and hierarchical, the second based on group rights and ethnically defined autonomous regional states—constituted the EPRDF political system.

During the first decade of the EPRDF's rule under its new constitution (1995–2005), the regime managed to contain this contradiction. In part the TPLF remained in control in the center, whereas the newly formed regions were weak and dependent on the federal government for resources, and the newly created regionally based parties could not operate outside of the coalition. Also, the EPRDF merged the party with the state so that the party's Executive Committee controlled the resources—hence the policies of the regional states—and thereby held off centrifugal forces created by its ethnofederal constitutional structure. In the early years of the regime, the newly founded parties in the

Amhara, Oromia, and the SNNPR lacked the coherence to challenge the much more seasoned and cohesive Tigray wing of the party. As I discuss in Chapter Six, the non-TPLF parties experienced more turbulence within their central committees, making it harder for them to challenge the more experienced, close-knit TPLF. With leadership and resources controlled by the center, the autonomous regional institutions and parties had few options other than to play by the center's rules. Loyalty to the center rather than relationships with regional constituencies dominated Ethiopian politics.

At the same time, however, regional states and parties also controlled large bureaucracies and developed region-specific policies and patronage networks. Over time they increasingly positioned themselves as protectors of the interests of their ethnically defined bases. Competition over resources between regions (and hence ethnic groups) was common, as was obvious in political struggles over revenue-sharing formulas, in the careful ethnic balancing on the central Council of Ministers, and in violent conflicts over borders between and within regional states. As I explore further in later chapters, as the regional institutions settled into their new roles, they acquired greater authority over day-to-day politics in the regional states. The non-TPLF member parties developed more experienced leaders, and the organizational differences declined.

The ruling network managed to survive a brutal war with Eritrea from 1998 to 2000, in part by reactivating Ethiopian nationalist themes it had previously kept under wraps. The EPRDF also managed to get through a dangerous split within the TPLF that reverberated throughout the coalition in 2001. Within Oromia and the SNNPR, contentious decisions about designating regional capitals and creating new internal administrative boundaries resulted in violence. As I discuss in Chapter 5, the party faced a dangerous threat when it organized competitive multiparty elections in 2005 and lost a significant number of seats in Addis Ababa and in all four of the main regions. It responded by vastly expanding the size of the party and the links between the party and the government. The strong center continued to dominate the centrifugal dynamics within the ethnically defined regional states.

The Inner Life of a Strong Authoritarian Party

Recent research in comparative politics has established the link between political parties and durable authoritarianism. Party-based authoritarian regimes tend to be more stable than military or personalistic regimes, according to Geddes.[2] Building on this finding, Levitsky and Way argue that parties with origins in armed conflicts or national liberation struggles are likely to be strong as measured by organizational scope and cohesion.[3] "The identities, norms, and organizational structures forged during periods of sustained, violent, and ideologically driven conflict are a critical source of cohesion—and durability—in party-based authoritarian regimes."[4] This follows Huntington's logic: the strength and durability of a political party "derives more from its origins than from its character."[5] The key to durable authoritarianism, therefore, is not only the existence of a ruling party but also its origins.

Several mechanisms have been identified to explain the connections between regime durability and the presence of a strong authoritarian party. Strong parties facilitate intraelite accommodation, co-opt opposition, and institutionalize incentives that benefit loyalty and penalize defection.[6] Strong parties allow supporters to be rewarded and lengthen time horizons for career advancement, thereby encouraging long-term loyalty. Losers in power or policy struggles are more likely to remain loyal with the expectation of access to promotion and patronage in future rounds. "By regulating access to the spoils of public office and providing future opportunities for career advancement, ruling parties create incentives for regime elites to remain loyal."[7]

These scholars look at political parties as unified actors. In other words, a party is either strong or not, or built upon the legacies of armed struggle or not. Within the black box of the strong authoritarian party, however, intraparty dynamics are also essential to explaining regime durability. All political parties—including authoritarian parties—are composed of constituencies or factions with a variety of ideological, regional, and policy interests and perspectives. It is therefore necessary to investigate political parties as coalitions that require regular maintenance. The concept of party-based authoritarian regimes as posited by Levitsky and Way is insufficient for understanding the endogenous competition within such parties, critical to their durability.

There is a long tradition within the literature on political parties of examining the inner life of parties. Katz and Mair focus on intraparty processes to categorize different types of parties and their roles in modern democracies.[8] Competition among factions "may be such as to militate against any theories taking the party as a whole as the relevant unit of analysis."[9] Strong authoritarian parties must find the means to recruit new party leaders and discipline those who are disloyal or ineffective. Regional differences between wealthy regions and poor areas and between rural and urban constituencies create different interests in various parts of the ruling party that must be managed. Generational changes, particularly as the founding generation is replaced by a generation that worked its way up the party ladder, create another set of divergent agendas. Political competition is a feature within authoritarian parties, and this dynamic is critical to how such parties operate.

The EPRDF is a particularly interesting party to study in this way. On the one hand it is the epitome of a strong authoritarian party as envisioned by Levitsky and Way. It traces its origins to a victorious insurgent movement and has both considerable scope and cohesion. However, it is also a coalition of four distinct member parties, each created on the basis of an ethnic identity. Each of these regional parties has its own history and its own relationship to the armed struggle that created relative cohesion in some member parties but had far less significance for others. The constituencies each party notionally represents also vary considerably. The ruling coalition therefore consists of four parties, each with a specific ethnic identity, and variation across these constituent parties provides the bases for intraparty struggles to gain or retain dominance.

The Party-State: Balancing Democratic Centralism and Ethnofederalism

As I noted in Chapter 2, the TPLF insurgency followed classic Maoist guerrilla principles and operated on the basis of unified leadership that managed military and political affairs. The blurring of institutional roles present during the armed struggle remained after the transition, re-created in the relationship between the political party and the country. The party's Executive Committee and the executive branch's Council of Ministers "seem effectively to have been fused."[10] The EPRDF party-state functioned by straddling the roles of policymaking and implementation.

Scholars have long used the party-state as a concept to explain politics in places such as Côte d'Ivoire and Kenya.[11] A party-state is more than a single-party-dominant system; it is an institutional arrangement whereby the party becomes auxiliary to the executive. The party assumes the roles of transmitter and enforcer of policy decisions. Administrative bodies often carry out party tasks and, at the local level in particular, it is difficult to distinguish between party officials and civil servants. As Widner explains, "The party thus loses its function as a forum for interest-group bargaining and for interest aggregation—a function single-party-dominant systems still retain, to varying degrees—and acquires tasks performed by the executive in multiparty systems, including responsibility for socialization or public education and for certain forms of public order."[12]

In many key ways, however, Ethiopia is more than a party-state. The EPRDF not only plays roles performed by the executive, legislative, and judicial branches in multiparty systems but also has a large influence on the economy, the security forces, and civil society. The party controls mass organizations such as its Youth League and Women's League, each with more than a million members.[13] The TPLF controls a vast set of businesses through its party-based holding company, the Endowment Fund for the Rehabilitation of Tigray (EFFORT), and the other constituent parties operate similar but much smaller endowments.[14] One of the largest humanitarian organizations in Ethiopia is the TPLF-run Relief Society of Tigray (REST), and the party runs a major internationally registered charity, the Tigray Development Association (TDA), with a million members who raise money in the diaspora for schools, health clinics, and related development projects.[15]

The EPRDF, therefore, is more than a political party, and its ability to embed itself in a network of state, private business, and mass organizations at both the federal and regional state levels makes it hegemonic. Ethiopia is a party-business-nongovernment-organization-military-mass-organization-state, where the lines among all of these different facets of the EPRDF overlap and are blurred by design. When combined with the conviction that the party represents the "people," then the party-state-people complex is complete and impossible for the opposition to challenge without being categorized as "antipeople," "antidevelopment," or "antipeace."

At the core of its domination is the EPRDF's control over the large and effective security services. The blurred lines between the state and the party extend to the security services, where party loyalists occupy top positions and the police and intelligence services are perceived as operating on behalf of the ruling party. This results in the security services being "easily perceived as partisan executive agencies."[16] Although the rank and file of the army reflect the diverse makeup of Ethiopia, the top military leadership for the first twenty-seven years of the regime was overwhelmingly from Tigray and dominated by the leaders of the TPLF's armed struggle.

The EPRDF has these hegemonic characteristics, but it has also put in place a set of institutions that have empowered ethnically defined political parties and regional states. These contrasting logics—one highly centralizing and the other favoring autonomy—have been at the core of the party since its creation. These tensions between the logic of military discipline and democratic centralism, on the one hand, and the logic of group rights and ethnofederalism, on the other, have their origins in how the TPLF operated during the armed struggle and its ideological positions going back to its student movement origins. There was no contradiction within a hierarchical, Tigray-nationalist organization for most of the civil war because the TPLF operated in a Tigrayan context. Democratic centralism and nationalism did not contradict each other during the years the TPLF operated solely in Tigray. After the insurgency left Tigray and moved toward Addis Ababa through lands inhabited by Amhara and then Oromo, however, it had to develop the means to both retain its centralizing tendencies and incorporate non-Tigrayan populations into its realm of operations.

In other words, the TPLF-led EPRDF faced two different ways to organize its regime. One would be to emphasize the strong, disciplined hierarchy the TPLF embodied, which would build on historic patterns of autocracy in Ethiopia. Another would be to emphasize group rights, self-determination up to and including independence, and ethnically defined political structures. This would be consistent with the TPLF's positioning on the national question and would allow the TPLF to expand in order to rule multiethnic Ethiopia. The EPRDF pursued both. The puzzle of Ethiopian politics is how the EPRDF managed to live within that contradiction for nearly three decades and whether the party could reform without overcoming these contrasting logics.

The Noncompetitive Elections of 1995 and 2000

As I discussed in the context of the 1992 local polls, elections in Ethiopia provide insights into the EPRDF's transformation from a regionally focused insurgent group into a powerful, national political party. The question is not whether elections were free and fair or whether they advanced liberal democracy: they were not, and they did not. However, they did serve essential functions in the construction of the powerful authoritarian party. Electoral processes consolidated power and served as means both to maintain discipline in the party and to marginalize opposition. Furthermore, the EPRDF sought to build a revolutionary democracy that operated according to different imperatives than the liberal democracy promoted by many donors and international advocacy organizations.

Elections mattered to the EPRDF: the ruling party carefully recorded the number of people registered, the number who turned out, and the final tallies of their votes. Party congresses were held with great fanfare and televised speeches. Party leaders presented platforms written in considerable detail. The EPRDF member parties presented their common platforms in meetings held across the country. The party went to great lengths to organize well-managed, orderly electoral processes and reacted with great umbrage when international observers or media criticized its processes. In the EPRDF's conception of revolutionary democracy, good governance required participation but in the form of mass organizations and high, peaceful turnout rather than through determinative roles in the selection of the country's top decisionmakers. Tronvoll argues that Ethiopian elections should be understood in their "nonelectoral context," but it was the EPRDF's performance and ability to shape party building that made the elections matter.[17]

Ethiopia is by no means unique in using elections for reasons unrelated to meaningful participation. Electoral processes often are used by authoritarian regimes to consolidate power and to demonstrate the ruling party's dominance.[18] Elections and strong political parties thereby contribute to "authoritarian resilience," as noted by scholars with reference to China, Iran, Syria, and Zimbabwe.[19] These elections therefore serve the purposes of the ruling party rather than serving as processes that determine who rules.

1995 Elections

The May 1995 regional and national elections were the first held under the new constitution.[20] As described above, the 1992 regional elections had empowered ethnic regions and ethnic parties affiliated with the ruling party and had created facts on the ground that would characterize future polls. The 1995 voting marked the culmination of a four-year campaign by the EPRDF to transform the government from the brutal Derg, which engaged in endless civil war, to a peaceful one-party federal republic structured around ethnically defined regions. The political transformation since 1991 and the nonparticipation of opposition parties determined the outcome of the 1995 election in advance.[21] Only one small national organization, a few minor ethnic or regionally based groups, and some generally weak independents challenged the powerful incumbent party. Although not competitive, the 1995 elections were important and provided further opportunities for the EPRDF to consolidate its power and for the opposition to try without success to shape the institutions of political contestation.

Although 1995 was the first election under the new constitution, with its ethnically defined regions, almost all political parties already were organized on the basis of ethnicity. Politics structured around ethnicity had created key facts on the ground. Not only the EPRDF but also most of the opposition was organized around ethnicity, including the Oromo Liberation Front (OLF), the All-Amhara People's Organization (AAPO), and the Southern Ethiopia People's Democratic Coalition (SEPDC), often called the Southern Coalition. A small multiethnic party, the Ethiopian National Democratic Party (ENDP), did run and won a single seat. But the EPRDF's strategy of building a coalition of ethnically defined parties to compete in ethnically defined constituencies led to overwhelming advantages for the incumbents and insurmountable challenges for actors who favored a pan-Ethiopian political agenda.

The election campaign was relatively quiet, registration topped 21 million, and turnout was 94 percent.[22] Although the EPRDF operated as a well-integrated coalition across the four main regions, each regional state had its own story during the elections. In 1995 the TPLF, not surprisingly, won every seat in Tigray, its northern base.[23] The ANDM demonstrated its ability to mobilize the population and won all but one constituency in the Amhara region. Overall the 1995 elections provided the opportunity for the TPLF and ANDM to demonstrate their control over their respective regional states and to marginalize opposition.

In the large Oromia region, the OPDO won all but 3 of the 177 constituencies. It campaigned on the common EPRDF five-year plan but also championed cultural issues such as the use of the Oromo language in schools and the adoption of the Latin alphabet. Despite these appeals, the population in many areas continued to regard the OPDO as seriously compromised by its association with the EPRDF, which many Oromos saw as another northern, or *neftenya* (the term for imperial military overlords) regime. Many voters continued to express their preference for the OLF, which had called for a boycott and urged Oromos to "disobey the occupation forces by keeping away from voting stations."[24] Compared to the sophisticated organizational capacity and skilled leadership demonstrated by the more experienced TPLF and ANDM, the OPDO relied more on intimidation and patronage to dominate the region's politics. Still, notably, in many areas, including those where the OLF historically had high levels of support, such as Wellega, the OPDO managed to mobilize a large turnout for uncontested races. Vulnerable citizens, when faced with the OLF's call for boycotting the elections and OPDO *kebele* leaders' demand for participation, voted in high numbers. The election also provided the opportunity for the OPDO to arrest some of its opponents by labeling them as supporters of the banned OLF. In comparison with the TPLF and the ANDM, the OPDO relied upon higher levels of repression in order to maintain similar levels of control over Oromia.

Following the 1992 local elections, the transitional regime merged a number of smaller regional states into the SNNPR, which thereby became a conglomeration of dozens of smaller nationalities, none of which had close to a majority across the region. As many as thirty-two parties participated in the 1995 elections, but only those affiliated with the EPRDF, grouped within the Southern Ethiopian People's Democratic Front (SEPDF, later reorganized as the SEPDM), won seats. Again, although not competitive, the 1995 elections solidified the SNNPR as a regional state and the SEPDF as the dominant political party in the region. These elections therefore demonstrated that the SEPDF could win and control the region, but it remained a loose agglomeration of parties in comparison with its comember parties in the ruling coalition.

Addis Ababa, a chartered city outside the ethnically structured regions, had considerably more political space than the rural areas did. Numerous political organizations and independents that represented an alternative to the ruling coalition were on the ballot in Addis Ababa, and independent media and civil society organizations were more present in the capital than anywhere else in the country. Turnout was also lower than in the more rural regions. Although the EPRDF controlled the city, two independents won seats in the capital district. There were contentious elections in the border regions, such as Somali, Gambela, and Benishangul-Gumuz, where the EPRDF did not compete. These contests were generally over rivalries between ethnic groups or clans with both sides pledging loyalty to (and hoping for patronage from) the incumbent EPRDF.[25]

One of the most striking characteristics of the 1995 elections was the extent to which the EPRDF demonstrated its strength as a party across Ethiopia. By May 1995, a well-led, well-financed, and well-institutionalized hierarchy that controlled nearly all aspects of the political process replaced the somewhat loose, inchoate coalition of 1992. The party had a comprehensive, five-year plan of action that all EPRDF candidates adopted and promoted as their platform. In addition to dominating the political agenda by the force of its organizational capacity, the ruling party enjoyed the enormous benefits of incumbency. State-owned media provided a means for the ruling party to get its message to the countryside, and local administration invariably supported candidates from the ruling party.

The Donor Election Unit (DEU), an internationally supported electoral observation group, issued a report that concluded, "The May 1995 Ethiopian elections had large numbers of candidates, large numbers of voters, a generally effective administration, and was conducted in a peaceful manner. Elections, however, are about choice. For the reasons stated in this report, the ability of the Ethiopian people to use the ballot effectively to choose their leaders is still limited."[26] Many Ethiopians understood that the outcome was a foregone conclusion but felt it prudent to do as the local officials requested and turn out to vote. An Oromo farmer expressed a common attitude toward participation: "I was afraid. The Government said I should vote, so I voted. What could I do?"[27] The power of the emerging party-state was clear. The dominance of the EPRDF was virtually complete.

2000 Elections

The pattern of noncompetitive, boycotted elections continued in almost every constituency in Ethiopia in the national elections in 2000 and the local elections of 2001.[28] The exceptions were in urban areas (again, particularly Addis Ababa) and a few districts in the SNNPR. The numbers were never sufficient to threaten the ruling party's hold on power either regionally or in the center. Regardless, opposition parties such as the Hadiya National Democratic Organization (HNDO) faced intimidation and harassment, and election day brought widespread rigging. Despite these manipulations, the HNDO won six of the seven seats in the Hadiya zone, as well as another six seats elsewhere in the country.

Local elections in 2001 brought further evidence of intimidation. The EPRDF swept local elections even in constituencies where the opposition had done well in the national elections the year before. In general, the opposition SEPDC candidates withdrew because they feared for the safety of their families and constituents if they remained in the contest. Voter turnout again was high, pointing to the EPRDF's mobilizing capacity and dominance. In Addis Ababa, observers reported kebele officials and EPRDF party cadres acting to ensure high voter turnout. A voter is reported to have said, "I voted because the kebele officials told me [to] when they walked door to door, campaigning for the elections. Even if it is not written in any law that I have to vote, it is compulsory. As long as we are under this government we have to do it. Otherwise we have no rights."[29]

The 1995 and 2000 elections demonstrated the oppositions' vulnerabilities and the EPRDF's ability to mobilize the population to participate in a process that affirmed and solidified the ruling party's preeminence. An organization that a few years earlier had been a regionally focused rebel group in the far north was now a formidable political party that could turn out enormous numbers of voters across the diverse country. Elections were a moment for the ruling party to demonstrate its power nationwide through mass mobilization and a performance that highlighted the fact that they had no viable opposition. There was no choice but the EPRDF.

Foreign Policy and Regional Relationships

In addition to its ability to dominate in domestic politics, the EPRDF demonstrated considerable skill in managing the opportunities and risks posed by its regional and international position. Ethiopia's foreign policy under the EPRDF has been driven in part by the recognition that regional and international developments shape domestic stability and prosperity and that domestic politics are linked with external policies. The Ethiopian government's Foreign Affairs and National Security Policy and Strategy document of 2002 explicitly conceptualized foreign policy as subservient to domestic policies, notably domestic economic development. "It is clear to see that our foreign relations and national security policy and strategy can only have relevance if it [*sic*] contributes to the fight against poverty and promotes speedy economic development, democracy, and peace."[30] The regional and international, therefore, are local, and a key dimension of the EPRDF's political success has been its ability to find opportunities in and manage risks from its external relationships.

The United States and other major international donors welcomed the new regime in 1991 and began to provide significant development support. Washington regarded Prime Minister Meles Zenawi as one of the "impressive new generation of African leaders" in the 1990s. In the 2000s Ethiopia became an important security partner in the "global war on terrorism." In addition, Ethiopia served as a key case in demonstrating how the millennium development goals might be met and received significant assistance from Washington, London, the European Union, and major foundations as a result. Ethiopia played key roles in regional peacekeeping, providing particularly critical troops to UN peacekeeping operations in different parts of Sudan and, more controversially, to the Africa Union mission in Somalia.

For Ethiopia, the regional is also the local.[31] The relationship with the Eritrean People's Liberation Front (EPLF) during the war and the state of Eritrea afterward has been a critical dimension of domestic security. The Ethiopia-Eritrea border conflict between 1998 and 2000 set Addis Ababa back many years in terms of development, and the unimplemented peace agreement led to eighteen years of costly stalemate. Eritrea and Ethiopia sponsored each other's rebel groups, meaning domestic politics and regional insecurity were intertwined. The Somali regional state in Ethiopia and Somalia are linked even more intricately. Insecurity on one side of the border generally spilled over into the neighboring side, resulting in part in a highly militarized Somali regional state. The borders with Sudan and southern Sudan have often been difficult to manage because refugees and populations who straddle the border are often engaged in political, economic, and insurgent activities in more than one country. The movement of Nuer refugees from southern Sudan into western Ethiopia shaped political dynamics within Gambela, for example.

The Ethiopia-Eritrea Border War and Its Aftermath

The Ethiopia-Eritrea border conflict reflects how the legacies of the armed struggle shaped regional relations and how a border conflict can provide a rationale for authoritarian governance.[32] In May 1991, when the EPRDF seized power in Addis Ababa, the EPLF occupied Eritrea. As did the war in Ethiopia, the Eritrean armed struggle ended in rebel victory, not a negotiated settlement. In April 1993, Eritreans voted overwhelmingly for independence in a UN-monitored referendum. Addis Ababa welcomed this outcome, but many Ethiopians blamed the EPRDF for surrendering not only what they regarded as a historic part of Ethiopia but also access to the sea, leaving Ethiopia landlocked. In fact, the EPRDF could not have prevented the EPLF from achieving its long-sought goal of independence. For the next several years, the two states seemed prepared to put past conflicts behind them and cooperate in a broad range of economic and diplomatic spheres.[33]

By 1998, however, relations had degenerated. Disputes between Addis Ababa and Asmara arose over Ethiopia's access to Eritrean ports; the relationship of the Ethiopian currency, the *birr*, to the new Eritrean currency, the *nakfa*; and the precise location of the poorly demarcated border between them, among other disagreements. The classic imperatives of nation-state building drove both regimes to set unconditional goals and refuse compromise on the vital issues of territoriality, legitimacy, and identity. In May 1998, Eritrean armed forces attacked the disputed border town of Badme, a use of military force that quickly escalated into full-scale war.[34] The historical links and rivalries between the two ruling parties and leaders made the violence particularly bitter. An estimated hundred thousand people were killed, a million displaced, and a generation of development opportunities squandered.

After a period of military stalemate, Addis Ababa launched a major offensive in May 2000 that forced Asmara to pull its troops back to prewar positions. After difficult negotiations led by Algeria and the United States, the warring parties signed an agreement in December 2000. The Algiers Agreement established a cease-fire and created a twenty-five-kilometer temporary security zone to be patrolled by the UN Mission in Ethiopia and Eritrea (UNMEE), the Eritrea-Ethiopia Border Commission (EEBC) to delimit the border, and a claims commission to assess liability for war damages. On the issue of the border, the EEBC decision was to be final and binding. In April 2002, the EEBC issued its determination and ruled that the symbolically important town of Badme was on the Eritrean side of the border. Badme was not the underlying cause of the conflict, but each regime used it as the marker of whether it had "won" or "lost" the war, and hence whether the terrible sacrifices each made in the conflict were justified or in vain. The control of this small, desolate town therefore became linked directly to the political fortunes of both regimes.[35]

At first Ethiopian leaders objected to the border ruling. They later declared acceptance in principle but insisted further talks on implementation were needed.[36] Asmara took the position that international law required Ethiopia to abide by the final and binding EEBC decision and that the international community had a responsibility to compel Ethiopia to leave Eritrean territory. This created a stable—if costly—stalemate that showed little movement to resolution until a new government in Ethiopia broke the impasse in 2018. This brutal war had important reverberations across Ethiopia in general, and Tigray in particular, where the TPLF faced a nearly fatal split in 2001. The struggle led by the EPLF for self-determination in Eritrea, along with the TPLF and then the EPRDF's war against the Derg, had been intertwined from the start. Ethiopia's relations with Eritrea had major political implications for politics within the EPRDF and between the EPRDF and its opposition.

The Ethiopia-Eritrea War and Ethiopian Nationalism

The EPRDF took power in 1991 with a deep skepticism of Ethiopian nationalism. A senior EPRDF leader stated, for example: "We say there is no country called Ethiopia, no state that defends the interests of this multiethnic community grouped under the name Ethiopia. That's why we've been immersed in wars for the last 30 years. So we must start again, from scratch."[37] Ethiopian nationalism, however, remained a potent force. It was always powerful in the diaspora but also remained available as a focus for mobilization domestically, particularly in Amhara and urban areas. In 1998, during the border war with Eritrea, Ethiopian nationalism burst into the open.[38] Without the EPRDF's endorsement, a large nationalist rally in support of Ethiopia's war effort was organized, and only at the last minute did the government assign the mayor of Addis Ababa to address the large crowd. Clapham writes:

> The "invasion" by Eritrea of what was perceived by Ethiopians as "their" territory thus prompted a far wider and more nationalist

> Ethiopian response than could otherwise have been expected from a small local conflict over land that most Ethiopians had never heard of. This response was not promoted by the government in Addis Ababa, which was taken completely by surprise, and had in any event been promoting a very different conception of Ethiopia as a congeries of disparate nationalities. . . . The rejoicing that greeted the victory at Badme in February 1999, when Ethiopia recaptured a significant part of the territory that had been seized by Eritrea nine months earlier, was popular rather than government orchestrated.[39]

Ethiopians were elated by their victory and took great pride in dominating their regional rival. "They were thrashed, they were kicked out, they were destroyed," government spokesperson Selome Tadesse said.[40]

As a consequence of the war, pan-Ethiopian identity—*Ethiopiawinet* (Ethiopia first)—based on a concept of identity that transcends ethnic identities and harkens back to the glories of the imperial era, again became a focal point for political discourse.[41] The public expression of Ethiopian nationalism put the ANDM in a difficult position because many members of its notional constituency self-identified as Ethiopian rather than Amhara.[42] This revival of pan-Ethiopian identity provided the basis for new opposition movements, as would become apparent in the 2005 elections, and shaped the discourse during the protests of 2016.[43]

Ethnofederalism in Practice

Ethnofederalism created an administrative structure that replicated the political structure of the EPRDF. The four principal regional states ranged from the small and cohesive Tigray to the huge and historically marginalized Oromia to the multiethnic SNNPR. Although the center retained dominance, each regional state also had its own political narrative and each regional party its own set of challenges. Despite the fact that the EPRDF has ruled since 1991, the history of each regional state reveals considerable political dynamism and interregional variation.

The Tigray National Regional State

As noted in Chapter 2, the TPLF emerged from the protracted war in Tigray with cohesive leadership and a disciplined organization that had experience in administering liberated territory as a consequence of its victory in the armed struggle. The TPLF as a political party and as the leading element in the EPRDF coalition continued to operate in ways that developed out of its wartime experiences and organizational structures and norms. Democratic centralism, which shaped how the rebels made decisions during the civil war, for example, remained fundamental to how the party made decisions after it seized power.

Although Meles was clearly the leader of the TPLF from 1991 until his death in 2012, its powerful Central Committee and officials based in the Tigray regional state rather than in Addis Ababa provided a degree of counterbalance, particularly in the 1990s. TPLF officials in Mekele (the regional capital in Tigray), for example, blocked Meles's plans to privatize the government-owned Electric Power Corporation.[44] A number of top TPLF leaders, such as Gebru Asrat, Tigray regional state president from 1991 to 2001, never joined the leadership in Addis Ababa but remained in powerful positions in Tigray until the 2001 split. Intra-TPLF competition shaped how the TPLF engaged with the larger EPRDF coalition.

The Tigray National Regional State received significant resources outside of its share of federal grants, which all the regional states received. The REST was created by the TPLF during the war and remained a party-run humanitarian organization that brought in support from international donors and played a major role in food distribution, agriculture, and resource management. The Tigray Development Association (TDA), also run by the TPLF, mobilized resources from the diaspora to support development projects. According to Solomon, these kinds of "off-budgetary" resource flows to Tigray equaled the level of resources transferred from the federal government.[45] The REST, TDA, and Tigray regional state institutions were so interlinked that it was hard to make a distinction between the party-run nongovernmental organizations (NGOs) and the party-run regional government.

As noted above, relations with the now independent neighboring state of Eritrea to the north had special significance to Tigrayans. After the 1998–2000 border war, old divisions between leaders who remained primarily focused on Tigray and those who played leadership roles in the EPRDF and the national coalition and who often held positions in the executive branch erupted. In 2001 the TPLF Central Committee split and voted fifteen to thirteen to support Meles against a faction of senior members of the party that included other party founders and military heroes from the struggle.[46] Differences regarding how Meles had pursued the war with Eritrea and his willingness to engage in negotiations were a key source of the grievances behind the split, but there were other issues as well. Meles prepared a paper on "Bonapartism" that criticized members of the TPLF leadership for decay and lack of connection to their constituencies. The party debated this paper for a month, indicating that there was a struggle for control of the party—and the country— behind these seemingly obscure Marxist debates. The dissenters, including party stalwarts such as Gebru, Siye Abraha (founding member of the TPLF and former minister of defense and chair of EFFORT), and

Tewolde Woldemariam (deputy chair of the TPLF) walked out of the party Central Committee meeting, providing Meles and his faction the opportunity (if not the legal authority) to expel them from the organization. With his position within the TPLF gravely weakened, Meles and his allies turned to the other member parties of the EPRDF.

At first, several leaders such as Kuma Demeksa (OPDO) and Abate Kisho (SEPDM) sided with the Siye group, and divisions became apparent. In July 2001, for example, the OPDO split into pro- and anti-Meles factions.[47] However, the ANDM and its leader, Addisu Legesse, rallied behind Meles. The EPRDF engaged in a rigorous process of self-examination (*gimgema*) and purged thousands of individuals who supported the dissenters in the TPLF as well as in the OPDO and SEPDM. A number of those associated with Meles's rivals were arrested and charged with corruption or, in the case of the OPDO and SEPDM, of "narrow nationalism." Leaders loyal to Meles's faction assumed leadership positions in the member parties, such as Haile-mariam Desalegn (the future prime minister) in the SEPDM and Abadula Gemeda in the OPDO. Many of the dissidents were officials in the party, whereas many affiliated with Meles had positions in the central government bureaucracy. Therefore, part of the post-2001 *tehadso* (renewal, or reform) involved increasing the role of the state relative to the party. With the EPRDF's leadership role reduced, the four member parties began to lose their authority and on-the-ground capacity to mobilize, as would be evident in the 2005 elections.

This struggle at the heart of the TPLF illustrates that the hard-won cohesion of the leadership rooted in the armed struggle required constant attention and that wartime coherence could break down under stress. The TPLF's legacy of wartime discipline did not prevent factionalism and a split that nearly destroyed the party. The contradiction between power centers based in the regional states and in the center manifested as two competing factions within the TPLF. The tactics of using organizational procedures to expel dissidents and to build alliances in the larger EPRDF to remain dominant within the TPLF showed that the party as an organization, rather than a single individual or governing clique, mattered at the top. Intra-TPLF power struggles were linked to larger competition among the other three members of the EPRDF coalition.

The Amhara National Regional State

The Amhara National Regional State (ANRS) illustrates the potential for regional states to develop institutional autonomy and direct links to their populations. Many correctly note that Ethiopia was a highly centralized regime under the EPRDF and that Addis Ababa controlled most of the finances upon which the regional states relied. At the same time, however, the ethnoregional states had often overlooked significance. The ANRS, for example, is the second-largest regional state in Ethiopia, with a population of 21 million.[48] It has its own constitution; its own elected council; regional bureaus of transport, health, and education; its own system of courts and prisons; and so forth. Long lines of farmers wait to make their cases to Amhara regional court officials to adjudicate land disputes, indicating that authority to decide issues fundamental to everyday life is located in the regional state. The Administration and Security Bureau has built a 100,000-member local militia in the rural areas— "almost a regional army," according to one ANRS official in 2011.[49]

The ANDM developed out of the Ethiopian People's Democratic Movement (EPDM), which, like the TPLF, had specific legacies from the armed struggle. It began as a faction that broke away from the Ethiopian People's Revolutionary Party (EPRP) and had been active in Amhara areas in Wollo. As a result, it had its own history of resistance to the Derg and came to resent EPRDF narratives that emphasized the central role of the TPLF while saying little about Amhara resistance. Key ANDM figures such as Tamrat Layne (future deputy prime minister), Bereket Simon (future communications minister), and Tefera Walwa (future minister of defense) had been leaders in the EPRP in the 1970s and EPDM in the 1980s. Although the EPDM was originally multiethnic, in 1994 it transformed into the ANDM to fit the ethnic party structure of the EPRDF. The ANDM, therefore, had claims to engaging in the armed struggle and the legitimacy such participation brought but also had a complicated relationship to the idea of an Amhara—rather than Ethiopian—identity.

The ANDM faced the challenge of mobilizing the Amhara ethnic group because a significant number of Amhara historically self-identify as members of the pan-Ethiopian nation. Appeals to the history of the Amhara past for ethnic mobilization is dissonant because the most salient symbols and narratives are imperial and Ethiopian.[50] The EPDM/ANDM therefore faced a dilemma, given the ethnofederal structures put in place. An EPDM member stated, "Today politics in Ethiopia is based on ethnicity. There are ethnic groups that have very strong ethnic sentiments and very strong ethnic-based political organizations. . . . In the face of this reality, those ethnic groups that are not organized, like the Amhara, will become underdogs and trail behind. . . . The only way out is to organize on the basis of ethnicity."[51] Another ANDM leader who participated in the EPDM during the struggle similarly said, "At first EPDM's multiethnic organization was essential, but later it had to be organized as an ethnic nationalist party to serve the interest of the Amhara people."[52]

The history of Amhara association with the Ethiopian nation-state therefore made it difficult for the ANDM to mobilize around Amhara nationalism rather than the historical Ethiopian identity.[53] On one level, the ANDM operated in a manner similar to the TPLF. The EPDM/ANDM joined the TPLF to form the EPRDF, and the ANDM had control over the Amhara regional state in the same way the TPLF had control over the Tigray region. As I discuss below, each had the same number of representatives in the EPRDF Executive Committee, where key decisions were made. Despite these formal similarities, the TPLF's position as the defender of the Tigray people during the civil war was not replicated with the ANDM and the Amhara population. Resentment against perceived lack of respect by the TPLF fueled a sense of grievance within the Amhara National Regional State that erupted in 2016.

Oromia

Oromia is the largest and most populated regional state in the Ethiopian federation. The Ethiopian Central Statistical Agency estimated its 2017 population at more than 35.5 million (approximately the size of Uganda or Morocco), making up 38 percent of Ethiopia's total population. Oromia virtually divides Ethiopia geographically, with the Amhara and Tigray regions to the north and the SNNPR to the south. It shares borders with the Somali, Afar, Benishangul-Gumuz, and Gambela regional states, surrounds key cities such as Addis Ababa and Harar, and borders the city of Dire Dawa. It is difficult to conceptualize Ethiopia as a viable territorial state without Oromia.

The region became part of the Ethiopian state with Menelik's imperial expansion in the nineteenth century. Many Oromos resented efforts to favor Amharas over Oromos and to repress organizations with Oromo identities, such as the Mecha and Tulama Self-Help Association, in the mid-1960s. In the 1970s, the OLF developed out of the student movement and fought for self-determination. The OLF, however, had difficulties mobilizing across the broad and diverse Oromo population and controlled relatively little territory under the Derg (I discuss this in Chapter 5).

The OPDO faced specific challenges in becoming an effective constituent party in the ruling coalition. Many Oromos were conscripted into the Derg Army during the civil war, but fighting within the region was limited compared with that in Eritrea and northern Ethiopia. The

EPRDF formed the OPDO from prisoners of war and deserters of the Derg Army. A few, such as Kuma (president of Oromia, minister of defense, and mayor of Addis Ababa), had first joined the multinational EPDM and then left that movement to help form the OPDO to create an Oromo party within the ruling coalition. Although the TPLF and the ANDM could make claims to legitimacy derived from the armed struggle, it was more difficult for the OPDO.

The OPDO quickly took several steps that met key Oromo nationalist aspirations. It adopted the Latin alphabet (rather than the *fidels* of the Semitic Amharic alphabet), made claims on Addis Ababa as its regional capital, and changed names of cities from their imperial names back to the original Afan Oromo names.[54] In the 1990s, however, the OLF retained considerable support in Oromia and in the Oromo diaspora, and the OPDO relied more on direct use of force to maintain its hold on power than was necessary in the northern regions. The introduction of the EPRDF into remote areas of Oromia led local intra-Oromo struggles to become entangled with national politics. For example, in Moyale, along the Ethiopia-Kenya border, the candidates on the ballot in 1992 were from the Gabra and Garri clans, not the large Borana clan, because the Borana were perceived to be close to the OLF.[55] In Bale, the Christian Shewa Oromo tended to support the OPDO, whereas the Muslim Arsi Oromo favored the OLF or the Islamic Front for the Liberation of Oromia.[56] The Oromos are a diverse population, creating challenges for any political party that seeks to claim sole legitimate authority.

Although the Oromo population is overwhelmingly rural, cities play an important symbolic role in its politics. Addis Ababa is in the middle of the Oromo region and is called Finfine (its Afan Oromo name) by Oromo nationalists. As is the case in many countries, Ethiopia decided to make its national capital an autonomous jurisdiction, but the 1995 constitution recognized that the Oromo people have a special status relative to the capital. Plans to expand Addis Ababa into the Oromo regional state without consulting with the Oromos triggered demonstrations in 2014 and remained explosive in 2018. The ancient city of Harar is another particular case. The Harari, despite their small population, were recognized as a national group and hence given the Harar region as their national regional state. Harar regional state, however, is majority Oromo. Finally, Dire Dawa has been contested by both the Oromo and the Somali regional states and, after a period of conflict, was declared a chartered city in 1993. Some Oromo nationalists believe that the EPRDF regime is deliberately denying the Oromos their fair share of resources, increasingly focused in the cities.[57]

In addition, as cities expand they come into conflict with Oromos in the adjoining rural areas.

In 2000, many Oromos protested the plan to move the Caffee Oromia (the parliament of the regional state) and Oromo regional state ministries from Addis Ababa to Adama (the city that used to be called Nazaret). Many saw this move as diminishing Oromo claims on Addis Ababa, putting the OPDO in the position of enforcing an unpopular move and undermining its nationalist credibility. Although opposition to the move was popular among many Oromos, OPDO officials felt it necessary to threaten "drastic measures" against anyone opposing the move.[58] A major demonstration in Meskel Square in the center of Addis Ababa in January 2004 ended with police beating and arresting protesters.[59] The Oromo organization Mecha and Tulama Self-Help Association was perceived as encouraging dissent, and some of its leadership was also arrested. Protests spread to university and high school students in Oromia. From the vantage point of the Oromo people, OPDO's acceptance of the order "amounted to national suicide because it surrendered the rights of the Oromo people, thereby preventing them from exercising any form of influence or control over the city [Addis Ababa]."[60] In 2000 the OPDO failed to find a way to position itself as sympathetic to the aspirations of its base while remaining loyal to the powerful center.

The OPDO leadership faced splits and purges during the crisis in 2001 that split the TPLF. Kuma, then-president of Oromia and secretary general of the OPDO, along with three OPDO Central Committee members, were suspended, and OPDO member Almaz Mako, the speaker of the House of Federation, fled into exile.[61] Abadula Gemeda rose in prominence by rallying to Meles's side of the struggle. The OPDO faced internal crises, pervasive corruption, and difficulty in establishing connections to its constituency. In 2003, for example, then-president of Oromia Junedin Sado fought with the chair of the OPDO, Abadula.[62]

Many Oromos welcomed the EPRDF's ethnofederalism, but the OPDO as a party had several difficulties in establishing itself as the hegemonic party in Oromia. The OLF had prior claims as the defender of Oromo rights, and the TPLF's role in creating the OPDO from prisoners of war led to questions related to the OPDO's autonomy and legitimacy. In addition, all Oromo political organizations struggled to unite the vast and diverse Oromo people, who include Muslims, Orthodox Christians, and Protestants; farmers and pastoralists; and populations with different experiences within Ethiopia. The structural challenge to the OPDO resulted in Oromia remaining relatively weak within the EPRDF, despite its size and population.

The Southern Nations, Nationalities, and People's Region (SNNPR)

In 1991 the EPRDF invited a number of newly formed parties with nominal links to the many small and marginalized communities in southern Ethiopia to participate in the Transitional Government of Ethiopia (TGE).[63] In 1992, twenty of these small parties created a coalition, the SEPDF, that joined the EPRDF as the fourth member party. In 2003 this coalition merged into a single political party, the SEPDM. The SNNPR is extremely diverse, and the region's populations are united principally by their status as historically neglected peoples. The SNNPR, therefore, is organized differently than the Tigray, Amhara, and Oromo regional states, where one ethnic group and one ethnic party control an ethnically defined regional state.[64] The SEPDM is a multiethnic coalition within the larger EPRDF multiethnic coalition.

The SEPDM has a mixed record that reflects the diverse socioeconomic terrain of the region. In the SNNPR, the many small groups fear domination by the region's larger groups, such as the Wolayita, Sidama, Hadiya, Gamo, Kaficho, and Gedeo. The Sidama do not want to live in *woredas* where the majority is Wolayita, and the Wolayita do not want to be minorities in woredas dominated by the Sidama.[65] Internal regional boundaries, therefore, have critical implications for local power and identity politics, and SNNPR politics are often riven with intraethnic competition.

In many areas with local rivalries, whereas one group reaches out to the SEPDM for support, the other is in opposition. In 1991 the Sidama Liberation Movement (SLM) was one of the ethnonational organizations invited by the EPRDF to participate in the TGE. Soon, however, the EPRDF recruited its own Sidama People's Democratic Organization (SPDO).[66] The EPRDF regarded the SLM as a movement of the traditional aristocracy and recruited younger, less elite leadership for the SPDO.[67] Many Gurage favored the opposition, for example, whereas many Siltes (who have contentious relationships with the Gurage) have allied with the SEPDM/EPRDF.[68] In Gedeo those who favor closer relations with the ruling party are concentrated in the Gedeo People's Democratic Movement, whereas those in the antigovernment camp have set up the rival Gedeo People's Democratic Organization, a member of the opposition SEPDC.[69] To a significant extent all politics is local in the SNNPR, and decisions regarding cooperation with the EPRDF often link back to quite parochial rivalries and local claims to power.

For some groups marginalized under the imperial and Derg regimes, the early years of the EPRDF seemed like a honeymoon. The Konso, for example, received recognition and control over a "special woreda," a self-governing semiautonomous unit. Local Konso-speaking people replaced the Amharic speakers from non-Konso regions as administrators and officials. The challenge of finding skilled professionals to staff the Konso Ministry of Health, Ministry of Education, court system, and so on resulted in "nearly 100 percent employment for Konso people with education."[70] This shift in power to the Konso and other historically marginalized groups in southern Ethiopia contrasted with the previous regimes' efforts to disparage local cultures and encourage conversion to Orthodox Christianity and the Amharic language.

At first, a significant number of TPLF officials operated in the SNNPR, a necessity given that the EPRDF had limited connections to locally led political institutions or organized loyalists in the region. Over time, the SEPDF recruited local officials, particularly younger officials happy to replace the old elite. In contrast to the TPLF, which could draw upon those who had demonstrated their commitment in Tigray during the war, the SEPDF attracted careerists who saw advantages in working with the ruling party. In 2001, during the *tehadso* period, launched following the TPLF party splits, a leadership shakeup in the SEPDF resulted in a new set of leaders and the removal of most of the TPLF cadres.

In the early years of the EPRDF's reign, the party created a number of new local government units as a way to manage interethnic disputes. For example the North Omo Nationality Zone originally had lumped together the Wolayita, Gamo-Gofa, and Daro communities. Wolayitas, however, demanded their own separate nationality zone. After a brief period of violence, the EPRDF divided the North Omo Nationality Zone into three nationality zones (Wolayita, Daro, and Gamo-Gofa) and two special woredas for the Basketo and Konta peoples. Similarly the Keffa and Sheka zone had been split to provide separate local government areas for the Keffico and Shekich peoples.[71] Later, efforts to merge the special zone for the Konso people with those for the Dirashe, Burji, and Amaro peoples to form a new Segen Area People's Zone generated protests and conflict as the Konso perceived this move as reducing their power.[72]

In November 1999, protests in Soddo, in the Wolayita region of the SNNPR, ended in violence with some ten persons killed and as many as a thousand arrested. Local Wolayita speakers were protesting the creation of a new language called Wagagoda that would combine Wolayita, Gamo-Gofa, and Dawro into a new hybrid.[73] The new language was designed for classroom use but generated strong opposition and was eventually dropped. The Wolayita feared that losing their distinct language and identity would lessen their stature in the new political and economic order. Language and a sense of group history are fundamental to forming and retaining a sense of identity, and a claim to a distinct identity was key to making claims for a distinct woreda or zone.[74]

A peaceful Sidama mobilization in 2002 against a planned change in the administrative status of the capital, Awassa, ended with police shooting into the crowd, killing between fifteen and thirty-eight people.[75] Protesters, estimated to number seven thousand, had obtained advance permission to march. The demonstrators carried Ethiopian flags and signs that said, "The Constitutional Rights of the Sidamo Zone people should be respected" and "We have no objections to EPRDF's policies." But when they arrived at the city limits, they were met with machine-gun fire, according to witnesses interviewed by the Ethiopian Human Rights Council.[76] The European Union described the shooting into unarmed crowds as an "atrocity."[77] Ethnofederalism often generated a series of new conflicts because different constituencies perceived the new order as disadvantaging them, often relative to a neighboring group.

The SNNPR, therefore, shared historical marginalization in ways similar to that of Oromia. Of greater immediate concern to local political leaders, however, were intraregional rivalries. The sense of a "southern" identity was not developed in the same way Tigray or Oromo identities were. Although the SEPDM and the TPLF were both constituent parties within the EPRDF and had equal representation on the EPRDF's Executive Committee, each had vastly different origins and constituencies. Rivalries among the various groups in the SNNPR shaped regional politics, as seen in the demonstrations in Soddo in 1999 and Awassa in 2002. Language policies, intraregional state boundary conflicts, and the contentious politics of where regional capitals would be located kept SNNPR politics internally focused and made the fragmented SEPDM a difficult political base for national leadership.

Somali, Afar, Benishangul-Gumuz, Gambela, and Harar
Parties that are not members of the EPRDF coalition govern the Somali, Afar, Benishangul-Gumuz, Gambela, and Harari regions. These parties, however, almost always act as affiliates of the ruling party rather than as opposition parties. There is competition among these parties for a larger share of federal resources, along with campaigns to get more of their respective party members appointed to high office. Not surprisingly, the affiliate parties generally seek to win support from the center by supporting rather than opposing the dominant party.

The Somali National Regional State (SNRS) is a partial exception. In the SNRS (a region with a larger population than Tigray) the EPRDF aligned with the Ogaden National Liberation Front (ONLF) for a period after the 1992 local elections. The ONLF won the 1992 elections, and the ONLF-controlled regional assembly demanded the constitutional right to self-determination in February 1994. The Ethiopian Somali Democratic League (ESDL), composed of representatives from non-Ogadeni clans, replaced the ONLF and pursued regional policies that met with the EPRDF's approval. Senior official Abdulmejid Hussein led the ESDL and its successor party, the Somali People's Democratic Party (SPDP).[78] The ONLF engaged in limited armed resistance against the EPRDF until 2006, when the civil war between the ONLF and the EPRDF escalated.

Benishangul-Gumuz is a multiethnic region along the border with Sudan. The region is 25 percent Berta, 22 percent Amhara, 21 percent Gumuz, and 14 percent Oromo. The Derg moved many highland Amharas and Oromos to the region as part of its resettlement policies of the 1980s. As a result, there are often tensions between the Berta and Gumuz peoples and the "highlanders," who occupy a significant portion of land and resources. From 1991 to 1995 the Benishangul People's Liberation Movement (BPLM) governed the region, but difficult relations with the EPRDF led the ruling party to form the Benishangul-Gumuz People's Democratic Unity Front, which has controlled the region since 1996.[79]

Gambela is also along the Sudanese border and is inhabited by the Nuer and Anuak peoples, along with a population of highlanders relocated to the region. The Anuak-dominated Gambela People's Liberation Movement (GPLM) had fought the Derg in a loose alliance with the EPRDF. This relationship, however, was difficult because the GPLM's political agenda focused on removing highlanders (which included Tigrayans and Amharas) from the region. After the transition the Anuak-led GPLM and Nuer had continuing clashes. In 1998 the federal government pressured the GPLM to merge with the Nuer-dominated Gambela People's Democratic Unity Party to form the Gambela People's Democratic Front.[80]

Finally, Harar, the historic walled city, is recognized as the Harari People's National Regional State (HPNRS). The Adare are the notional nationality in the city, but a significant Oromo population inhabits HPNRS, particularly in the surrounding countryside. Urban areas such as Addis Ababa, Dire Dawa, Adama, Gondar, and Hawassa are generally more multiethnic. As a party that self-consciously saw its base as among the rural peasants and that viewed urban dwellers with suspicion, the EPRDF did not have well-developed policies for urban development for its first decade of rule.[81] Urban areas remained a highly contentious issue in the identity politics of 2018.

Politics in these regions are fascinating and enormously complex. The Somali region, in particular, has a long history of opposition, a prolonged civil war, and brutal counterinsurgency operations that had national and regional implications.[82] In recent years large-scale land leases of agricultural land in Gambela to international investors and the building of the Grand Ethiopian Renaissance Dam in Benishangul-Gumuz have created considerable controversy.[83] The EPRDF makes its claims to legitimacy in part by pointing to the manner in which these historically marginalized regions benefited from the 1991 transition. To keep my focus on the EPRDF and its transformation from insurgency to powerful authoritarian party, however, I will not investigate in depth the local politics and non-EPRDF party dynamics in these regions.

Conclusion

This chapter has demonstrated that local dynamics shape Ethiopian politics beyond the overarching story of how "the" EPRDF or "the" TPLF dominated politics. The EPRDF is a powerful ruling party that has dominated Ethiopia and exhibited considerable central authority over the vast and diverse country. Elections in 1995 and 2000 served as opportunities to consolidate power and build the party's scope and reach. At the same time, however, the EPRDF is a fragile coalition of disparate constituent parties that have divergent legacies from the war and varied experiences as postwar administrations and parties. Internal contention within the EPRDF and struggles over intraparty conflicts characterized the first decade of the party's rule. Although many analysts focus on politics in Addis Ababa and among the top leadership of the EPRDF, there was important political contestation in the OPDO and within the Amhara National Regional State, among other players. In other words, both a strong center and important political processes in the regional states characterized the EPRDF and Ethiopian politics.

Notes

1. Cited in Stig Jarle Hansen, "Organizational Culture at War: Ethiopian Decision Making and the War with Eritrea (1998–2000)," PhD diss., Aberystwyth University, 2006, 156–157.
2. Barbara Geddes, "Authoritarian Breakdown: Empirical Test of a Game Theoretic Argument," paper presented at the American Political Science Association Meeting, 1999.

3. Steven R. Levitsky and Lucan A. Way, *Competitive Authoritarianism: Hybrid Regimes After the Cold War* (Cambridge, UK: Cambridge University Press, 2010); Beatriz Magaloni, *Voting for Autocracy: Hegemonic Party Survival and Its Demise in Mexico* (Cambridge, UK: Cambridge University Press, 2006); Jennifer Gandhi, *Political Institutions Under Dictatorship* (Cambridge, UK: Cambridge University Press, 2008); Jason Brownlee, *Authoritarianism in an Age of Democratization* (Cambridge, UK: Cambridge University Press, 2007). For a review, see Beatriz Magaloni and Ruth Krischeli, "Political Order and One-party Rule," *Annual Review of Political Science* 3 (2010): 123–143.

4. Steven R. Levitsky and Lucan A. Way, "Beyond Patronage: Violent Struggle, Ruling Party Cohesion, and Authoritarian Durability," *Perspectives on Politics* 10, no. 4 (2012): 870.

5. Samuel P. Huntington, *Political Order in Changing Societies* (New Haven, CT: Yale University Press, 1968), 424.

6. Milan W. Svolik, *The Politics of Authoritarian Rule* (Cambridge, UK: Cambridge University Press, 2012).

7. Steven Levitsky and Lucan Way, "The Durability of Revolutionary Regimes," *Journal of Democracy* 24, no. 3 (2013): 8.

8. Richard S. Katz and Peter Mair, eds., *How Parties Organize: Adaption and Change in Party Organizations in Western Democracies* (London: Sage, 1994); Daniela Giannetti and Kenneth Benoit, eds., *Intra-Party Politics and Coalition Governments* (London: Routledge, 2009).

9. Richard S. Katz and Peter Mair, "The Evolution of Party Organizations in Europe: The Three Faces of Party Organization," *American Review of Politics* 14 (Winter 1993): 593.

10. Sarah Vaughan and Kjetil Tronvoll, *The Culture of Power in Contemporary Ethiopian Political Life,* SIDA Studies No. 10 (Stockholm: Swedish International Development Cooperation Agency 2003), 17.

11. Aristide Zolberg, *Creating Political Order: The Party-States of West Africa* (Chicago: Rand McNally, 1967).

12. Jennifer Widner, *The Rise of the Party State in Kenya: From Harambee! to Nyayo!* (Berkeley: University of California Press, 1992), 7.

13. Jean-Nicolas Bach, "*Abyotawi* Democracy: Neither Revolutionary nor Democratic—a Critical View of EPRDF's Conception of Revolutionary Democracy in Post-1991 Ethiopia," *Journal of Eastern African Studies* 5, no. 4 (2011): 641–663. On the size of these leagues, see www.eprdf.org.et.

14. Sarah Vaughan and Mesfin Gebremichael, *Rethinking Business and Politics in Ethiopia: The Role of EFFORT, the Endowment Fund for the Rehabilitation of Tigray,* Africa Power and Politics Program Research Report No. 2 (London: Overseas Development Institute, August 2011).

15. Tigray Development Association (TDA), http://www.tdaint.org/. These funds supplement the block grant to the Tigray National Regional State from the federal government.

16. Erwin van Veen, *Perpetuating Power: Ethiopia's Political Settlement and the Organization of Security* (The Hauge: Clingendael Institute, September 2016), 28.

17. Kjetil Tronvoll, "Ambiguous Elections: The Influence of Non-Electoral Politics in Ethiopian Democratisation," *Journal of Modern African Studies* 47, no. 3 (2009): 449–474.

18. Andreas Schedler, ed., *Electoral Authoritarianism: The Dynamics of Unfree Competition* (Boulder, CO: Lynne Rienner, 2006); Jennifer Gandhi and Ellen Lust-Okar, "Elections Under Authoritarianism," *Annual Review of Political Science* 12 (June 2009): 403–422.

19. Andrew J. Nathan, "Authoritarian Resilience," *Journal of Democracy* 14, no. 1 (January 2003): 6–17; Minxin Pei, "Is CCP Rule Fragile or Resilient?" *Journal of Democracy* 23, no. 1 (January 2012): 27–41; Steven Heydemann and Reinoud Leenders, eds., *Middle East Authoritarianisms: Governance, Contestation, and Regime Resilience in Syria and Iran* (Palo Alto, CA: Stanford University Press, 2013); Michael Bratton, *Power Politics in Zimbabwe* (Boulder, CO: Lynne Rienner, 2014).

20. Terrence Lyons, "Closing the Transition: The May 1995 Elections in Ethiopia," *Journal of Modern African Studies* 34, no. 1 (March 1996): 121–142. Much of the analysis in this section is based on the author's role as senior adviser to the Donor Election Unit (DEU), which coordinated international teams to observe the 1995 elections. See "The Donor Election Unit's Leaked Report," *Ethiopian Register* 2, no. 5 (July 1995), 41–53. For another firsthand assessment, see USAID, "Lessons Learned from Elections in Ethiopia, 1992–1995 (and Some Thoughts on the Planned 2000 Elections)," June 17, 1999, http://pdf.usaid.gov/pdf_docs/PNACF945.pdf.

21. Some international election observers who came to Ethiopia were unhappy that the DEU briefing material began with the conclusion that the outcome was clear before the first vote was cast.

22. Africa Elections Database, http://africanelections.tripod.com/et.html #1995_House_of_Peoples_Representatives_Election.

23. Although independent candidates did appear on the ballot in Tigray, at least some interviewed by election observers stated they had been selected by the party to run as independents, and the party helped them collect the requisite signatures to get on the ballot. Candidates, interviews with author, Addis Ababa, 1995.

24. "Ethiopia: Boycott Call," *Indian Ocean Newsletter* 668 (April 22, 1995). In many parts of western Oromia, informants claimed that the OLF was active "at night" and "in the rural areas" despite being absent from the formal political process. Informants, interviews with author in Arsi, Wellega, and Bale as part of the DEU, 1995.

25. Donor Election Unit, "Final Analytical Summary of Donor Election Unit Reports: The 7 May 1995 Ethiopian Elections" (Addis Ababa: Donor Election Unit, May 30, 1995).

26. Donor Election Unit, "Final Analytical Summary of Donor Election Unit Reports."

27. Quoted in Stephen Buckley, "Ethiopia Takes New Ethnic Tack: Deliberately Divisive," *Washington Post*, June 18, 1995, A2.

28. This section draws upon the reports of Norwegian observers published in Siegfried Pausewang and Kjetil Tronvoll, eds., *The Ethiopian 2000 Elections: Democracy Advanced or Restricted?* (Oslo: Norwegian Institute of Human Rights, 2000); and Siegfried Pausewang and Lovise Aalen, *Withering Democracy: Local Elections in Ethiopia, February/March 2001,* Working Paper 2001:07 (Oslo: Nordem, 2001).

29. Pausewang and Aalen, *Withering Democracy.*

30. Federal Democratic Republic of Ethiopia, Ministry of Information, *Foreign Affairs and National Security Policy and Strategy* (Addis Ababa: Federal Democratic Republic of Ethiopia, November 2002), 1.

31. I thank Ken Menkhaus for helping me think through these points.

32. I first presented some of this analysis in Terrence Lyons, *Avoiding Conflict in the Horn of Africa: U.S. Policy Toward Ethiopia and Eritrea,* Special Report no. 21 (New York: Council on Foreign Relations, December 2006); and Terrence Lyons, "The Ethiopia-Eritrea Conflict and the Search for Peace in the Horn of Africa," *Review of African Political Economy* 36, no. 120 (2009): 167–180. See also Kjetil Tronvoll, *War and the Politics of Identity in Ethiopia: The Making of Enemies and Allies in the Horn of Africa* (Oxford, UK: James Currey, 2009).

33. For a sense of the early optimism, see Amare Tekle, ed., *Eritrea and Ethiopia: From Conflict and Cooperation* (Lawrenceville, NJ: Red Sea, 1994).

34. See Eritrea-Ethiopia Claims Commission, partial award, *Jus Ad Bellum*, Ethiopia's Claims 1–8, The Hague, December 19, 2005, http://www.pca-cpa.org/upload/files/FINAL%20ET%20JAB.pdf.

35. Isaias Afewerki said, "Pulling out of Badme may be likened to insisting that the sun will not rise in the morning. . . . It is unthinkable." Cited in Kjetil Tronvoll, "Borders of Violence—Boundaries of Identity: Demarcating the Eritrean Nation-State," *Ethnic and Racial Studies* 22, no. 6 (November 1999): 1048.

36. In a September 2003 letter to UN secretary-general Kofi Annan, Prime Minister Meles Zenawi dug in his heels and characterized the EEBC decision as "totally illegal, unjust, and irresponsible" and called for an "alternative mechanism" to demarcate the boundary. See President of the Eritrea-Ethiopia Boundary Commission to the Secretary-General, letter, October 7, 2003, reprinted in "Progress Report of the Secretary-General on Ethiopia and Eritrea," December 19, 2003, S/2003/1186.

37. Dawit Yohannes, legal adviser to Meles Zenawi, quoted in Michaela Wrong, "Ethiopia Buries the African 'Nation State,'" *Financial Times*, May 5, 1995.

38. Dominique Jacquin-Berdal and Martin Plaut, *Unfinished Business: Ethiopia and Eritrea at War* (Trenton, NJ: Red Sea, 2004), 109.

39. Christopher Clapham, "War and State Formation in Ethiopia and Eritrea," paper prepared for Failed States conference, Florence, 2001, 11. See also Christopher Clapham, "Post-Crisis Ethiopia: The Trajectories of Crisis," *Review of African Political Economy* 36, no. 120 (2009): 181–192.

40. David Gough, "Ethiopia Elated at Victory in Border War with Eritrea," *Guardian,* May 25, 2000, http://www.theguardian.com/world/2000/may/26/ethiopia.

41. Tronvoll, *War and the Politics of Identity in Ethiopia*, 139–143. See also Franklin Stevens, "Regime Change and War: Domestic Politics and the Escalation of the Ethiopia-Eritrea Conflict," *Cambridge Review of International Affairs* 16, no. 1 (2003).

42. Assefa Fisseha, "Theory Versus Practice in the Implementation of Ethiopia's Ethnic Federalism," in David Turton, ed., *Ethnic Federalism: The Ethiopian Experience in Comparative Federalism* (Oxford, UK: James Currey, 2006), 147.

43. Tronvoll, "Ambiguous Elections," 467. Jean-Nicolas Bach, however, cautions against overstating the shift from ethnic federalism to Ethiopianess.

See Bach, "Compromising with Ethiopianness After 1991: The Ethiopian Festival of the Millennium (September 2007–September 2008), *Northeast African Studies* 13, no. 2 (2013): 93–122.

44. Paulos Milkias, "Ethiopia, the TPLF, and the Roots of the 2001 Political Tremor," *Northeast African Studies* 10, no. 2 (2003): 16.

45. Solomon Negussie, *Fiscal Federalism in the Ethiopian Ethnic-based Federal System* (Ottawa: Forum of Federations, 2008), 111.

46. Paulos, "Ethiopia, the TPLF, and the Roots of the 2001 Political Tremor," 20. See also Medhane Tadesse and John Young, "TPLF: Reform or Decline?" *Review of African Political Economy* 97 (2003): 389–403.

47. "OPDO on the Verge of Major Split," *Indian Ocean Newsletter,* July 21, 2001.

48. This population is larger than that of most African states—higher than the populations of Zimbabwe, Rwanda, Senegal, and Zambia, for example. It is, however, only the second-highest population in Ethiopia (the population of Oromia region is larger).

49. Interviews with author, Addis Ababa and Bahir Dar, 2011. This pattern of locally controlled security forces is present in the other regions as well. Interviews with author in Hawassa and Arba Minch, 2011.

50. Mackonen Michael, "What Is Amhara?" *African Identities* 6, no. 4 (November 2008): 393–404; Takkele Taddese, "Do the Amhara Exist as a Distinct Ethnic Group?" in *Ethnicity and the State in Eastern Africa,* ed. Mohamed A. Salih and John Markakis (Stockholm: Elanders Gotab, 1992).

51. Andargachew Tsige, a former member of EPDM, quoted in Tegegne Teka, "Amhara Ethnicity in the Making," in *Ethnicity and the State in Eastern Africa,* ed. Mohamed A. Salih and John Markakis (Stockholm: Elanders Gotab, 1992), 730.

52. Alemnew Mekonnen, ANDM Central Committee member, interview, "Strengthening Democratic Nationalism," *Ethiopian Reporter,* https://archive english.thereporterethiopia.com/content/strengthening-democratic-nationalism.

53. Similar dynamics shaped the political opposition as the All-Amhara People's Organization struggled to mobilize pan-Ethiopian nationalists on the basis of Amhara identity. See Chapter 5.

54. Debre Zeit's name was changed back to Bishoftu, and Nazaret back to Adama, among many others.

55. Marco Bassi, "The Politics of Space in Borana Oromo, Ethiopia: Demographics, Elections, Identity, and Customary Institutions," *Journal of Eastern African Studies* 4, no. 2 (2010): 231.

56. Terje Østebø, "Islam and Politics: The EPRDF, the 2005 Elections, and Muslim Institutions in Bale," in *Contested Power in Ethiopia: Traditional Authorities and Multi-party Elections,* ed. Kjetil Tronvoll and Tobias Hagmann (Leiden: Brill, 2011), 189.

57. Interviews with author, Addis Ababa, 2011, 2012, and 2013.

58. "Tough Luck on the Oromos," *Indian Ocean Newsletter* 916 (September 9, 2000).

59. "Oromos Are Riled Up," *Indian Ocean Newsletter* 1071 (January 10, 2004).

60. Getahun Benti, "A Blind Without a Cane, a Nation Without a City: The Oromo Struggle for Addis Ababa," in *Contested Terrain: Essays on Oromo*

Studies, Ethiopianist Discourse, and Politically Engaged Scholarship, ed. Ezekiel Gebissa (Trenton, NJ: Red Sea, 2009), 155.

61. Mohammed Hassen, "Conquest, Tyranny, and Ethnocide Against the Oromo: A Historical Assessment of Human Rights Conditions in Ethiopia, ca. 1880s–2002," in Ezekiel Gebissa, ed., *Contested Terrain: Essays on Oromo Studies, Ethiopianist Discourse, and Politically Engaged Scholarship,* ed. Ezekiel Gebissa (Trenton, NJ: Red Sea, 2009), 53. Almaz Mako received asylum in the United States and joined the opposition Oromo Liberation Front. Kuma Demeksa rejoined the OPDO after a few years and served as minister of defense from 2005 to 2008.

62. "Rifts Within OPDO Leadership," *Indian Ocean Newsletter* 1050 (July 12, 2003); "Oromos Are Riled Up"; interviews with author, Washington, DC, 2017.

63. The United Nations maintained a twenty-four-page list of party acronyms in the early 1990s. See "Alphabet Soup: Election 1995 Special!," UN Emergency Prevention and Preparedness Group, May 3, 1995, found at http://www.africa.upenn.edu/eue_web/soup_may.htm.

64. The Somali and Afar regions also consist of predominantly a single ethnic group, whereas Gambela, Benishangul-Gumuz, and Addis Ababa are multiethnic.

65. Lovise Aalen, *The Politics of Ethnicity in Ethiopia: Actors, Power, and Mobilisation Under Ethnic Federalism* (Leiden: Brill, 2011), 174.

66. Lovise Aalen, "Two Stories Told: The 2001 Local Elections in Kambata, Tambaro, Hadiya, and Sidama," in *Ethiopia 2001: Local Elections in the Southern Region,* Report 3/2002 (Oslo: Nordem, 2002).

67. Vaughan and Tronvoll, *Culture of Power in Contemporary Ethiopian Political Life,* 191. Many elementary school teachers, for example, joined the SPDO.

68. Lahra Smith, "Voting for an Ethnic Identity: Procedural and Institutional Responses to Ethnic Conflict in Ethiopia," *Journal of Modern African Studies* 45, no. 4 (2007): 565–594; author's field notes, Butajira, 2005. See also Makoro Nishi, "Making and Unmaking of the Nation-State and Ethnicity in Modern Ethiopia: A Study on the History of the Silte People," *African Studies Monographs* (March 2005): 157–168.

69. Siegfried Pausewang, "A Population Resisting Local Control and Intimidation? The Elections in Gedeo, Southern Region," in *Ethiopia Since the Derg: A Decade of Democratic Pretension and Performance,* ed. Siegfried Pausewang, Kjetil Tronvoll, and Lovise Aalen (London: Zed, 2002).

70. Elizabeth Watson, "Capturing a Local Elite: The Konso Honeymoon," in *Remapping Ethiopia: Socialism and After,* ed. Wendy James, Donald L. Donham, Eisei Kurimoto, and Alessandro Triulzi (Oxford, UK: James Currey, 2002), 200. In a later article, Watson analyzes intra-Konso violent conflict between different groups on the basis of economics and religion. See Watson, "Making a Living in the Postsocialist Periphery: Struggles Between Farmers and Traders in Konso, Ethiopia," *Africa* 76, no. 1 (February 2006): 70–86.

71. Zemelak Ayitenew Ayele, "The Politics of Sub-national Constitutionalism and Local Government in Ethiopia," *Perspectives on Federalism* 6, no. 2 (2014): 89–115; Lahra Smith, "The Politics of Contemporary Language Policy in Ethiopia," *Journal of Developing Societies* 24, no. 2 (2008): 208.

72. Author's fieldwork in Arba Minch and Konso, 2011. For background, see Misganaw Addis Modes, *Practice of Self-Government in the Southern Nations, Nationalities, and People's Regional State: The Case of the Segen*

Area People's Zone, master's thesis, Addis Ababa University College of Law and Governance, 2014.

73. Ethiopian Human Rights Council, *Human Rights Violations in North Omo,* 27th Special Report, December 13, 1999.

74. Lahra Smith, *Making Citizens in Africa: Ethnicity, Gender, and National Identity in Ethiopia* (Cambridge, UK: Cambridge University Press, 2013).

75. Kjetil Tronvoll, "Human Rights Violations in Federal Ethiopia: When Ethnic Identity Is a Political Stigma," *International Journal on Minority and Group Rights* 15 (2008): 74; Ethiopian Human Rights Council, "Serious Human Rights Violations in Awassa and Its Environs," 51st Special Report, June 4, 2002. Some Sidama activists put the number of dead at sixty-nine. See United Sidama Parties for Freedom and Justice, "People of Sidama Globally Marks the 12th Anniversary of Looqqe Massacre," May 26, 2014, http://www.tesfanews.net/12th-sidama-looqqe-massacre-globally-markeds/.

76. Ethiopian Human Rights Council, "Serious Human Rights Violations in Awassa and Its Environs."

77. BBC, "EU Wants Ethiopian 'Atrocity' Investigation," July 16, 2002, http://news.bbc.co.uk/2/hi/africa/2131177.stm. EU ambassadors also raised questions about killings in Tepi following disputed elections in March 2002.

78. Tobias Hagmann and Mohamud Hussein Khalif, "State and Politics in Ethiopia's Somali Region Since 1991," *Bildhaan* 6, no. (2008).

79. Asnake Kefale, *Federalism and Ethnic Conflict in Ethiopia: A Comparative Regional Study* (London: Routledge, 2013), 249.

80. Dereje Feyissa, *Playing Different Games: The Paradox of Anywaa and Nuer Identification in the Gambella Region, Ethiopia* (New York: Berghahn, 2011).

81. Meheret Ayenew, "A Review of the FDRE's Urban Development Policy," in *Digest of Ethiopia's National Policies, Strategies, and Programs,* ed. Taye Assefa (Addis Ababa: Forum for Social Studies, 2008), 451–467.

82. Tobias Hagmann, "Beyond Clannishness and Colonialism: Understanding Political Disorder in Ethiopia's Somali Region, 1991–2004," *Journal of Modern African Studies* 43, no. 4 (December 2005): 509–536.

83. John Young, "Along Ethiopia's Western Frontier: Gambella and Beninshangul in Transition," *Journal of Modern African Studies* 37, no. 2 (June 1999): 321–346; Dereje, *Playing Different Games.*

5

Diverse Opposition

Political opposition in Ethiopia after the 1991 transition and the consolidation of the Ethiopian People's Revolutionary Democratic Front (EPRDF) took a number of forms. The ruling party, however, handily marginalized each in turn until 2005. Several parties that initially participated in the 1991 Transitional Government of Ethiopia (TGE)—notably the Oromo Liberation Front (OLF) and the Ogaden National Liberation Front (ONLF)—soon either left or were expelled from the Transitional Council of Representatives. In 1992 the OLF engaged in a short war with the EPRDF and quickly lost its military capacity. Similarly, but later, the ONLF collapsed as a military threat in the face of a brutal counterinsurgency campaign. Efforts to compel the EPRDF to participate in a national conference, such as the 1993 Paris Conference, also failed.[1] Opposition figures worked with the Carter Center, the US Congressional Task Force on Ethiopia, and mediators in Germany and Norway to convene talks between the opposition and the government, with little success.[2] The legally registered alternative political parties largely boycotted local elections in 1992, constituent assembly elections in 1994, and national elections in 1995 and 2000. In 1994, the EPRDF regime arrested the leader of the All-Amhara People's Organization (AAPO), Asrat Woldeyes, as well as leaders of the Omo People's Democratic Union in Jinka, in the Southern Nations, Nationalities, and People's Region (SNNPR). A few opposition parties participated in 2000 and 2001 and faced violent harassment as a consequence. Authorities suppressed demonstrations with force, as in Awassa in 2002 when a peaceful demonstration ended with a shower of bullets that killed dozens.[3]

With political space limited in Ethiopia, mobilization and debate within the diaspora became more important. Prior to 2005, the diaspora generally objected to political engagement with the EPRDF and called

109

for an "all parties' conference" as a prerequisite to joining the political process. For the most part, activists in North America and Europe rejected the new political order and lobbied donor governments and nongovernmental organizations (NGOs) such as the Carter Center to apply pressure on the ruling party to negotiate a power-sharing agreement. The EPRDF, however, had no intention of setting aside its victory and its plans for postwar governance to negotiate with opposition groups that refused to recognize it.[4]

From 1991 to 2005, the EPRDF positioned itself as the only party with the legitimacy to protect the rights of the masses and advance the people's aspirations to reduce poverty. To oppose the ruling party was to be labeled as antipeace and antidevelopment. The opposition's divisions and its strategy of boycotting elections and looking to the international community for support did little to alter the EPRDF's domination. It is notable that the impetus for the change of leadership in the EPRDF in 2018 came from pressure created by popular protests and from leaders within the party, not from opposition parties or electoral politics.

Opposition Parties in Authoritarian Systems

Opposition parties play important roles in authoritarian systems and can contribute to a regime's resilience and stability. All political systems generate opposition, and the roles and functions of opposition parties reveal a great deal about the nature of political authority.[5] Dahl calls opposition parties "very nearly the most distinctive characteristic of democracy itself" and the lack of a viable opposition "evidence, if not conclusive proof, of the absence of democracy."[6] Ruling and opposition parties play interactive roles under authoritarian political systems, and both are needed for the stability of the state.[7] It is sometimes difficult to know the extent to which autocrats are responsible for the weak opposition through repression, whether the opposition suffers from its own weaknesses, or both. As Rakner and van de Walle say about political opposition in Africa in general, "The persistent weakness of the opposition is both a consequence of democratic deficits and a cause of their continuation."[8]

It is not surprising that the legally registered alternative parties in Ethiopia have been weak and divided. They often have made blanket criticisms of the government rather than clearly articulating programs of reform.[9] Comparative research has found that ruling parties in dominant-party systems have "hyperincumbent" advantages because of their exclusive access to the administrative resources of the state.[10] In many instances, as in Ethiopia, the state controls significant portions of the economy, and private interests depend on remaining in the

regime's good graces to obtain government contracts, business per-
mits, and access to credit.[11] Without resources and with negligible
prospects of playing a significant role in government, opposition parties in noncompetitive systems are often reduced to "carping and snip-
ing rather than developing immediate alternatives."[12] It is also common in late democratizers, such as many African states, to have "a
proliferation of small, weak parties . . . devoid of organizational
extension and structure."[13] Many of the challenges the Ethiopian
opposition face, therefore, are similar to the hurdles other opposition
parties in authoritarian contexts face. Structural constraints rather than
bad decisions or an undemocratic disposition are principally responsible for Ethiopian opposition weaknesses.

The legally registered political opposition parties are often criticized for their unwillingness to create a united front. As Howard and
Roessler argue, the ability to form effective coalitions is vital if opposition is to challenge a powerful incumbent.[14] However, it is again not
surprising that weak political parties with disparate ideological positions, different historical paths of development, and leaders with strong
personalities struggle to unify. Opposition parties typically compete
among themselves as fiercely as they compete against the ruling party.
Particularly in a country as large and diverse as Ethiopia, it is inevitable
and healthy that different constituencies support different political agendas and associated organizations. Parties that mobilize constituencies in
southern Ethiopia, which have experienced the state as a source of marginalization, naturally have different political agendas from parties that
mobilize constituencies in the northern highlands, which have had different historical experiences.

Opposition Parties Under the EPRDF
The EPRDF transformed itself from an armed movement based in the
northern highlands of Tigray to a strong authoritarian political party that
controlled nearly all aspects of politics across the diverse state. In this
chapter I investigate the roles played by a range of opposition parties
from 1991 to 2004 (setting up my discussion of the important 2005
elections in Chapter 6). The opposition parties varied in terms of ideology and expressed goals. Some were panethnic Ethiopian nationalists,
whereas others sought to mobilize specific constituencies on the basis
of subnational identities. Some tried to position themselves as liberal
or social democratic alternatives rather than identity-based parties.
These various parties pursued different paths to participate in Ethiopian
politics. What they had in common between 1991 and 2004 was that

none became the kind of significant force that could engage with the ruling party on anything like equal terms.

The EPRDF was dismissive of opposition parties from the start. Even the concept of *teqawami* (opposition) has negative connotations, implying faultfinding, detracting, and creating obstacles—even rebellion. Within the EPRDF there is an "ideological unwillingness to engage in dialogue with alternative political perspectives, a sense that 'if you are not with us, you are against us.'"[15] In 1995 Meles Zenawi characterized the opposition as "anarchic," "rejectionist," "not constructive," and without a program. He noted that when the EPRDF proposed its first five-year plan, only foreigners and the International Monetary Fund (IMF) provided a critique, not the Ethiopian opposition.[16] The opposition suffered from the same political patterns of distrust that characterized the ruling party and the larger Ethiopian political culture. An opposition party leader said his party would not participate in the constituent assembly to draft the new constitution in 1994 because, if it did, the EPRDF would "steal" his party's good ideas.[17]

In a 2003 report, Tronvoll and Vaughan emphasized the suspicion of alternative ideas and distrust of competitive politics as among the fundamental questions facing the regime:

> Can a revolutionary party with an evangelical belief in the superiority of its own political program seek to establish a competitive electoral process as a desired goal in its own right? Could (should?) elections really be anything other than a means to an end, a process useful only for demonstrating anew the virtues of revolutionary democracy and democratic centralism? If the goal is winning at all costs, how can the contest be anything other than zero sum, how can "their gain" be anything other than "our loss?"[18]

The ruling party's concept of "revolutionary democracy" frames politics in ontological terms. As Abbink argues, "The [Tigray People's Liberation Front] TPLF/EPRDF sees itself as a vanguard party that is invincible" and "convinced that it has the solution for everything."[19] When the ruling party defines itself as the party of the masses, it is hard to mobilize an opposition. The EPRDF treated alternative political parties as if they were illegitimate and motivated only by personal gain rather than the interests of the citizens. The government regularly accused the opposition of serving the interests of the old Derg regime or representing "antipeace" elements, often labeling them "narrow nationalists" and "chauvinists."[20]

The nature of federalism in Ethiopia had the intention and the effect of creating decentralized and ethnically based competition for local political office, thereby making it more difficult for alternatives to the ruling party to develop. With a few exceptions in urban areas, the overwhelming majority of constituencies is designed to be monoethnic. It is therefore necessary for a political party to win in hundreds of ethnically configured constituencies to win national power. Even local victories are problematic because resources to fund local administrations come from the center and hence depend upon good relations with the ruling party. An Ethiopian nationalist or nonethnic party might wish to participate in elections and take the country in a different direction, but under the ethnofederal system the only realistic way to do this is to win a majority of seats in the various ethnically defined districts. Furthermore, the electoral system of majoritarian, first-past-the-post seats means that unless an opposition party can win a plurality in an ethnically defined constituency, it cannot win a seat in Parliament. Only the ruling party is set up to compete in this way, and only the ruling party has the resources to support campaigns across the hundreds of constituencies necessary to win control of the central government.[21]

The EPRDF has put in place the rules for political competition without consulting the opposition. The ruling party, for example, developed the map of ethnically defined states unilaterally. The National Electoral Board of Ethiopia (NEBE) was appointed by the ruling party without prior consultation with opposition parties and has operated in a manner that emphasizes formal rule-based processes rather than problem solving or consensus building as the best way to run elections and other political processes. The EPRDF and NEBE do not see elections as processes that require the support of key stakeholders but rather as a unilaterally determined set of procedures. Electoral rules have sometimes included high signature thresholds for candidate registration, enforcement of regulations that prevented the opposition from registering the symbols they wished to use in campaigns, and encouragement of microparties and independent candidates that split the vote and made it more difficult for the opposition to coordinate or win in a majoritarian electoral system.[22] As a consequence, Ethiopia had dozens and dozens of political parties, but only the EPRDF had the capacity to mobilize and "compete" for national power. Ethiopia from 1991 to 2004 was both a formal multiparty and effective authoritarian system. The EPRDF alone determined political outcomes.

Most fundamentally, the political economy and coercive power of the EPRDF party-state made it extremely difficult for opposition parties to be viable. Resources in private hands were limited, and most businesspeople were wary (for good reason) of being identified with the opposition. The EPRDF held televised telethons in which major business owners publicly pledged significant funds in support of the ruling party. Even state-owned businesses contributed to the ruling party's campaign fund-raising.[23] Few wished to be publicly identified as less than generous to the party that shaped economic opportunities. Although opposition parties sometimes had offices in Addis Ababa and could be seen at embassy receptions and press conferences at major hotels, it was nearly impossible for them to open rural offices or even rent a room for a party meeting in a private hotel or restaurant outside of the capital.[24]

EPRDF cadres—present in every *kebele* and responsible for allocation of scarce resources—were the politicians/administrators most familiar to rural Ethiopians. Given the economic insecurity of many small-scale farmers, "as long as the peasants in Ethiopia rely on the state for daily survival, and as long as agents of the ruling party act on the behalf of the state and control their means of survival to the advantage of the party, the people will continue to vote for the EPRDF."[25] Furthermore, the EPRDF had an insurmountable advantage in its ability to use government resources for partisan political purposes. As noted by international observers of the 1995 elections, for example, "The EPRDF-affiliated party had large offices provided by the government and had access to government vehicles and other material support. The boundaries between party business and regional and local government business often were vague or not recognized."[26] Similar patterns were reported in other elections.

Finally, the EPRDF has a clear pattern of intimidating and harassing opposition party candidates. The US Department of State said that the 1992 elections were "flawed by numerous irregularities, including fraud, harassment, intimidation, and political assassination."[27] As a result of this intimidation, only token opposition participated in the 1992 (local), 1994 (constituent assembly), and 1995 (national) elections. In 2000 and 2001, few members of opposition parties participated in specific areas of the SNNPR (such as in the Hadiya zone), and they suffered significant violence as a consequence.[28] By remaining out of the elections, however, the leaders of the opposition played a central part in the consolidation of the EPRDF's control. The opposition boycott did little to halt the EPRDF's growing dominance and consolidation of power and nothing to establish a basis for opposition growth.[29]

Mapping the Diverse Opposition

Most of the opposition political parties and movements have their origins in some of the same founding experiences as the EPRDF, notably the student movement, the Red Terror, and the subsequent period of protracted armed struggle by national liberation movements.[30] In this section I examine the different elements within the opposition, with a particular emphasis on their diverse relationships to the armed struggle and engagement in the early transitional process, which established the new rules. I also outline how the opposition sought to compel the EPRDF to engage with it in various ways, generally with little success. In addition, different regions have different historical experiences of the state, resulting in different political orientations. For groups that represented interests in northern Ethiopia (Tigray and Amhara), a strong government was needed to provide economic resources to desperately poor areas, whereas in the Oromo and southern regions central authorities historically extracted wealth and were repressive.[31] Opposition parties based in these two different areas generally have different political goals and mobilize constituencies in distinctive ways.

Pan-Ethiopian and Amhara Opposition Parties

One set of alternative parties emphasized a pan-Ethiopian identity and criticized the ethnonational provisions of the 1995 constitution. Some in this camp originated in the Ethiopian People's Revolutionary Party (EPRP) and the remnants of the student movement that survived the Red Terror. The EPRP was a multiethnic movement and emphasized class analysis and the need to create a "people's democracy" in its opposition to the imperial order of the early 1970s.[32] Some of its adherents went on to form the Ethiopian People's Democratic Movement (EPDM), which joined with the TPLF to form the EPRDF in 1989. Other opponents remained active as exiles and played important roles in diaspora politics as the champions of a pan-Ethiopian, nonethnic identity. Meison, the EPRP's archrival during the 1970s, also survived as a faction in exile and endorsed a nonethnic concept of Ethiopia. Another less influential element in the Ethiopian nationalist camp was the Ethiopian Democratic Union (EDU), initially composed of members of the old imperial order but later transformed into the nationalist Ethiopian People's Democratic Alliance. Most in this stream of nonethnic opposition (including EDU, EPRP, Meison, along with the Tigray People's Democratic Movement [TPDM]) joined the Coalition of Ethiopian Democratic Forces (COEDF) after 1991.

The distinct meanings of *Amhara* as an identity in Ethiopia made basing opposition among the Amhara difficult. There have long been Amhara-speaking, Orthodox Christian, highland, ox-plow agriculturalists in northern Ethiopia who self-identify as Amhara, although regional identities such as Gojjami or Shewan often mattered more. At the same time, as part of the empire-building process, elites from peripheral areas could become Amharaized and join the dominant social strata. To be Amhara generally required deemphasizing (or even denying) those aspects of one's culture that reflected one's origin. Many of the cities throughout the empire had significant Amhara populations. This group often self-identifies as Ethiopian, associates itself with the symbols and glories of the ancient empire, and rejects what it sees as parochial, ethnic identities.[33]

After the 1991 transition, the AAPO mobilized one group of this identity. Asrat formed the organization to defend the rights of the Amhara people, whom some thought the EPRDF targeted with its policies. Attacks on Amharas at places such as Arbagugu and Bedeno fed this narrative.[34] The AAPO stated:

> The events which brought about the founding of the AAPO were the anti-Ethiopian and anti-Amhara policies which TPLF/EPRDF pursued immediately after its accession to power on the basis of its Charter for the transition period and the muzzle of the gun. Set on imposing the dictatorial hegemony of a particular ethnic group, Ethiopia's sovereignty, the unity of its people, and its territorial integrity were, in fact, contemptuously violated.[35]

The regime arrested Asrat and charged him with fomenting violence and ethnic dissent in 1994. The AAPO did not participate in the elections in 1992, 1994, or 1995. Elements of the party transformed into the multiethnic All-Ethiopia Unity Party and the Ethiopian Democratic Party, which then joined the Coalition for Unity in Democracy (CUD) in 2005 and Medrek in 2010 as "liberal" parties that endorsed individual rights.[36]

The AAPO presented itself as the champion of the Amhara cause and therefore a direct challenge to the Amhara National Democratic Movement (ANDM), the EPRDF's Amhara wing. The Amhara opposition had a difficult and ambivalent relationship with the idea of pan-Ethiopian nationalism, and some in the opposition resisted mobilizing as Amharas rather than as Ethiopians. Some pan-Ethiopianists who believed in *Ethiopiawinet* (Ethiopia first) opposed the AAPO for fear that it would contribute to dividing the Ethiopian nation. The EPRDF and others sought to label this constituency "Amhara chauvinist" and link it to the old political order, but many within it insisted it was built upon a nonethnic agenda of "Ethiopian unity."[37]

The OLF and the Oromo Opposition

The OLF had its own history of armed resistance and as the champion of Oromo nationalism during the imperial and Derg regimes. As I discussed in Chapter 2, it developed out of the student movement in a manner similar to the early TPLF and engaged in a protracted rural insurgency against the Derg. The OLF had a military presence in Hararghe, Bale, Arsi, and Sidamo in the 1980s and controlled an area along the Sudanese border in 1991. Although it had less military success than the TPLF did, it remained a powerful, symbolic force that championed the concept of an Oromo nation and rejected the historic domination of the Oromos by the Amharas. Other Oromo parties such as the Oromo National Congress (ONC), United Oromo People's Liberation Front, Oromo Abo Liberation Front, and Islamic Front for the Liberation of Oromia emerged, but all failed to sustain the symbolic profile of the OLF.[38]

The OLF adopted a platform of self-determination that, if fully enacted, would virtually divide Ethiopia in two. Many of the neighboring populations, specifically in the SNNPR and Somali regions, feared that a more autonomous Oromo state would encroach on their interests. After leaving the TGE in 1992 and losing its military capacity, the OLF operated in exile, with irregular clandestine operations. It based itself in Nairobi for a time, was expelled by the Kenyan government, and then after 2000 set up its offices in Asmara, Eritrea. The Oromo diaspora, particularly communities in northern Europe, Minneapolis, and Toronto, provided sustained and critical financial and diplomatic support.[39] In addition to the challenges of being based in Asmara and the diaspora, the OLF experienced different factions breaking away and for a period of time fighting each another.

Many Oromos have an overarching attachment to Oromo nationalism, but the population is divided (broadly) into Muslims in the East and Christians in the West. The Oromo Muslim pastoralists of Borana, near the Kenyan border, practiced distinct variations of Oromo culture and pursued livelihoods quite different from the Oromo grain farmers in agriculturally rich Arsi, the wealthy Oromo khat merchants around Harar, the Protestant Oromo professionals of western Wellega, and the relatively Amharaized Oromos of Shewa. Oromos had differing perspectives on whether their goal should be independence, autonomy, or greater representation within the Ethiopian state. Throughout these challenges many Oromos, both in the diaspora and at home, remained committed (at least emotionally) to the OLF and regarded the Oromo People's Democratic Organization (OPDO), the EPRDF's Oromo wing, as compromised by its affiliation with the TPLF. Although the OPDO lacked the OLF's nationalist pedigree, it was able to enact popular nationalist aspirations. Under the OPDO, schools, courts, and other public offices operated in the Afan Oromo language for the first time.

Opposition Oromo parties, such as the ONC, later renamed as the Oromo People's Congress (OPC), operated as legally registered parties.[40] They positioned themselves as supportive of Oromo nationalist positions on issues such as opposition to moving of the Oromo National Regional State capital from Addis Ababa to Adama. The ONC competed in and won seats in the 2000 elections. The OLF, however, remained a powerful symbol of Oromo nationalism and retained significant popularity and sympathy although it was largely not present as an organization. According to Schaeffer, politics in western Oromia boiled down to the EPRDF/OPDO forces, perceived as the latest incarnation of the *neftenya* ("men with guns" or northern occupying forces), against the opposition, seen as the OLF.[41] The EPRDF labeled any antiregime talk pro-OLF, and "the OLF remained the devil the regime painted on the wall to secure control over the population."[42]

Opposition in Southern Ethiopia

Alternatives to the EPRDF's affiliated parties in southern Ethiopia appeared from several sources. In a few instances prior experiences with resistance created a local organization that could claim legitimacy as a national liberation front, as was the case with the Sidama Liberation Movement (SLM). In other cases local notables, displeased with the alliances the EPRDF affiliates made with other elites or more often with lower-status individuals, mobilized. Some of these participated in the TGE, formed in 1991, such as Beyene Petros, a Hadiya National Democratic Organization (HNDO) member who served as deputy minister of education. In March 1992 a number of parties formed the Southern Ethiopia People's Democratic Coalition (SEPDC), often called the Southern Coalition. Many of these ethnically oriented opposition parties shared the EPRDF's emphasis on group rights and self-determination and opposition to Amhara domination. In this view the problem with the EPRDF was not that it favored ethnofederalism but rather that northern leaders in the ruling coalition dominated southern Ethiopia and did not allow sufficient autonomy or self-determination. Some SEPDC parties, such as the HNDO, competed in 2000 and won seats in Parliament, although opposition supporters suffered significant repression in response.

To illustrate the fragmented nature of political organization in southern Ethiopia, the SEPDC was formed by the Burji People's Democratic Organization, the Gedeo People's Democratic Organization (GPDO), Gurage People's Democratic Front, the HNDO, the Kaffa People's Democratic Union, the Omotic People's Democratic Front, the SLM, the Wolayita People's Democratic Front, and the Yem National

Democratic Movement. In November 1992 (after the regional elections) the Dawro People's Democratic Movement, the Kabena National Democratic Organization, the Omo People's Democratic Union, and the Tembaro People's Democratic Union joined. The EPRDF southern wing had its own set of analogue parties, many of which positioned themselves as the representatives of the same constituencies. The Southern Ethiopian People's Democratic Front (SEPDF) included the Bench People's Revolutionary Democratic Movement; the Burji People's United Democratic Movement; the Dawero People's Revolutionary Democratic Organization; the Denta, Debamo, Kitchenchla Democratic Organization; the Dirashe People's Democratic Organization; the Donga People's Democratic Organization; Gamo Democratic Unity; Gedeo People's Democratic Movement; Gurage People's Revolutionary Movement; Hadiya People's Democratic Organization; Kebena Nationality Democratic Organization; Kembata People's Democratic Organization; Konso People's Democratic Organization; Kore Nationality Unity Democratic Organization; Shekecho People's Democratic Movement; Sidama People's Democratic Organization; Southern Omo People's Democratic Movement; Tembaro People's Democratic Organization; Wolayita People's Democratic Organization; and the Yem People's Democratic Front. The point of this list is not to present exotic sounding names but to underline that southern Ethiopian politics is generally locally organized by relatively small ethnic groups split between those who support the government and those who support the opposition.[43]

Opposition Strategies: Calls for All-Party Conferences

One important opposition strategy in the 1990s focused on appealing to the West, particularly the United States, to use its apparent influence to convince the EPRDF to engage in talks with the goal of forming a new transitional government that would include all political parties. Rather than negotiate with the EPRDF as the legitimate incumbent party because it had won the armed struggle, many in the opposition wanted to have an all-party conference not dominated by insurgent groups. In February 1994 a number of Ethiopian opposition groups met with former president Jimmy Carter in Atlanta to explore opportunities for talks prior to the Constitutional Convention. The initiative faltered, however, when Meles's regime declined Carter's offer to mediate. The incumbent regime in Addis Ababa insisted that opposition parties make public commitments to abide by the transitional charter and foreswear violence, whereas many of the opposition movements insisted on talks without preconditions.[44]

In February 1995, the US Congressional Task Force on Ethiopia brought leaders from the major opposition movements—the OLF, COEDF, AAPO, and SEPDC—to Washington, DC, as well as Dawit Yohannes (a founder of the EPRDF) as the government's special envoy.[45] The task force hoped to broker a deal to get the opposition to participate in the next round of elections. The EPRDF again insisted that opposition groups accept the constitutional framework already in place as a precondition for participation and future talks back in Ethiopia. Three of the four opposition parties argued for negotiations without preconditions, refused to accept a constitutional framework they had not participated in constructing, and did not end their electoral boycott.[46] As in the earlier Carter talks, the lack of parity between the ruling EPRDF and the weak and divided opposition provided little scope or incentive for an agreement.

The SEPDC, led by Beyene, who had participated in the TGE, continued talks in Addis Ababa with the encouragement of the Donors' Group.[47] The opposition party raised concerns regarding the imprisonment on political grounds of a number of its officials, including the leadership of the Omo People's Democratic Union. Six Western ambassadors traveled to Jinka to investigate. Despite the dubious charges, they failed to get the prisoners released or cases reviewed.[48] The leaders of the SEPDC were denied permission to open a political office or hold a rally in Hosaina, and their request for a six-month delay in the election date was summarily dismissed. Despite considerable pressure on Beyene by donors, talks ultimately ended without an agreement, and the SEPDC declined to participate in the 1995 elections.[49]

In the end, these different efforts at negotiation resulted in little. The EPRDF perceived these initiatives as leveraging international pressure to obtain concessions for the opposition. In control in Ethiopia and on good terms with the major international donors, the ruling party saw no reason to make the major compromises demanded by the opposition. The donors were not willing to risk damaging their friendly relations with the EPRDF by placing conditions on their assistance or diplomatic support. Without any form of parity between the two sides, and with the EPRDF's power secure, the prospect of successful talks was slim. The ruling party advanced along the course it had planned, with a well-organized constituent assembly, a new constitution, and national elections in 1995 and 2000, with little opposition participation and little donor pressure.

The non-EPRDF parties were a diverse group of organizations. A number of these parties demonstrated a commitment to the electoral process and were consistently legally registered by the NEBE. The

SEPDC and the ONC participated in elections since 2000 and took up their seats as the loyal opposition in Parliament. It is not surprising that the opposition in a state without a tradition of democracy would have been weak and fractious. The EPRDF controlled the enormous power of the state and dominated the economy. Furthermore, different historical experiences with the central state and with Ethiopian nationalism naturally generated different political goals. At the same time, the ruling party systematically and successfully applied pressure, arrested leaders, and generally eliminated political space, making it impossible for any type of alternative party to participate effectively.

Opposition Politics in the Diaspora

With limited political space within Ethiopia, opposition politics shifted as activists and media in the diaspora became more important. In Ethiopia, as well as in many countries such as Croatia, the Dominican Republic, Liberia, and Sri Lanka, diaspora networks have been critical in determining political outcomes in homeland countries. Recent scholarship has noted that political dynamics around the world have been transformed by globalization and the development of innovative transnational social networks. These new political processes are rooted in communities and networks increasingly less restricted by geographical location. As a result, the relevant constituencies participating in a particular political campaign can live in different countries or move between locations. Networks of activists and supporters are less bound by the need to work in close proximity to their homeland or to accept notions that actors outside a state are not members of communities rooted within a specific territory.[50] Although politics has been delinked from territory with regard to processes and actors, this does not mean transnational politics generally focuses on universal issues such as global social justice and cosmopolitan democracy. Rather, much of the new transnational politics is intensely focused on specific locations, identities, and issues. Politics remains fundamentally about local, parochial issues even though political processes are increasingly transnational.[51]

Diaspora groups created by conflict and sustained by traumatic memories tend to compromise less and, therefore, reinforce and exacerbate the protracted nature of conflicts. In some cases, such as the Armenian, Irish, Tamil, or segments of the Ethiopian diasporas, this tendency to frame homeland conflict in categorical, hard-line terms strengthens confrontational leaders and organizations and undermines others seeking compromise. In other cases, diaspora groups have transformed themselves from supporters of militant elements to key partners with peacemakers, as seen in the Irish American diaspora and the Good Friday agreements, or supporters of homeland political reforms and development.[52] Conflict-generated diasporas therefore often have the resources and the ability to frame conflicts in ways that fundamentally alter local political dynamics.

The Ethiopian diaspora in North America has its origins in Ethiopia's violent political transitions and protracted conflicts. Many of those who have migrated to the United States since the 1970s remained linked to networks rooted in the Ethiopian student movement. In Washington, Minneapolis, Toronto, and other cities with significant diaspora communities, social and professional organizations contributed to a web of relationships and social capital that in turn was used by political organizations to mobilize the community to support movements engaged in political struggles in the homeland.[53] In creative ways, leaders and organizations based in the diaspora developed new forms of mobilization, communication, and political action to press for political change in Ethiopia.

Although relatively few in numbers, there was a vocal group of partisan political leaders, organizations, and media (particularly websites and social media) in the diaspora. These groups ran the full gamut of political viewpoints, and squabbles are characteristic of diaspora politics. Given the official embassy's active engagement and profile, those who supported the government had less need to establish independent diaspora organizations or media, leaving these organizations and publications more often in the hands of opposition leaders. Organizations close to the government such as the Tigray Development Association (TDA), however, held regular and quite successful fund-raising events in North America, and an important pro-TPLF website operates out of California (aigaforum.com).[54] The Ethiopian Embassy in Washington created an office dealing with diaspora relations, and the Ethiopian Ministry of Foreign Affairs had a general directorate in charge of Ethiopian expatriate affairs. The EPRDF government regarded the diaspora both as a threat and as a community to woo.

Before the 1991 transition the various actors involved in the armed struggle against Mengistu Haile Mariam's regime were active abroad. The Eritrean People's Liberation Front (EPLF), often the most organized of the diaspora fronts, had well-developed initiatives to lobby, engage media, and raise funds, as did the TPLF, the EPRP, and the OLF.[55] In the 1980s, regular conferences at universities in New York, Howard University in Washington, and Stanford University brought activists, academics, and leaders of the exiled opposition together. The Voice of America created an Amharic channel for opposition voices to counter the Derg's control over media. Meles, the leader of the TPLF, toured the United States in the late 1980s, meeting with diaspora leaders, activists, advocates, the media, and the think tank community.[56]

The power of the diaspora was apparent in 1995. As noted above, the opposition SEPDC entertained the idea of engaging with the EPRDF regime and competing in elections. Before returning to Ethiopia, the coalition's leader, Beyene, traveled to several cities in the United States to make speeches and consult diaspora leaders. The diaspora vehemently objected to the idea of participation in elections under the EPRDF and labeled Beyene a traitor who had been given money and buses to launch his own business by the regime. Unable to ignore this pressure, the SEPDC ultimately boycotted the election.[57] Many of the most vigorous and dedicated supporters of Oromo self-determination and the OLF were in the diaspora. These stalwarts insisted on uncompromising and unqualified demands—liberation of all Oromia by any means necessary—and supported OLF military leaders who pursued this agenda. The same was true of the ONLF, which had an active network and engaged in significant fund-raising in the diaspora.[58]

As the EPRDF limited political space for opposition politicians and independent civil society leaders to operate within Ethiopia, the diaspora became an increasingly important arena in shaping Ethiopia's politics. Some of the most vocal members of the diaspora in North America and Europe positioned themselves as categorically rejecting not only the EPRDF but also the entire post-1991 political order. The diaspora's ability to serve as a gatekeeper for Ethiopian opposition politics, in part a consequence of its financial power and its ability to engage in political speech, made transnational networks an essential dimension of political outcomes.

Conclusion

The transformation of the EPRDF into a powerful authoritarian party is reflected in the story of Ethiopia's various opposition movements. As detailed here, many streams of opposition originated in the student movement of the early 1970s. Since 1991, some objected to the EPRDF's emphasis on ethnic federalism and identified as pan-Ethiopian nationalists. Some of these in turn eventually formed organizations such as the AAPO. Others, such as the OLF, had a distinctive history of resistance and did not want to be a junior partner within the EPRDF. Still others mobilized among the relatively small communities in southern Ethiopia and often accepted the principle of ethnic self-determination but argued that the EPRDF continued past patterns of northern authorities imposing their will on marginalized southern communities.

The opposition tried many different strategies to prevent or alter the EPRDF's plans but generally failed. Efforts to get the international community to apply meaningful pressure, along with election boycotts, all failed. Many activists in the diaspora sought to shape political outcomes from abroad. But overall, the victorious EPRDF kept the opposition divided and intimidated and used its dominant position to put in place a political system that reinforced the ruling party's position and made it difficult for opposition to mobilize.

Notes

1. Asnake Kefale, "The (Un)making of Opposition Coalitions and the Challenge of Democratization in Ethiopia, 1991–2011," *Journal of Eastern African Studies* 5, no. 4 (2011): 681–701.

2. "Carter Center Statement on Ethiopia Negotiations," *News from the Carter Center*, March 23, 1994; "Norway's Mediation in an Impasse," *Indian Ocean Newsletter* 1108 (October 30, 2004). The author participated in the talks organized by the Carter Center and the US Congressional Task Force on Ethiopia.

3. Ethiopian Human Rights Council, "Serious Human Rights Violations in Awassa and Its Environs," 51st Special Report, June 4, 2002.

4. Interviews with author, Washington, DC, 1993–1995.

5. Lisa Anderson, "Lawless Government and Illegal Opposition: Reflections on the Middle East," *Journal of International Affairs* 40, no. 2 (1987): 219.

6. Robert Dahl, ed., *Political Opposition in Western Democracies* (New Haven, CT: Yale University Press, 1996), xv–xvi. See also Giovanni Sartori, *Party and Party Systems: A Framework for Analysis* (Cambridge, UK: Cambridge University Press, 1976), 63.

7. I. William Zartman, "Opposition as Support for the State," in *Beyond Coercion: The Durability of the Arab State,* ed. Adeed Dawisha and I. William Zartman (New York: Croom Helm, 1988), 6.

8. Lise Rakner and Nicolas van de Walle, "Opposition Weakness in Africa," *Journal of Democracy* 20, no. 3 (July 2009): 109.

9. Jennifer A. Widner, "Political Parties and Civil Societies in Sub-Saharan Africa," in *Democracy in Africa: The Hard Road Ahead,* ed. Marina Ottaway (Boulder, CO: Lynne Rienner, 1997), 68.

10. Kenneth F. Greene, "Opposition Party Strategy and Spatial Competition in Dominant Party Regimes: A Theory and the Case of Mexico," *Comparative Political Studies* 35, no. 7 (September 2002): 755–783; Ethan Scheiner, *Democracy Without Competition in Japan: Opposition Failure in a One-party Dominant State* (Cambridge, UK: Cambridge University Press, 2006).

11. Leonardo R. Arriola, *Multiethnic Coalitions in Africa: Business Financing of Opposition Election Campaigns* (Cambridge, UK: Cambridge University Press, 2012).

12. Alan Arian and Samuel H. Barnes, "The Dominant Party System: A Neglected Model of Democratic Stability," *Journal of Politics* 36, no. 3 (1974): 598. However, see Andreas Ufen, "The Transformation of Political Party Opposition in Malaysia and Its Implications for the Electoral Authoritarian Regime," *Democratization* 16, no. 3 (June 2009): 604–627, for an account of how a divided opposition can come together in a unified party after forty years.

13. Carrie Manning, "Assessing African Party Systems After the Third Wave," *Party Politics* 11, no. 6 (2005): 716.

14. Marc Morjé Howard and Philip G. Roessler, "Liberalizing Electoral Outcomes in Competitive Authoritarian Regimes," *American Journal of Political Science* 50, no. 2 (April 2006): 365–381. See also Staffan I. Lindberg, *Democracy and Elections in Africa* (Baltimore: Johns Hopkins University Press, 2008).

15. Sarah Vaughan and Kjetil Tronvoll, *The Culture of Power in Contemporary Ethiopian Political Life,* SIDA Studies No. 10 (Stockholm: Swedish International Development Cooperation Agency, 2003), 120.

16. See Harold G. Marcus, "A Breakfast Meeting with Prime Minister Meles," October 20, 1996, http://www.h-net.org/~africa/confrpt/melesbreakfast .html. The author participated in this meeting.

17. Interview with author, Addis Ababa, 1995.

18. Vaughan and Tronvoll, *Culture of Power in Contemporary Ethiopian Political Life*, 157.

19. Jon Abbink, *Political Culture in Ethiopia: A Balance Sheet of Post-1991 Ethnically Based Federalism* (Leiden: African Studies Centre, 2010), 3.

20. Interviews with author, Addis Ababa, June 2016.

21. Elliot Green, "Decentralization and Political Opposition in Contemporary Africa: Evidence from Sudan and Ethiopia," *Democratization* 18, no. 5 (October 2011): 1067–1086.

22. International consultants and election observers have raised these concerns since 1992. See John M. Cohen, William Hammink, and Emmy Simmons, *Evaluation Report: Ethiopia Democracy/Governance Support Project,* 1994, http://pdf.usaid.gov/pdf_docs/PDABK181.pdf; National Democratic Institute, *An Evaluation of the June 21, 1992, Elections in Ethiopia* (Washington, DC: National Democratic Institute, 1992); Keith Klein, *Pre-Election Technical Assessment: Ethiopia May 1994* (Washington DC: International Foundation for Electoral Systems, May 1994); Gary Ouellet, *Recommendations Report: Ethiopia* (Washington, DC: International Foundation for Electoral Systems, July 1994); Donor Election Unit, *Final Analytical Summary of Donor Election Unit Reports: The 7 May 1995 Ethiopian Elections* (Addis Ababa: Donor Election Unit, May 30, 1995); "Lessons Learned from Elections in Ethiopia, 1992–1995 (and Some Thoughts on the Planned 2000 Elections)," June 17, 1999, 12, http://pdf.usaid.gov/pdf_docs/PNACF945.pdf; European Union Election Observation Mission, *Ethiopia: Legislative Elections 2005—Final Report,* http://ec .europa.eu/external_relations/humanrights; Carter Center, *Observing the 2005 Ethiopia National Elections: Carter Center Final Report* (Atlanta, GA: Carter Center, December 2009), http://www.cartercenter.org/resources/pdfs/news/peace _publications/election_reports/Ethiopia-2005-Finalrpt.pdf.

23. "The Recent TPLF Fundraising and the Diaspora's Foul Play," Abbay Media, November 6, 2008, http://abbaymedia.com/the-recent-tplf-fundraising -and-the-diasporas-foul-play/.

24. Author interviews in Ethiopia, 1992, 1995, 2005, 2011.

25. Lovise Aalen, "Two Stories Told: The 2001 Local Elections in Kambata, Tambaro, Hadiya, and Sidamo," in *Ethiopia 2001: Local Elections in the Southern Region,* Report 3/2002 (Oslo: Nordem, 2002).

26. Donor Election Unit, *Final Analytical Summary of Donor Election Unit Reports*, 8. Similar credible complaints have been raised after every election.

27. The US Department of State said that the 1992 elections were "flawed by numerous irregularities, including fraud, harassment, intimidation, and political assassination." US Department of State, Ethiopia Human Rights Practices, January 31, 1993, http://dosfan.lib.uic.edu/ERC/democracy/1993_hrp_report/93hrp_report_africa/Ethiopia.html. For further examples from the 1995 elections, see Donor Election Unit, *Final Analytical Summary of Donor Election Unit Reports.*

28. Kjetil Tronvoll, "Voting, Violence, and Violations: Peasant Voices on the Flawed Elections in Hadiya, Southern Ethiopia," *Journal of Modern African Studies* 39, no. 4 (2001): 697–716.

29. A Western diplomat said, "The tragedy of this election is that there will be no opposition. But you have to put just as much responsibility on the opposition that failed to breathe life into the system as on the Government. There is no tradition of political tolerance in Ethiopia. Politics is extremely polarized. You are either for or against the Government." Quoted in Donatella Lorch, "Ethiopia Holding Elections in Federal System," *New York Times,* May 7, 1995.

30. With the exception of the Ethiopian People's Revolutionary Party, there is little written on Ethiopian opposition parties. For exceptions, see Sandra Fullerton Joireman, "Opposition Politics and Ethnicity in Ethiopia: We Will All Go Down Together," *Journal of Modern African Studies* 35, no. 3 (September 1997): 387–407; John Young, "Regionalism and Democracy in Ethiopia," *Third World Quarterly* 19, no. 2 (1998): 191–204; Asnake, "(Un)making of Opposition Coalitions and the Challenge of Democratization in Ethiopia."

31. Asnake distinguishes between "liberal" parties such as the All-Ethiopian Unity Party and the Ethiopian Democratic Party, and ethnic parties such as the Southern Ethiopian Democratic Coalition and the Oromo National Congress. Asnake, "(Un)making of Opposition Coalitions and the Challenge of Democratization in Ethiopia," 682–683. Stevens Tucker suggests a more fine-grained typology based on the party's position with regard to the transitional period. He suggests four significant categories of opposition: radical proponents of the unitary state (COEDF is his example), proponents of a new political order (AAPO, CAFPDE), a loyal opposition (ENDP), and radical nationalists with secessionist tendencies (OLF, ONLF). Tucker, *Ethiopia in Transition, 1991–1998* (Geneva: UNHCR Writenet, 1998).

32. Kiflu Tadesse, *The Generation* (Trenton, NJ: Red Sea, 1993).

33. Mackonen Michael, "What Is Amhara?" *African Identities* 6, no. 4 (November 2008): 393–404.

34. These massacres were against Amharas living in Oromo areas. Some claim the OLF, rather than the OPDO, was responsible for these massacres in the early days of the transition and in the tense period prior to the 1992 elections. See "OLF Officially Condemned for Bedeno Massacre," *Indian Ocean Newsletter* 530 (May 5, 1992).

35. All-Amhara People's Organization (AAPO), press conference, Addis Ababa Hilton Hotel, September 26, 1994.

36. Teshome B. Wondwosen, "Ethiopian Opposition Political Parties and Rebel Fronts: Past and Present," *International Journal of Human and Social Sciences* 4, no. 1 (2009): 60–68.

37. Takkele Taddese, "Do the Amhara Exist as a Distinct Ethnic Group?" in *Ethnicity and the State in Eastern Africa,* ed. Mohamed A. Salih and John Markakis (Stockholm: Elanders Gotab, 1992).

38. Anonymous, "Thoughts on Oromiya," November 5, 1996.

39. On the Oromo diaspora, see Atsuko Karin Matsuoka and John Sorenson, *Ghosts and Shadows: Construction of Identity and Community in an African Diaspora* (Toronto: University of Toronto Press, 2001).

40. After the National Electoral Board of Ethiopia (NEBE) recognized a splinter group as the legitimate ONC, this party, led by Addis Ababa University professor Merera Gudina, was forced to change its name to the Oromo People's Congress.

41. Charles Schaefer, "'We Say They Are *Neftenya*; They Say We Are OLF,'" in *Contested Power in Ethiopia: Traditional Authorities and Multi-party Elections,* ed. Kjetil Tronvoll and Tobias Hagmann (Leiden: Brill, 2011), 195.

42. Terje Østebø, "Islam and Politics: The EPRDF, the 2005 Elections, and Muslim Institutions in Bale," in *Contested Power in Ethiopia: Traditional Authorities and Multi-party Elections,* ed. Kjetil Tronvoll and Tobias Hagmann (Leiden: Brill, 2011), 174.

43. See UN Emergency Prevention and Preparedness Unit, "Alphabet Soup," May 3, 1995, http://www.africa.upenn.edu/eue_web/soup_may.htm.

44. "Carter Center Statement on Ethiopia Negotiations"; author's field notes, Atlanta, 1994.

45. Dawit was well known in the Washington diaspora, where he supported himself driving a taxi while attending Georgetown University Law School.

46. "Ethiopia: Negotiations in Washington," *Indian Ocean Newsletter* 658 (February 11, 1995), 3; author field notes, Washington, DC, 1995.

47. SEPDC leaders had been arrested in Jinka, and despite the intervention of a group of Western ambassadors, remained in prison. The SEPDC doubted that guarantees from donors could protect their ability to participate in opposition politics.

48. See US Department of State, *Ethiopia Human Rights Practices* (Washington, DC: US Department of State, 1995).

49. Interviews with author, Addis Ababa, Hosaina, and Awassa, 1995. For context, see Terrence Lyons, "Closing the Transition: The May 1995 Elections in Ethiopia," *Journal of Modern African Studies* 34, no. 1 (March 1996): 121–142.

50. Miles Kahler and Barbara Walter, eds., *Globalization, Territoriality, and Conflict* (Cambridge, UK: Cambridge University Press, 2006).

51. Terrence Lyons and Peter Mandaville, "Thinking Locally, Acting Globally: Towards a Transnational Comparative Politics," *International Political Sociology* 4, no. 2 (June 2010): 124–142; Terrence Lyons and Peter Mandaville, eds., *Politics from Afar: Transnational Diasporas and Networks* (Oxford, UK: Oxford University Press, 2012); Rey Koslowski, ed., *International Migration and the Globalization of Domestic Politics* (London: Routledge, 2005); Nadje Al-Ali and Khalid Koser, eds. *New Approaches to Migration? Transnational Communities and the Transformation of Home* (London: Routledge, 2002).

52. Feargal Cochrane, "Mediating the Diaspora Space: Charting the Changing Nature of Irish-America in the Global Age," in *Politics from Afar: Transnational Diasporas and Networks,* ed. Terrence Lyons and Peter Mandaville (Oxford, UK: Oxford University Press, 2012).

53. Addis Getahun Solomon, *The History of Ethiopian Immigrants and Refugees in America, 1900–2000: Patterns of Migration, Survival, and Adjustment* (New York: LFB Scholarly, 2007).

54. Ethiopian News Agency, "TDA Organizes Fund-Raising Night in Seattle," *Ethiopian Herald,* August 22, 2006. Note that the state-run media in Ethiopia

covers fund-raising events in the North American diaspora, further suggesting the influential links between homeland and diaspora communities.

55. The African National Congress (ANC) and other insurgent groups also had de facto embassies during their respective national liberation struggles. See Stephen Ellis, *External Mission: The ANC in Exile, 1960–1990* (Oxford, UK: Oxford University Press, 2013). See also Bridget L. Coggins, "Rebel Diplomacy: Theorizing Violent Non-state Actors' Strategic Use of Talk," in *Rebel Governance in Civil War,* ed. Ana Arjona, Nelson Kasfir, and Zachariah Mampilly (Cambridge, UK: Cambridge University Press, 2015).

56. The author participated in a small meeting in a church basement in Washington, DC, at this time.

57. "Ethiopia: Negotiations in Washington."

58. Terrence Lyons, "Transnational Politics in Ethiopia: Diaspora Mobilization and Contentious Politics," in *Politics from Afar: Transnational Diasporas and Networks,* ed. Terrence Lyons and Peter Mandaville (Oxford, UK: Oxford University Press, 2012); Terrence Lyons, "Transnational Advocacy: Genocide or Terrorism?" *Genocide Studies and Prevention* 13, no. 2 (2019).

6

Elections and the
Closing of Political Space

In this chapter I consider several mechanisms the Ethiopian People's Revolutionary Democratic Front (EPRDF) used to sustain its dominance as a political organization. In earlier chapters I focused on how the ruling party used elections to consolidate and demonstrate its power and to marginalize the opposition. In this chapter I examine how the 2005 election did not follow the path of earlier or later elections and represented the political space opening significantly. In the aftermath, however, the EPRDF effectively shattered the opposition and made it virtually impossible for human rights groups or independent journalists to operate. Along with these forms of repression, the EPRDF had internal party processes that helped it balance the need for a strong center with the institutionalization of ethnically defined parties and regional states. In this chapter I examine variations of appointments to regional body central committees to see how the Tigray People's Liberation Front (TPLF) remained central to the coalition but also how this role declined over time. The legacies of the armed struggle in the form of a cohesive, disciplined party affected coalition dynamics but faded with the passing decades.

In the aftermath of the election the government arrested opposition leaders and cracked down on civil society and independent media, effectively closing the brief political opening of 2005. It issued new proclamations curtailing civil groups and used antiterrorism laws against independent journalists, bloggers, and opposition leaders. The EPRDF expanded its party membership from 700,000 to 8 million and effectively formed a powerful, authoritarian party-state.[1] As a consequence, the EPRDF and its affiliated parties won 99.6 percent of the seats in Parliament in the 2010 elections and 100 percent in 2015. This story of competition followed by a big crackdown illustrates both the strength of the ruling party and its vulnerability.

Competition in 2005

By 2005, Ethiopia had held a series of elections in which the ruling party effectively monopolized power by controlling the electoral process, arresting opponents, and intimidating opposition supporters. This pattern was broken in 2005, when a number of procedural openings and a decision by the opposition to participate made the election competitive across the key regions of the country.[2] Live televised debates on matters of public policy, opposition party access to state-owned media, and political meetings in the countryside all culminated in a million people rallying in Meskel Square in the center of Addis Ababa to listen to opposition speakers on the last day of campaigning. These unprecedented events made it clear that the 2005 elections represented a decisive moment in Ethiopia's political development. In contrast with earlier elections, 2005 offered most voters a meaningful choice, and many perceived for the first time that change was possible through the ballot box.

The EPRDF in general and the TPLF in particular went through a major split in 2001 that threatened the survival of the ruling alliance. However, in the end, Prime Minister Meles Zenawi's faction survived and consolidated its hold on party leadership. In the aftermath of the crisis the EPRDF purged a number of high-level officials from all four of its constituent parties. This reformed and perhaps still unsettled EPRDF participated in the 2005 election. Despite apparent party unity, the depth of Meles's support and the fault lines of 2001 remained in question. The ability of newly appointed leaders such as Hailemariam Desalegn in the Southern Ethiopian People's Democratic Front (SEPDF) and Abadula Gemeda in the Oromo People's Democratic Organization (OPDO) to mobilize votes was untested.

A few opposition parties competed in and won a few seats in the 2000 elections, notably the Oromo National Congress (ONC) and the Hadiya National Democratic Organization (HNDO). In 2004 elements within the leadership of the banned Oromo Liberation Front (OLF) considered entering Ethiopian politics to participate in the 2005 elections. This plan, however, posed grave risks to the ruling party. The OLF had the potential to win significant votes at the expense of the OPDO, and the EPRDF could not operate as a national party without a viable constituent party in Oromia. In the end, the OLF did not participate in 2005 but—in contrast with earlier elections—did not condemn those Oromo parties that did.[3]

Two opposition coalitions competed in 2005. The United Ethiopian Democratic Forces (UEDF) coalition formed following a 2003 party conference in the United States and included the ONC, parts of the All-

Ethiopia Unity Party, and the Council of Alternative Forces for Peace and Democracy in Ethiopia (CAFPDE, which included the Southern Ethiopia People's Democratic Coalition [SEPDC], or Southern Coalition). The coalition's leaders were Merera Gudina of the ONC and Beyene Petros of the HNDO/SEPDC, two professors from Addis Ababa University who had won seats in the 2000 elections. As evidenced by voting patterns, the UEDF had pockets of support in parts of the South (particularly in Beyene's home region of Hadiya) and in parts of Oromia (Merera's home area around Ambo in eastern Wellega), as well as in Arsi. The second opposition alliance was the Coalition for Unity and Democracy (CUD), comprising Rainbow Ethiopia, elements of the All-Ethiopia Unity Party, the Ethiopian Democratic Union (EDU), and the Ethiopian Democratic League. Leaders included Hailu Shawel (president of the All-Ethiopia Unity Party and formerly one of the founders of the All-Amhara People's Organization [AAPO]), Berhanu Nega (a professor of economics), and Lidetu Ayalew (the firebrand from the Ethiopian Democratic Party). The CUD had a significant following in urban areas, the Amhara region, and the Gurage zone, in southern Ethiopia.[4] Another opposition party that competed was the Oromo Federal Democratic Movement (OFDM), led by Bulcha Demeksa, a prominent banker with support in western Wellega. All three of these opposition groups decided to participate in the elections only in late 2004 or early 2005. As late as February 2005, the opposition continued to raise the potential that it would boycott again until the regime responded to questions of electoral procedures, the presence of international observers, and issues of intimidation.[5] In the end, the opposition parties decided to participate and compete throughout the main population centers of Ethiopia.

Most Ethiopians saw more political debate and more candidates actively and peacefully soliciting support than ever before in history. One leading opposition candidate went on a tour across southern Ethiopia, making speeches from the back of a truck and meeting voters in the markets and along farm roads.[6] The most important difference in 2005 was that the EPRDF's top leadership told the party's local cadres to allow the opposition to operate. After this political space was opened, the opposition parties quickly and effectively launched campaigns. The campaign season reached its peak on May 8 when an estimated million Ethiopians rallied in Meskel Square in a peaceful political rally.

Why did the EPRDF organize competitive elections for the first time in 2005? International donors had long raised the importance of "free and fair" elections with Ethiopian officials, but the regime had resisted these entreaties without serious consequences in 1995 and 2000 (and would do so with regard to later elections as well). It seems more likely that intra-EPRDF dynamics better explain the change. The EPRDF was still reorganizing after the shock of the 2001 party splits, and an electoral victory perceived as legitimate might shore up support for the leadership and marginalize its competitors. In early 2005 the opposition seemed disorganized and fractured, without a clear plan regarding how to compete in the elections. Although opposition support in Addis Ababa and a few other cities seemed apparent, the EPRDF had reason to anticipate that it would win in the rural constituencies, where 85 percent of Ethiopians live. The ruling party was surprised at the breadth of the opposition victory but retained control over the security services and therefore had alternatives to accepting an undesirable outcome.

Although the campaign season was an impressive display of the capacity of Ethiopians to manage a competitive election, there were several signs of the regime's intention to retain control. US-based nongovernmental organizations (NGOs) working on democracy for the US Agency for International Development (USAID) were expelled in March 2005. Some thirty Ethiopian organizations formed a coalition with plans to field 3,000 domestic observers. The National Electoral Board of Ethiopia (NEBE), however, refused at first to register them, forcing the coalition to go to court. When the coalition members finally won their case, it was too late to deploy a significant observation mission.[7]

Electoral procedures collapsed on the evening of polling day after the tabulation began and the scale of the opposition vote became apparent. Both the opposition and the government claimed victory, and Meles imposed a ban on public political meetings. Under intense political pressure, procedures for accounting for the movement of ballot boxes and tabulation sheets failed, making it impossible to track results from polling place to the NEBE, where the final figures were tabulated. According to official results, as shown in Table 6.1, the combined opposition increased its representation in Parliament from 12 to 173 (32 percent of total seats).[8]

Analyzing the Results

Regardless of the controversies over the vote count, the results as announced by the NEBE and accepted by the EPRDF pointed to many and diverse constituencies that chose alternatives to the ruling party when given the opportunity. Although much analysis focused on the important question of which party won, the results also provide insights into Ethiopian political views at the subregional level. Results in Afar, Benishangul-Gumuz, Dire Dawa, Gambela, Harar, and Somali—where

Table 6.1   Final Results of the 2005 Election

	EPRDF and Affiliates	CUD	UEDF	Others
Oromia	109	16	41	11
Amhara	88	50		
SNNPR	92	18	12	1
Tigray	38			
Addis Ababa		23		
Somali	23			
Benishangul-Gumuz	8	1		
Afar	8			
Gambela	3			
Dire Dawa	1	1		
Harar	2			
Total seats	372	109	53	12
Percentage of seats	68%	20%	10%	2%

EPRDF did not compete but had relationships with affiliate parties—had their own complex microdynamics, but I will not analyze them here.[9]

The official results suggest a complex and dynamic political picture. In addition to doing particularly well in urban areas and poorly in Tigray (as predicted), the opposition surprisingly extended its victory throughout the key constituencies in Amhara, Oromo, and the Southern Nations, Nationalities, and People's Region (SNNPR). In Addis Ababa, the CUD won an overwhelming victory and captured all 23 seats in contention, many with 75–80 percent of the vote. In Tigray, the TPLF won all 38 seats handily. In the Amhara region, the EPRDF member party Amhara National Democratic Movement (ANDM) won approximately 64 percent of the 138 seats, doing particularly well in East Gojjam and North Wollo zones. The CUD ran well in West Gojjam, North Shewa, and the area around Dessie. Widespread violence and intimidation, substantiated by international observers' reports, were a particular problem in Ankober (North Shewa) and in parts of East Gojjam and South Gondar.

In Oromia, Ethiopia's most populous region, the ruling OPDO captured approximately 62 percent of the 178 seats, winning large numbers of seats in the rural zones of Hararghe, Illubabor, and Jimma. The ONC (part of the UEDF) did well in West Shewa (ONC leader Merera won 83 percent in his constituency in the city of Ambo) as well as in East Wellega and even remote Borana.[10] The opposition won seats in Arsi (central Oromia) as well. The OFDM captured 11 seats, most in West Wellega, where its mobilization on the basis of traditional leadership worked. The CUD carried a number of seats in West Shewa (the area immediately around Addis Ababa) as well as some urban areas in Wellega.

The combined opposition therefore won votes across Oromia's 177 constituencies, with the UEDF winning 41 seats (17 percent of the total), the OFDM winning 11 seats (4 percent), the CUD 16 seats (7 percent), and the ruling OPDO 109 seats (62 percent).[11] As Arriola puts it, "Once the results were posted outside polling states, as required by the electoral law, Oromo voters discovered that their coethnics held a broad range of preferences."[12] Many analysts explain opposition votes as anti-EPRDF rather than in favor of any particular opposition party, and as in many elections elsewhere in the world this is undoubtedly an important rationale.[13] Furthermore, many leaders in the ONC and OFDM agreed that their supporters would have voted for the outlawed OLF given the opportunity.[14]

In the SNNPR, the ruling party won 92 of 123 seats (75 percent). The opposition CUD did well in the Gurage area in addition to winning some urban seats in Hawassa and Arba Minch. The SEPDC (part of the UEDF coalition) won nearly all the seats in Hadiya (Beyene's home area, where the opposition had won in 2000). Reports of violence and intimidation were particularly strong and substantiated in the area around Hossana.[15] In Wolayita, local rivalries with the Hadiya people led some voters who opposed the EPRDF to choose the CUD over the UEDF because the HNDO played a key role in the UEDF.[16] In South Omo, opposition parties recruited candidates from traditional authorities: UEDF candidates included the brother of the Maale king and a brother of one of the richest Maale chiefs, and the CUD recruited two candidates from the family of the Baaka king.[17] Therefore, as in Oromia, a complicated pattern of voting, explained in part by different preferences in urban as opposed to rural constituencies and in part by the particular support for "favorite sons," suggests the diverse political views among the many constituencies in the SNNPR.

In 2005, therefore, millions and millions of voters, rural and urban, from across the broad ethnically and religiously diverse Ethiopia, turned out and voted for the opposition. There is a tendency to ask which alliance of parties won the most seats overall, but that question obscures important microdynamics and localized politics. Four different parties, for example, won seats in Oromia, and parochial issues and local rivalries often shaped outcomes in the SNNPR. The notion that there was one political narrative and that all Ethiopians accepted it seems to have been thoroughly refuted. In general, the opposition did relatively better in the more urban constituencies (most notably Addis Ababa), but the breadth of this result indicates that significant numbers of rural Ethiopians voted for the opposition in the three main regions of the country. As expected, the EPRDF did better in poorer and more rural constituencies and in many Islamic communities, where voters reacted against the Orthodox Christian symbols used by the CUD.[18] In some constituencies the EPRDF won with a plurality when the opposition ran more than one candidate. In others the EPRDF was unopposed because the opposition lacked the resources and organizational capacity to mount campaigns in the remote countryside. The opposition's share of the votes, therefore, came despite it joining the political process less than six months before the election and either splitting the vote or not competing for a number of the seats the EPRDF won unopposed.

Furthermore, although the provisional results announced by the NEBE indicated that the EPRDF had an overall majority of seats, many key leaders of the party lost their positions in Parliament. Dawit Yohannes (speaker of Parliament), Abadula Gemeda (chair of the OPDO and former minister of national defense), Tefera Walwa (minister of capacity building), Bereket Simon (minister of information), Addisu Legesse (deputy prime minister, former president of the Amhara National Regional State, and chair of the ANDM), Genet Zewde (minister of education), Getachew Belay (minister of revenue), Arkebe Oqubay (mayor of Addis Ababa), and Junedin Sado (president of Oromia) all lost their seats. In this way the 2005 results represented a sharp rebuke of the EPRDF top leadership.[19]

Controversy over the election outcome created a dangerous political crisis in Ethiopia.[20] The opposition rejected the EPRDF's claims of victory and fomented a series of protests, a taxi strike, and student demonstrations in May and June 2005. International observers such as the Carter Center released statements noting monitor reports of improperly secured ballot boxes and intimidation and harassment of opposition agents and called on all sides to pursue legal channels to investigate complaints and resolve disputes.[21] As tensions escalated, the NEBE postponed further announcements of results, and the political parties negotiated a multiphased review process that included ad hoc complaint review boards and complaint investigation panels. These ad hoc committees, however, re-created the imbalance of power between the ruling party and the opposition, and the opposition parties withdrew from the process. As a consequence, in the twenty-eight districts that eventually revoted, the EPRDF won twenty-five.[22]

The opposition did not accept the official results. International observers also noted problems with the count and with intimidation of the opposition. Neither the Carter Center nor the EU took positions on the question of the electoral outcome, but they did express their views regarding the flawed postelection processes. The Carter Center's final report concluded

> The May elections marked an historic event in the country, as Ethiopia witnessed its first genuinely competitive campaign period with multiple parties fielding strong candidates. Unfortunately, what began with a comparatively open period of campaigning and an orderly voting process on election day was followed by flawed counting and tabulation processes in many areas; repeated incidents of serious postelection violence, including the killing of many dozens of people during electoral protests; a significant delay in finalizing election results; and an ineffective complaints review and investigation process. In spite of the positive preelection developments, therefore, the Carter Center concludes that the 2005 electoral process did not fulfill Ethiopia's obligations to ensure the exercise of political rights and freedoms necessary for genuinely democratic elections.[23]

The European Union's conclusion was virtually identical to that of the Carter Center:

> The 2005 parliamentary elections were the most competitive elections Ethiopia has experienced, with an unprecedented high voter turnout. However, while the preelection period saw a number of positive developments and voting on 15 May was conducted in a peaceful and largely orderly manner, the counting and aggregation process[es] were marred by irregular practices, confusion and a lack of transparency. Subsequent complaints and appeals mechanisms did not provide an effective remedy. The human rights situation rapidly deteriorated in the postelection day period when dozens of citizens were killed by the police and thousands were arrested. Overall, therefore, the elections fell short of international principles for genuine democratic elections.[24]

There was controversy regarding these observer reports. The head of the EU observer mission, member of the European Parliament Ana Gomez, had a more confrontational style than did former president Jimmy Carter. The Ethiopian government claimed that the Carter Center report endorsed the election and that the EU report was biased for political reasons. Both groups, however, reached similar final assessments, and neither concluded that the 2005 elections met criteria for "genuine democratic elections." Both of the major international observer groups refrained from validating the ruling party victory for the same reason—the counting process was so chaotic and nontransparent that international observers could not assess the outcome.[25]

Beforehand, most observers expected the EPRDF to win the May 15 elections handily.[26] The ruling party had the overwhelming advantages of incumbency, particularly in the rural areas, where local government and party officials controlled access to land and fertilizer, keys to survival of many small-scale farmers. The EPRDF and allied parties controlled regional state administrations, the state-owned media, and an overwhelming majority of the seats in Parliament. Contrary to these expectations, however, significant numbers of small-scale farmers and small-town residents voted against the ruling party and its local representatives. Widescale and deeply felt anger about how the EPRDF operated explained part of this pattern. At the local levels in particular, observers regularly reported resentment over how *kebele* officials abused their power. After fourteen years, many Ethiopians had had enough and were ready for a change.

Many voters presumably responded to the well-known impulse to throw out incumbents when economic conditions are poor and government policies are perceived to have failed. Some (particularly in the urban areas and the Amhara region) clearly supported the CUD's platform with regard to Ethiopian nationalist unity in contrast with the ruling party's commitment to ethnic federalism. Others saw leaders of the UEDF and OFDM as more authentic and legitimate representatives of their ethnic group or nationality than were the constituent parties in the EPRDF coalition.[27] Many knew little about the new opposition parties and coalitions but wanted to cast a vote against the ruling party. Multiple factors, including ethnic solidarity, urban-rural distinctions, class, nationalism, religion, and perceptions of the performance of local officials shaped how Ethiopians exercised their choices. The official election outcome demonstrated a series of specific microcontests that showed the EPRDF doing well in many critical constituencies, the CUD doing well in others, and the UEDF and OFDM in yet others. This complicated electoral outcome reflected the diverse political aspirations of the population, a direct rebuke of the incumbent ruling party, which insisted that it alone understood the needs of the Ethiopian masses.

Postelection Crackdown

In this dangerous context the two opposition coalitions engaged in a lengthy and sometimes public series of consultations to plan their next steps. Some favored a strategy of taking up their seats in Parliament and in the Addis Ababa regional government and using these positions to build stronger opposition in preparation for local elections in 2006 and the next round of national elections in 2010. Escalating violence, these leaders argued, would only play into the hands of the EPRDF, which had overwhelming military dominance. Others, however, argued that accepting results they and their supporters believed were fraudulent would make a mockery of democracy. The EPRDF's unilateral decision to change the rules of Parliament to make a 51 percent majority necessary to place an item on the agenda (rather than the twenty signatures previously required) reinforced the opposition's belief that the incumbent regime would never allow it to play a meaningful role.[28] Some opposition leaders argued for a boycott rather than participation in Parliament based on the "daylight robbery" of opposition votes.[29] The only way to replace the EPRDF was through a people's power movement of mass demonstrations, according to this viewpoint.

Some of the most vocal elements in the diaspora advocated this latter position and accused those willing to participate in Parliament of betraying their cause. Given the critical role of transnational networks, key opposition leaders traveled to Europe and North America at the same time public meetings were being organized in Addis Ababa and other core opposition constituencies. In September 2005 some CUD leaders, such as Berhanu and Lidetu, urged participation, whereas others, notably Hailu, promised cheering diaspora audiences he would boycott. This transnational debate within the opposition was extensive and included vigorous participation from actors based in Ethiopia, actors based in the diaspora, political leaders traveling between Ethiopia and North America, and some who had recently returned to Ethiopia from abroad.

When the new Parliament met on October 11, most opposition leaders took their seats, but others, particularly leading members of the CUD, refused. This decision to boycott represented a historical missed opportunity to advance political reform in Ethiopia. On November 2 and 3, violence exploded across Addis Ababa. "This is not your run-of-the-mill demonstration. This is an Orange Revolution gone wrong," Meles said, referring to the successful 2004 people's power protests in Ukraine.[30] In December 2005, 131 opposition politicians (including 10 elected members of Parliament), journalists, and civil society leaders were charged with crimes that included treason.[31] The space for a more open and democratic Ethiopia that seemed possible during the spring ended with key opposition leaders in prison and civil society silenced. The EPRDF effectively criminalized dissent, and the 2005 political opening closed.

The international community's response to the 2005 election crisis illustrates the limits of external leverage over a regime such as the

EPRDF. In the immediate aftermath of the postelection violence and crackdown, major donors responded with clear statements criticizing its government and with the suspension of significant levels of assistance. In November 2005, the Development Assistance Group for Ethiopia (DAG) adopted a tough posture and stated, "These disturbances weaken the environment for aid effectiveness and poverty reduction. . . . As a result of the situation, the DAG is collectively reviewing development cooperation modalities to Ethiopia."[32] In December 2005 international donors put $375 million in budget support on hold, sending another message that business as usual would not be possible in the context of this political crisis. In January 2006, a US Department of State press release expressed concern that "steps that appear to criminalize dissent impede progress on democratization."[33] These statements and concrete actions represented the most significant international pressure on the EPRDF since 1991.

The EPRDF, however, remained unmoved. The regime repeatedly stated that the elections were free and fair; the response of the security forces to demonstrations appropriate; and the charges against opposition politicians, journalists, and civil society leaders based on solid evidence and long-standing Ethiopian law. Over the course of the next year, the international community eventually shifted its focus to other issues. Washington in particular became increasingly concerned about the threat from "radical Islamic groups" operating in the Horn of Africa and looked to Addis Ababa for cooperation and intelligence sharing. Other donors wished to move on with the discussion of poverty reduction or investments. Ethiopia's intransigence led diplomats to accept a status quo they concluded would not change and to get on with other business.

Closing of Political Space: Civil Society and the Media

Ethiopia has a rich tradition of community-based organizations that engage at the grassroots in the form of self-help, such as *iddir* (burial associations).[34] During the famine of the 1980s there was an increase in organizations, particularly linked to religious institutions, engaged in humanitarian assistance. In the period between 1991 and 2005, more organizations began to engage in advocacy work. Action Professionals Association for the People, Hundee Oromo Grassroots Organization, the African Initiative for a Democratic World Order, and the Organization for Social Justice (OSJ) were active in the areas of good governance and rights-based development. The Ethiopian Human Rights Council produced a series of reports on conditions in the countryside. The Ethiopian Women Lawyers Association (EWLA) filled a significant need by representing women in cases of domestic violence and with regard to property rights. EWLA also advocated for reform of Ethiopia's family laws and an increase in the age of marriage from fifteen to eighteen. In 2005 Inter-Africa Group organized televised debates, and other NGOs engaged in civic education with the support of international donors. A number of NGOs, such as the OSJ, organized a network to monitor the elections.

In its concept of revolutionary democracy and later the developmental state, the EPRDF regarded NGOs as illegitimate, given the party's position that it already represented the people.[35] The appropriate way for citizens to participate was through party-controlled mass organizations that mobilized the population on the basis of gender, age, and occupation. The regime regarded NGOs as selfish institutions pursuing narrow interests—"rent seeking," in the EPRDF's parlance—opportunistic briefcase organizations without a serious presence in the countryside, that is, "inauthentic, undemocratic, unaccountable, [and] locally illegitimate."[36] Ruling authorities blamed foreign-funded NGOs for stirring up opposition and for being part of a conspiracy to overthrow the constitution, following recent patterns of peoples' power movements such as the Orange Revolution in Ukraine. "Collective participation" through party-sponsored institutions served developmental state policy and prevented the opposition from organizing.[37] Participation, in other words, denoted a particular instrumental role of controlling the population in a top-down approach organized by the party-state structure.

The EPRDF responded to the challenge of the 2005 electoral crisis by demonstrating its extraordinary strength in using the levers of its power and its considerable organizational capacities to dominate all aspects of political life. In combination, the Anti-Terrorism Proclamation and the Charities and Societies Proclamation (CSP) of 2009 largely eliminated what were already weak independent media and fledgling civil society institutions. The CSP restricted the ability of organizations engaged in human rights work and democracy promotion to operate in the country, and many closed or changed their mandates to become service delivery organizations. The EPRDF justified this new policy by emphasizing that "local" (but not "foreign") civil society could engage in advocacy around human rights and democracy. Given that local civil society depended on international financial support, this effectively decimated advocacy. As Tronvoll concludes, this represented the "reinterpretation of human rights and democratic values away from being universal standards."[38] In addition, the 2009 antiterrorism proclamation advanced an extremely broad definition so that nearly all forms of protest risked being classified as terrorism. In the context of a weak court system, these threats had a chilling effect. The ruling party vastly increased its ability to penetrate and monitor activities in the country and expanded its membership dramatically. Finally, the ruling party and the government consolidated their links, allowing the party to use its domination of government-owned media, control over development and humanitarian assistance, and professional opportunities through government jobs and university positions to stimulate increased party membership.[39]

Upon taking power in 1991, the EPRDF's provision of space for independent media served to distinguish the new regime from the prior military junta and to make claims that the regime was liberalizing. The EPRDF at first allowed print media to flourish. According to Stremlau, more than 200 newspapers and 87 magazines were founded in Ethiopia between 1992 and 1997.[40] The print media generally positioned themselves as hostile to the EPRDF, but by and large the regime ignored the press as being marginal to its core rural constituency.[41] Radio and television, far more important media for communication, remained under state control. After 2005, however, almost all media willing to criticize the regime were closed. The EPRDF engaged in ambitious efforts to block critical websites and blogs and even interrupted text-messaging services to make opposition mobilization more difficult. The ruling party periodically cut off the internet (the state-owned telecommunications firm controlled all incoming lines) and jammed radio stations such as the Voice of America and the Amharic service of Deutsche Welle.

2010 Elections: A Return to Noncompetitive Elections

Alongside the limitations on space for civil society, independent media, and opposition political parties, the EPRDF vastly increased its ability to penetrate and monitor activities in the country and expanded its membership dramatically. The EPRDF grew from 700,000 members in 2005 to 6.5 million by 2013 and 8 million by 2015.[42] In addition, the ruling party and the government further consolidated their links, allowing the party to use its domination of government-owned media, control over development and humanitarian assistance, and professional opportunities through government jobs and university positions to build party membership. One-to-five networks linked every five people to a party-affiliated leader in a system of information gathering and monitoring.

The effectiveness of these strategies was clear in the April 2008 local elections. A weak and divided opposition faced harassment and only managed to register some sixteen thousand candidates for the nearly 4 million posts up for election.[43] Even parties that participated in Parliament found it impossible to select candidates or to campaign, particularly in the Oromia region. In addition to restricting political space, the ruling party deepened its control over the smallest subcommunity level of administration, the *kebele* councils. Although kebeles are quite small, some of the councils expanded to 300 members. The EPRDF pointed to this expansion of direct participation as an indicator of the democratic nature of these institutions.[44] Some 4 million Ethiopians in a country that at the time numbered approximately 75 million served on EPRDF-controlled local councils. The scale of the election made it virtually impossible for opposition parties to run sufficient candidates to play more than a symbolic role. The Ministry of Foreign Affairs blamed the opposition for its poor showing: "Rather than put the blame on others they should have concentrated on improving their own position and leaving the final judgment to the people."[45] Tronvoll and Aalen, two longtime observers, characterize the elections as "seriously flawed" and argue that the ruling party engaged in a "nationwide strategy to intimidate, harass, and restrict the registration of opposition candidates."[46]

The national elections of 2010 returned to the patterns seen in 1995 and 2000.[47] Long before the March 23, 2010, polls it was clear that open political space had virtually disappeared. As with the pattern in earlier elections, the opposition objected to the composition of the NEBE, lack of access to state-controlled media, and restrictions on its ability to organize. According to one Canadian observer, the ruling party "unapologetically utilized the state machinery to facilitate its reelection."[48] Elements of the shattered CUD participated, and many of the parties in the UEDF reorganized and ran as the Forum for Democratic Dialogue (or Medrek, the Amharic word for forum), a loose coalition. The ruling EPRDF and its affiliated parties won 545 of the 547 seats, an astonishing 99.6 percent. Medrek won a single seat, and another went to an independent.[49] Leaders who chose to pursue opposition politics through legally registered parties and electoral participation had nothing to show for their efforts. All of the prominent opposition leaders lost their positions in Parliament, even in Addis Ababa, where the opposition had won in a landslide in 2005. Members of the opposition who argued that the EPRDF would never allow for a peaceful transfer of power through the ballot box pointed to this result and called for armed struggle.

Initial international reactions to this result were incredulous. The European Union electoral observation mission concluded that the poll did not meet international standards and was not fair because of a playing field that was "not sufficiently balanced, leaning in favor of [the] ruling party in many areas."[50] Meles responded to criticism by attacking the West in general and international human rights organizations in particular. He warned the opposition not to try to override the vote "because I will not bow to pressure from foreign forces."[51] Banners in English at a postelection EPRDF rally exclaimed, "We Have Spoken!" and "Don't Second Guess Us!"[52] Human Rights Watch in particular was accused of interfering in Ethiopian politics.

It is not surprising that vulnerable, risk-averse voters chose the ruling party.[53] In contrast to the competitive 2005 election, EPRDF domination by 2010 was so complete that there were no viable alternatives. Voters' choices that resulted in the 99.6 percent victory for the EPRDF were shaped by perceptions regarding closing political space, criminalization of dissent, and increased use of state resources to strengthen the ruling party in the years between 2005 and 2010.

The Death of Meles

Meles died in August 2012, marking the end of an era in contemporary Ethiopian politics. He died of an infection following a medical procedure in a hospital in Belgium. After defeating the brutal Derg regime in 1991, Meles headed the powerful party-state that ruled the country through a massive transformation. Many reflections on Meles's leadership have pointed to his personal qualities and his complicated and often quite contentious legacies. Former US ambassador to the UN Susan Rice, for example, gave a laudatory speech at his funeral, calling him "an uncommon leader, a rare visionary, and a true friend to me and many."[54] However, it is a mistake to think of his tenure as a period of one-man rule or his death as creating either a political vacuum or an opportunity for liberal reform. Power, authority, and resources never rested in Meles's hands alone.

Meles left behind a larger set of connected interests that included key figures in each of the ethnic parties that made up the EPRDF coalition; powerful economic institutions and mass organizations controlled by leading members of the ruling party; and, most importantly, the large and disciplined military and security services. This order remained fundamentally in place even after Meles's passing. Although formal authority shifted to Deputy Prime Minister Hailemariam, it was clear that power remained embedded within this network of party, economic, and military institutions. Meles's death did not provide opportunities for the shattered, repressed, and increasingly ineffectual opposition to engage in politics effectively. Hailemariam worked hard to link his every initiative to Meles, who became a larger-than-life figure after his death.

Some complained that Hailemariam mentioned Meles's legacy in virtually every speech, suggesting that the post-Meles transition remained more in the realm of personnel than ideas.[55]

Institutionally, the EPRDF remained a coalition of ethnically based parties that differed sharply in terms of size, experience in the liberation struggle, and capacity to administer their respective regions. The inherent tension between centralized power and ethnically and regionally based parties remained strong. This underlying ethnic positioning was evident when Hailemariam, from the SNNPR, appointed leaders of the Tigray, Amhara, and Oromo wings of the party as deputy prime ministers so that each constituent party retained a seat at the table.[56]

The initial post-Meles government appointments reflected the continued importance he placed on ethnic balancing in the distribution of power. Hailemariam's first cabinet gave eight positions to the OPDO (31 percent), seven to the ANDM (27 percent), seven to the Southern Ethiopian People's Democratic Movement (SEPDM; 27 percent), two to the TPLF (8 percent), and two to affiliated parties from the country's peripheral regions. This ethnoregional composition was virtually identical to that of the cabinets formed by Meles in 2005 and 2010 and suggested that ethnic balancing was one mechanism to sustain the equilibrium between the center and the ethnically defined regions.

The 2015 Elections

The 2015 elections were the first polls without Meles leading the party. Although the succession of Hailemariam went smoothly, the regime faced important questions and potential instability on several fronts. Among the constituent parties of the EPRDF coalition there was competition to see which party would get the most powerful positions in the coalition and the government. Politics within the ruling coalition and its constituent parties became increasingly important, whereas legal alternative parties played an increasingly marginal role.

Despite allegations of harassment and political favoritism by the NEBE, several opposition parties campaigned in the weeks prior to election day and participated. The Oromo Federalist Congress held large rallies in Ambo and areas of western Oromia.[57] Beyene also campaigned in his constituency of Hadiya and expected the opposition to win at least a few seats to assuage the international community. Beyene argued that running in elections mattered regardless of winning seats. "Even if we don't win, we want to do the politics."[58]

With the opposition in disarray and the EPRDF using its capacity to mobilize Ethiopians at the grassroots, the outcome of the election was a foregone conclusion. The EPRDF and its affiliated parties surpassed their 2010 results and increased their share of seats in Parliament from 99.6 to 100 percent. The member parties also won 100 percent of the seats in their respective regional states. Although met with incredulity abroad, this outcome was meant as an unambiguous message to the party's own rank and file. It signaled that the EPRDF, despite the death of its party founder and longtime leader, would continue to function as before, regulating access to office from the top down. It also communicated to the party's cadres that defection was pointless: there were no political alternatives outside the ruling party.

Strategies to Maintain a Strong Authoritarian Party

As indicated above, the EPRDF demonstrated its ability to use the levers of power and access to resources to dominate politics from 1991 to 2015. The party's power, however, relied upon mechanisms beyond patronage and coercion. In Chapter 2 I argue that the legacies of the civil war, in terms of leadership cohesion, hierarchical discipline, experience with military governance in liberated territory, and the initial legitimacy earned by wartime sacrifice and success established key initial conditions for the victorious rebel movement to control postwar politics. In addition, as I discuss in Chapter 3, the nature of the war-to-peace transition following military victory allowed the EPRDF to put in place rules that favored political movements based on ethnicity and that institutionalized ethnofederal regional states. These processes and mechanisms facilitated the creation of the EPRDF as a powerful, dominant, ruling party, as I detail in Chapter 4, and marginalized the political opposition, as I outline in Chapter 5. Noncompetitive elections and the ability of the party-state to reward loyalists and coerce opposition consolidated the party's grip on power. The EPRDF managed to remain dominant through 2015 by balancing the dynamics of centralized, hierarchical power on the one hand and autonomous, ethnically defined parties and regions on the other.

In this section I investigate intra-EPRDF politics as suggested by variations among the four constituent parties with regard to promotion to their respective central committees. These mechanisms facilitated the two contradictory logics at the core of the EPRDF's governance—top-down, democratic centralism on the one hand and ethnofederal, autonomous political institutions on the other—to remain in rough balance from 1991 to 2016. As I argue in Chapter 9, intraparty contradictions also played a central part in the political crisis of 2016 and the leadership change in 2018.

The first, centralizing logic was exemplified in the composition of the EPRDF's Executive Committee. This committee operated as a politburo and was the pinnacle of the democratic centralist system, where policy debates were settled and then communicated down to lower levels. It was organized on the basis of all four constituent parties being equal members of the coalition. Each party—the ANDM, the OPDO, the SEPDM, and the TPLF—appointed nine members, regardless of the size of the population each represented. This structure allowed the TPLF's more experienced and more cohesive party leadership to control the Executive Committee and thereby dominate the ruling coalition and the federal government.

The second, ethnic-balancing logic distributed positions proportionate to population size. Cabinet positions, for example, generally included appointments roughly in proportion to the respective populations. From 2000 to 2015, the ethnic composition of the cabinet remained stable.[59] Many observers said that although the formal distribution of offices was ethnically balanced relative to population, the TPLF remained first among equals and controlled power through informal mechanisms. There was undoubtedly considerable truth to this, but also, over time, officials in control of large ministries typically had access to appointments and budget decisions that allowed them to expand and consolidate power.[60] On the basis of demography, therefore, the EPRDF Executive Committee had an overrepresentation of members from the TPLF, but the cabinet roughly followed the statewide population ratios.

Intraparty Dynamics:
Variation in Central Committee Appointments

One can better understand that the EPRDF was composed of a coherent ex-rebel core but also a diverse set of constituent parties by comparing patterns of regional party appointments.[61] Although the party's internal deliberations were generally opaque, new Central Committee members were selected by the four member parties' congresses, and the outcomes were announced publicly. Although the TPLF's Central Committee proved to be a remarkably consistent body, with little turnover from 2001 to 2013, the Central Committees of the ANDM, OPDO, and SEPDM were almost entirely remade through high rates of personnel turnover.

The regional parties of the EPRDF had their own procedures for selecting their respective Central Committees. Individuals joined the ANDM, OPDO, SEPDM, and TPLF—not the EPRDF coalition—and the constituent parties were responsible for membership and internal party governance. The regional parties held congresses every two to three years, usually more or less simultaneously. One of the main purposes of these meetings was to elect the regional party Central Committees. The formal rules of the regional parties, although hierarchical, emphasized the "direct participation" of the membership base in leadership selection. The key mechanism for selecting party leadership began with a bottom-up process of selecting delegates to the party congresses. Membership in the ANDM, for example, began with individuals joining local-level institutions known as *hewas*, where they started as provisional members vetted at the *sretawi dirgit* (basic organization) level. A regional congress organizing committee proposed the agenda for the party congress and selected the delegates to attend. This committee achieved its mandate by coordinating with lower-level party organs such as the *sretawi dirgit* and *hewas*. The OPDO organized its congresses in a similar manner.[62] The resulting congresses were large events and provided the arena for local competition within the regional parties. The 2018 OPDO congress, for example, included some 6,000 delegates.[63]

Taken together, the data on Central Committee appointments indicate a considerable degree of asymmetry in member party institutionalization despite the EPRDF's continuous monopoly on national power since 1991. However, as the data also show, the variation between the TPLF and the other regional parties has declined in recent years. By the mid-2010s, the ANDM and the OPDO had Central Committees that more closely resembled that of the TPLF and, therefore, were positioned better to compete with the TPLF in intra-EPRDF struggles for power. This more symmetric distribution of power across the coalition member parties led to a new alignment of power within the coalition in 2018.

One of the most evident differences among EPRDF constituent party Central Committees is the size of their membership. Across all four parties, the mean number of Central Committee members was sixty. However, as shown in Figure 6.1, the parties varied widely in this respect. Between 2001 and 2013, the ANDM had a mean of sixty-one members, the OPDO sixty-three, and the SEPDM sixty-nine, whereas the TPLF had a mean of forty-five members. Creating cohesive leadership within the TPLF Central Committee, therefore, was a significantly less complicated challenge than in the other, larger party Central Committees.

The different sizes of the regional party Central Committees were a result, in part, of the differences in population among the four regions each party represented. According to the 2017 estimated census, Oromia was the country's largest region, with more than 35 million inhabitants, whereas Tigray had only 5 million inhabitants. Nevertheless, despite the fact that larger party Central Committees formed in more populous

Figure 6.1   Size of Regional Party Central Committees

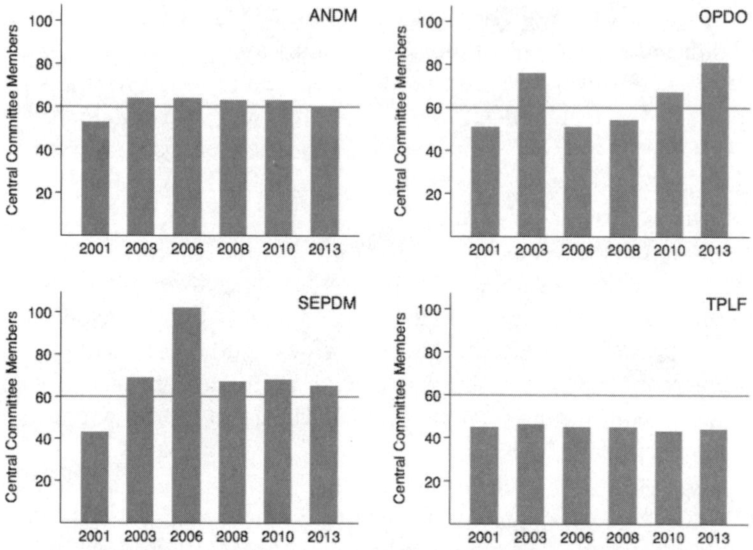

regions, representational disparities remained, as illustrated in Figure 6.2. For the TPLF, there was approximately 1 Central Committee member for every 95,877 inhabitants of Tigray. Each member of the other party Central Committees represented anywhere from two to five times the number of citizens: 1 SEPDM member for every 224,515 inhabitants of the SNNPR, 1 ANDM member for every 273,239 inhabitants of the Amhara National Regional State, and 1 OPDO member for every 502,935 inhabitants of Oromia. Given that the Central Committee of each regional party was supposed to play an integral role in linking the party to the constituency, such numbers provide some insight into why that challenge was been greater in regions such as Oromia. As was the case regarding the size of the EPRDF Central Committee, the relatively low ratio of Central Committee members to population advantaged the TPLF relative to the other three members of the ruling coalition and fostered TPLF leadership coherence.

The EPRDF's member parties varied significantly in the extent to which their Central Committees were composed of new members and the extent of those members' turnover. Figure 6.3 indicates that one of the mechanisms for ensuring the cohesion and stability of the TPLF was restricted addition of new members. In the five party congresses

**Figure 6.2   Popular Representation in Regional Party
Central Committees**

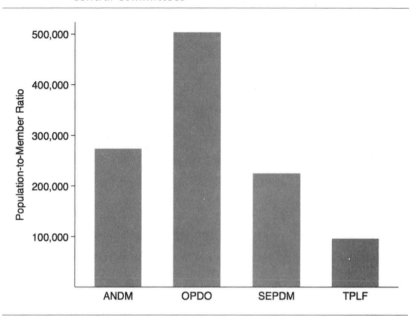

held between 2003 and 2013, the TPLF added an average of eight new
Central Committee members, representing about 18 percent of the
total committee. The other regional parties consistently absorbed far
more new members at each party congress. The ANDM had an average of nineteen new members (31 percent) appointed, the OPDO an
average of twenty-seven new members (40 percent), and the SEPDM
an average of thirty-five new members (45 percent).

Therefore, the dominance of the TPLF within the EPRDF coalition
after 1991 might have been magnified by the fact that its own Central
Committee members were far more likely to remain in place when compared with its regional counterparts. This churning within the ANDM
OPDO, and SEPDM Central Committees, in contrast with the stability
in the TPLF, was another indicator of how intra-EPRDF processes reinforced and sustained the TPLF's initial advantages as the oldest party in
the coalition, which benefited from the organizational legacies of the
armed struggle. The data show a similar story with regard to the pace
at which EPRDF Central Committee members were replaced in contrast
with the length of tenure on regional party Central Committees.[64]

Figure 6.3   New Membership in Regional Party Central Committees

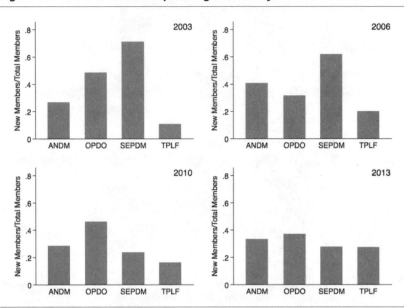

Over time, however, these advantages declined. The wartime legacies faded with fewer Ethiopians having a direct memory of the victory. By 2015 the TPLF's advantage had eroded, and the leadership of all four parties converged in terms of seniority and experience. The constant change in the size and composition of the OPDO and SEPDM Central Committees in the early 2000s was tempered to resemble the more stable patterns of the ANDM and TPLF. Figure 6.3, for example, shows that new membership in regional party Central Committees was significantly different in 2003, but by 2013 all four central committees had converged and only a few new members joined each committee. In other words, by the mid-2010s the EPRDF began to function as a coalition of more-or-less similar parties in contrast with the EPRDF in the early 2000s, when the TPLF had the experience, coherence, and seniority to dominate.

Conclusion

Ethiopia since 1991 had in place many of the key institutions and processes necessary for democracy. Elections were held regularly, Parliament included multiple political parties, the prime minister faced questions, and opposition leaders met with foreign diplomats and international media openly. On a more fundamental level, however, political space was hollow, and democratic institutions lacked substance. Conditions that would allow for an independent press, for opposition parties to mobilize without intimidation, and for civil society to serve as a check on the government were not in place. The 2005 elections demonstrated high levels of opposition across the main regions but failed to usher in an orderly transition based on peaceful multiparty competition. The EPRDF recognized the threat posed by democracy and took steps to increase party membership and to build the links between the party and the government. This closing of political space led to elections in 2010 and 2015 in which the EPRDF and its affiliates won virtually every seat.

Internal party dynamics and processes also shaped the EPRDF's durability. The pattern of ethnic balance at the cabinet level, along with the constituent party balance in the Executive Committee, provided arenas for both the centralizing and autonomous dynamics of the political system to be institutionalized. The different sizes and rates of turnover in the OPDO and SEPDM relative to the relative stability in the ANDM and TPLF provided evidence of another mechanism that served to strengthen the center and keep those parties that represented historically marginalized areas weak and divided. In Chapter 9, I argue that the trend of reducing turnover in Parliament and the equalization of tenure in the different Central Committees contributed to the crisis within the EPRDF coalition in 2016.

Notes

1. *EPRDF in Brief,* www.eprdf.org.et, 3.

2. As explained above, because I am primarily interested in the ways in which the ruling EPRDF shapes Ethiopian politics, in this chapter I emphasize the political processes in the Oromia, Amhara, SNNPR, Tigray, and Addis Ababa regions, where 90 percent of votes were cast. I mostly omit the processes in the Somali, Afar, Benishangul-Gumuz, Gambela, and Harar regions.

3. Ethiopian opposition leaders, interviews with author, Washington, DC, 2006. See also "No Illusions About the Elections," *Indian Ocean Newsletter* 1129 (April 2, 2005).

4. For thoughtful consideration of the ideological positions of the CUD and their relationships to the student movement, see Elleni Centime Zeleke, "When Social Science Concepts Become Neutral Arbiters of Social Conflict: Reading the Ethiopian Federal Elections of 2005 Through the Ethiopian Student Movement of the 1960s and 1970s," *Northeast African Studies* 16, no. 1 (2016): 107–139.

5. Interviews with author, Addis Ababa, January 2005.

6. Interview with author, Addis Ababa, May 2005.

7. The National Electoral Board of Ethiopia (NEBE) argued only groups that had listed election observation as one of their functions in their registration documents could be granted credentials to observe. See Carter Center, *Observing the*

152   *The Puzzle of Ethiopian Politics*

2005 Ethiopia National Elections: Carter Center Final Report (Atlanta, GA: December 2009), 19, http://www.cartercenter.org/resources/pdfs/news/peace _publications/election_reports/Ethiopia-2005-Finalrpt.pdf.

8. The Gambela People's Democratic Movement won three seats.

9. For excellent analyses of the 2005 elections in the periphery, see Kjetil Tronvoll and Tobias Hagmann, eds., *Contested Power in Ethiopia: Traditional Authorities and Multi-party Elections* (Leiden: Brill, 2012). On Gambela, see Dereje Feyissa, "Electoral Politics in the Nuer Context," in *Contested Power in Ethiopia*. On Somali, see Tobias Hagmann, "Fishing for Votes in the Somali Region: Clan Elders, Bureaucrats, and Party Politics in the 2005 Elections," in *Contested Power in Ethiopia*.

10. The Borana story had its own microdynamics of intraclan rivalries that went back to 1992. See Marco Bassi, "The Politics of Space in Borana Oromo, Ethiopia: Demographics, Elections, Identity and Customary Institution," *Journal of Eastern African Studies* 4, no. 2 (2010): 238; Marco Bassi, "Customary Institutions in Contemporary Politics in Borana Zone, Oromiya, Ethiopia," in *Contested Power in Ethiopia: Traditional Authorities and Multi-party Elections,* ed. Kjetil Tronvoll and Tobias Hagmann (Leiden: Brill, 2012).

11. On voting patterns in western Oromia, see Charles Schaefer, "'We Say They Are *Neftenya*; They Say We Are OLF,'" in *Contested Power in Ethiopia: Traditional Authorities and Multi-party Elections,* ed. Kjetil Tronvoll and Tobias Hagmann (Leiden: Brill, 2012); and for the Bale region of Oromia, see Terje Østebø, "Islam and Politics: The EPRDF, the 2005 Elections, and Muslim Institutions in Bale," in *Contested Power in Ethiopia*.

12. Leonardo R. Arriola, "Protesting and Policing in a Multiethnic Authoritarian State," *Comparative Politics* 45, no. 2 (January 2013): 152. See also Leonardo R. Arriola, "Ethnicity, Economic Conditions, and Opposition Support: Evidence from Ethiopia's 2005 Elections," *Northeast African Studies* 10, no. 1 (2008): 115–144.

13. Schaeffer, "'We Say They Are *Neftenya*,'" 205.

14. Interviews with author, Addis Ababa and Ambo, 2005 and 2006, respectively.

15. Interviews with author, Addis Ababa, 2005. See also Data Dea Barata, "Family Connections: Inherited Status and Parliamentary Elections in Dawro, Southern Ethiopia," in *Contested Power in Ethiopia: Traditional Authorities and Multi-party Elections,* ed. Kjetil Tronvoll and Tobias Hagmann (Leiden: Brill, 2012), 98.

16. Lovise Aalen, "A Revival of Tradition? The Power of Clans and Social Strata in the Wolyata Elections," in *Contested Power in Ethiopia: Traditional Authorities and Multi-party Elections,* ed. Kjetil Tronvoll and Tobias Hagmann (Leiden: Brill, 2012), 127. See also interviews with author, Addis Ababa, 2005.

17. Donald L. Donham, "The 2005 Elections in Maale: A Reassertion of Traditional Authority or the Extension of a Nascent Public Sphere?" in *Contested Power in Ethiopia: Traditional Authorities and Multi-party Elections,* ed. Kjetil Tronvoll and Tobias Hagmann (Leiden: Brill, 2012), 253.

18. See the excellent analysis of opposition voters in Arriola, "Ethnicity, Economic Conditions, and Opposition Support"; Leonardo R. Arriola, "The Ethiopian Voter: An Assessment of Economic and Ethnic Influences with Survey Data," *International Journal of Ethiopian Studies* 3, no. 1 (Winter/Spring 2007).

19. The EPRDF took these lost races to the complaint investigation panels and succeeded in winning back these seats because the opposition eventually chose not to participate in the process of recasting the votes.

20. Agence France-Presse, "Ethiopian PM Cracks Down After Opposition Protests in Election," May 16, 2005, http://www.sudantribune.com/spip.php?page=imprimable&id_article=9589.

21. Carter Center, "Postelection Statement on Ethiopian Elections," June 3, 2005, https://www.cartercenter.org/news/documents/doc2115.html.

22. The EPRDF therefore gained control of twenty-five out of twenty-eight contested seats through this process—approximately 10 percent of its total number of seats. However, twenty-two were constituencies in which complaints had been filed against the ruling party and, in some cases, constituencies in which the opposition had won by considerable margins in May. The Carter Center observed these complaint procedures and concluded that the process "did not . . . provide an impartial and effective process for reviewing and investigating complaints. As a result, the CIP process did not overcome the opposition's fundamental lack of confidence in the electoral process and was not able to deliver an outcome acceptable to key political actors." Carter Center, *Observing the 2005 National Ethiopian Elections*, 31.

23. Carter Center, *Observing the 2005 National Ethiopian Elections*, 3. Note that the final report elaborates on the preliminary statements issued in 2005.

24. European Union Election Observation Mission, *Ethiopia Legislative Elections 2005: Final Report,* http://www.eods.eu/library/FR%20ETHIOPIA%202005_en.pdf.

25. For a contrary view, see Patrick Gilkes, "Elections and Politics in Ethiopia, 2005–2010," in *Understanding Contemporary Ethiopia: Monarchy, Revolution, and Meles Zenawi,* ed. Gérard Prunier and Éloi Ficquet (London: Hurst, 2015).

26. This was my assessment prior to the elections.

27. I have drawn these conclusions from my discussions with dozens of international observers, my interviews with many Ethiopian political party officials, and my field notes from 2005.

28. The EPRDF also changed the rules to limit the authority and tax base of the Addis Ababa regional government, where the opposition had won all of the seats.

29. Hailu Shawel, leader of the CUD, said: "This was daylight robbery. The whole machinery of the government went to war to overturn these results." Marc Lacey, "Ethiopia's Capital, Once Promising, Finds Itself in Crisis," *New York Times*, November 14, 2005.

30. David Mageria, "Ethiopian Protestors Face Treason Charge," Reuters, November 10, 2005.

31. In July 2007, most of the major opposition political leaders arrested following the electoral crisis of 2005 and convicted of treason were pardoned after they signed documents admitting responsibility for the violence. In December 2008 one key CUD leader, Birtukan Mideska, was rearrested after she suggested the pardon was part of a political negotiation. The opposition was forced to devote much of its energy to these cases of arrests, trials, and negotiations, making the work of building party capacity impossible.

32. Statement by the Development Assistance Group, Addis Ababa, November 11, 2005.

33. US Department of State, "Ethiopian Political Violence," November 7, 2005; Statement by the Development Assistance Group, Addis Ababa, November 11, 2005; US Department of State, "Political Dissent and Due Process in Ethiopia," press release, January 6, 2006.

34. Stefan Dercon, "Group-based Funeral Insurance in Ethiopia and Tanzania," *World Development* 34, no. 4 (April 2006): 685–703; Elias Yitbarek, "The Role of *Iddir* in Neighbourhood Upgrading in Addis Ababa, Ethiopia," *Journal of Ethiopian Studies* 41, nos. 1–2 (June–December 2008): 187–197.

35. I have benefited from discussions with Seife Ayalew on this point.

36. Kendra E. Dupuy, James Ron, and Aseem Prakash, "Who Survived? Ethiopia's Regulatory Crackdown on Foreign-funded NGOs," *Review of International Political Economy* 22, no. 2 (2015): 425.

37. Sarah Vaughan and Kjetil Tronvoll, *The Culture of Power in Contemporary Ethiopian Political Life,* SIDA Studies No. 10 (Stockholm: Swedish International Development Cooperation Agency, 2003), 15.

38. Kjetil Tronvoll, "The 'New' Ethiopia: Changing Discourses of Democracy," in *Contested Power in Ethiopia: Traditional Authorities and Multi-party Elections,* ed. Kjetil Tronvoll and Tobias Hagmann (Leiden: Brill, 2012), 276.

39. Simegnish Yekoye Mengensha, "Silencing Dissent," *Journal of Democracy* 27, no. 1 (January 2017): 89–94. For details see Human Rights Watch, *Development Without Freedom: How Aid Underwrites Repression in Ethiopia* (New York: Human Rights Watch, October 19, 2010).

40. Nicole Stremlau, "The Press and Political Restructuring of Ethiopia," *Journal of Eastern African Studies* 5, no. 4 (2011): 716–732.

41. Ignio Gagliardone, "New Media and the Developmental State in Ethiopia," *African Affairs* 113, no. 451 (April 2014): 279–299.

42. *EPRDF in Brief,* www.eprdf.org.et, 3.

43. Michael Deibert, "Politics-Ethiopia: A Tangled Political Landscape Raises Questions About U.S. Ally," InterPress Service, June 2, 2008, http://www.ipsnews.net/2008/06/politics-ethiopia-a-tangled-political-landscape-raises-questions-about-us-ally/.

44. Marco di Nuzio, "'Do Not Cross the Red Line': The 2010 General Elections, Dissent, and Political Mobilization in Urban Ethiopia," *African Affairs* 113, no. 452 (July 2014): 414.

45. Ethiopian Ministry of Foreign Affairs, "A Week in the Horn," April 18, 2008, https://mfaethiopiablog.wordpress.com/category/a-week-in-the-horn/.

46. Lovise Aalen and Kjetil Tronvoll, "The 2008 Ethiopian Local Elections: The Return of Electoral Authoritarianism," *African Affairs* 108, no. 430 (2008): 114.

47. On the 2010 elections, see Kjetil Tronvoll, "The Ethiopian 2010 Federal and Regional Elections: Re-establishing the One-party State," *African Affairs* 110, no. 438 (2011): 121–136.

48. Glenn Brigaldino, "Elections in the Periphery: Ethiopia Hijacked," *Review of African Political Economy* 38, no. 128 (June 2011): 327.

49. National Electoral Board of Ethiopia, "Provisional Election Result," https://web.archive.org/web/20100527040550/www.electionethiopia.org/en.

50. Barry Malone and David Clarke, "Ethiopia's Meles Urges Recognition of Poll Win," Reuters, May 25, 2010, http://ca.reuters.com/article/idCA TRE64N2YS20100525. The State Department similarly noted, "a number of

laws, regulations and procedures implemented since the previous parliamentary elections in 2005 created a clear and decisive advantage for the ruling party throughout the electoral process." Assistant Secretary of State for Public Affairs Philip J. Crowley, Daily Press Briefing, Washington, DC, May 26, 2010.

51. See clip of Meles Zenawi's speech on Al Jazeera, http://www.youtube .com/user/AlJazeeraEnglish#p/search/0/mQj1JZmnfSE.

52. Voice of America, "EU: Ethiopian Election Unbalanced," http://www1 .voanews.com/english/news/africa/Ethiopias-Ruling-Coalition-Winning-in -Landslide-94811604.html. See also Ministry of Foreign Affairs, "Second Guessing the Will of the Ethiopian People: Unacceptable," May 26, 2010, http://waltainfo.com/index.php?option=com_content&task=blogcategory&id =26&Itemid=90.

53. Abiye Teklemariam, "The Rational Decision Is to Elect EPRDF," blog, http://addisnegeronline.com/2010/05/the-rational-decision-is-to-elect-the-eprdf/.

54. "Remarks by Ambassador Susan E. Rice, U.S. Permanent Representative to the United Nations, at the Funeral of Prime Minister Meles Zenawi of Ethiopia," Addis Ababa, September 2, 2012.

55. Lovise Aalen, "Ethiopia After Meles: Stability for How Long?" *Current History* 113 (May 2014): 193.

56. Prime Minister Hailemariam Desalegn, an ethnic Wolayita, was joined by Demeke Mekonnen (ANDM), Debretsion Gebremichael (TPLF), and Muktar Kedir (OPDO). The 1995 Constitution defines the deputy prime minister position as occupied by a single individual.

57. See the photographs published in "Oromo Federalist Congress (OFC) Criss-crossing Oromia with Huge Turnouts at Campaign Rallies," May 8, 2005, http://finfinnetribune.com/Gadaa/2015/05/oromo-federalist-congress-ofc-criss -crossing-oromia-with-huge-turnouts-at-campaign-rallies/. Merera Gudina's party changed its name from the Oromo National Congress (ONC) to the OFC after the National Electoral Board of Ethiopia (NEBE) recognized a breakaway faction as the legal leadership of the ONC.

58. Quoted in Marthe van der Wolf, "Ethiopian Opposition Hopes to Overcome Intimidation, Steep Odds," Voice of America, May 19, 2015, http://www .voanews.com/content/ethiopian-opposition-hopes-to-overcome-intimidation -steep-odds/2777472.html.

59. I thank Leonardo Arriola for sharing data with me for this chart.

60. Leonardo R. Arriola and Terrence Lyons, "Ethiopia's 100% Election," *Journal of Democracy* 27, no. 1 (January 2016): 76–88.

61. In this section I draw from a collaborative project with Leonardo R. Arriola, Seife Ayalew, and Josef Woldenses. See Leonardo R. Arriola, Terrence Lyons, Seife Ayalew, and Josef Woldenses, "The Ethiopian People's Revolutionary Democratic Front: Authoritarian Resilience and Intra-Party Dynamics," paper presented at the annual meeting of the American Political Science Association, Philadelphia, Pennsylvania, September 2016; and Arriola, Lyons, Ayalew, and Woldenses "Organizing for Long-Term Rule: How Intra-Party Leadership Competition Explains Authoritarian Party Durability in Ethiopia," paper presented at the African Studies Association annual meeting, Atlanta, Georgia, November 2018.

62. This section is based on the rules of the ANDM and OPDO (in Amharic and Afan Oromo, respectively) and on interviews with party officials in Ethiopia and the United States.

63. Fana, "9th Organizational Conference of OPDO Kicks Off Today," September 19, 2018, https://fanabc.com/english/2018/09/9th-organizational -conference-of-opdo-kicks-off-today/. In 2018 the ANDM had 2,000 delegates and the TPLF 1,600. See "ANDM 12th Congress to Recreate a Party of Change," Borkena.com, September 27, 2018, https://borkena.com/2018/09/27/andm-12th -congress-to-recreate-a-party-of-change/; Bamlak Tadesse, "Mekelle: TPLF Holds 13th Organizational Conference," AFRO 105.3FM, September 26, 2018, http://www.afro105fm.com/afrofm.com/2018/09/26/mekelle-tplf-holds-13th -organizational-conference/.

64. The patterns are the same for length of tenure, number of new appointments per congress, and number of one-term appointments across the four parties. See Arriola, Lyons, Seife, and Woldenses, "Organizing for Long-Term Rule."

7

The Developmental State

When the Ethiopian People's Revolutionary Democratic Front (EPRDF) seized power in 1991, it took over an economy that had suffered from protracted civil war, lacked major marketable natural resources, was extremely drought prone, was experiencing rapid population growth, and was at the center of a highly conflicted, poverty-stricken region. The Derg, inspired by the Soviet model, was a strict regime that controlled most aspects of the economy, notably free trade of agricultural commodities. Furthermore, the Derg pursued policies of forced villagization and resettlement that greatly disrupted social and economic life, although it abandoned these tactics in the waning years of its rule.[1] Overall economic growth from 1981 to 1992 was 0.5 percent and, by the end of the Derg era, was shrinking by 1.2 percent a year.[2]

By 2015 the EPRDF claimed credit for the economic transformation of both urban and rural life. With economic growth rates at twice the African average, large segments of Ethiopian society attained a level of stability, if not prosperity, unprecedented in the country's modern history. In addition to the high modernist projects such as the Grand Ethiopian Renaissance Dam (GERD) and massive new construction in Addis Ababa, there were new regional universities, industrial parks, local health clinics, and roads that allowed farmers access to markets and services. The EPRDF rose to power over a poor, largely agrarian state but took important steps toward its goal of transforming Ethiopia into a modern, middle-income, industrial state.

The EPRDF's post-1991 order emphasized ethnofederalism mediated by a strong central party. The victorious insurgents ruled with the conviction that the vanguard party could be used to transform the economy if wise leadership controlled policy and focused on poverty reduction without distraction from independent civil society groups or

157

opposition parties. After the war with Eritrea (1998–2000), the 2001 split within the Tigray People's Liberation Front (TPLF), and the electoral crisis of 2005, the EPRDF launched an ambitious set of economic policies labeled the Growth and Transformation Plan (GTP), designed to use a developmental state model to foster rapid economic expansion and alleviate poverty. The logic of the developmental state reinforced power at the center and top-down links to the smallest village. It also contributed to regional conflicts regarding the distribution of benefits because the government controlled where investments were made and how profits were distributed.

The EPRDF presented its political and economic policies as indispensable to promote peace and development, thereby positioning all opposition parties as warmongers who stood in the way of Ethiopia's modernization. The government's *Foreign Affairs and National Security Policy and Strategy* paper from 2002—immediately after the war with Eritrea—stated, "The main source of our vulnerability to threats is our poverty and backwardness."[3] Poverty, therefore, was identified as the existential threat and the EPRDF top-down plans to address it essential to national security. The regime claimed legitimacy insofar as it pursued the interests of the masses in terms of poverty reduction and improved service provision.[4] Prime Minister Meles Zenawi wrote that the "single-minded pursuit of accelerated development" was the fundamental source of legitimacy for the developmental state. The autonomy of the state was essential so that it might "pursue its development project without succumbing to myopic interests."[5] Providing new economic opportunities through the implementation of what the regime claimed were irrefutably correct policies justified the EPRDF's continued domination.

Evolution of Economic Policies Under the EPRDF

After the 1974 Ethiopian revolution, the Derg tried to legitimize its power through state-led development, Ethiopian nationalism, and the creation of a strong, centralized administration. After nationalizing all land, the Derg targeted funds to large, mechanized state-owned farms and largely ignored small-scale landholders and pastoralists. "Marxist modernism," in Donham's phrase, even reached the historically marginalized southern marches of Ethiopia.[6] The consequences for the Ethiopian economy were dire, leading to widespread poverty and hunger.

During the period of armed struggle (1974–1991), the TPLF advocated a Marxist-Leninist form of revolutionary democracy and a peasant-focused solidarity economy. As noted above, the TPLF emphasized equality, redistributed land in areas it controlled during the war, and engaged in extensive humanitarian activities. The EPRDF's founding 1989 program clearly reflected these links to Marxist-Leninist thinking, promising to "crush the ownership of dependent capitalism and imperialism" and bring the main economic institutions under government control.[7]

However, upon taking power two years later in 1991, the EPRDF initially shifted (at least rhetorically) toward markets and free trade and built good relations with international financial institutions, donors, and private foundations.[8] During the transitional period, economic policies emphasized limiting the government's involvement in various activities such as marketing agricultural products and reducing investments in inefficient state-owned farms and accepting the need for private investment and free trade. In 1992, the Transitional Government of Ethiopia (TGE) devalued its national currency, introduced a new labor code, and enacted a donor-funded reform program that included privatization and liberalization of the private sector and international trade.[9] Although it adopted some market-friendly measures, the EPRDF retained ownership of all land and refused to accept the kind of structural adjustment policies promoted by the international financial institutions in the 1990s.[10]

In the 1990s, the EPRDF emphasized agricultural growth and small landholder production in particular. The Ministry of Finance and Economic Development stated in 1993, "Peasant farmers and pastoralists constitute the cornerstone" of economic development.[11] The agricultural development–led industrialization program emphasized the small-farm sector raising productivity to increase food security and produce a surplus. The emphasis on small-scale farmers tapped into the narrative of equity and fairness that went back to the "Land to the Tiller" slogans of the student movement in the 1970s and the policies followed in liberated territory during the armed struggle.[12]

The war with Eritrea (1998–2000) represented a significant disruption in the Ethiopian economy. According to a report by the Ethiopian Economic Policy Research Institute, the war cost Ethiopia more than $2.9 billion. The size of the national army increased from 60,000 to 350,000 (reversing a generally successful demobilization), and spending on the military increased from $95 million to $777 million, making up nearly 50 percent of the country's total recurrent expenditure.[13]

After the war with Eritrea and the political crisis of the 2005 election, the EPRDF transformed its economic policies. The 2006 Plan for Accelerated and Sustained Development to End Poverty added the commercialization of agriculture and the acceleration of private-sector development to the prior small-scale farmer emphasis.[14] GTP I (2010–2015) and II (2015–2020) emphasized massive investment in infrastructure and commercial agriculture as the backbone of economic growth and aspired to turn Ethiopia into a middle-income country.[15] The GTP included an industrial policy to protect fledgling Ethiopian firms from competition.[16]

The Developmental State in Ethiopia

Chalmers Johnson advances the concept of the developmental state to describe Japan's rapid industrialization and the similar processes in Korea and Taiwan.[17] Economic growth and poverty alleviation were the core missions of these postwar states, justifying widescale government intervention in their economies. The model assessed outcomes in terms of economic goals met rather than processes of participation and good governance. To deliver the desired economic outcomes, the developmental state had to be autonomous and able to act unencumbered by the interests of particular constituencies.[18] In contrast with the Washington Consensus and policies of structural adjustment, the state was seen as the solution rather than the problem.

Ethiopia differs from the East Asian model with regard to the importance of an independent state bureaucracy. The classic archetype emphasized a neutral bureaucracy that could implement policies on the basis of technocratic merit. Ethiopia, particularly after 2005, linked party membership to the recruitment and promotion of civil servants. When an EPRDF official was asked about the politicization of the bureaucracy, he replied that it was "by design. . . . We cannot envisage a developmental state without the EPRDF [because] there are no other parties with the comprehensive understanding like we have."[19] Party leadership rather than technocratic teams drove developmental state policies in Ethiopia.

The ideology of the developmental state is important in Meles's writings. He explicitly challenges neoliberal orthodoxy: "The neoliberal paradigm is a dead end incapable of bringing about the African renaissance, and . . . a fundamental shift in paradigm is required to effect a revival."[20] He rejects the model of the "night watchman state," which merely protects property rights and enforces contracts. He argues that the "neoliberal assumption of efficient competitive markets has no basis in fact or theory."[21] Many of Meles and his colleagues' ideas for the developmental state come from their analysis of conditions in Ethiopia rather than from the Japanese or Chinese models.

The theories of the developmental state reinforced the top-down system of political control of the EPRDF. The way the state interacted with the rural population disempowered the most vulnerable groups by prioritizing technical knowledge over local practices.[22] The government's distribution of key agricultural inputs, such as improved seeds and fertilizers, served as a powerful mechanism of control and domination.[23] From the party-state's viewpoint, the people were subjects to be moved and retrained as necessary to advance the kinds of development it prioritized.[24] Furthermore, Ethiopian development plans were framed around a kind of "high modernism" that features showpiece projects such as massive road-building projects. The developmental state was a project to promote state-led development that follows a logic developed of top-down, expert-based knowledge. State-managed development was inherently nonparticipatory because unaccountable central authorities made key decisions.

Ethiopia had an extensive network of development agents (DAs) throughout the country. The DAs were appointed by *woreda* officials and were not necessarily from the communities to which they were assigned. DAs sometimes did not speak the local language or have knowledge of the local agricultural practices. Villagers were encouraged to participate in multiple meetings where they were instructed by agents on how to increase production and thereby meet the goals of the GTP. Quotas were set by the central government and translated down through the bureaucracy to the local level, where the farmers were pressured to sign up for programs.[25] In Planel's research, for instance, many farmers felt compelled to buy fertilizer from the DAs regardless of whether they thought they needed it for their specific crops or soil types.[26] Agricultural specialists could tell by viewing fields during harvest time which farmers had good relations with the local DA and therefore received their fertilizer at the optimal time and which had difficult relations with local officials and therefore received their allotment late in the growing season.[27]

GTP I argued that agriculture would remain "the engine of growth," but the "key actor in the sector's development will not be the semisubsistence small farmers."[28] The GTP channeled significant money to promising "model farmers" through microfinance and small-enterprise development. The political one-to-five networks were used to link "model farmers" to others in the community.[29] This represented an important shift from the EPRDF's initial focus on small-scale farmers and agricultural-led development. Class differentiation, seen as a danger during the time of the armed struggle and early years of the regime, became accepted and seen as necessary for modernization. As Lefort points out, there was a political logic in this process because local elites who had supported the opposition in 2005 elections became model farmers and were thereby co-opted by the ruling party. Some became recipients of government support and joined the ruling party.[30]

The developmental state had enormous capacity to regulate life at the grassroots and therefore complemented the democratic centralism of the EPRDF. Even remote villages were linked in multiple ways to the state. Land registration, for example, extended the state's power into the countryside and empowered local administrative structures with increased authority over land and control over the people who used it.[31] Local DAs and Land Administration Committees served as agents of the state and as the mechanism to extend the state's reach deep into the countryside.[32] The local administrative structures were primarily concerned with implementing government-initiated policies rather than representing local interests. According to Chinigò, some peasants said that joining the ruling party was necessary in order to register their land, and if local officials accused farmers of failing to use land "productively," they could seize it.[33] The developmental state not only promised rapid economic development but also controlled the population and thereby marginalized opposition and strengthened the dominant ruling party.

Similar mechanisms for building networks were created in urban and periurban areas. In 2005, unemployed urban youth were perceived as agents of opposition, leading to a new vagrancy proclamation and efforts to regulate this population. In part to manage this problem, the government supported microloans for unemployed youths trying to establish themselves in small businesses. This development initiative simultaneously created the structures to connect these potentially disruptive populations with the state. For unemployed youths in periurban areas, following the government's advice to register at the *kebele*, join a one-to-five network, engage in sanctioned activities sponsored by the party, and participate in savings and credit through state microfinance institutions both potentially provided employment, on the one hand, and allowed the government to monitor and tame the behavior of this population on the other.[34]

The ideology of the developmental state and the huge state-led investments in GTP I and II contributed to significant economic growth. This process of change resulted in massive urban development, dramatic expansion of the road and railroad networks, new regional universities, and improvement in human development indicators in part because of the development of rural health centers and schools. Chinese loans resulted in major expansion of infrastructure, including new roads, a new railroad linking Addis Ababa with the port of Djibouti, and a new light-rail system in the capital. This kind of development legitimized the EPRDF by providing jobs and services. It also deepened the ruling party's ability to monitor and control the population.

However, as often happens with rapid economic growth, expectations grew faster than the state's ability to provide jobs and other benefits. Powerful narratives developed that those close to the regime, particularly those from Tigray, received vastly disproportional profits, whereas those in rural areas remained unemployed and landless. These narratives were particularly powerful in Oromia, which had a deeper historical sense of marginalization. In addition, the Ethiopian developmental state acquired land from small-scale farmers to build infrastructure and then leased it to private, international investors to build large-scale mechanized farms. The small-scale farmers typically received less compensation than they felt they deserved, and grievances grew as state-collected rent far exceeded its payments to the farmers.

The Challenges of Drought and Humanitarian Relief

Practices of international development programs and humanitarian relief provide a window into the connections between economic and political processes and how the ruling party used them to remain dominant. Ethiopia has a long history of engagement with external donors. Emperor Haile Selassie had extensive programs with US and European donors, including a large Peace Corps contingent in the 1960s. During the Derg regime, donor assistance for development largely receded, but international humanitarian assistance and the engagement of international nongovernmental organizations (INGOs) expanded dramatically. Particular during the Ethiopian famine of the mid-1980s, images of starving Ethiopians and pop stars making records to raise money dominated the international narrative of Ethiopia. Following the civil war, the victorious EPRDF (and the Eritrean People's Liberation Front [EPLF]) became donor darlings for a time and were lauded as a "new generation of African leadership" that was "pragmatic" and would deliver on development.

The EPRDF understood the powerful symbolism of famine because the emperor's silence on the 1973 famine in Wollo helped set the stage for the Ethiopian revolution. The 1984–1985 famine brought both tremendous suffering to Tigray and opportunities for the TPLF to build relations with local peasants and external donors. It used humanitarian assistance channeled through the Relief Society of Tigray (REST) in ways that generated popular support for the rebel movement and enhanced its authority.[35] Because vulnerable peasants depended on REST and the TPLF for food and security, the rebel movement deepened its penetration into the countryside. After the transition in 1991, the REST continued as a party-affiliated humanitarian organization that received large grants from international donors as well as donations from the Tigrayan diaspora.[36] These experiences underlined the political importance of relationships with the international community and contributed to the EPRDF's often tense relations with major donors and opposition to INGOs they felt worked against the government's priorities rather than supporting and complementing them.

Given the highly political nature of previous famines, it was not surprising that the EPRDF paid careful attention to food security. The TPLF "knew exactly how effectively subversive humanitarian assistance can be."[37] The regime created a National Disaster Prevention and Preparedness Committee and put in place extensive surveillance of nutrition and early warning systems so that drought or other shocks did not result in famine and the displacement of large populations. The EPRDF emphasized protecting livelihoods so that those unable to farm or maintain their herds for a season or two could quickly return to viable economic activity.[38]

In 2005, the government, along with development partners, initiated the Productive Safety Net Program (PSNP) to promote the capacity of rural people living in poverty to resist shocks and become food self-sufficient.[39] This program provided food and cash for a number of years and required recipients to work on projects designed to promote more resilient livelihoods, such as building community infrastructure and managing natural resources. The PSNP "provides transfers to the food insecure population in chronically food insecure woredas in a way that prevents asset depletion at the household level and creates assets at the community level."[40] A significant number of rural households graduated from the program every year. In part as a result of this framework and the investments made in the Famine Early Warning Systems Network, the government and donors were able to respond quickly to food insecurity in the context of irregular rains in 2015 and 2017. Some, however, argue that the PSNP is unlikely to deliver sustainable food security, particularly in highland Ethiopia, where a severe shortage of land makes sufficient production difficult. Although the program's impact on poverty reduction might be debatable, its ability to constrain urban migration and increase state control over the rural population is clear.[41]

Overall levels of donor funding to Ethiopia are high, but per capita levels are lower than in most developing countries. Ethiopia received $45 of official development assistance per capita in 2009, dropping to $32 per capita in 2015. The average in Africa in 2015 was $46 per capita.[42] The government in Addis Ababa had resisted accepting donor advice in a number of areas, notably liberalization of fertilizer markets and opening up the financial and telecommunications sectors to foreign investment.

These issues as well as lack of protection for intellectual property rights have delayed Ethiopia's accession to the World Trade Organization (WTO). The EPRDF saw the fertilizer, financial, and telecommunications sectors as politically important as part of its overall system of control. In addition, such sectors have been cash cows that help subsidize the regime's budget. In the 2000s and 2010s, Ethiopia, along with many other developing countries, diversified its sources of assistance and built relationships with new donors and investors from China, Turkey, India, and elsewhere.[43]

Party-, Military-, and Government-Owned Enterprises

Another key aspect of the EPRDF's economic policy was the manner in which it worked with party-owned and party-affiliated enterprises. The lines between the EPRDF and the private sector were deliberately blurred in many of the same ways the lines between the party and the state were. Different constituent units of the ruling coalition controlled party endowment funds used to invest in businesses that typically favored the party and its leadership. The first established and by far the largest in terms of assets was the Endowment Fund for the Rehabilitation of Tigray (EFFORT), controlled by the TPLF. Tiret, or Endeavor, was controlled by the Amhara National Democratic Movement (ANDM); Tumsa Endowment (previously known as Dinsho) by the Oromo People's Democratic Organization (OPDO); and the Wondo Group by the Southern Ethiopian People's Democratic Movement (SEPDM). According to Siye Abraha, EFFORT's onetime director, the other endowment funds were launched with money provided by the Tigrayan endowment.[44] EFFORT's Executive Committee is composed of seven members, all members of the TPLF Central Committee, making it clear this was a "party statal," or an enterprise that operated to benefit the party.[45] Azeb Mesfin served as chief executive officer of EFFORT until 2018 and declared that the endowment "is a property of the Tigray people" and that only the party could audit the fund's accounts.[46]

Vaughan and Mesfin note the nearly complete overlap between these nominally independent party endowments, the TPLF, and the government:

> Any serious difference of view between the Office of the Prime Minister [under Meles] and the EFFORT Board, for instance, would strike

at the heart of party cohesion. Most sources interviewed consider that, whatever formal legal differentiation there may be between EFFORT and the ruling party, politically unsanctioned commercial strategy on the part of the endowment-owned companies would be unthinkable.[47]

The World Bank further recognized that the playing field was tilted against enterprises not affiliated with the ruling party: "Endowment- and state-owned firms confront an investment climate that is substantially different from that faced by private enterprises, which may partially explain the fact that they appear to have greater access to policymakers, government as market, and the state-owned part of the financial sector."[48]

The party-owned enterprises were hybrids that pursued profits, provided some level of public goods, helped fund the ruling party, and enjoyed direct access to state authorities. Ethiopia combined statist and market approaches to economic growth, thereby making party-owned enterprises such as EFFORT and its affiliated party endowments key. According to press reports, EFFORT began with $100 million in capital but by 2017 was worth $3 billion.[49] Thanks to its party-owned enterprises, the EPRDF was "Africa's richest party."[50] When private companies competed with party-owned enterprises, the private companies suffered. The head of Ethiopian Amalgamated, a company founded in 1964 that grew into Ethiopia's largest agricultural supply company, ran afoul of the party-owned businesses, and the company went out of business. Its exiled owner-director distilled the lessons:

> Although the Ethiopian government overtly pledged allegiance to free market principles and invited the private sector to participate in the economic development of the country, it covertly pursued policies that favored party-owned enterprises to engage in commercial activities such as fertilizer importation and distribution to create steady revenue streams to finance party activities to the detriment of genuine private-sector companies and the poor Ethiopian farmers who live from hand to mouth."[51]

The close relationship between party and business in the state is not unique to Ethiopia. Similar party-business patterns existed in Taiwan.[52] Rwanda also has party businesses that promote development and channel funds to the ruling party during electoral campaigns.[53] In South Africa, business links between government procurement and ruling party–controlled businesses are called "tenderpreneurship."[54] The large share of the economy in the hands of party-businesses makes it more difficult for party members to freelance or to build autonomous bases of support. It is hard for a potential leader of a breakaway faction to envision financial support from the business community when many of the most important business leaders are party Central Committee members. At the same time, however, the near universal perception among Ethiopians that party-run businesses are given preferential treatment fed the narrative about corruption that contributed to the challenges to the regime in 2016 and 2017. Many of the most public winners in the process of implementing the GTP were perceived as TPLF owned or controlled, thereby linking development with inequality on the basis of ethnic identity in the minds of many aggrieved Ethiopians.

In many cases party stalwarts and, in particular, former insurgents were in charge of the large government-owned businesses. One important example was the Metals and Engineering Corporation (METEC). The purposes of METEC were to support key stakeholders in the public sector and to develop "private sector value chains and accelerate the technological capacity of the country."[55] Brigadier General and TPLF veteran Kinfe Dagnew founded the conglomerate of nine industries. METEC was the main contractor for the electromechanical and hydraulic steel structures of the GERD and was involved in other high-profile initiatives such as the light-rail project in Addis Ababa and equipment for key sugar processing factories.[56] METEC's establishment was justified by the GTP call for development and follows the model of Chinese People's Liberation Army and the business activities of the armed forces in other developing states. In another illustration of the blurred lines between civil business and the military, Ethiopian National Defense Forces (ENDF) officers working at METEC were regularly promoted to a higher rank within the ENDF.[57]

The failure of the Ethiopian Sugar Corporation (ESC) and the role of METEC illustrated the dangers of relying upon state- and military-controlled companies to foster rapid development. The GTP emphasized large-scale sugar plantations and processing as one of the priority areas for investment, with the goal of making Ethiopia one of the world's ten largest sugar producers by 2023.[58] Although GTP I called for the ESC to invest $4.6 billion in ten new processing plants to export 2.3 million metric tons of sugar by 2015, none of this happened, and Ethiopia remained a sugar importer.[59] The Kuraz Sugar Development Project, in the South Omo zone of the SNNPR, was one of the largest investments and included massive irrigation and the construction of five new processing plants. The ESC contracted with METEC for the construction of the factories. The political logic of this cooperation was clear. Abay Tsehaye, one of the founders of the TPLF, was the director general of ESC, and Kinfe, another TPLF veteran, ran

METEC.[60] However, high-level TPLF sponsorship did not prevent a huge scandal and a series of arrests in 2018.

The EPRDF retained state ownership over key sectors of the economy. Most importantly, all land is owned by the state, giving the regime enormous control over the most essential national asset. The Ethiopian Privatization Agency has sold a number of previously government-owned assets, including through a variety of employee buyout schemes in cases of small hotels and shops. Mohammed Al Amoudi, the Saudi billionaire investor with close ties to the EPRDF, bought many of the larger assets—including hotels, tanneries, mining companies, and the Pepsi bottling company.[61] In all of these transactions, lack of government transparency led critics to question whether privatization was used to benefit ruling party supporters in a type of crony capitalism.[62]

The regime did not privatize certain parts of the economy. The government-owned Ethiopian Telecommunications Corporation was a monopoly that registered every SIM card and mobile phone and strictly monitored and regulated access to the internet, cutting it off during times of political crisis.[63] Mobile-phone penetration was much lower than the African average, and only 2.5 percent had access to the internet (in Kenya, by comparison, 40 percent had access).[64] Prime Minister Hailemariam Desalegn reportedly dubbed the telecom industry a "cash cow," generating more than $300 million for the government's coffers.[65]

Perceptions of corruption increased in the 2010s.[66] Many suggest that businesses owned by Tigrayans or by people close to the ruling party have tremendous advantages. There are periodic arrests of business and political leaders on charges of corruption, but the popular narrative is that the "big fish" are never charged and anyone who faces jail has fallen afoul of the EPRDF.[67] The Federal Ethics and Anti-Corruption Commission of Ethiopia had a high profile but was perceived by many as protecting powerful political interests.[68] It is notable, for example, that Siye and Abate Kisho (president of the SNNPR until 2001) were investigated for corruption only after falling out with Meles in 2001.

Transformation of the Countryside: Dam Building and Land Leasing

A particular manifestation of the developmental state and the regime's high modernist approach was Ethiopia's emphasis on large dams such as the Tendaho (on the Awash River in the East), Tekkeze (Africa's tallest dam, on a tributary to the Nile in the North), T'ana Beles (on the Blue Nile, or Abay, as it is called in Ethiopia), and most importantly the

GERD (on the Blue Nile/Abay). These projects had the potential to generate electricity needed domestically and also great potential as an export regionally. Along with electricity, the dams promised the possibility of large-scale irrigated agriculture for export using foreign capital, technology, and markets.

These megadams, however, also served as symbols of the powerful state and were the epitome of large, top-down, centrally controlled investments. In this way the developmental state's economic policies reinforced the centralizing logic of the EPRDF and caused tensions with the autonomous institutions put in place in the 1995 constitution. Regional state bureaus and local party officials generally were marginalized as Addis Ababa determined where to invest, whom to compensate, and who would receive the largest share of the benefits. The local residents of the areas along the rivers that were dammed, for example, generally were not consulted and received what many regarded as insufficient compensation for their lost livelihoods.

The GERD was expected to be the largest hydroelectric dam in Africa when completed. It was a matter of significant pride that voluntary contributions by Ethiopians, including many in the diaspora, financed the dam. Egypt objected to the dam, pointing to its need for the Nile water to survive and referencing earlier treaties (not signed by Ethiopia) that divided the water between Egypt and Sudan. Rainfall in the Ethiopian highlands represents 86 percent of the flow in the Nile River.[69] Addis Ababa has stated that the GERD will be used exclusively for producing electric power, not for irrigation, and that the water flow will not be affected, although Cairo has not indicated it accepts these assurances. The GERD was the emblematic image of the developmental state. Meles blasted anyone who raised questions about the dams. In 2010 he said of his critics: "They don't want to see developed Africa; they want us to remain undeveloped and backward to serve their tourists as a museum."[70]

The Gibe III dam was at the center of a major agricultural development project in southern Omo, in the SNNPR. The Kuraz Sugar Development Project was key to the GTP II plan to increase production, processing, and exports of sugar but was subject to serious delays and controversies over payments to military-controlled companies.[71] The vast scale of the project, including massive land clearance, irrigation, roads, housing and services for workers, and factory construction—and the remoteness of the region in southwestern Ethiopia, near the border with South Sudan—has hampered progress and resulted in missed deadlines. Plans included the villagization of the local population (predominantly small groups such as the Me'en/Bodi, Mursi, Nyangatom, and Suri), in what some activists have called forced eviction. In South Omo there were persistent reports of human rights violations but fewer reports of sustained protests.[72] The Gibe III dam ended the practice of flood-recession agriculture, and the movement of livestock was hindered by the new infrastructure. Furthermore, the project raised concerns about the environmental impact of the project on Omo National Park and the water flow into Lake Turkana, across the border in Kenya.[73]

Related to the investments in dams was the leasing of large tracts of land to domestic and foreign developers to encourage cash crop production for exportation. Rice, sugar, and crops for biofuel received major investments. The most important leases were in the regions along the border with South Sudan, particularly Gambela. However, controversies over what opponents called "land grabs" reinforced the narratives about corruption, lack of transparency, and the widespread perception that political and particularly Tigrayan elites at the center benefited, whereas those displaced were not consulted and received only token compensation. National regional states came under increased pressure to advocate for local priorities rather than the center's plans with regard to the distribution of the benefits of these developments.

In some cases the central government did not recognize pastoralists' or shifting cultivators' rights over land they did not use year-round. The EPRDF's development strategy never considered pastoralists an important element of its plans and had no long-term alternative to sedentarization.[74] The minister for agriculture and rural development was clear: "We are not really appreciating pastoralists remaining as they are. We have to improve their livelihood by creating job opportunities. Pastoralism, as it is, is not sustainable. We want to change the environment."[75]

In Gambela, Saudi Star, a company established by Saudi Ethiopian business tycoon Al-Amoudi, leased land to produce high-quality rice for the Saudi market. Local populations claimed their land was taken with minimal compensation. Anuak militants attacked the Saudi Star farm in April 2012. The Indian company Karuturi also leased, but did not develop, large blocks of land in Gambela and western Oromia.[76] In the Afar region, the large, state-owned ESC developed irrigated sugar plantations along the Awash River. There were clashes periodically when the Tendaho Dam was closed, preventing Afar herders from accessing water for their animals.

Regardless of the long-term or macrolevel improvements in Ethiopia's standard of living from these land leases, in the short run specific communities, particularly in Oromia and the developing regional states, suffered displacement and the loss of their livelihoods. Dessalegn Rahmato argues that the fundamental issue is how land rights belonging to individuals and communities were being transferred by the state without due compensation.[77] The activities under the GTP emphasized central investment and government determination of how costs were allocated and profits distributed, and in these ways reinforced the centralizing tendencies of the EPRDF.

Conclusion

Under the EPRDF, Ethiopia moved from an economy that had virtually collapsed under the Derg to one that showed important improvements in poverty reduction, the expansion of infrastructure, and early signs of new developments in energy and agricultural exports and processing. This transformation was driven in part by the EPRDF's ability to sustain general stability and attract donor support, along with its developmental state policies, which targeted state investments in key areas of infrastructure and rural development. At the same time, however, this economic system relied heavily on state resources and the activities of party- and military-run enterprises. Furthermore, many Ethiopians perceived that economic growth provided most of its benefits to a few political elites and those in Tigray, whereas the majority received meager compensation. These grievances were framed in general as allegations of corruption and in particular as unjustified displacement of populations without adequate compensation. Although the top-down economic policies of the developmental state reinforced the strong authoritarian political system of the EPRDF, the grievances about inequality fed mass protests and violence in 2016.

Notes

1. Göte Hansson, *The Ethiopian Economy, 1974–1994: Ethiopia Tikdem and After* (London: Routledge, 1995); David L. Bevan, "The Fiscal Dimensions of Ethiopia's Transition and Reconstruction," WIDER Discussion Paper No. 2001/56 (August 2001).

2. Nat Colleta, Markus Kostner, and Ingo Wiederhofer, *Case Studies in War to Peace Transition: The Demobilization and Reintegration of Ex-combatants in Ethiopia, Namibia, and Uganda* (Washington, DC: World Bank, 1996), 109.

3. Federal Democratic Republic of Ethiopia, *Foreign Affairs and National Security Policy and Strategy* (Addis Ababa: Federal Democratic Republic of Ethiopia, 2002), 37, http://www.aictda.gov.et/doc/Foreign-English-Policy.pdf.

4. Meles Zenawi, "African Development: Dead Ends and New Beginnings," paper presented at the Initiative for Policy Dialogue, Africa Task Force Meeting, University of Manchester, August 3–4, 2006.

5. Meles Zenawi, "States and Markets: Neoliberal Limitations and the Case for a Developmental State," in *Good Growth and Governance in Africa: Rethinking Development Strategies,* ed. Akbar Noman, Kwesi Botchwey, Howard Stein, and Joseph E. Stiglitz (Oxford, UK: Oxford University Press, 2012), 167.

6. Donald Donham, *Marxist Modern: An Ethnographic History of the Ethiopian Revolution* (Berkeley: University of California Press, 1999).

7. "Programme of the Ethiopian People's Revolutionary Democratic Front," *People's Voice: Publication of the Tigray People's Liberation Front* 11, no. 1, Special Issue (1989): 12.

8. Jean-Nicolas Bach, *"Abyotawi* Democracy: Neither Revolutionary nor Democratic—a Critical View of EPRDF's Conception of Revolutionary Democracy in Post-1991 Ethiopia," *Journal of Eastern African Studies* 5, no. 4 (2011): 644–645, makes a convincing argument that revolutionary democracy and liberalism are not opposites but rather feed each other.

9. Pramila Krishnan, Tesfaye Gebre Selassie, and Stefan Dercon, "The Urban Labour Market During Structural Adjustment: Ethiopia 1990–1997," WPS/98-1 (Oxford, UK: Centre for the Study of African Economics, 1998), 2.

10. Transitional Government of Ethiopia (TGE), *Ethiopia's Economic Policy During the Transitional Period* (Addis Ababa: TGE, November 1991), 15.

11. Ethiopian Ministry of Planning and Economic Development, "An Economic Development Strategy for Ethiopia: A Comprehensive Guidance and a Development Strategy for the Future" (Addis Ababa: Ethiopian Ministry of Planning and Economic Development, September 1993), 5; Stefan Dercon and Andrew Zeitlin, "Rethinking Agriculture and Growth in Ethiopia: A Conceptual Discussion," February 2009, 23, http://fac.dev.ids.ac.uk/pdf%20files/ethiopia%20paper1.pdf.

12. Davide Chinigò, "The Politics of Land Registration in Ethiopia: Territorialising State Power in the Rural Milieu," *Review of African Political Economy* 42, no. 144 (2015): 177.

13. Nita Bhalla, "War 'Devastated' Ethiopian Economy," *BBC News*, August 7, 2001, http://news.bbc.co.uk/2/hi/africa/1476618.stm.

14. Federal Democratic Republic of Ethiopia, Ministry of Finance and Economic Development, "A Plan for Accelerated and Sustained Development to End Poverty" (Addis Ababa: Federal Democratic Republic of Ethiopia, September 2006); Dercon and Zeitlin, "Rethinking Agriculture and Growth in Ethiopia."

15. Ethiopian Ministry of Finance and Economic Development, "Growth and Transformation Plan" (Addis Ababa: Ethiopian Ministry of Finance and Economic Development, 2010).

16. Arkebe Oqubay, *Made in Africa: Industrial Policy in Ethiopia* (Oxford, UK: Oxford University Press, 2015).

17. Chalmers Johnson, *MITI and the Japanese Miracle: The Growth of Industrial Policy, 1925–1975* (Palo Alto, CA: Stanford University Press, 1982).

18. Thandika Mkandawire, "Thinking About Developmental States in Africa," *Cambridge Journal of Economics* 25, no. 3 (2001): 289–314. On the related concept of developmental patrimonialism as applied in Africa, see David Booth and Frederick Golooba-Mutebi, "Developmental Patrimonialism? The Case of Rwanda," *African Affairs* 111 (2012): 379–403.

19. Cited in Lovise Aalen, "Ethiopia After Meles: Stability for How Long?" *Current History* 113 (May 2014): 194. This quote also exemplifies the EPRDF's hyperconfidence in its unique abilities.

20. Meles, "States and Markets," 140.

21. Meles, "States and Markets," 163. See also Arkebe, *Made in Africa*, for more comprehensive details.

22. David J. Spielman, Dawit Kelemwork Makonnen, and Dawit Alemu, "Seed, Fertilizer, and Agricultural Extension in Ethiopia," in *Food and Agriculture in Ethiopia: Progress and Policy Challenges,* ed. Paul A. Dorosh and Shahidur Rashid (Philadelphia: University of Pennsylvania Press, 2012).

23. Teferi Abate Adem, "The Local Politics of Ethiopia's Green Revolution in South Wollo," *African Studies Review* 55, no. 3 (December 2012): 81–102.

24. James C. Scott, *Seeing Like a State: How Certain Schemes to Improve the Human Condition Have Failed* (New Haven, CT: Yale University Press, 1999). As noted by Jon Abbink, "Modernization ideology is alive and well in Ethiopia, which . . . is showing itself to be a classic high-modernist state indeed, bent on technology-driven 'development' and top-down planning at all costs by a self-declared all-knowing state elite." Abbink, "Dam Controversies: Contested Governance and Developmental Discourse on the Ethiopian Omo River Dam," *Social Anthropology* 20, no. 2 (2012): 128.

25. Kaatje Seegers et al., "Be Like the Bees: The Politics of Mobilizing Farmers for Development in Tigray, Ethiopia," *Africa* 109, no. 430 (2009): 91–109.

26. Sabine Planel, "A View of a Bureaucratic Developmental State: Local Governance and Agricultural Extension in Rural Ethiopia," *Journal of Eastern African Studies* 8, no. 3 (2014): 420–437. See also Kassa Belay, "Constraints to Agricultural Extension Work in Ethiopia: The Insider's View," *South African Journal of Agricultural Extension* 31 (2002): 63–79.

27. Interviews with author, Amhara Region, 2016.

28. Ethiopian Ministry of Finance and Economic Development, "Growth and Transformation Plan."

29. Asnake Kefale, "Narratives of Developmentalism and Development in Ethiopia: Some Preliminary Explorations," paper presented at the Fourth European Conference on African Studies, Uppsala, Sweden, June 15–18, 2011, http://www.nai.uu.se/ecas-4/panels/41-60/panel-57/Asnake-Kefale-Full-paper.pdf.

30. René Lefort, "Free Market Economy, 'Developmental State,' and Party-State Hegemony in Ethiopia: The Case of the 'Model Farmers,'" *Journal of Modern African Studies* 50, no. 4 (2012): 681–706.

31. Desalegn Rahmato, *The Peasant and the State: Studies in Agrarian Change in Ethiopia, 1950s–2000s* (Addis Ababa: Addis Ababa University Press, 2009).

32. Paulos Chanie, "Clientelism and Ethiopia's Post-1991 Decentralization," *Journal of Modern African Studies* 45, no. 3 (September 2007): 355–384.

33. Davide Chinigò, "The Politics of Land Registration in Ethiopia: Territorialising State Power in the Rural Milieu," *Review of African Political Economy*, 42, no. 144 (2015): 183.

34. Davide Chinigò, "'The Peri-urban Space at Work': Micro and Small Enterprises, Collective Participation, and the Developmental State in Ethiopia," paper presented at the International Conference of Ethiopian Studies, Warsaw, 2015.

35. Peter Gill, *Famine and Foreigners: Ethiopia Since Live Aid* (Oxford, UK: Oxford University Press, 2010). Also REST officials, interviews with author, Addis Ababa, 2011.

36. For a description, see Relief Society of Tigray 2012 Annual Report, http://www.tigraionline.com/rest-annual-report-2012.pdf

37. Patrick Gilkes, cited in Sue Lautze, Angela Raven-Roberts, and Teshome Erkineh, *Humanitarian Governance in the New Millennium: An Ethiopian Case Study* (London: Humanitarian Policy Group, February 2009), 20.

38. Sue Lautze, Angela Raven-Roberts, and Teshome Erkineh, *Humanitarian Governance in the New Millennium: An Ethiopian Case Study* (London: Humanitarian Policy Group, February 2009).

39. Sarah Coll-Black, Daniel O. Gilligan, John F. Hoddinott, Neha Kumar, Alemayehu Seyoum Taffesse, and William Wiseman, "Targeting Food Security Interventions in Ethiopia: The Productive Safety Net Programme," in *Food and Agriculture in Ethiopia: Progress and Policy Challenges,* ed. Paul A. Dorosh and Shahidur Rashid (Philadelphia: University of Pennsylvania Press, 2012).

40. Federal Democratic Republic of Ethiopia, Ministry of Agriculture and Rural Development, *Productive Safety Net Programme: Programme Implementation Manual* (Addis Ababa: Federal Democratic Republic of Ethiopia, 2004), 2.

41. Tom Lavers, "Food Security and Social Protection in Highland Ethiopia: Linking the Productive Safety Net to the Land Question," *Journal of Modern Africa Studies* 51, no. 3 (2013): 459–485.

42. World Development Indicators, https://knoema.com/WBWDIGDF2017Jul /world-development-indicators-wdi.

43. Christine Hackenesch, *Competing for Development? The European Union and China in Ethiopia,* Discussion Paper 3/2011 (Stellenbosch: University of Stellenbosch, Centre for Chinese Studies, 2011); Agnieszka Paczynska, ed., *The New Politics of Aid: Emerging Donors and Conflict Assisted States* (Boulder, CO: Lynne Rienner, 2019).

44. US Embassy in Addis Ababa, "Party-Statals: How the Ruling Party's Endowments' Operate," cable, March 19, 2009, https://wikileaks.org/plusd /cables/09ADDISABABA677_a.html. Seye lost his position at EFFORT during the 2001 split within the TPLF. In this same cable, Seye confirms that the party-statals receive preferential treatment relative to private business enterprises.

45. In this section I draw upon Sarah Vaughan and Mesfin Gebremichael, *Rethinking Business and Politics in Ethiopia: The Role of EFFORT, the Endowment Fund for the Rehabilitation of Tigray,* Africa Power and Politics Program Research Report 2 (London: Overseas Development Institute, August 2011).

46. Cited in Daniel Berhane, "'TPLF Firms' Recovering from Debts, Losses: CEO Azeb Mesfin," Hornaffairs.com, August 13, 2014, http://hornaffairs .com/en/2014/08/13/ethiopia-tplf-effort-company-azeb-mesfin/; US Embassy in Addis Ababa, "Party-Statals."

47. Vaughan and Mesfin, *Rethinking Business and Politics in Ethiopia*, 33.

48. World Bank, *Toward the Competitive Frontier: Strategies for Improving Ethiopia's Investment Climate* (Washington, DC: World Bank, 2009), 58.

49. Omar Uliah, "Analysis: Inside the Controversial EFFORT," *Addis Standard,* January 16, 2017, http://addisstandard.com/analysis-inside-controversial-effort/.

50. Berhanu Abegaz, "Political Parties in Business: Rent Seekers, Developmentalists, or Both?" *Journal of Development Studies* 49, no. 11 (2011): 1467.

51. Abegaz, "Political Parties in Business," 1481.

52. Mitsutobo Matsumoto, "Political Democratization and KMT Party-owned Enterprises in Taiwan," *Developing Economies* 40, no. 3 (2002): 359–380.

53. EFFORT operates in ways similar to the Rwandan Patriotic Front's party-owned investment firm, Tri-State Investments/CVL. See Booth and Golooba-Mutebi, "Developmental Patrimonialism?"

54. Roger Southall, *Liberation Movements in Power: Party and State in Southern Africa* (Oxford, UK: James Currey, 2013), 277.

55. For background see METEC's homepage http://www.metec.gov.et/index .php/en/about-us. See also "State-Owned METEC Has Big Ideas," *Indian Ocean Newsletter,* 1362, August 30, 2013.

56. METEC's homepage, http://www.metec.gov.et/index.php/en/.

57. For some context see Erwin van Veen, *Perpetuating Power: Ethiopia's Political Settlement and the Organization of Security* (The Hague: Clingendael Institute, September 2016).

58. "Ethiopia: Boosting Sugar Industry," editorial, *Ethiopian Herald* (government-owned newspaper), March 4, 2016, http://allafrica.com/stories /201603041123.html.

59. William Davidson, "Ethiopian China-Backed Sugar-Export Hits Cash, Design Snags," *Bloomberg*, June 13, 2016, found at http://www.bloomberg.com /news/articles/2016-06-13/ethiopian-china-backed-sugar-export-push-hits-cash -design-snags.

60. In May 2016 the House of People's Delegates held a hearing to question the sugar corporation regarding its ability to meet only 44 percent of its annual plan and for the failure of METEC to deliver on its commitment with regard to the factory at Kuraz, despite having received 97 percent of its payment. Representatives of the sugar corporation suggested that they had no ability to take action against the military-run METEC for its failure to meet its obligations. See Benedikt Kamski, "The Kuraz Sugar Development Project (KSDP) in Ethiopia: Between 'Sweet Visions' and Mounting Challenges," *Journal of Eastern African Studies* 10, no. 3 (2016): 568–680. Scandals relating to METEC received considerable attention under Prime Minister Abiy Ahmed in 2018, and its leadership—including top TPLF military officials—was sacked and arrested.

61. For details, see US Embassy in Addis Ababa, "Privatization or Monopolization in Ethiopia?" January 11, 2008, https://www.wikileaks.org/plusd /cables/08ADDISABABA82_a.html. Al Amoudi was arrested and charged with corruption in Saudi Arabia in November 2017 and was held in the Ritz Carlton.

62. Mesfin Negash, "Rethinking Corporate Governance in Ethiopia," http:// ethiomedia.com/accent/rethinking_corporate_governance_in_ethiopia.pdf.

63. The economic costs of these shutdowns are large. See James Jeffrey, "Ethiopia's Internet Crackdown Hurts Everyone," *Integrated Regional Information Networks News*, November 17, 2016, https://www.irinnews.org/analysis /2016/11/17/ethiopia%E2%80%99s-internet-crackdown-hurts-everyone.

64. "Telecoms in Ethiopia: Out of Reach," *Economist* August 24, 2013.

65. "Telecoms in Ethiopia."

66. Janelle Plummer, ed., *Diagnosing Corruption in Ethiopia: Perceptions, Realities, and the Way Forward for Key Sectors* (Washington, DC: World Bank, 2012).

67. Aaron Maasho, "Ethiopia Arrests State Minister of Finance on Suspicion of Corruption," Reuters, August 4, 2017, https://www.usnews.com/news/world /articles/2017-08-04/ethiopia-state-minister-for-finance-arrested-on-corruption -charges-state-tv. See also interviews with author in Addis Ababa and Bahir Dar, 2011, 2015, 2016, 2017.

68. Regional states have established their own ethics commissions as well. Tewodros Mezmur and Raymond Koen, "The Ethiopian Federal Ethics and Law Anti-corruption Commission: A Critical Assessment," *Law, Democracy, and Development* 15 (2011): 1–29.

69. Michael Hammond, "The Grand Ethiopian Renaissance Dam and the Blue Nile: Implications for Transborder Water Governance," *Global Water Forum* (February 18, 2013), http://www.globalwaterforum.org/2013/02/18/the-grand-ethiopian-renaissance-dam-and-the-blue-nile-implications-for-transboundary-water-governance/.

70. Darren Taylor, "Huge Dam Endangers Thousands in Ethiopia and Kenya, Say Activists," Voice of America, April 7, 2011, http://www.voanews.com/content/huge-dam-endangers-thousands-in-ethiopia-and-kenya-say-activists—119465734/160054.html.

71. Kamski, "Kuraz Sugar Development Project (KSDP) in Ethiopia."

72. Human Rights Watch, *"What Will Happen If Hunger Comes?" Abuses Against the Indigenous Peoples of Ethiopia's Lower Omo Valley,* 2012, https://www.hrw.org/report/2012/06/18/what-will-happen-if-hunger-comes/abuses-against-indigenous-peoples-ethiopias-lower.

73. See Benedict Moran, "A Way of Life Under Threat in Kenya as Lake Turkana Shrinks," *Integrated Regional Information Networks News,* May 22, 2017, https://www.irinnews.org/feature/2017/05/23/way-life-under-threat-kenya-lake-turkana-shrinks. For dire projections of some of the dam's impact on the regional environment, see International Rivers' advocacy reporting, www.internationalrivers.org.

74. Tom Lavers, "Patterns of Agrarian Transformation in Ethiopia: State-mediated Commercialisation and the 'Land Grab,'" *Journal of Peasant Studies* 39, nos. 3–4 (2012): 799. See Meles Zenawi, Thirteenth Annual Pastoralists' Day celebration speech, Jinka, South Omo, January 25, 2011.

75. BBC, "Land Grab Fears for Ethiopian Rural Communities," December 16, 2010, http://www.bbc.com/news/business-11991926.

76. In March 2016, the Ethiopian government suspended India's Karuti Global contract for 100,000 hectares of land in western Gambela. Davidson, "Ethiopian China-Backed Sugar-Export Hits Cash, Design Snags."

77. Dessalegn Rahmato, "Land to Investors: Large-Scale Land Transfers in Ethiopia," paper presented at Forum for Social Science, Addis Ababa, 2011, http://www.landgovernance.org/system/files/Ethiopia_Rahmato_FSS_0.pdf.

8

Popular Uprising

In the aftermath of the May 2015 election, in which the Ethiopian People's Revolutionary Democratic Front (EPRDF) and its affiliates won 100 percent of the seats, Ethiopia appeared stable and the ruling party in firm control. Arriola and Lyons comment that the "elections confirm that authoritarian rule will persist in Africa's second most populous country for the foreseeable future."[1] By October 2016, however, the Ethiopian government was clearly in its worse crisis since coming to power in 1991. A wave of popular uprisings and violence began in Oromia, spread to the Amhara National Regional State (ANRS), and shook the country.[2] Regional officials in the Oromo People's Democratic Organization (OPDO) and the Amhara National Democratic Movement (ANDM), the two largest constituent parties in the ruling coalition, seemed incapable or unwilling to end the protests and reassert the center's authority. The EPRDF struggled to come up with a reasonable plan to deal with the crisis. The security forces made mass arrests and caused significant casualties. Most tragically, on October 2, 2016, the Oromo thanksgiving celebration, Irreecha, ended in tear gas, a stampede, and dozens if not hundreds of deaths. One week later, on October 9, the Ethiopian government announced a state of emergency.

The state of emergency was an extraordinary step that suggested the old ways of governing no longer could contain the protests or address the underlying grievances. Since coming to power in 1991, the EPRDF sustained its control by balancing two contradictory logics. The first was the centralizing, top-down logic of a strong authoritarian party that built upon the legacies of the armed struggle. The other was a logic based on ethnofederalism, institutionalized in ethnically defined regional states and parties, which contributed to identity politics. In 2016, efforts by the center to reestablish the balance between these two dynamics and roll back the gains made by the centrifugal forces of autonomy failed. The inability either to repress or co-opt dissent without deploying the state's coercive apparatus suggested that the principles that governed Ethiopian politics since 1991 had lost their equilibrium and that the post-1991 dispensation was at risk of collapse.

The 2016 crisis helps one see both the contradictory dynamics operating in Ethiopia and the challenges of either rebalancing these dynamics or finding a new modus vivendi to retain the EPRDF's domination. The ruling party had increasingly begun to operate as a coalition of four different member parties, each with specific identities, interests, and leadership claims. The massive protests both reflected and accelerated a crisis of legitimacy for the EPRDF. At the same time, however, the confrontations on the streets allowed elements within two of its key members—the OPDO and ANDM—to construct new populist claims of legitimacy and challenge the old distribution of power within the coalition. The demonstrations, therefore, had the capacity to undermine the past political order and create opportunities for new leadership to rebalance the party and sustain its domination.

Waves of Protests

The underlying grievances in Ethiopia are easier to identify than answers regarding the timing and the dynamics of the wave of popular protests in 2016. Despite figures suggesting rapid overall growth in the economy from 2005 to 2015, unemployment—particularly youth unemployment—remained high. Many people in rural areas saw few prospects for economic advancement, and even those who could find jobs as casual laborers had no job security or benefits. The insistent government-sponsored narrative about the "Ethiopian Renaissance," when contrasted with the people's experience of everyday poverty, generated cynicism and despair. "We can't eat GDP growth!" said some desperate citizens. In urban areas, inflation was a major concern, even among professionals, and housing was unaffordable. There were particular frustrations among the increasing numbers of young people who had the opportunity to attend university but lacked the prospect of meaningful employment after graduation. Increased urbanization, education, literacy, and mobility created rising expectation the Ethiopian economy struggled to meet and the political system could not manage. Most dangerously, these economic grievances were linked to a pervasive perception that most of the benefits of economic development had gone to Tigray or to a few corrupt elites collaborating with the Tigray People's Liberation Front (TPLF).

These economic hardships overlay deep resentment related to the lack of political space and freedoms. The ruling party restricted civil society, the media, and opposition political parties in ways that many Ethiopians perceived as unfair. The EPRDF had created a rigid political system with limited resilience. As indicated dramatically in 2005, many Ethiopians wished to be represented by a party other than the EPRDF. The 2010 and 2015 elections had led many Ethiopians to conclude that change through electoral processes was impossible. Many disengaged from electoral politics or resigned themselves to joining the ruling party as a necessary condition for professional advancement or access to land, fertilizer, and government services. A few took up arms and threatened to remove the regime by any means necessary.

Precedents and Past Protests

Since 1991, opposition in Ethiopia took a number of forms, and the EPRDF marginalized each in turn. In 1992 the Oromo Liberation Front (OLF) engaged in a short war with the EPRDF but quickly lost its military capacity. Similarly, the Ogaden National Liberation Front (ONLF) collapsed as a military threat in the face of a successful—but brutal—counterinsurgency campaign in 2007. Efforts to compel the EPRDF to participate in all-party national conferences failed, as with the 1993 Paris Conference and the efforts led by the Carter Center and the US Congressional Task Force on Ethiopia in the early 1990s. The prospects for opposition parties to find avenues to influence their government through elections seemed promising in 2005 but soon collapsed in the face of the postelection crisis, arrests, and criminalization of dissent.[3]

Demonstrations in 2012 by Ethiopian Muslims, who make up approximately 40 percent of the population, provided another model of politics outside of the vanguard ruling party. The demonstrations began in response to government interference in the Ethiopian Islamic Affairs Supreme Council. The movement was extraordinarily disciplined and nonviolent and succeeded in part by focusing on a specific set of issues framed as nonpolitical. Creative new models of demonstrations, such as mass marches following Friday prayers and holding up "yellow cards" to suggest the government was being given a warning as in a football match, seemed to suggest wider opportunities for nonviolent mobilization. Muslim activists insisted they operated within the framework of the Ethiopian constitution and were not linked to foreign extremists, despite repeated but specious allegations from the government. The documentary "Jihadist Crackdown," screened on Ethiopia's state-run television network, linked the Ethiopian Muslim protests to

Boko Haram and compared the protests in Ethiopia with violence in Nigeria and elsewhere.[4]

Demonstrations were held after Friday prayers in Addis Ababa and, notably, in other towns across Ethiopia. An arbitration committee of elders stepped forward to engage with the regime. Rather than accept their suggestion to hold talks with a key constituency, however, the EPRDF treated Muslim leaders as criminals working against the interests of peace and development. In August 2015, courts in Ethiopia sentenced eighteen leaders to twenty-two years in prison each for terrorism.[5] The EPRDF previously had marginalized armed resistance, calls for third-party negotiations, and opposition party participation in elections. Now it had criminalized and suppressed the model of organized, peaceful, constitutional, narrowly focused, multiethnic protests.

The Oromo Protests of 2016

The next important round of demonstrations took place in Oromia and not only reflected current demands for equal treatment and economic opportunities but also resonated with deep historical grievances of Oromo marginalization. The immediate spark was the April 2014 leak of draft plans many Oromos perceived as designed to expand the jurisdiction of the Addis Ababa federal district at the expense of some of the most industrialized—and hence valuable—areas of Oromia. What was framed as a technocratic document to integrate infrastructure and services highlighted contrasting narratives about whether the centralized developmental state or identity politics and ethnic autonomy would shape Ethiopia's political future. Addis Ababa—or Finfine, as some called it in reference to its original Afan Oromo name—had long been an important and contentious symbol for many Oromos.[6] Section 49(5) of the 1995 Constitution states, "The special interest of the state of Oromia in Addis Ababa, regarding the provision of social services or the utilization of natural resources and other similar matters, as well as joint administrative matters arising from the location of Addis Ababa within the state of Oromia, shall be respected." In 2000 the EPRDF announced its intention to move the capital of Oromia to Adama, setting off violent demonstrations by Oromos who saw this as an effort to undermine Oromo claims on Addis Ababa. In addition to these symbolic issues, a number of midlevel OPDO cadres had been engaged in brokering lucrative business deals and land contracts in the *woredas* adjacent to Addis Ababa, and it seemed these Oromo elites risked being bypassed if the areas were removed from Oromia's jurisdiction. In April and May 2014, deadly protests erupted on college campuses in western Oromia (in Ambo, Nekemte, and Jimma) but were quickly suppressed.[7]

In November 2015, another round of protests broke out in Ginchi, a small town west of Addis Ababa where the government allegedly planned to clear a forest to make room for a development project.[8] The protests rapidly spread across Oromia, often erupting in relatively small towns. News of different protests soon spread through social media and diaspora-based news sites. The demonstrations received widespread international attention when Feyissa Lilesa crossed the finish line in second place at the 2016 Olympics marathon and flashed the crossed arms symbol to show solidarity with the Oromo protests.

Although connected by a common narrative about historical marginalization, the protests also focused on specific complaints regarding working conditions and control of land.[9] Protests in the Guji zone, for example, mentioned conditions for gold miners in Shakiso, and protests in West Wellega similarly targeted the marble mine near Mendi. One of the largest demonstrations in Ambo mobilized an estimated 25,000 people and spilled into the city center, where government buildings were damaged. Farmers in Gudet protested that OPDO officials enriched themselves selling land on the edge of town to developers and using the profits to build homes near the capital.[10] On August 6, 2016, protesters demonstrated in some two hundred towns across the Oromia region.[11] In some cases foreign investments, such as floriculture enterprises, were the focus of demonstrations, particularly regarding compensation for leased land and unregulated environmental degradation.[12] In some cases the protests took an anti-Tigray turn and targeted buses built by TPLF-owned companies and threatened Tigray businesspeople. In other places demonstrators looted local government offices; in Ejere they burned down the homes of local officials.[13] The protests, therefore, were driven by localized economic grievances but were connected across Oromia and in the diaspora by a shared narrative of historical marginalization and perceptions that corruption benefited TPLF leaders.

Local OPDO authorities at first appeared helpless and disoriented, either unable or unwilling to restore order.[14] Although some in the EPRDF leadership condemned the demonstrations, others in the OPDO began to speak sympathetically of them.[15] OPDO authorities reportedly turned a blind eye to the protests in some instances. In other cases security forces—often the Ethiopian federal police rather than the Oromia regional police—responded with deadly fire. Civilians in small towns in places such as Dodola (West Arsi), Boru Jawi (East Arsi), and Haramaya (East Hararghe), did not back down when police were sent to quell the disturbances.[16] Many protesters were high school students, and some were even younger. No overarching body coordinated the protests, but rather young people mobilized spontaneously in reaction to hearing about others protesting.[17] Over time a group of young activists known as the Qeerroo began coordinating the events. In the past, security forces making mass arrests suppressed demonstrations. In 2016, however, protests spread and escalated.

The unrest predominantly occurred across Oromia, with some notable events in the ANRS as well. Despite the diversity within Oromia, demonstrations took place in areas populated by Muslims, Orthodox Christians, and protestants, in areas of settled agriculturalism and pastoralism, in urban areas, and in small rural market towns. Although the crisis threatened the EPRDF as a ruling party, the demonstrations and the violence were less evident in the regional states of Tigray and the Southern Nations, Nationalities, and People's Region (SNNPR).

The Oromo protests were transnational in that they seemed both inspiring to and inspired by young diaspora nationalists operating on social media. The Oromo Media Network (OMN) and Facebook and Twitter accounts linked disparate protests and coordinated solidarity rallies in major Western capitals. Individuals such as OMN's Jawar Mohammed; Awol Allo, who often wrote for *Al Jazeera*; and Mohammed Ademo, editor of OPride.com articulated a renewed sense of Oromo nationalism. Oromo nationalists declared, "I am an Oromo first!" and provoked those who insisted on a unified Ethiopian identity. Cooperation between disaffected Oromo students on the streets across Oromia and savvy mobilizers operating from media platforms in the diaspora challenged the OPDO by making it difficult for the party to be simultaneously loyal to the EPRDF in the center and responsive to the Oromos on the street.[18]

The regime responded as it had to political protests following the 2005 elections and the Muslim protests of 2012. It characterized the demonstrators as enemies working with foreign interests seeking to destabilize Ethiopia and derail the government's progress. Government spokesperson Getachew Reda, for example, claimed naive protesters had been misled by radical, antipeople terrorists working on behalf of "narrow nationalists" and external enemies such as Eritrea.[19] Authorities used mass arrests and deadly force to regain control of the streets. The government closed down key social media sites, notably WhatsApp and Twitter, to prevent access to news and interrupt the coordination of demonstrations. As federal police stepped in to replace Oromia regional police reluctant to break up demonstrations, arrests and casualties increased.

The tragic climax of this phase of mobilization took place in early October 2016, when significant casualties occurred in Bishoftu. These deaths occurred during the symbolically important Irreecha holidays, a time of thanksgiving for the harvest for many Oromos. Huge crowds of pilgrims gathered on the banks of Lake Hora, a crater lake, for ritual washing. Not surprisingly, given the tense atmosphere and the demonstrations suppressed violently across Oromia the prior year, many participants chanted antiregime slogans and crossed their arms as a sign of defiance. At one point, a young man from the crowd jumped onstage, grabbed the microphone, and began shouting "Down, Down Woyane" (a common nickname for the TPLF). The crowd began to surge, and security personnel set off tear gas, presumably to disperse the crowd. In the ensuing—and unsurprising—stampede, more than fifty and perhaps several hundred pilgrims died.[20]

The demonstrations created a crisis within the OPDO and thus within the larger EPRDF coalition. The independent newsmagazine *Addis Standard* commented, "The current Oromo protests have, more than any time in the past, . . . opened the doors for sincere reflections on the legitimacy and relevance of the party that constitutes the larger share to the coalition of the ruling EPRDF."[21] Without a unified Oromo wing, the EPRDF could not function as a national party. At the same time, however, the OPDO could not exist as more than a regional party, cut off from national resources and patronage and without its connection to the ruling coalition. OPDO leaders faced criticism that they exhibited "narrow nationalism" if they advanced Oromo interests, demonstrating their autonomy and legitimacy. At the same time, they risked denunciation from Oromo activists as puppets of the *neftenya* if they remained loyal to the EPRDF and did not promote Oromo interests. In 2016 and 2017, however, some leaders such as Lemma Megersa (president of Oromia) and Abiy Ahmed (deputy president of Oromia) sought to strengthen their authority and position the OPDO against the TPLF by aligning with the populist demands of the Oromo street protesters.

Amhara National Regional State Protests

During the early summer of 2016, the ANRS seemed relaxed compared with Oromia.[22] By July, however, a specific controversy over whether the Welkait zone should be part of Tigray or ANRS sparked a protest.[23] Violence erupted when security forces sought to arrest the leaders of the Welkait Amhara Identity Committee, and major demonstrations followed in Gondar and Bahir Dar.[24] Members of the ANDM joined the demonstrators in support of this symbolic cause for many Amharas.

Political leaders emphasized their differences with the TPLF as a means to accelerate Amhara identity construction. Amharas who perceived their political leaders as having served twenty-five years as the TPLF's junior partner were frustrated, and they welcomed the opportunity to demonstrate their Amhara pride. Social media broadcast videos of Amhara demonstrators shooting automatic weapons in the air, which had not occurred during Oromo protests. Such an open display of weapons in a demonstration indicated to EPRDF leaders that conflict in the Amhara region had significant potential to escalate and that the ANDM might no longer be a reliable partner.

The ANDM had its origins in the Ethiopian People's Revolutionary Party (EPRP) and had joined the EPRDF as the multiethnic Ethiopian People's Democratic Movement (EPDM). Ethiopian nationalist and Amhara identities are intertwined in ways that have made mobilizing as Amharas difficult. In the mid-2010s, however, a new process of identity construction among Amharas began to develop. In the diaspora, leaders who had long insisted on an Ethiopian identity began to emphasize their "Amharaness" and insist on Amhara rights as a nationality distinct from that of Ethiopia.[25] On social media, the hashtag #AmharaResistance sought to connect the protests in Gondar and Bahir Dar to identity building.[26]

The ANDM went through a process of recasting its origins and developed a new narrative about Amhara nationalism. Instead of emphasizing the TPLF's role in creating the ANDM, the party highlighted its independent role in the armed struggle against the Derg. The ANDM thirty-fifth anniversary celebrations in November 2015, for example, were replete with such references. The head of the ANDM Central Committee office emphasized that the ANDM "gave sanctuaries to TPLF fighters who were strategically backpedaling" as the Derg launched a major offensive. TPLF fighters bristled at claims that they had ever "backpedaled."[27] Key TPLF leaders began to label popular ANRS president Gedu Andargachew and other reformers "Amhara chauvinists" who "pined for the old order."[28] As with the OPDO officials, some ANDM leaders aligned themselves with the populist mood on the streets rather than with orders from Addis Ababa to reimpose control. With both the OPDO and ANDM—the two largest member parties in the coalition—looking toward their bases and identity politics for legitimacy, the EPRDF centralizing project was at risk of collapse.

SNNPR Protests

Protests in the SNNPR received far less attention than the Oromia and Amhara protests. Mobilization in the SNNPR during 2016 followed yet another, more locally focused dynamic. The Konso people protested the creation of the Segen Area People's Zone, which merged Konso, Dirashe, Amaro, and Burji special woredas. Some Konsos believed this would disadvantage them.[29] Contention around inter- and intraregional borders was a constant source of conflict because each border created "winners" and "losers," generally perceived in ethnic terms. Attachment to an SNNPR identity was much weaker than attachment to the Tigray, Amhara, and Oromia National Regional States. The Konso demonstrations were led by traditional leaders as opposed to the more diffuse mobilization in the Oromia and Amhara regions. The EPRDF's failure to consult them before creating the new zone sparked the protests. Police arrests of these traditional leaders resulted in escalation. For example, in March 2016 Kala Gezahegn, a Konso traditional leader, was arrested while seeking to engage in talks with SNNPR authorities. Thousands took to the streets to protest, three persons reportedly were killed, and the dispute subsequently became more entrenched.[30]

The Konso protests received little notice in the main diaspora media. Although there were intense debates about the relationships between the protests in Oromia and Amhara regions, few noted the demonstrations in the SNNPR. Despite the transformation of ethnic relations since 1991, political discourse in the center largely ignored the SNNPR and the developing regional states (Afar, Somali, Gambela, and Benishangul-Gumuz). In a moment of heightened identity politics, for instance, the Southern Ethiopian People's Democratic Movement (SEPDM) amalgamation of small ethnic groups riven by rivalries made it hard for southerners to take up national leadership roles. Conflicts between Sidama and Wolayita and a host of other rivalries had the potential to escalate, and this always made the SNNPR a difficult base upon which to build power.

The State of Emergency

By fall 2016 violence had spread throughout the Oromia and Amhara regions and reached its symbolic height in the deaths at the Irreecha festival. In October 2016, the EPRDF regime declared a state of emergency to restore order. The decree was extraordinarily broad in its provisions. It allowed the government, in the form of command posts under the authority of the Ethiopian National Defense Force (ENDF), to spread out across the country, arrest without a court order, enforce a curfew, and ban a full range of political activities. In many ways, the decree put in place de facto martial law. The EPRDF claimed the state of emergency was necessary because externally supported extremists had taken over what had started as legitimate expression of grievances. The EPRDF pointed to alleged acts of extreme violence and stated that the government's loss of control of the countryside made the declaration necessary, a narrative distinctly different from the "Ethiopia Rising" story the regime had promoted for so many years, essential for attracting foreign investment.[31]

Under the state of emergency, tens of thousands of civilians were detained without trials and held in reeducation camps. In the Tolay military camp in southwestern Oromia, for example, detainees spent a month learning about the benefits of the "Ethiopian Renaissance" and the dangers of "color revolutions." Prime Minister Hailemariam Desalegn attended the "graduation" ceremony marking their release, reminded the former detainees of their constitutional right to free expression, and simultaneously warned them that they would "pay a price" if they ever resorted to violence. Graduates even received T-shirts emblazoned with the slogan "Never Again." According to an Ethiopian journalist present for the occasion, "For many observers, there was a cruel irony to seeing a government educating people about their right to protest, having imprisoned thousands over the past few months for exercising it."[32]

The EPRDF framed the state of emergency as a means to restore order so it could "improve service delivery," addressing what the regime regarded as the population's economic grievances. Some within the regime insisted the only problems facing Ethiopia were "threats related to lack of good governance, rent-seeking, and corruption that are the results of the wrong perception of leadership."[33] Some characterized the demonstrations as a "bump in the road" in fulfilling the promise of the developmental state.[34] In private discussions, top EPRDF leaders expressed, "We know that we are 100 percent responsible for the crisis in Oromia. We alone will fix it."[35] It was possible, with this orientation, for the party to admit mistakes without altering its way of operating. Protesters were simply ill informed and exploited by enemies of Ethiopia.

The state of emergency was not necessary for the regime to employ its coercive apparatus against demonstrators. In fact, the regime had set up command posts, arrested thousands, and cut social media connections prior to the declaration. Declaring a state of emergency was necessary, however, to signal key parts of the ANDM and OPDO that they would be sidelined in managing the affairs of their respective regions and that the federal government would now end the demonstrations the regional governments were unwilling to contain. The EPRDF, from the center, saw armed ANDM militias protecting mass demonstrations in Bahir Dar calling for the return of land in the Tigray National Regional State and rec-

ognized this as an unprecedented challenge from the regional party structures against central control. Officials in the OPDO tolerated antiregime
protests, some of which targeted Tigrayan or foreign investments. Many
in the ruling party felt it necessary for the center to discipline these significant elements in the coalition by rolling back some of the authority
built up in the regional states and parties. Disorder on the streets and
challenges within the party were connected.

After declaring the state of emergency, the EPRDF announced it was
engaging in a process of "deep reform," but its proposed changes did not
address the core, structural challenges facing the regime. The regime
called on the people to redouble their efforts against chauvinism and
parochialism in support of the Growth and Transformation Plan (GTP).[36]
The party promised an "inclusive political dialogue" but did not change
the civil society and antiterrorism proclamations or release key political
prisoners. Rather than interpreting the wave of protests as a clear signal
that the relationship between the ruling party and the population needed
to be restructured, the EPRDF recommitted itself to its existing policies
and patterns of governance and to small technocratic, course corrections.
In August 2017, the regime lifted the state of emergency.[37]

The federal project at the center of the 1995 Constitution had, as
one of its stated goals, empowered political institutions and bureaucracies based in the ethnically defined regional states. Not surprisingly,
after twenty-five years these regional states developed their own identities and political agendas. By 2016 the sense of Oromo nationalism
and Amhara identity threatened the center, and the center fought back.
Key leaders in the OPDO and ANDM, however, had gained sufficient
legitimacy by aligning with the protesters and reformers in the party
that they could retain their positions.

In late 2016, therefore, the EPRDF was in a two-pronged crisis of
popular mobilization that could only be contained through a state of
emergency and elements within the ruling coalition who perceived that
aligning with populist sentiments had political advantages. The intra-
EPRDF coalition dynamics that had favored the TPLF and the strong
center had collapsed as the OPDO and ANDM increasingly pursued
their own agendas. Although the different member parties had increasingly open disagreements with each other, they also depended on the
larger coalition to survive. The EPRDF needed the OPDO, or it lacked
an instrument to govern Ethiopia's largest region. The OPDO could not
function outside of the ruling coalition, or it would lose its raison
d'être relative to competing Oromo parties without an alliance with
northern political interests.

In December 2017, the EPRDF's Executive Committee met behind closed doors for eighteen days to devise a response to the ongoing crisis. Although the party accepted responsibility for the emergency, it reaffirmed that its own ideology and political path was fundamentally correct. It also used blunt language to promise that "all forms of protest, [and] resistance, will be stopped" and to state that "all national parties should relentlessly struggle against all parasites [i.e., corrupt officials] in their respective states which they govern."[38] Repression and mass arrests failed in 2016 and 2017, but the ruling party seemed to redouble its commitment to use force. On February 15, 2018, Hailemariam resigned, reportedly forced out by his wing of the ruling coalition for failing to advocate effectively for the region's interests. This announcement was surprising in its timing, but Hailemariam was a relatively weak placeholder who recently had lost influence to the military and intelligence services. Hailemariam later suggested that the TPLF's continued hold on power made it impossible for him to move forward with reforms.[39] There was no clear successor within the party.

Fundamentally the EPRDF coalition lost popular legitimacy, but some of its constituent parties increased their local authority by aligning with growing nationalism, populism, and calls for deep political reform. The resignation of Hailemariam further emboldened the opposition and made it harder for the regime to return to the prior order based on strong central control. In recognition of the continuing crisis, the EPRDF reimposed the state of emergency following Hailemariam's resignation.

Conclusion

The EPRDF's rapid shift from winning 100 percent of the seats in the May 2015 elections to declaring two states of emergency in an incomplete effort to regain control over the street protests demonstrated both the strength and vulnerability of the ruling party. The party encompassed two dynamics in tension. On the one hand the party exemplified centralized, top-down, disciplined administration, reflecting in part its origins in the victorious insurgent movement. At the same time, the ruling coalition encompassed four diverse, ethnically defined parties and a constitutional order that empowered ethnically defined regional states. From 1995 to 2015, the strong center kept the centrifugal pressures in check, but by 2016 the grievances exploded and leaders with bases of power in the regional states perceived political options beyond patient loyalty to the center. In Oromia, historical narratives of marginalization, along with more contemporary competition over the fruits of regional development and the role the OPDO should play, fed a set of locally organized demonstrations that began peacefully but were met with repression and escalated into widescale violence. In the Amhara region, the local perception that the ANDM should demonstrate that it was willing to fight for Amhara interests fed a conflict over a border region with Tigray that quickly escalated into massive demonstrations and violence. In Konso, along the Somali-Oromia border, and elsewhere in Ethiopia, the central government's ability to manage dynamics in the regional states faced new limits, and regionally based leaders asserted remarkable independence.

Notes

1. Leonardo R. Arriola and Terrence Lyons, "Ethiopia: The 100% Election." *Journal of Democracy,* 27, no. 1 (January 2016): 76.

2. Adam Branch and Zachariah Mampilly, *Africa Uprising: Popular Protests and Political Change* (London: Zed, 2015).

3. Asnake Kefale, "The (Un)making of Opposition Coalitions and the Challenge of Democratization in Ethiopia, 1991–2011," *Journal of Eastern African Studies* 5, no. 4 (2011): 681–701.

4. "Ethiopia's Muslim Protests," *Integrated Regional Information Networks News,* November 15, 2012, http://www.irinnews.org/analysis/2012/11/15 /ethiopia%E2%80%99s-muslim-protests.

5. "Ethiopia: Federal High Court Found Kedir Mohammed Yusuf et al. Guilty of Terrorism, Violating Penal Code," *Addis Standard,* December 21, 2016. For context, see Terje Østebø, "Salafism, State Politics, and the Question of 'Extremism' in Ethiopia." *Comparative Islamic Studies* 8, nos. 1– 2 (2014): 165–184; Jon Abbink, "Religious Freedom and Political Order: The Ethiopian 'Secular State' and the Containment of Muslim Identity Politics," *Journal of Eastern African Studies* 8, no. 3 (2014): 346–365.

6. Other cities with large Oromo populations such as Harar and Dire Dawa had been carved out of the Oromia National Regional State earlier.

7. Human Rights Watch, *Ethiopia: Brutal Crackdown on Protests*, May 5, 2014, https://www.hrw.org/news/2014/05/05/ethiopia-brutal-crackdown-protests. See also Paul O'Keefe, "Ethiopia Crackdown on Student Protests Taints Higher Education Success," *Guardian,* May 22, 2014, https://www.theguardian.com /global-development/poverty-matters/2014/may/22/ethiopia-crackdown-student -protest-education.

8. Mahlet Fasil and Tsedale Lemma, "Oromo Protests: Defiance Amidst Pain and Suffering," *Addis Standard,* December 16, 2015, http://addisstandard .com/oromo-protests-defiance-amidst-pain-and-suffering/.

9. Michael Day, "Ethiopia Security Forces Kill up to 50 People in Crackdown on Peaceful Protests," *Independent,* December 17, 2015.

10. William Davidson, "How Long Can Ethiopia's State of Emergency Keep the Lid on Anger?" *Guardian,* February 12, 2017, https://www.theguardian .com/global-development/2017/feb/12/ethiopia-state-of-emergency-anger-oromo -people?CMP=share_btn_fb.

11. Awol Allo, "Ethiopia's Unprecedented Nationwide Oromo Protest: Who, What, Why?" *African Arguments,* August 8, 2016, http://africanarguments.org/2016

/08/06/ethiopias-unprecedented-nationwide-oromo-protests-who-what-why/. See also Opride, "Several Dozens Killed as #OromoProtests Sweep Oromia," https://www.opride.com/2016/08/06/oromoprotests-all-you-need-to-know-live-blog/.

12. Human Rights Watch, *"Such a Brutal Crackdown": Killings and Arrests in Response to Ethiopia's Oromo Protests* (New York: Human Rights Watch, 2016), 14.

13. Paul Schemm, "A State of Emergency Has Brought Calm to Ethiopia, but Don't Be Fooled," *Washington Post,* December 24, 2016.

14. Kalkidan Yibeltal and Tesfalem Waldyes, "OPDO: Lost, Confused, and at a Crossroads," *Addis Standard,* August 15, 2016, http://addisstandard.com/opdo-lost-confused-crossroads-2/.

15. Lemma Megersa, then the speaker of the Caffee Oromia (the Oromia Regional State Assembly), reportedly said, "As far as the Integrated Master Plan is concerned, even if it is for the benefit of the Oromo people, even if it were to pour gold on us, it will not be implemented if rejected by the public." TPLF stalwart Abay Tsehaye, however, insisted the plan would be implemented regardless of public opinion, and the ruling authorities would "mercilessly silence" those who dared to oppose it. See timeline in https://www.opride.com/2016/03/24/purging-opdo-and-rhetorical-gymnastics-won-t-quell-oromo-protests/.

16. For detailed data on time, place and, casualties, see the ACLED database, https://www.acleddata.com/data/.

17. Many claimed that the Qeerroo, a traditional age set of young Oromo men, played a key role in coordinating these protests, but it seems the Qeerroo was more a consequence than an instigator of the uprising.

18. William Davison, "Oromo Nationalism on the Rise in Ethiopia," Al Jazeera, August 1, 2014, http://www.aljazeera.com/indepth/features/2014/07/oromo-nationalism-rise-ethiopia-201472981456841809.html.

19. Getachew said, "An organized and armed terrorist force aiming to create havoc and chaos has begun murdering farmers, public leaders, and other ethnic groups residing in the region." *Sudan Tribune,* "Ethiopia's Opposition Leaders Implicated in Oromia Violence," February 28, 2016, http://sudantribune.com/spip.php?frame&page-imprimable&id_article=58167. "Narrow nationalist" is the label usually applied to the Oromo Liberation Front.

20. Many reports claim much higher casualties. For a moving account and pictures from Zacharia Abubeker, a photographer on the scene, see http://zachabubeker.com/news/irreecha. Abubeker wrote, "It was difficult to determine if people were surprised that protest had manifested and continued to grow, or if they had hopefully anticipated this event."

21. Kalkidan and Tesfalem, "OPDO."

22. The author spent two weeks in May 2016 teaching at Bahir Dar University, where things appeared relaxed.

23. This area had been part of the Amhara-dominated Gondar region until 1991, and its population became majority Tigray as a result of the resettlement of Tigray refugees along the rich agricultural land on the border with Sudan. For context, see Laura Hammond, *This Place Will Become Home: Refugee Repatriation to Ethiopia* (Ithaca, NY: Cornell University Press, 2004).

24. BBC, "Ethiopia Protests: 'Nearly 100 Killed' in Oromia and Amhara," August 8, 2016, http://www.bbc.com/news/world-africa-37015055.

25. René Lefort, "Ethiopia's Crisis," OpenDemocracy, November 19, 2016, https://www.opendemocracy.net/ren-lefort/ethiopia-s-crisis.

26. For a sample of the often convoluted diaspora debates, see Seifu Adem, "War of Words Between AG7 (ESAT) and Leaders of #AmharaResistance," November 20, 2016, http://ayyaantuu.net/war-of-words-between-ag7-esat-and -leaders-of-amhararesistance/. Amhara nationalism in the diaspora often built upon fears that the Orthodox Christian church was under attack by Muslims and evangelical Christians.

27. Daniel Beyene, "Ethiopia: ANDM Anniversary Augments Democratic Nationalism," *Ethiopian Herald,* November 10, 2015, http://allafrica.com/stories /201511100713.html.

28. See Amanuel Tesfaye, "Commentary: The Birth of Amhara Nationalism— Causes, Aspirations, and Potential Impacts," *Addis Standard,* May 4, 2018, http://addisstandard.com/commentarythe-birth-of-amhara-nationalism-causes -aspirations-and-potential-impacts/.

29. Abate Seyoum, "Ethiopia: What Was Troubling Konso?" *Addis Standard,* April 25, 2016, http://allafrica.com/stories/201604251712.html.

30. William Davidson, "Ethiopia's Clampdown on Dissent Tests Ethnic Federal Structure," *Guardian,* April 8, 2016, https://www.theguardian.com /global-development/2016/apr/08/ethiopia-clampdown-dissent-ethnic-federal -structure. See also Association for Human Rights in Ethiopia, "AHRE Urges Ethiopia to End the Atrocities and Human Rights Abuses Against the Konso People," September 20, 2016, https://ahrethio.org/2016/09/20/ahre-urges-ethiopia -to-end-the-atrocities-and-human-rights-abuses-against-the-konso-people/.

31. Interviews with author, Washington, DC, October 2016. See also the letter to the editor by an official at the Ethiopian embassy in Washington, DC. Tesfaye Wolde, "Ethiopia's State of Emergency Will Work," *Washington Post,* October 16, 2016, https://www.washingtonpost.com/opinions/ethiopias-state -of-emergency-will-work/2016/10/16/52f87c0a-923b-11e6-bc00-1a9756d4111b _story.html?utm_term=.3ce0d2c62f3d.

32. Kalkidan Yibeltal, "Never Again? Inside Ethiopia's 'Retraining' Programme for Thousands of Detained Protesters," *African Arguments*, January 28, 2017, http://africanarguments.org/2017/01/26/never-again-inside-ethiopias-retraining -programme-for-thousands-of-detained-protesters/.

33. "Ethiopia: Deep Reform Improving Economic Environment," *Ethiopian Herald*, May 21, 2017.

34. High-level EPRDF official, interview with author, Addis Ababa, 2016.

35. Interviews with author, Washington and New York, 2017.

36. Bilal Derso, "Ethiopia: EPRDF to Expand, Consolidate Deep Reform," *Ethiopian Herald,* March 9, 2017.

37. Felix Horne, "State of Emergency Ends in Ethiopia: Government Should Use Reform, Not Force, to Avoid More Protests," Human Rights Watch, August 7, 2019, https://www.hrw.org/news/2017/08/07/state-emergency-ends-ethiopia.

38. "EPRDF's Executive Committee Statement," *Ethiopian Herald,* January 2, 2018, https://allafrica.com/stories/201801020439.html.

39. "Many in the TPLF felt that even after Meles, that their experience gave them the exclusive right to rule. Whenever I brought new reforms before the EPRDF, these were always undermined by the TPLF, who felt that they owned the existing order." Hailemariam Dessalegn, quoted in Greg Mills, "Ethiopia's Need for 'Deep Renewal,'" *Daily Maverick*, August 14, 2018, https://www .dailymaverick.co.za/article/2018-08-14-ethiopias-need-for-deep-renewal/.

9
The Ethiopian Transformation?

In the previous chapters, I emphasized how the legacies of the civil war; the war-to-peace transition, which resulted in ethnofederal politics and institutions; and the consequent contradictions between centralizing and autonomous dynamics explain the puzzle of Ethiopian politics. The crisis of 2016 and the proclamation of the state of emergency, however, pointed to the limits of this model to ensure stability. The legitimacy and leadership coherence that developed from winning the war faded, and the high growth associated with the developmental state's successes created new grievances and relative deprivation that reinforced ethnic identities. The ruling Ethiopian People's Revolutionary Democratic Front (EPRDF) went through an important realignment of leadership in 2018 many observers have characterized as a political transformation. Many have emphasized the charisma and leadership of the new prime minister in their efforts to understand the pace of change. Here, however, I continue to focus on the organizational dimensions of politics and argue that there has been continuity underneath the symbolically important generational and regional change within the party's leadership. At the end of 2018 the EPRDF remained the most powerful political actor in Ethiopia and the only actor with the ability to mobilize across the diverse state. There was little evidence that it intended to surrender it position of dominance. In a historical transition, the distribution of power within the coalition shifted from the long-dominant Tigray People's Liberation Front (TPLF) toward the long-marginalized Oromo wing of the party. The EPRDF, as the ruling coalition, however, still comprised four ethnically defined but dissimilar parties and needed to balance centralizing and autonomous dynamics.

My discussion in earlier chapters highlighted the importance of the constituent parties in the EPRDF—the TPLF, Amhara National

Democratic Movement (ANDM), Oromo People's Democratic Organization (OPDO), and Southern Ethiopian People's Democratic Movement (SEPDM)—and therefore helps one understand the 2018 transition. The member parties had their own histories and identities and administered regional states that had their own budgets, civil services, and security forces. The TPLF, in part because of the legacies of the armed conflict, dominated the coalition, particularly in the early years. By the mid-2010s, however, the newer constituent parties had developed into powerful institutions of their own. Each member party was positioned between the federal government and ordinary people as the de facto promoter and defender of its ethnically defined constituency. In other words, the OPDO was the embodiment of the government for the Oromo, the ANDM for the Amhara, and so on. When the opportunity arose in 2018, key leaders in the OPDO had the capacity to act. This shift in the distribution of power within the governing coalition and the ensuing proclamations of new policies were important but did not represent a fundamental rupture or transformation of the powerful authoritarian party that has ruled Ethiopia since 1991.

The Rise of the Populist Reformers

As a result of the protests, violence, mass arrests, and proclamation of the state of emergency in 2016 (extended until July 2017), the EPRDF coalition lost popular legitimacy. However, some of its member parties, notably the OPDO, increased their own local authority by aligning with growing nationalism, populism, and calls for deep political reform. A populist position allowed longtime OPDO stalwarts to champion a critique of the ruling party and the TPLF in particular, despite their positions within the Executive Committee and their control of Oromia.

The new leadership moved the ruling party in both the direction of populism and the reconsolidation of power. As a matter of discursive style, the new leadership emphasized the need for a mass base against a corrupt "old" regime. As Cheeseman argues, populism in Africa entails politicians articulating "shared narratives of exclusion in order to integrate diverse constituencies into a united campaign."[1] Populism and a common narrative about the corrupt "other" helped obscure cleavages between different regional states and ethnic communities.[2]

The OPDO long had struggled to overcome its origins as an instrument of the TPLF and to become recognized as the authentic guardian of Oromia and defender of Oromo nationalism. The 2016 protests provided that opportunity. To speak out against the Addis Ababa master plan and the heavy-handed security forces arresting protesters in Oromia allowed OPDO politicians to position themselves on the side of the demonstrators. To support making Afan Oromo an additional official working language of Ethiopia allowed the OPDO to straddle the contradictory imperatives of loyalty to the EPRDF and solidarity with the young Oromos protesting in the streets.

In the interregnum following Hailemariam Desalegn's resignation, many Oromo nationalists rallied around Lemma Megersa, the president of the Oromia National Regional State. Lemma, an EPRDF loyalist, had made a career within the OPDO serving as Oromia police commissioner and head of the Oromia Administration and Security Bureau. However, as speaker of the Caffee Oromia (Oromia Regional State Assembly) at the height of the 2016 protests, Lemma vowed to "address the legitimate concerns of the youth." Lemma distanced himself from the EPRDF and said, "I took the oath of office to serve my people, not shadowy elements hiding behind the cover of strict adherence to party dogma."[3] Oromo nationalists and reformers designated "Team Lemma" as the vanguard of a new kind of Oromo politics.[4] It seemed clear to many that only an Oromo-led government would have a chance to end the protests that continued to rock Ethiopia.

The Oromo reform group within the OPDO did not initiate or direct the Oromo protests but criticized the state's violent reaction and aligned with the demands for reform. No longer willing to accept a position subservient to the TPLF, Oromo nationalist reformers promised to make the advancement of Oromia their priority. Supported by the young Oromo street protesters as well as powerful media voices such as the Oromo Media Network (OMN), based in the diaspora, this leadership became an alternative to the "old" EPRDF. It promised to create a "new" EPRDF. Lemma, however, was a member of the Caffee Oromia, not the Parliament, and, therefore, could not become prime minister. Therefore Abiy Ahmed, his ally and then deputy president of Oromia, became the standard-bearer for this reformist, populist group.

On March 27, after a period of contentious and indecisive meetings, the EPRDF's Executive Council selected OPDO leader Abiy Ahmed as party chair and prime minister. Within the EPRDF coalition, the ANDM joined the OPDO in backing Abiy's candidacy, but the TPLF—long the coalition's dominant member—reportedly did not.[5] The symbolism of an Oromo head of government elicited jubilation among many. It is hard to overstate how important seeing an Oromo take the oath of office and pictures of his family dressed in traditional Oromo clothing meant to many who felt historically marginalized. The deeply held narrative that Oromos needed independence because they could never be first-class citizens in Ethiopia immediately became unsettled and complicated, with new opportunities foreseeable.

Shock Therapy and Medemer

Rather than moving incrementally, Abiy advanced rapidly on a range of fronts in a kind of shock therapy that did not allow time for opposition to mobilize. The new government invited long-exiled opposition figures to return—including groups such as Ginbot 7, the Oromo Liberation Front (OLF), and the Ogaden National Liberation Front (ONLF), which had previously been labeled "terrorists"—and released political prisoners.[6] Abiy lifted the state of emergency and the ban on websites and independent media.[7] He removed two long-serving and seemingly untouchable senior security officials—Getachew Assefa, the intelligence chief, and Samora Yunis, the army chief, both senior TPLF leaders.[8] Regarding the economy, Abiy proclaimed that privatization would accelerate and include key national assets such as Ethio Telecom and symbolic enterprises such as Ethiopia Airlines.[9] Finally, Abiy promised to honor the Algiers peace agreement with Eritrea, flew to Asmara to meet with President Isaias Afewerki, and opened border crossings.[10] Ethiopians (and international observers) were stunned by the suddenness and expansiveness with which these changes occurred.

Some of the most dramatic changes were in style and symbolism. The offer to normalize relations with Eritrea had been on the table for years, the need for foreign exchange made more rapid privatization inevitable, and the retirement of Samora had been in the works before Abiy came to power. The new prime minister spoke about love—"Love always wins"—and reconciliation, and had an informal style (often appearing in public in T-shirts or modern interpretations of traditional Ethiopian clothing). Ethiopian political observer Solomon Dersso wrote, "As opposed to the dominant political vocabularies such as 'democratic centralism' [and] 'anti-peace or anti-democratic forces,' he introduces a new discourse preaching love, inclusivity, and unity, widely applauded among the wider public, particularly the youth."[11] Abiy stated that his tenure would be guided by *medemer*, the Amharic word for addition, which suggested coming together without abandoning diversity. As Abiy put it in May 2018, *medemer* was "tender love instead of abject cruelty, peace instead of conflict, love over hate, forgiveness over holding [a] grudge, pulling instead of pushing."[12] Abiy's personal imprint on these dramatic moves led analysts to report on "Abiymania," to compare him to Barack Obama, and to report that people in Addis Ababa "talk quite openly about seeing him as the son of God or a prophet."[13] In August

2018, Abiy visited the United States, where he presided over jubilant meetings with members of the diaspora. In a large meeting at the convention center in Washington, DC, he emphasized his message of unity and said, "If you want to be the pride of your generation, then you must decide that Oromos, Amharas, Wolayitas, Gurages, and Siltes are all equally Ethiopian."[14]

In addition to continuity within the ruling structures, the underlying political economy, which generated the protests in 2016, remained unchanged. Grievances remained about the lack of jobs, along with perceptions that the developmental state benefited certain elites rather than average Ethiopians. The euphoria in 2018 that Ethiopia had stepped back from the brink and that a new generation of leaders from previously marginalized groups had moved into top positions provided breathing space for reform but did not end the economic and political grievances behind the protests. Fisher and Meressa call it the "growing gap between aspirational discourses at the top and unresolved ethnonationalist conflicts on the ground."[15]

The new leadership demonstrated that it had sufficient support to move against powerful elements of the old regime. In the context of the upsurge of violence along the border with Oromia and in Jijiga, Addis Ababa removed longtime Somali National Regional State (SNRS) president Abdi "Iley" Mohamoud Omar. Abdi had long been protected by key elements of the security services, in part because of his role in support of the Ethiopian military interventions in Somalia, but with the change of leadership he became vulnerable and was deposed and arrested. METEC, the military-owned industrial enterprise, faced scrutiny despite the number of top military on its board. In November 2018, Major General Kinfe Dagnew's arrest while reportedly trying to flee from Tigray into Sudan was televised. According to the indictment, Kinfe and other senior military and industrial leaders conspired to conduct international procurement worth approximately $2 billion without following legal procedures.[16]

Engaging with Eritrea was another major change of direction. On July 9, 2018, Ethiopia and Eritrea signed the "Joint Declaration of Peace and Friendship," which reopened diplomatic relations between the two countries, along with transportation and communication links. The symbolism of Abiy flying to Asmara to shake hands with Isaias was remarkable. Ethiopia had long insisted that talks and normalization of relations should precede final border demarcation, whereas Eritrea insisted that Ethiopia withdraw from occupied territory first. These seemingly irreconcilable positions generated a costly stalemate for almost fifteen years, until the dramatic meeting. With the TPLF no longer leading the EPRDF, the Eritrean regime was prepared to make a settlement. Opening the border created a series of emotional scenes as relatives who had not seen each other since 1998 reestablished contact. This mattered most in Tigray, and the open border stimulated trade and people-to-people diplomacy to reconnect the two communities through the Zalambessa border crossing.

Although the symbolic meeting and claims that a "bridge of love" opened the border, many fundamental issues remained unresolved. Negotiations on port access, finalization of the border demarcation, and a host of other disputes required difficult work. Ethiopia and Eritrea both benefit from a "soft" border that allows economic and social interactions to flourish. However, a considerable political shift will be necessary to transform one of the world's most militarized borders into one that brings the benefits of exchange.

The first nine months of the new leadership's tenure emphasized changes that could be made by proclamation or appointment from above rather than policy changes that required parliamentary approval and more complex implementation. Until the EPRDF had its party meetings in September 2018, the new leadership's relationships to the constituent parties was not fully defined. It is hard to assess at the time of this writing the degree to which institutionalization of the new policy will take place. Key appointments to committees reviewing the Charities and Societies Proclamation (CSP), the National Electoral Board of Ethiopia (NEBE), and the Supreme Court, however, indicate deep reforms are under consideration. These reforms, however, do not challenge the centrality of the EPRDF as the dominant political party.

Continued Instability

The protests of 2016 resulted in the EPRDF's intraparty crisis and the collapse of local security in many rural areas, particularly in Oromia and along the borders between regional states. In May 2018, violence between Gedeo (in the Southern Nations, Nationalities, and People's Region [SNNPR]) and Guji (in Oromia) left an estimated million people displaced.[17] An additional million remained displaced as a result of earlier violence along the Somali-Oromia border.[18] In June 2018, Abiy lifted the state of emergency, and violence escalated in numerous parts of Ethiopia: in the Sidama and Wolayita communities (in the SNNPR); Jijiga (in the SNRS) in June; Shashamene and eastern Hararghe (in Oromia) in August; Burayu (in Oromia on the outskirts of Addis Ababa), Gurage (in the SNNPR), the Benishangul-Gumuz region in September;[19] and Moyale (in Oromia) in December. Oromo leaders expressed their alarm that insecurity had resulted in the killing of "dozens" of Oromia police.[20] Considerable controversy focused on the return of OLF fighters and whether they had been disarmed.[21] Each of these examples had specific causes and dynamics. In the absence of a strong government that could ensure law and order, a wide variety of parochial grievances, political posturing, local rivalries, score settling, and violent economic predation escalated.

These distinct conflicts reflected that the Ethiopian state had not yet reconstructed local security systems that had collapsed during the period of mass protests. They underlined that although Abiy was enormously popular, consolidation of power in the EPRDF had not penetrated many parts of the countryside. Local security structures based upon regional state police forces struggled to maintain order in a context of heightened identity politics and a central government preoccupied with national issues. Although in many ways the EPRDF remained a powerful authoritarian party in the center, its ability to control at the grassroots—a core characteristic until the demonstrations—had eroded.

Violence in Burayu, on the outskirts of Addis Ababa, in September 2018 illustrated how the opening political space resulted in clashes.[22] Political actors long in exile returned home and organized mass rallies to project their strength and popularity. That month, after both parties held rallies in Addis Ababa in quick succession, Oromo activists removed flags associated with Ginbot 7 and instead painted the OLF flag on buildings and pavements. Fights between supporters of the two groups escalated, and the Oromia regional police seemed unable or unwilling to prevent the deadly violence that ensued. Nearly thirty people were killed, thousands were displaced, and significant destruction of property occurred.[23]

Abiy responded to the Burayu clashes with uncharacteristic sternness. Rather than his usual tone of love and reconciliation, he warned those engaging in violence not to test the regime, or it would respond with its far superior coercive capabilities. Some 3,000 young men were quickly arrested in one night, with 1,200 held for "reeducation."[24] The state's ability to sustain order without returning to the days of heavy-handed repression remained in question.

Challenges to the EPRDF

Along with increased violence and political insecurity in the aftermath of the demonstrations and inauguration of the new leadership, Ethiopia experienced an upsurge in the salience of identity politics. Ethnicity, of course, had been at the core of the EPRDF's federal structures enshrined in the 1995 Constitution. The success of the OPDO and ANDM to adopt populist positions in defense of their ethnic constituencies led others to recognize new political opportunities. The return of exiled politicians (notably members of the OLF), the rise of new hypernationalist groups such as the National Movement of Amhara (NAMA), and increased momentum of campaigns to create new regional states for the Sidama and others in the SNNPR added more energy to the chaotic politics of transition.

Each member party of the EPRDF faced new pressures from opposition parties or advocacy groups that demanded more action to defend their ethnic interests. Despite its significant advantage as the agent of change that brought Oromos to top positions in Ethiopian politics, the OPDO faced a range of opposition within Oromia. The OPDO faced competition from some of the registered political parties, most notably the Oromo Federalist Congress, led by Merera Gudina and Bekele Gerba. Although the OLF returned from exile, and its flag and history remained powerful symbols of Oromo pride, the organization's ability to mobilize at the grassroots remained uncertain. The OLF had splintered multiple times, and some senior leaders, notably Lencho Letta, chose to join the OPDO, whereas others such as Dawud Ibsa insisted that the OLF had legitimate political rights in Oromia. The Oromo youth who mobilized during the demonstrations—known as the Qeerroo—meanwhile positioned themselves as an autonomous force for reform. The Qeerroo did not demobilize in many places and grew frustrated with the slow pace of change despite Abiy's rise to power. Jawar Mohammed, who ran the important OMN and advanced Oromo nationalism on social media, declared, "We have two governments in Ethiopia: Abiy's government and the Qeerroo government."[25]

Another challenge for the OPDO was that although Abiy was widely popular, the party's cadres at the *kebeles* and *woredas* were not. Many of the protests had been against local OPDO leaders perceived as corrupt or insufficiently committed to protecting Oromo interests. The new leadership of the OPDO worked as fast as it could to reform the old OPDO from the grassroots up and replaced thousands of cadres, but many stalwarts remained in place despite popular anger. The party reportedly purged some forty thousand cadres, but this was a fraction of the total, and the new leadership could not recruit replacements quickly enough, leaving a power vacuum and local government paralysis.[26]

In 2016 the ANDM allowed Amhara mobilization around the Welkait issue to reinforce the party's claims to represent the Amhara against the "other." In particular, the Amhara party had no intention of accepting orders from the Tigrayan leaders. Although the ANDM repositioned itself as the defender of the Amhara, it faced competition from other, more hard-line political actors. NAMA, a new non-

EPRDF party, positioned itself to challenge the ANDM with a narrative of Amhara's past glories and current victimhood under the EPRDF.[27] In contrast with other non-EPRDF parties that lacked the resources to build organizational infrastructure, NAMA seemed well funded and quickly opened up offices across the Amhara National Regional State (ANRS).[28]

At a time when ethnic polarization was high, divisions within the multiethnic SNNPR resulted in a cascade of demands for the creation of new national regional states outside the SNNPR. The SEPDM faced a major intraparty crisis when the Sidama demanded a vote to leave the SNNPR and create its own national regional state, with all of the consequent conflict over borders. The population of the Sidamo zone is estimated at three million, larger than a number of current national regional states. The call for separation included a demand that Hawassa, the SNNPR capital, become the capital of the new Sidamo national regional state, threatening the interests of other southern peoples in that city. The prospect of the Sidamo zone leaving the SNNPR led to some in Hadiya, Gamo-Gofa, Kambata, and Bench Maji to request referendums on separating from the SNNPR.[29] There seemed to be a race among the different zones in the SNNPR to leave before the national regional state was no longer viable.

If the SEPDM broke into smaller ethnic parties, it is unclear how the EPRDF would decide who represented the seats reserved for the SEPDM on the EPRDF Executive Council. There might be ways to develop more autonomy for the different constituencies within the SNNPR while retaining the SEPDM as an overarching alliance within the EPRDF. Given the often violent conflicts around internal borders, however, a new dispensation within the SNNPR has the potential to escalate quickly and in ways that neither the SNNPR internal security nor federal forces could manage.

The TPLF, in its own way, adopted the populist position of defending its people against "others" who intended them harm. TPLF chair Debretsion Gebremichael characterized the EPRDF's crackdown on corruption in METEC, where the top leadership was from the TPLF, as "targeting individuals accused of corruption . . . being used to bring Tigrayan people to their knees."[30] Pressure from Amhara on the question of Welkait has left many Tigrayans feeling besieged and perceiving that only the TPLF can protect them. Some TPLF activists responded to the threat by highlighting how the ANDM treated the Qemant minority within the Amhara state.[31] In addition, TPLF officials quickly pointed out that Tigray remained calm, whereas the other major regions experienced turmoil.[32] Many senior TPLF leaders were alarmed by the new direction of the coalition they created and the ideology of revolutionary democracy, and they insist the developmental state is the best path forward. Some of these fears and resentments encourage the notion of an Agazian movement, creating a "greater Tigray" with Eritrea, but this seems unrealistic given the current alignments of local and regional power.[33]

2018 Party Congresses

Against the backdrop of these promises and continued instability, particularly on the borders between regions, each of the four constituent parties of the EPRDF coalition held party congresses in September 2018 in advance of the EPRDF's Eleventh Congress in October.

Despite its apparent loss of influence on the national scene, the TPLF remained overwhelmingly dominant within the Tigray National Regional State. Debretsion remained as chair of the TPLF. Some regarded Debretsion as a reformer, whereas others saw him as a representative of the older generation of former fighters.[34] Some senior leaders, notably former Tigray regional president Abay Woldu, left the Central Committee. In a provocative move, the TPLF named Getachew Assefa, the controversial former head of intelligence sacked by Abiy, to its Central Committee. In the Amhara region, the ANDM rebranded itself as the Amhara Democratic Party (ADP) and retained most of its top leadership. In line with the heightened salience of identity politics across Ethiopia, the ADP increasingly emphasized the party's commitment to defending Amhara national interests. The OPDO also rebranded itself as the Oromo Democratic Party (ODP), complete with new logos and songs, and retired most of its original leadership. Finally, in the SNNPR, the party retired former prime minister Hailemariam and other leaders, and a younger generation took over the SEPDM's top leadership positions.

All four constituent parties met for the Eleventh EPRDF Congress in early October 2018. In a clear indication that this was now at least formally under the control of the new generation of reformers, the EPRDF Congress endorsed Abiy as party leader and prime minister by a vote of 176 to 1. The ODP came out of these party meetings with a new, younger set of colleagues and a more consolidated position. The Oromo and Amhara wings of the ruling coalition rebranded themselves with new names and symbols. The party's ideological direction was far less clear than it once was, but the EPRDF remained by far the dominant party in Ethiopia.

With this mandate, Abiy quickly named a new cabinet. The number of members of the cabinet was reduced from twenty-eight to twenty, and half of the members were women, including several appointed to what are traditionally seen as power portfolios. Muferiat Kamil was named to the new Peace Ministry, which oversees intelligence and security; Aisha Mohammed joined as minister of defense; Adanech Abebe as minister of revenue; and Getlework Gebregziabher as minister of trade and industry. Abiy also nominated Sahle-Work Zewde as Ethiopia's first woman president. These moves to increase the participation of women in government had enormous symbolic importance in a country that remains highly patriarchal in many ways. Fitsum Arega, then the prime minister's chief of staff, tweeted, "In a patriarchal society such as ours, the appointment of a female head of state not only sets the standard for the future but also normalizes women as decisionmakers in public life."[35] In contrast with the pattern Hailemariam followed when he succeeded Meles Zenawi and expanded his cabinet to keep more senior leaders in the government, Abiy again dramatically chose to make a break with the past and bring in a new group of supporters.

The long-term future of the new leadership, which took power in March 2018 and was affirmed in the party congresses of October and November 2018, was impossible to know at the time of this writing. The EPRDF faces challenges on multiple fronts, and frustrations are growing. The new leadership in general and Abiy in particular made dramatic pronouncements and appointments, and the excitement in Addis Ababa was palpable. However, in other ways, the EPRDF as a political organization remains dominant and is likely to remain so. The protests and the OPDO and ANDM's use of populism to advance to power pointed to the importance of populist identity politics in 2018 and likely in the period leading up to the next round of national elections in 2020. The party congresses all spoke to the roles the respective parties committed to play to protect the interests of their ethnic constituencies. Each member party of the EPRDF faced new pressures from opposition parties or advocacy groups that demanded more action to defend their ethnic interests.

Although intracoalition tensions and internal maneuvering remained major issues in 2018, none of the four constituent parties had a clear path to national power except through the EPRDF. As a result, the ruling party was unlikely to break apart under its internal pressures. If the ANDM/ADP and OPDO/ODP, for example, left the EPRDF, they would be relegated to regional parties without a means to compete for national power and resources.

The post-2018 EPRDF remained the only political organization with the means to mobilize nationwide and operate at both the federal level and local levels of the most important regional states. Political actors such as the NAMA, or Sidama separatists or various Oromo parties might well win significant votes in their respective regions by outbidding the EPRDF member parties and championing popular, if divisive, positions. But it will be difficult for any to win regionwide, and it is difficult to imagine a coalition of ultranationalist opposition parties because many mobilize around identifying other nationalists as the enemy. Given that central resources remain fundamental to running the national regional states, a party that is only competitive in one region would be disadvantaged.

Abiy was immensely popular in late 2018. But the EPRDF in general and OPDO/ODP in particular are not. The majority of the local party officials remain in place despite the dramatic changes at the top levels of the party. In elections, voters select local candidates, and only those in Abiy's home constituency of Agaro (southwestern Oromia) will have the chance to vote for him. The anger against woreda-level OPDO/ODP officials that animated the protests of 2016 remains and will challenge incumbents in the next elections.

For elections to be competitive, the EPRDF must do more than provide the legal space for opposition parties to operate. The huge state-party apparatus put in place after 2005 links individual voters to the EPRDF through extensive patronage and surveillance. No opposition party will have close to this kind of rural penetration, and none will have the resources of the ruling party. It is difficult to see, therefore, how the opposition will be able to win in a majority of the 547 constituencies to form a new government. It is possible that members of the opposition parties will be able to win 15 or 25 percent of the seats, as they did in 2000, but in the heavily majoritarian system of Ethiopia, controlling a majority of legislative seats provides the opportunity to appoint all executive and judicial positions. As in 2005, it is possible that the opposition might win a majority in the Addis Ababa regional assembly, and that would create potentially important opportunities to demonstrate policy ideas and show the opposition's capacity to manage public affairs.

Conclusion

It is dangerous to make predictions about the future of a political regime when the leadership has been in power for less than a year. Ethiopia remains in a crisis without a clear path forward. The displacement crisis is still enormous, underlying economic challenges difficult to resolve, and despite Abiy's popularity, significant political actors wish to advance other agendas. Many longtime observers of Ethiopian politics argue that 2018 represented the end of one era and the emergence of a new order. Lefort, for example, argues that Abiy represents a "radical departure" and that "stone by stone he is dismantling the authoritarian edifice erected since 1991."[36] Others suggest Abiy is a hero who will rescue Ethiopia from its "winter of despair."[37]

However, my focus on the structures of the EPRDF suggests that there is considerable continuity despite the dramatic change of top leadership in the party. There is no question that Abiy brought in a new style of politics and has opened up political space closed since 2005. The normalization of relations with Eritrea and the replacement of Somali National Regional State president Abdi were significant changes from past policies. The EPRDF, however, overwhelmingly remains the most powerful political party in Ethiopia. In 2018 it continued to occupy 100 percent of the seats in Parliament and key regional state legislatures. Alternative leaders have not yet had the time, resources, or opportunities to develop the kind of grassroots organizational infrastructure to compete with the longtime ruling party. Many have recently returned from exile or have been released from prisons.

The characteristics of the EPRDF also have endured. The legacies of the armed struggle in terms of a disciplined core and hierarchical control have diminished, whereas the power of the regionally based member parties has increased. However, the difficult balance between positions that favor unity and authority at the federal level and those that reflect the desire of many for more autonomy continue to characterize the post-2018 regime. In other words, the new party leadership has not replaced the contradictory logics of centralization and autonomy at the core of the EPRDF since it took power. Competition among the four member parties is in the open, and the instability of the SEPDM in particular is evident. But contentious politics within the ruling coalition is not new. Each member party has strong incentives to remain within the EPRDF to have access to the resources that remain concentrated at the center. Although tensions are high within the coalition, each constituent party would face difficult political prospects if it sought to operate as an independent party.

Notes

1. Nic Cheeseman, "Populism in Africa and the Potential for 'Ethnically Blind' Politics," in *Routledge Handbook of Global Populism,* ed. Carlos de la Torre (London: Routledge, 2018), 365. For comparative considerations, see Steven Levitsky and Kenneth M. Roberts, "Latin America's 'Left Turn': A Framework for Analysis," in *The Resurgence of the Latin American Left,* ed.

Steven Levitsky and Kenneth M. Roberts (Baltimore: Johns Hopkins University Press, 2011), 6–7. Many populist movements focus on urban areas, but in Ethiopia the ruling party continued to have uncertain relations with the ethnically mixed populations in many major cities.

2. For a view that explicitly challenges the argument that Abiy is a populist, see Tom Gardner, "Abiy Ahmed Is Not a Populist," *Foreign Policy,* December 5, 2018, https://foreignpolicy.com/2018/12/05/abiy-ahmed-is-not-a-populist-ethiopia -eprdf-tplf-modi-erdogan-populism/.

3. Opride, "Lemma Megersa: Opride's Oromo Person of the Year 2017 Runner Up," https://www.opride.com/longform/lemma-megersa-oprides-oromo -person-of-the-year-2017-runner-up/.

4. The coterie for change within the OPDO included Abiy Ahmed (prime minister, chair of the EPRDF, and chair of the OPDO), Lemma Megersa (president of the Oromia National Regional State), Addisu Arega (Oromia National Regional State Communications Bureau, later head of OPDO political mobilization), Shimelis Abdissa (head of Urban Affairs, Oromia), Adanech Abebe (mayor of Adama, later head of OPDO Central Office), Takele Uma Banti (Oromia Transportation, later deputy mayor of Addis Ababa), and a small circle of others.

5. Jonathan Fisher and Meressa Tsehaye Gebrewahd, "'Game Over?' Abiy Ahmed, the Tigrayan People's Liberation Front, and Ethiopia's Political Crisis," *African Affairs* (2018), report that Abiy won 108 votes, the TPLF's Debretsion won 2, and SEPDM's Shiferaw Shigute won 58. After the ANDM's support for Abiy was clear, the outcome was clear.

6. Al Jazeera, "Andargachew Tsige Pardoned by Ethiopia," May 26, 2018, https://www.aljazeera.com/news/2018/05/andargachew-tsige-pardoned-ethiopia -180526163642586.html. For context, see Michael Woldemariam, "Can Ethiopia's Reforms Succeed?" *Foreign Affairs,* September 11, 2018, https://www.foreignaffairs .com/articles/east-africa/2018-09-10/can-ethiopias-reforms-succeed.

7. Paul Schemm, "Ethiopia Moves to Lift State of Emergency Two Months Early as Tensions Ease," *Washington Post,* June 2, 2018, https://www.washingtonpost .com/world/africa/ethiopia-moves-to-lift-state-of-emergency-two-months-early-as -tensions-ease/2018/06/02/2f1fa6ec-6669-11e8-a768-ed043e33f1dc_story.html ?utm_term=.2e8e6b8d13fe.

8. Samora's retirement had been in the works for some time, but Getachew's removal was more surprising and might have reflected intra-TPLF divisions.

9. Paul Schemm, "Ethiopia Says It Is Ready to Implement Eritrea Peace Deal and Privatize Parts of the Economy," *Washington Post,* June 5, 2018, https:// www.washingtonpost.com/world/africa/ethiopia-says-its-ready-to-implement -eritrea-peace-deal-and-privatize-parts-of-the-economy/2018/06/05/f5813936 -68e4-11e8-9e38-24e693b38637_story.html?utm_term=.1904f2721215.

10. Fergal Keene, "Can Ethiopia's Abiy Ahmed Make Peace with 'Africa's North Korea?'" BBC, July 10, 2018, https://www.bbc.com/news/world-africa-44771292.

11. Solomon Dersso, "Ethiopia's Spring of Hope and Winter of Despair," August 7, 2018, https://solomondersso.wordpress.com/2018/08/07/ethiopias- spring-of-hope-and-winter-of-despair/.

12. Translated excerpt from Yilma Bekele, "Discourse on the Concept of Medemer," Ethioexplorer.com, July 20, 2018, https://ethioexplorer.com/discourse -on-the-concept-of-medemer-%E1%88%98-%E1%8B%B0-%E1%88%98-%E1 %88%AD-yilma-bekele/.

13. *Economist,* "Abiymania: Ethiopians Are Going Wild for Abiy Ahmed," August 18, 2018, https://www.economist.com/middle-east-and-africa/2018/08/18/ethiopians-are-going-wild-for-abiy-ahmed. Jenni Marsh, "Why Ethiopians Believe Their New Prime Minister Is a Prophet," CNN, August 29, 2018, https://www.cnn.com/2018/08/26/world/abiymania-ethiopia-prime-minister-abiy-ahmed/index.html.

14. Hannah Giorgis, "Abiy Ahmed Meets the Ethiopian Diaspora," *Atlantic,* August 4, 2018, https://www.theatlantic.com/entertainment/archive/2018/08/abiy-ahmed-meets-the-ethiopian-diaspora/566591/.

15. Fisher and Meressa, "'Game Over?'"

16. Mahlet Fasil and Yared Tsegaye, "Analysis: Inside Ethiopia's Trial of Grand Corruption: Who Is Accused of What?" *Addis Standard,* December 11, 2018, http://addisstandard.com/analysis-inside-ethiopias-trial-of-grand-corruption-who-is-accused-of-what/.

17. UN Office for the Coordination of Humanitarian Affairs, *Ethiopia Humanitarian Bulletin* 63 (September 3–15, 2018), https://reliefweb.int/report/ethiopia/ethiopia-humanitarian-bulletin-issue-63-3-16-september-2018.

18. UNOCHA and Ethiopian Commissioner of the National Disaster Risk Management Commission, "Ethiopia: Immediate Humanitarian Funding Priorities," August 13, 2018, https://www.humanitarianresponse.info/files/documents/files/ethiopia_immediate_humanitarian_funding_priorities_3_aug_2018_.pdf.

19. Wolde Tadesse, Jason Mosley, and Angela Raven-Roberts, "Strains Down South: Ethiopia's National Reforms Rouse Local Tensions," *African Arguments,* June 19, 2018; UN Office for the Coordination of Humanitarian Affairs, *Ethiopia Humanitarian Bulletin* 64 (September 17–30, 2018), https://reliefweb.int/report/ethiopia/ethiopia-humanitarian-bulletin-issue-64-17-30-september-2018; Ermias Tasfaye and Solomon Yimer, "Tens of Thousands Flee Benishangul After Oromia Border Dispute Flares," *Ethiopia Insight,* October 4, 2018, https://www.ethiopia-insight.com/2018/10/04/tens-of-thousands-flee-benishangul-after-oromia-border-dispute-flares/.

20. Yared Tsegaye, "Amid the Killing of Dozens of Oromia Police and Unknown Numbers of Civilians ODP Admits Deteriorating Security, Vows to Bring Rapid Change," *Addis Standard,* November 30, 2018, http://addisstandard.com/news-amid-killing-dozens-oromia-police-unknown-numbers-civilians-odp-admits-deteriorating-security-vows-bring-rapid-change/; Nizar Manek and Ermias Tasfaye, "Mob Killings Split Ethiopians as Political Fault Lines Test Abiy's Big Tent," *Ethiopia Insight,* September 26, 2018, https://www.ethiopia-insight.com/2018/09/26/mob-killings-split-ethiopians-as-political-fault-lines-test-abiys-big-tent/.

21. Abdurazak Kedir Abdu, "The OLF Is Dead, but Its Oromo Struggle Lives," *Ethiopia Insight,* January 19, 2019, https://www.ethiopia-insight.com/2019/01/19/the-olf-is-dead-but-its-oromo-struggle-lives/.

22. Interviews with author, Addis Ababa, September 2018.

23. Andualem Sisay, "28 Killed and over 2,500 Arrested After Addis Clashes," *East African,* September 24, 2018, https://www.theeastafrican.co.ke/news/ea/Scores-killed-and-others-arrested-after-Addis-clashes/4552908-4775844-9jd60az/index.html.

24. Hadra Ahmed and Joseph Goldstein, "Thousands Are Arrested in Ethiopia After Ethnic Violence," *New York Times,* September 24, 2018, https://www.nytimes.com/2018/09/24/world/africa/ethiopia-ethnic-violence-arrests.html.

25. Alemayehu Weldemariam, "Domestic Despair Shadows Abiy's Diplomatic Waltz," *Ethiopian Insight*, September 18, 2018, https://www.ethiopia-insight.com/2018/09/18/domestic-despair-shadows-abiys-diplomatic-waltz/.

26. Interviews with author, Washington, DC, 2018.

27. Interviews with author, Addis Ababa, September 2018.

28. Some suggest that Amharas from Gojjam dominate NAMA, pointing to intragroup rivalries that might limit NAMA's appeal.

29. Brook Abdu, "Kaffa Zone Council Votes for Statehood," *Reporter,* November 15, 2018, https://www.thereporterethiopia.com/article/kaffa-zone-council-votes-statehood; Yohanan Yokamo, "Sidama Referendum Should Proceed Without Further Delay," *Ethiopia Insight,* January 12, 2019, https://www.ethiopia-insight.com/2019/01/12/sidama-referendum-should-proceed-without-further-delay/. Such divisions recall the regional states that existed before the creation of the SNNPR in 1995.

30. "Ethiopia PM Conducting Political, Ethnic Witch-hunt—Tigray Chair," *Africa News,* November 20, 2018, http://www.africanews.com/2018/11/20/tigray-chair-says-ethiopia-pm-conducting-political-and-ethnic-witch-hunt/.

31. William Davison, Solomon Yimer, and Kibreab Beraki, "Violent Qemant Dispute Fueling Explosive Amhara-Tigray Divide," *Ethiopia Insight,* December 16, 2018, https://www.ethiopia-insight.com/2018/12/16/violent-qemant-dispute-fueling-explosive-amhara-tigray-divide/.

32. René LeFort, "Ethiopia: Climbing Mount Uncertainty," *Open Democracy,* October 21, 2018, https://www.opendemocracy.net/ren-lefort/ethiopia-climbing-mount-uncertainty.

33. Tesfay Nigus, "The Agazian Movement: Exhuming a Corpse?" *Horn Affairs*, March 18, 2017, https://hornaffairs.com/2017/03/18/agazian-movement-exhuming-corpse/.

34. Interviews with author, Addis Ababa and Washington, DC, 2018.

35. Paul Schemm, "Ethiopia Appoints First Female President in Its Modern History in Latest Reform," *Washington Post,* October 25, 2018, https://www.washingtonpost.com/world/africa/ethiopia-appoints-first-female-president-in-its-modern-history-in-latest-reform/2018/10/25/3514d3a4-d82b-11e8-a10f-b51546b10756_story.html?utm_term=.0aa88ceaffc4.

36. René LeFort, "Pacified Politics or Risk Disintegration? A Race Against Time in Ethiopia," *Open Democracy*, August 21, 2018, https://www.opendemocracy.net/ren-lefort/pacified-politics-or-risk-disintegration-race-against-time-in-ethiopia.

37. The reference to Dickens is from Solomon Dersso, although he does not emphasize the personality of Abiy in his analysis. See Dersso, "Ethiopia's Spring of Hope and Winter of Despair."

10

Continuity and Change

In this final chapter I summarize the narrative of Ethiopia's political history to explain how the nature of the Ethiopian civil war and the war-to-peace transition resulted in an authoritarian system in which a strong center balanced subnational identities and institutions. I argue that, though this regime has been stable since 1991, it has within it contradictory logics of centralization and regional autonomy. The Ethiopian People's Revolutionary Democratic Front (EPRDF) has been simultaneously a powerful, centralized party and a coalition of quite different member organizations. The demonstrations in 2016 and the change of leadership in 2018 are the outcomes of these contradictions. Between 1995 and 2016, the autonomous logic as promised in the Constitution increased, whereas the centralizing logic of the victorious insurgent group declined. I also discuss the contributions of the Ethiopian case to the theoretical arguments about authoritarian stability, the importance of intraparty dynamics, the roles of political parties and elections in authoritarian contexts, and how institutions established to shape successful war-to-peace transitions might create the conditions for a strong regime that has the ability to undergo a major leadership change and remain dominant.

The Puzzle of Ethiopian Politics

The political history of Ethiopia since 1991 has been shaped by the transformation of the Tigray People's Liberation Front (TPLF), a small Marxist-Leninist insurgent group based in northern Ethiopia, into the powerful EPRDF. The EPRDF has its origins as a victorious insurgent movement and, as a consequence, has developed into a disciplined and cohesive hierarchical organization. The imperatives of transforming a Tigray-based military movement into a political organization that drew

209

from large and diverse communities who had not participated in the armed struggle contributed to putting in place an ethnofederal system that institutionalized the political salience of ethnic and regional identities.

The TPLF created the EPRDF, a coalition that eventually included four ethnically defined constituent parties: the TPLF, the Amhara National Democratic Movement (ANDM), the Oromo People's Democratic Organization (OPDO), and the Southern Ethiopian People's Democratic Movement (SEPDM). The TPLF was battle hardened and experienced in military governance. The ANDM, however, had far less wartime experience, the OPDO was created late in the war and much of its early leadership had been TPLF prisoners of war, and the SEPDM had no prior existence before the transition. Important insurgent groups such as the Oromo Liberation Front (OLF) were not part of the EPRDF.

EPRDF rule was based on a balance between centralizing dynamics, such as the TPLF's legacies from the war and the ensuing hierarchical vanguard party, and institutions that empowered regionally and ethnically based political actors. Between 1991 and 2015, a strong center sustained equilibrium between these contradictory logics, one strengthening the federal government, the EPRDF Executive Committee, and the centralizing dynamics of the developmental state and the second favoring ethnically defined regions, ethnic political parties, mobilization around identity, and local control over resources. In 2016 this balance broke down. The accumulation of grievances, a slowing economy, and escalating intracoalition competition between the four constituent parties broke into the open in the 2016 protests in the Oromia and Amhara regions. The disruption of the equilibrium between centralizing and autonomous dynamics provided the opportunity for new leadership to position itself as both sympathetic with the grievances of the demonstrators and a possible force that could consolidate power and save the EPRDF.

The Legacies of the War and Durable Authoritarianism

The Ethiopian case speaks to several theoretical concerns regarding transitions from war to peace and the durability of authoritarian political order. It supports the contention that strong authoritarian parties often have their origins in national liberation movements. It demonstrates further, however, that the nature of the war-to-peace transition is another mechanism that shapes what type of postwar political party the insurgent group can become. In Ethiopia, these processes generated a strong authoritarian ruling party that consisted of different member parties.

The TPLF seized power with relatively coherent leadership, high levels of solidarity, and effective command-and-control systems that then shaped postconflict political party building. War generates specific social processes and incentives for particular types of institutions characterized by vertical command structures. They are quite different from political parties with their origins in labor unions and social movements.[1] The Ethiopian case demonstrates the importance scholars such as Arjona, Staniland, Mampilly, and others place on understanding insurgent groups as creators of specific kinds of political order because the logics of such orders shape postwar politics.[2] This is particularly true following rebel victory. Because the rebels won the war in Ethiopia, these wartime institutions remained most powerful as they transformed into political parties operating in the postwar state.

Levitsky and Way, among other scholars of authoritarian regimes, have developed a compelling argument to explain how authoritarian political parties with origins in national liberation movements are typically strong in terms of organizational scope and cohesion.[3] Strong parties often create stable authoritarian systems by facilitating intraelite accommodation, co-opting opposition, and institutionalizing incentives to reward loyalty and penalize defection.[4] Strong parties allow loyalists to be reliably rewarded and lengthen their time horizons for career advancement, thereby creating incentives for long-term loyalty.[5] Losers in power or policy struggles are likely to remain loyal with the expectation of access to patronage and power in future rounds. The resilient authoritarian party literature helps explain how the TPLF served as the strong center within the EPRDF and how the wartime legacies of leadership cohesion and experience in regional administration led to the authoritarian ruling party.

War-to-Peace Transitions and Postwar Politics

The Ethiopia case, however, also suggests that the initial benefits derived from the legacies of the armed struggle are further shaped in important ways by the nature of the war-to-peace transition. There is more than one path to connect a rebel movement to the postwar political order. Along with the endowment of a coherent and disciplined organization with experience in military governance of liberated territory, the process of moving from war to peace has its own role in shaping postwar politics. In Ethiopia, the war-to-peace transition created a coalition of vastly different constituent parties, a different model than the cohesive, hierarchical organizational consequences of winning the war. The victorious insurgents in Uganda, Rwanda, and elsewhere faced different challenges in consolidating power and did not face the kind of political and social landscape in Ethiopia.

The larger literature on war-to-peace transitions focuses on the liberal peace model and emphasizes cases in which civil war ends in stalemate, followed by a negotiated settlement, a significant role for the international community in sponsoring postconflict elections, transitional justice processes, and demobilization of soldiers.[6] In many cases, the war-to-peace imperatives entail overcoming security dilemmas and lack of trust between the government and rebel forces.[7] Various power-sharing formulas are often used to increase the chances of sustained peace.[8]

This literature—and the critique of this literature—provides limited leverage on the key questions raised by cases in which the war ends in victory for one or another side and how this set of cases of war termination differ from those that ended in stalemate and the intervention of the international community.[9] In Ethiopia as well as Uganda and Rwanda, the war-to-peace transition was under the supervision of the insurgent movements that won the war.[10] Victory made the war-to-peace transition an exercise in power consolidation and broadening, not power sharing as in the liberal peace model. The imperative in general is to consolidate power and in particular to develop mechanisms to extend the wartime organization into a ruling system that incorporates communities not directly involved in the war.

The most fundamental challenge facing the victorious rebels is organizational enlargement: How can a cohesive rebel movement bring in new constituencies and simultaneously maintain control? How can a rebel movement that developed in one particular region or within one identity group expand to effectively govern areas outside of its core area of operation? Regardless of how diverse the insurgent movement is, there will undoubtedly be some communities that joined the struggle earlier, some that supported insurgents that did not win the war, and some that experienced more fighting than others. To successfully govern, the rebel movement must move beyond its wartime base and incorporate sufficient constituencies outside the insurgent alliance that had less direct involvement in the armed struggle.

In Ethiopia this meant transforming the largely Tigrayan rebel army into a civilian ruling party that included the Oromos, Amharas, and the many groups of southern Ethiopia outside the war zones. The TPLF sought to resolve this challenge by supporting the creation of non-Tigrayan, ethnically defined parties that could administer their respective territories and serve as member parties in a ruling coalition. The border regions of Somali, Afar, Benishangul-Gumuz, and Gambela were administered through affiliates not part of the ruling party. The EPRDF coalition provided a mechanism for the TPLF to develop coalition partners that could govern in Oromia and in the Southern Nations, Nationalities, and People's Region (SNNPR). The insurgent force became the core of a broad, multiethnic coalition of parties. But, over time, the initial advantage the TPLF enjoyed as the original founder of the EPRDF shrank as the other constituent parties developed their own leaderships, institutional capacities, and relationships with their constituencies. Therefore, it is important to examine the intracoalition dynamics of the EPRDF to understand politics in post-1991 Ethiopia.

In contrast to the theories that argue insurgents are likely to create strong authoritarian parties, the Ethiopia case suggests the operation of another set of mechanisms linked to the war-to-peace transition. Along with the initial endowments of coherence and hierarchy associated with successful insurgent movements, the demands of transforming from a wartime institution into a party capable of governing a diverse state shape postwar politics. The strength of the TPLF follows the logic of postinsurgent political parties, but the EPRDF coalition owes its character to the exigencies of broadening the rebel movement from Tigray into a multiethnic coalition of different constituent parts. As a result, the EPRDF has a dual nature, in part cohesive and hierarchical and in part diverse and structured asymmetrically.

From 1991 to 2015, with a few exceptions such as the 2001 party split and the 2005 electoral crisis, the center of the EPRDF and the dominance of the TPLF kept the centrifugal forces of regional states and ethnic parties in check. By 2016, however, prolonged demonstrations and protests suggested that the equilibrium had been disrupted. As the legacies of victory that made the TPLF so powerful in the 1990s began to fade in the 2010s, the logic of ethnofederalism and the promise of autonomy included in the 1995 Constitution challenged the center.

In 2018, Abiy Ahmed and other OPDO leaders managed, although remaining within the EPRDF, to position themselves as connected with the anger and rising Oromo nationalism that came out of the protests. They questioned EPRDF policies with regard to the federal security services operating in Oromia, for example, and managed to remain in the party's top leadership. Following Prime Minister Hailemariam Desalegn's resignation, an alliance between the OPDO and the ANDM provided the backing for Abiy to rise to the top position in the EPRDF.

As I have argued previously, this change of leadership did not mean the EPRDF as a powerful authoritarian party had been vanquished. The coalition structure and the contradictions between centralized power and ethnofederal autonomy remained. The shift of power within the coalition from the TPLF to the OPDO mattered in many important ways but did not structurally transform the EPRDF. Rather, it offered a way for the party to reconsolidate power. The new leaders continue to operate within institutions forged by the victorious insurgents and the war-to-peace transition that resulted in ethnofederalism.

Notes

1. David Close and Gary Prevost, "Introduction: Transitioning from Revolutionary Movements to Political Parties and Making the Revolution 'Stick,'" in *From Revolutionary Movements to Political Parties,* ed. Kalowatie Deonandan, David Close, and Gary Prevost (New York: Palgrave Macmillan, 2007), 9.

2. Ana Arjona, *Rebelocracy: Social Order in the Colombian Civil War* (Cambridge, UK: Cambridge University Press, 2016); Paul Staniland, *Networks of Rebellion: Explaining Insurgent Cohesion and Collapse* (Ithaca, NY: Cornell University Press, 2014); Zachariah Cherian Mampilly, *Rebel Rulers: Insurgent Governance and Civilian Life During War* (Ithaca, NY: Cornell University Press, 2011).

3. Steven R. Levitsky and Lucan A. Way, *Competitive Authoritarianism: Hybrid Regimes After the Cold War* (Cambridge, UK: Cambridge University Press, 2010).

4. Jennifer Gandhi, *Political Institutions Under Dictatorship* (Cambridge, UK: Cambridge University Press, 2008).

5. Jason Brownlee, *Authoritarianism in an Age of Democratization* (Cambridge, UK: Cambridge University Press, 2007).

6. Anna K. Jarstad and Timothy D. Sisk, eds. *From War to Democracy: Dilemmas of Peacebuilding* (Cambridge, UK: Cambridge University Press, 2008); Christoph Zürcher et al., eds., *Costly Democracy: Peacebuilding and Democratization After War* (Palo Alto, CA: Stanford University Press, 2013).

7. Stephen John Stedman, "Spoiler Problems in Peace Processes," *International Security* 22, no. 5 (1997): 5–53; Desirée Nilsson and Mimmi Söderberg Kovacs, "Revisiting an Elusive Concept: A Review of the Debate on Spoilers in Peace Processes," *International Studies Review* 13, no. 4 (December 2011): 606–626.

8. Caroline A. Harzell and Matthew Hoddie, *Crafting Peace: Power-Sharing Institutions and the Negotiated Settlement of Civil Wars* (University Park: Pennsylvania State University Press, 2007).

9. Oliver P. Richmond and Roger Mac Ginty, "Where Now for the Critique of the Liberal Peace?" *Cooperation and Conflict* (2014); Neil Cooper, "Review Article: On the Crisis of the Liberal Peace," *Conflict, Security, and Development* 7, no. 4 (December 2007).

10. Terrence Lyons, "The Importance of Winning: Victorious Insurgent Groups and Authoritarian Politics," *Comparative Politics* 48, no. 2 (January 2016): 167–184; Terrence Lyons, "Victorious Rebels and Postwar Politics," *Civil Wars* 18, no. 2 (2016): 160–174; Giulia Piccolino, "Peacebuilding and Statebuilding in Post-2011 Côte d'Ivoire: A Victor's Peace?" *African Affairs* 117, no. 468 (July 2018).

Acronyms

AAPO	All-Amhara People's Organization
ADP	Amara Democratic Party
ALF	Afar Liberation Front
ANDM	Amhara National Democratic Movement
ANRS	Amhara National Regional State
CAFPDE	Council of Alternative Forces for Peace and Democracy in Ethiopia
COEDF	Coalition of Ethiopian Democratic Forces
CUD	Coalition for Unity in Democracy
DA	development agent
DAG	Donor Assistance Group
ECHA'AT	Ethiopian Oppressed People's Revolutionary Struggle
EDU	Ethiopian Democratic Union
EEBC	Eritrea-Ethiopia Border Commission
EFFORT	Endowment Fund for the Rehabilitation of Tigray
ENDF	Ethiopian National Defense Force
EPDM	Ethiopian People's Democratic Movement
EPLF	Eritrean People's Liberation Front
EPRDF	Ethiopian People's Revolutionary Democratic Front
EPRP	Ethiopian People's Revolutionary Party
ESAT	Ethiopian Satellite Television
ESC	Ethiopian Sugar Corporation
ESDL	Ethiopian Somali Democratic League
EWLA	Ethiopian Women Lawyers Association
GERD	Grand Ethiopian Renaissance Dam
GPLM	Gambela People's Liberation Movement
GTP	Growth and Transformation Plan
HNDO	Hadiya National Democratic Organization

HPNRS	Harari People's National Regional State
Meison	All-Ethiopia Socialist Movement
METEC	Metals and Engineering Corporation
MLLT	Marxist-Leninist League of Tigray
NAMA	National Movement of Amhara
NEBE	National Electoral Board of Ethiopia
ODP	Oromo Democratic Party
OFDM	Oromo Federal Democratic Movement
OLF	Oromo Liberation Front
OMN	Oromia Media Network
ONC	Oromo National Congress
ONLF	Ogaden National Liberation Front
OPDO	Oromo People's Democratic Organization
ORA	Oromo Relief Association
OSJ	Organization for Social Justice
PSNP	Productive Safety Net Program
REST	Relief Society of Tigray
SEPDC	Southern Ethiopia People's Democratic Coalition
SEPDF	Southern Ethiopian People's Democratic Front
SEPDM	Southern Ethiopian People's Democratic Movement
SLM	Sidama Liberation Movement
SNNPR	Southern Nations, Nationalities, and People's Region
SPDO	Sidama People's Democratic Organization
SPDP	Somali People's Democratic Party
SPLM	Sudan People's Liberation Movement
TDA	Tigray Development Association
TGE	Transitional Government of Ethiopia
TNO	Tigray National Organization
TPLF	Tigray People's Liberation Front
UEDF	United Ethiopian Democratic Forces
UNMEE	United Nations Mission in Ethiopia and Eritrea
USAID	US Agency for International Development
WPE	Workers' Party of Ethiopia`
WSLF	Western Somali Liberation Front

Selected Bibliography

Aalen, Lovise. "Ethiopia After Meles: Stability for How Long?" *Current History* 113 (May 2014).
———. *Ethnic Federalism in a Dominant Party State: The Ethiopian Experience, 1991–2000.* Bergen: Chr. Michelsen Institute, 2002.
———. *The Politics of Ethnicity in Ethiopia: Actors, Power, and Mobilisation Under Ethnic Federalism.* Leiden: Brill, 2011.
———. "A Revival of Tradition? The Power of Clans and Social Strata in the Wolyata Elections." In *Contested Power in Ethiopia: Traditional Authorities and Multi-party Elections,* edited by Kjetil Tronvoll and Tobias Hagmann. Leiden: Brill, 2012.
———. "Two Stories Told: The 2001 Local Elections in Kambata, Tambaro, Hadiya, and Sidama." In *Ethiopia 2001: Local Elections in the Southern Region.* Report 3/2002. Oslo: Nordem, 2002.
Aalen, Lovise, and Kjetil Tronvoll. "The 2008 Ethiopian Local Elections: The Return of Electoral Authoritarianism." *African Affairs* 108, no. 430 (2008).
Abbink, Jon. "Authority and Leadership in Surma Society (Ethiopia)." *Africa* 52, no. 3 (1997): 317–342.
———. "Ethnic-based Federalism and Ethnicity in Ethiopia: Reassessing the Experiment After 20 Years." *Journal of Eastern African Studies* 5, no. 4 (2011): 596–618.
———. *Political Culture in Ethiopia: A Balance Sheet of Post–1991 Ethnically Based Federalism.* Leiden: African Studies Centre, 2010.
———. "Religious Freedom and Political Order: The Ethiopian 'Secular State' and the Containment of Muslim Identity Politics." *Journal of Eastern African Studies* 8, no. 3 (2014): 346–365.
Addis Getahun Solomon. *The History of Ethiopian Immigrants and Refugees in America, 1900–2000: Patterns of Migration, Survival, and Adjustment.* New York: LFB Scholarly, 2007.
Ahmed Hassan Omer. "Close Yet Far: Northern Shewa Under the Derg." In *Remapping Ethiopia: Socialism and After,* edited by Wendy James, Donald L. Donham, Eisei Kurimoto, Alessandro Triulzi. Oxford, UK: James Currey, 2002.
Al-Ali, Nadje, and Khalid Koser, eds. *New Approaches to Migration? Transnational Communities and the Transformation of Home.* London: Routledge, 2002.

Amare Tekle, ed. *Eritrea and Ethiopia: From Conflict and Cooperation*. Lawrenceville, NJ: Red Sea, 1994.

Andargachew Tiruneh. *The Ethiopian Revolution: 1974–1987—a Transformation from an Aristocratic to a Totalitarian Autocracy*. Cambridge, UK: Cambridge University Press, 1993.

Andebrhan Welde Giorgis. *Eritrea at a Crossroads: A Narrative of Betrayal and Hope*. Houston, TX: Strategic, 2014.

Anderson, Lisa. "Lawless Government and Illegal Opposition: Reflections on the Middle East." *Journal of International Affairs* 40, no. 2 (1987).

Aregawi Berhe. "The Origins of the Tigray People's Liberation Front." *African Affairs* 103, no. 413 (2004).

———. *A Political History of the Tigray People's Liberation Front (1975–1991): Revolt, Ideology, and Mobilisation in Ethiopia*. Los Angeles: Tsehai, 2009.

———. "Revisiting Resistance in Italian-occupied Ethiopia: The Patriots' Movement (1936–1941) and the Redefinition of Post-war Ethiopia." In *Rethinking Resistance: Revolt and Violence in African History,* edited by Jon Abbink, Klaas van Walraven, and Mirjam de Bruijn. Leiden: Brill, 2003.

Arian, Alan, and Samuel H. Barnes. "The Dominant Party System: A Neglected Model of Democratic Stability." *Journal of Politics* 36, no. 3 (1974).

Arjona, Ana. *Rebelocracy: Social Order in the Colombian Civil War*. Cambridge, UK: Cambridge University Press, 2016.

Arjona, Ana, Nelson Kasfir, and Zachariah Cherian Mampilly, eds. *Rebel Governance in Civil Wars*. Cambridge, UK: Cambridge University Press, 2015.

Arkebe Oqubay. *Made in Africa: Industrial Policy in Ethiopia*. Oxford, UK: Oxford University Press, 2015.

Arriola, Leonardo R. "Ethnicity, Economic Conditions, and Opposition Support: Evidence from Ethiopia's 2005 Elections." *Northeast African Studies* 10, no. 1 (2008): 115–144.

———. *Multiethnic Coalitions in Africa: Business Financing of Opposition Election Campaigns*. Cambridge, UK: Cambridge University Press, 2012.

———. "Protesting and Policing in a Multiethnic Authoritarian State." *Comparative Politics* 45, no. 2 (January 2013).

Arriola, Leonardo R., and Terrence Lyons. "Ethiopia's 100% Election," *Journal of Democracy* 27, no. 1 (January 2016): 76–88.

Arriola, Leonardo R., Terrence Lyons, Seife Ayalew, and Josef Woldenses, "The Ethiopian People's Revolutionary Democratic Front: Authoritarian Resilience and Intra-party Dynamics." Paper presented at the annual meeting of the American Political Science Association, September 2016, Philadelphia, PA.

Asafa Jalata. *Contending Nationalisms of Oromia and Ethiopia: Struggling for Statehood, Sovereignty, and Multinational Democracy*. Binghamton, NY: Global Academic Press, 2010.

———. *Oromia and Ethiopia: State Formation and Ethnonational Conflict, 1868–1992*. Boulder, CO: Lynne Rienner, 1993.

———. "The Struggle for Knowledge: The Case of Emergent Oromo Studies." *African Studies Review* 39, no. 2 (September 1996): 95–123.

Asnake Kefale. "Federal Restructuring in Ethiopia: Renegotiating Identity and Borders Along the Oromo-Somali Ethnic Frontiers." *Development and Change* 41, no. 4 (July 2010): 615–635.

———. *Federalism and Ethnic Conflict in Ethiopia: A Comparative Regional Study*. London: Routledge, 2013.

———. "Narratives of Developmentalism and Development in Ethiopia: Some Preliminary Explorations." Paper presented at the Fourth European Conference on African Studies, Uppsala, Sweden, June 15–18, 2011.

———. "The (Un)making of Opposition Coalitions and the Challenge of Democratization in Ethiopia, 1991–2011." *Journal of Eastern African Studies* 5, no. 4 (2011): 681–701.

Assefa Fisseha. "Theory Versus Practice in the Implementation of Ethiopia's Ethnic Federalism." In *Ethnic Federalism: The Ethiopian Experience in Comparative Federalism,* edited by David Turton. Oxford, UK: James Currey, 2006.

Awet T. Weldemichael. "Formative Alliances of Northeast African Insurgents: Eritrean Liberation Strategy and Ethiopian Armed Opposition, 1970s–1990s." *Northeast African Studies* 14, no. 1 (2014): 83–122.

Bach, Jean-Nicolas. "*Abyotawi* Democracy: Neither Revolutionary nor Democratic—a Critical View of EPRDF's Conception of Revolutionary Democracy in Post-1991 Ethiopia." *Journal of Eastern African Studies* 5, no. 4 (2011): 641–663.

———. "Compromising with Ethiopianness After 1991: The Ethiopian Festival of the Millennium (September 2007–September 2008)." *Northeast African Studies* 13, no. 2 (2013).

Bahru Zewde. *A History of Modern Ethiopia, 1855–1974.* Addis Ababa: Addis Ababa University Press, 1992.

Barth, Fredrik. *Ethnic Groups and Boundaries: The Social Organization of Cultural Difference.* Boston: Little, Brown, 1969.

Bassi, Marco. "Customary Institutions in Contemporary Politics in Borana Zone, Oromiya, Ethiopia." In *Contested Power in Ethiopia: Traditional Authorities and Multi-Party Elections,* edited by Kjetil Tronvoll and Tobias Hagmann. Leiden: Brill, 2012.

———. "The Politics of Space in Borana Oromo, Ethiopia: Demographics, Elections, Identity, and Customary Institutions," *Journal of Eastern African Studies* 4, no. 2 (2010).

Baxter, P. T. W. "Ethiopia's Unacknowledged Problem: The Oromo." *African Affairs* 77, no. 308 (July 1978): 283–296.

Baxter, P. T. W., Jan Hultin, and Alessandro Triulzi, eds. *Being and Becoming Oromo: Historical and Anthropological Enquiries.* Lawrenceville, NJ: Red Sea, 1996.

Bereket Habte Selassie, *Conflict and Intervention in the Horn of Africa.* New York: Monthly Review, 1980.

Berhanu Abegaz. "Political Parties in Business: Rent Seekers, Developmentalists, or Both?" *Journal of Development Studies* 49, no. 11 (2011): 1467–1483.

Bevan, David L. "The Fiscal Dimensions of Ethiopia's Transition and Reconstruction." WIDER Discussion Paper No. 2001/56, August 2001.

Bongartz, Maria. *The Civil War in Somalia: Its Genesis and Dynamics.* Uppsala: Nordiska Afrikainstitutet, 1991.

Booth, David, and Frederick Golooba-Mutebi. "Developmental Patrimonialism? The Case of Rwanda," *African Affairs* 111 (2012): 379–403.

Branch, Adam, and Zachariah Mampilly. *Africa Uprising: Popular Protests and Political Change.* London: Zed, 2015.

Bratton, Michael. *Power Politics in Zimbabwe.* Boulder, CO: Lynne Rienner, 2014.

Brigaldino, Glenn. "Elections in the Periphery: Ethiopia Hijacked." *Review of African Political Economy* 38, no. 128 (June 2011).

Brownlee, Jason. *Authoritarianism in an Age of Democratization.* Cambridge, UK: Cambridge University Press, 2007.

Caeyers, Bet, and Stefan Dercon. *Political Connections and Social Networks in Targeted Transfer Programmes: Evidence from Rural Ethiopia.* CSAE WPS/2008-33, September 2008. https://www.academia.edu/people/search ?utf8=%E2%9C%93&q=Political+Connections+and+Social+Networks.

Call, Charles T. *Why Peace Fails: The Causes and Prevention of Civil War Recurrence.* Washington, DC: Georgetown University Press, 2012.

Cheeseman, Nic. "Populism in Africa and the Potential for 'Ethnically Blind' Politics." In *Routledge Handbook of Global Populism,* edited by Carlos de la Torre. London: Routledge, 2018.

Chege, Michael. "The Revolution Betrayed: Ethiopia, 1974–1979." *Journal of Modern African Studies* 17, no. 3 (September 1979): 359–380.

Chinigò, Davide. "'The Peri-urban Space at Work': Micro and Small Enterprises, Collective Participation, and the Developmental State in Ethiopia." Paper presented at the International Conference of Ethiopian Studies, Warsaw, 2015.

———. "The Politics of Land Registration in Ethiopia: Territorialising State Power in the Rural Milieu." *Review of African Political Economy* 42, no. 144 (2015).

Chinigò, Davide, and Emanuele Fantini. "Thermidor in Ethiopia? Agrarian Transformations Between Economic Liberalization and the Developmental State." *EchoGéo* 31 (2015).

Christia, Fortini. *Alliance Formation in Civil Wars.* Cambridge, UK: Cambridge University Press, 2012.

Clapham, Christopher. "Controlling Space in Ethiopia." In *Remapping Ethiopia: Socialism and After,* edited by Wendy James, Donald L. Donham, Eisei Kurimoto, and Alessandro Triulzi. Oxford, UK: James Currey, 2002.

———. "Ethiopia and Eritrea: The Politics of Post-insurgency." In *Democracy and Political Change in Sub-Saharan Africa,* edited by John A. Wiseman. London: Routledge, 1995.

———. *Haile Selassie's Government.* London: Longman, 1969.

———. "Introduction: Analysing African Insurgencies." In *African Guerrillas,* edited by Christopher Clapham. Oxford, UK: James Currey, 1998.

———. "Post-war Ethiopia: The Trajectories of Crisis." *Review of African Political Economy* 36, no. 120 (2009): 181–192.

———. *Transformation and Continuity in Revolutionary Ethiopia.* Cambridge, UK: Cambridge University Press, 1988.

———. "War and State Formation in Ethiopia and Eritrea." Paper prepared for Failed States conference, Florence, 2001.

Close, David, and Gary Prevost. "Introduction: Transitioning from Revolutionary Movements to Political Parties and Making the Revolution 'Stick.'" In *From Revolutionary Movements to Political Parties,* edited by Kalowatie Deonandan, David Close, and Gary Prevost. New York: Palgrave Macmillan, 2007.

Cochrane, Feargal. "Mediating the Diaspora Space: Charting the Changing Nature of Irish-America in the Global Age." In *Politics from Afar: Transnational Diasporas and Networks,* edited by Terrence Lyons and Peter Mandaville. Oxford, UK: Oxford University Press, 2011.

Coggins, Bridget L. "Rebel Diplomacy: Theorizing Violent Non-state Actors' Strategic Use of Talk." In *Rebel Governance in Civil War,* edited by Ana Arjona, Nelson Kasfir, and Zachariah Mampilly. Cambridge, UK: Cambridge University Press, 2015.

Coll-Black, Sarah, Daniel O. Gilligan, John F. Hoddinott, Neha Kumar, Alemayehu Seyoum Taffesse, and William Wiseman. "Targeting Food Security
Interventions in Ethiopia: The Productive Safety Net Programme." In *Food
and Agriculture in Ethiopia: Progress and Policy Challenges,* edited by
Paul A. Dorosh and Shahidur Rashid. Philadelphia: University of Pennsyl-
vania Press, 2012.
Colleta, Nat, Markus Kostner, and Ingo Wiederhofer. *Case Studies in War to
Peace Transition: The Demobilization and Reintegration of Ex-combatants
in Ethiopia, Namibia, and Uganda.* Washington, DC: World Bank, 1996.
————. *The Transition from War to Peace in Sub-Saharan Africa.* Washington,
DC: World Bank, 1996.
Collier, Paul, V. L. Elliott, Håvard Hegre, Anke Hoeffler, Mara Reynald-Querol,
and Nicholas Sambanis. *Breaking the Conflict Trap: Civil War and Devel-
opment Policy.* Oxford, UK: Oxford University Press/World Bank, 2003.
Collier, Paul, Anke Hoeffler, and Dominic Rohner. "Beyond Greed and Griev-
ance: Feasibility and Civil War." *Oxford Economic Papers* 61 (2009): 1–27.
Cooper, Neil. "Review Article: On the Crisis of the Liberal Peace." *Conflict,
Security, and Development* 7, no. 4 (December 2007).
Crummey, Donald. "Banditry and Resistance: Noble and Peasant in Nineteenth-
century Ethiopia." In *Banditry, Rebellion, and Social Protest in Africa,*
edited by Donald Crummey. Oxford, UK: James Currey, 1986.
Dahl, Robert, ed. *Political Opposition in Western Democracies.* New Haven,
CT: Yale University Press, 1996.
Data Dea Barata. "Family Connections: Inherited Status and Parliamentary
Elections in Dawro, Southern Ethiopia." In Kjetil Tronvoll and Tobias Hag-
mann, eds. *Contested Power in Ethiopia: Traditional Authorities and Multi-
party Elections.* Leiden: Brill, 2012.
Dawit Wolde Giorgis. *Red Tears: War, Famine, and Revolution in Ethiopia.*
Trenton, NJ: Red Sea, 1988.
della Porta, Donatella. *Clandestine Political Violence.* Cambridge, UK: Cam-
bridge University Press, 2013.
Dercon, Stefan. "Group-based Funeral Insurance in Ethiopia and Tanzania."
World Development 34, no. 4 (April 2006): 685–703.
Dercon, Stefan, and Daniel Ayalew. "Where Have All the Soldiers Gone?
Demobilization and Reintegration in Ethiopia." *World Development* 26, no.
9 (1998): 1661–1675.
Dercon, Stefan, and Andrew Zeitlin. "Rethinking Agriculture and Growth in
Ethiopia: A Conceptual Discussion." February 2009. http://fac.dev.ids.ac.uk
/pdf%20files/ethiopia%20paper1.pdf.
Dereje Feyissa. "Electoral Politics in the Nuer Context." In *Contested Power in
Ethiopia: Traditional Authorities and Multi-party Elections,* edited by
Kjetil Tronvoll and Tobias Hagmann. Leiden: Brill, 2012.
————. *Playing Different Games: The Paradox of Anywaa and Nuer Identifi-
cation in the Gambella Region, Ethiopia.* New York: Berghahn, 2011.
Dereje Feyissa, and Markus Virgil Hoehn, eds. *Borders and Borderlands as
Resources in the Horn of Africa.* London: James Currey, 2010.
Dessalegn Rahmato. *Agrarian Reform in Ethiopia.* Trenton, NJ: Red Sea,
1985.
————. "The Unquiet Countryside: The Collapse of 'Socialism' and Rural Agi-
tation." In *Ethiopia in Change: Peasantry, Nationalism, and Democracy,*

edited by Abebe Zegeye and Siegfried Pausewang, 242–279. London: British Academic Press, 1994.

de Waal, Alex. "Ethiopia's Transition to What?" *World Policy Journal* 9, no. 4 (Fall–Winter 1992): 719–737.

———. *Evil Days: 30 Years of War and Famine in Ethiopia*. New York: Africa Watch, September 1991.

———. "The Theory and Practice of Meles Zenawi," *African Affairs* 112, no. 446 (January 2013): 148–155.

di Nuzio, Marco. "'Do Not Cross the Red Line': The 2010 General Elections, Dissent, and Political Mobilization in Urban Ethiopia." *African Affairs* 113, no. 452 (July 2014): 409–430.

Donham, Donald L. *Marxist Modern: An Ethnographic History of the Ethiopian Revolution.* Berkeley: University of California Press, 1999.

———. "The 2005 Elections in Maale: A Reassertion of Traditional Authority or the Extension of a Nascent Public Sphere?" In *Contested Power in Ethiopia: Traditional Authorities and Multi-party Elections,* edited by Kjetil Tronvoll and Tobias Hagmann. Leiden: Brill, 2012.

Donham, Donald L., and Wendy James, eds. *The Southern Marches of Imperial Ethiopia: Essays in History and Social Anthropology.* Athens: Ohio University Press, 2002.

Downs, Anthony. *An Economic Theory of Democracy.* Boston: Addison Wesley, 1957.

Duffield, Mark. *Global Governance and the New Wars: The Merging of Development and Security.* London: Zed, 2001.

Dupuy, Kendra E., James Ron, and Aseem Prakash. "Who Survived? Ethiopia's Regulatory Crackdown on Foreign-funded NGOs." *Review of International Political Economy* 22, no. 2 (2015).

Eide, Øyvind M. *Revolution and Religion in Ethiopia: The Growth and Persecution of the Mekane Yesus Church, 1974–1985.* Oxford, UK: James Currey, 2000.

Elias Yitbarek. "The Role of *Iddir* in Neighbourhood Upgrading in Addis Ababa, Ethiopia." *Journal of Ethiopian Studies* 41, nos. 1–2 (June–December 2008): 187–197.

Elleni Centime Zeleke. "When Social Science Concepts Become Neutral Arbiters of Social Conflict: Reading the Ethiopian Federal Elections of 2005 Through the Ethiopian Student Movement of the 1960s and 1970s." *Northeast African Studies* 16, no. 1 (2016): 107–139.

Ellis, Stephen. *External Mission: The ANC in Exile, 1960–1990.* Oxford, UK: Oxford University Press, 2013.

Elwert, Georg. "Markets of Violence." In *Dynamics of Collective Violence: Processes of Escalation and De-escalation in Violent Group Conflicts,* edited by Georg Elwert, Stephan Feuchtwant, and Dieter Neubert. Berlin: Duncker and Humblot, 1999.

Erlich, Haggai. *Ethiopia and the Challenge of Independence.* Boulder, CO: Lynne Rienner, 1986.

Ethiopian People's Revolutionary Democratic Front (EPRDF). *The Development Lines of Revolutionary Democracy.* Addis Ababa: EPRDF, 2000.

Fantahun Ayele. *The Ethiopian Military: From Victory to Collapse, 1977–1991.* Evanston, IL: Northwestern University Press, 2014.

Fekadu Adugna. "Overlapping Nationalist Projects and Contested Spaces: The Oromo-Somali Borderlands in Southern Ethiopia." *Journal of Eastern African Studies* 5, no. 4 (2011): 773–787.

Firebrace, James, and Gayle Smith. *The Hidden Revolution: An Analysis of Social Change in Tigray (Northern Ethiopia) Based on Eyewitness Accounts.* London: War on Want, 1982.

Fisher, Jonathan, and Meressa Tsehaye Gebrewahd. "'Game Over?' Abiy Ahmed, the Tigrayan People's Liberation Front, and Ethiopia's Political Crisis." *African Affairs* (2018).

Flores, Thomas, and Irfan Nooruddin. *Elections in Hard Times: Building Stronger Democracies in the 21st Century.* Cambridge, UK: Cambridge University Press, 2016.

Gagliardone, Ignio. "New Media and the Developmental State in Ethiopia." *African Affairs* 113, no. 451 (April 2014).

Gandhi, Jennifer. *Political Institutions Under Dictatorship.* Cambridge, UK: Cambridge University Press, 2008.

Gandhi, Jennifer, and Ellen Lust-Okar. "Elections Under Authoritarianism." *Annual Review of Political Science* 12 (June 2009): 403–422.

Gebre ab Barnabas and Anthony Zwi. "Health Policy Development in Wartime: Establishing the Baito Health Care System in Tigray, Ethiopia." *Health Policy and Planning* 12, no. 1 (1997).

Gebru Tareke. *The Ethiopian Revolution: War in the Horn of Africa.* New Haven, CT: Yale University Press, 2009.

Geddes, Barbara. "Why Parties and Elections in Authoritarian Regimes?" Paper presented at the annual meeting of the American Political Science Association, Washington, DC, 2005.

Getachew Woldemeskel. "The Consequences of Resettlement in Ethiopia." *African Affairs* 88, no. 352 (July 1989).

Getahun Benti. "A Blind Without a Cane, a Nation Without a City: The Oromo Struggle for Addis Ababa." In *Contested Terrain: Essays on Oromo Studies, Ethiopianist Discourse, and Politically Engaged Scholarship,* edited by Ezekiel Gebissa. Trenton, NJ: Red Sea, 2009.

Giannetti, Daniela, and Kenneth Benoit, eds. *Intra-party Politics and Coalition Governments.* London: Routledge, 2009.

Gilkes, Patrick. *The Dying Lion: Feudalism and Modernization in Ethiopia.* London: Julian Friedmann, 1975.

———. "Elections and Politics in Ethiopia, 2005–2010." In *Understanding Contemporary Ethiopia: Monarchy, Revolution, and Meles Zenawi,* edited by Gérard Prunier and Éloi Ficquet. London: Hurst, 2015.

———. *Ethiopia: Perspectives of Conflict, 1991–1999.* Bern: Swisspeace Foundation, 1999.

———. *Ethnic and Political Movements in Ethiopia and Somalia.* Fairfield, CT: Save the Children, May 1992.

Gill, Peter. *Famine and Foreigners: Ethiopia Since Live Aid.* Oxford, UK: Oxford University Press, 2010.

Gramsci, Antonio. *Selections from the Prison Notebooks,* edited by Quintin Hoare and Geoffrey Nowell Smith. New York: International, 1971.

Green, Elliot. "Decentralization and Political Opposition in Contemporary Africa: Evidence from Sudan and Ethiopia." *Democratization* 18, no. 5 (October 2011): 1067–1086.

Greene, Kenneth F. "Opposition Party Strategy and Spatial Competition in Dominant Party Regimes: A Theory and the Case of Mexico." *Comparative Political Studies* 35, no. 7 (September 2002): 755–783.

Guerorguiev, Dimitar D., and Paul J. Schuler. "Keeping Your Head Down: Public Profiles and Promotion Under Autocracy." *Journal of East Asian Studies* 16, no. 1 (March 2016): 87–116.

Hackenesch, Christine. *Competing for Development? The European Union and China in Ethiopia.* Discussion Paper 3/2011. Stellenbosch: University of Stellenbosch, Centre for Chinese Studies.

Hagmann, Tobias. "Beyond Clannishness and Colonialism: Understanding Political Disorder in Ethiopia's Somali Region, 1991–2004." *Journal of Modern African Studies* 43, no. 4 (December 2005): 509–536.

———. "Fishing for Votes in the Somali Region: Clan Elders, Bureaucrats, and Party Politics in the 2005 Elections." In *Contested Power in Ethiopia: Traditional Authorities and Multi-party Elections,* edited by Kjetil Tronvoll and Tobias Hagmann. Leiden: Brill, 2012.

———. "Punishing the Periphery: Legacies of State Repression in the Ethiopian Ogaden." *Journal of Eastern African Studies* 8, no. 4 (2014): 725–739.

Hagmann, Tobias, and Mohamud Hussein Khalif. "State and Politics in Ethiopia's Somali Region Since 1991." *Bildhaan: An International Journal of Somali Studies* 6, no. 6 (2008). http://digitalcommons.macalester.edu /bildhaan/vol6/iss1/6.

Halliday, Fred, and Maxine Molyneux. *The Ethiopian Revolution.* London: Verso, 1982.

Hammond, Jenny. *Fire from the Ashes: A Chronicle of the Revolution in Tigray, Ethiopia.* Lawrenceville, NJ: Red Sea, 1999.

———. "Garrison Towns and the Control of Space in Revolutionary Tigray." In *Remapping Ethiopia: Socialism and After,* edited by Wendy James, Donald L. Donham, Eisei Kurimoto, and Alessandro Triulzi. Oxford, UK: James Currey, 2002.

Hammond, Laura. *This Place Will Become Home: Refugee Repatriation to Ethiopia.* Ithaca, NY: Cornell University Press, 2004.

Hansen, Stig Jarle. "Organizational Culture at War: Ethiopian Decision Making and the War with Eritrea (1998–2000)." PhD diss., Aberystwyth University, 2006.

Hansson, Göte. *The Ethiopian Economy, 1974–1994: Ethiopia Tikdem and After.* London: Routledge, 1995.

Hartley, Aidan. *The Zanzibar Chest: The Story of Life, Love, and Death in Foreign Lands.* New York: Grove, 2004.

Hartzell, Caroline A., and Matthew Hoddie. *Crafting Peace: Power-sharing Institutions and the Negotiated Settlement of Civil Wars.* University Park: Pennsylvania State University Press, 2007.

Hendrie, Barbara. "'Now the People Are Like a Lord': Local Effects of Revolutionary Reform in a Tigray Village, Northern Ethiopia." PhD diss., University College London, 1999.

———. "The Politics of Repatriation: The Tigrayan Refugee Repatriation, 1985–1987." *Journal of Refugee Studies* 4, no. 2 (June 1991): 200–218.

Heydemann, Steven, and Reinoud Leenders, eds. *Middle East Authoritarianisms: Governance, Contestation, and Regime Resilience in Syria and Iran.* Palo Alto, CA: Stanford University Press, 2013.

Hiwot Teffera. *Tower in the Sky.* Addis Ababa: Addis Ababa University Press, 2012.

Hoben, Allan. *Land Tenure Among the Amhara of Ethiopia.* Chicago: University of Chicago Press, 1973.

Howard, Marc Morjé, and Philip G. Roessler. "Liberalizing Electoral Outcomes in Competitive Authoritarian Regimes." *American Journal of Political Science* 50, no. 2 (April 2006): 365–381.

Huang, Reyko. "Rebel Diplomacy in Civil War." *International Security* 40, no. 4 (2016): 89–126.

Human Rights Watch. *"Such a Brutal Crackdown": Killings and Arrests in Response to Ethiopia's Oromo Protests.* New York: Human Rights Watch, 2016.

Huntington, Samuel P. *Political Order in Changing Societies.* New Haven, CT: Yale University Press, 1968.

Ishiyama, John. "From Bullets to Ballots: The Transformation of Rebel Groups into Political Parties." *Democratization* 23, no. 6 (2016): 969–971.

Iyob, Ruth. "The Ethiopian-Eritrean Conflict: Diasporic vs. Hegemonic States in the Horn of Africa, 1991–2000." *Journal of Modern African Studies* 38, no. 4 (2000): 659–682.

Jacquin-Berdal, Dominique, and Martin Plaut. *Unfinished Business: Ethiopia and Eritrea at War.* Trenton, NJ: Red Sea, 2004.

Jarstad, Anna K., and Timothy D. Sisk, eds. *From War to Democracy: Dilemmas of Peacebuilding.* Cambridge, UK: Cambridge University Press, 2008.

Johnson, Chalmers. *MITI and the Japanese Miracle: The Growth of Industrial Policy, 1925–1975.* Palo Alto, CA: Stanford University Press, 1982.

Joireman, Sandra Fullerton. "Opposition Politics and Ethnicity in Ethiopia: We Will All Go Down Together." *Journal of Modern African Studies* 35, no. 3 (September 1997): 387–407.

Justino, Patricia, Tilman Bruck, and Philip Verwimp, eds. *A Micro-level Perspective on the Dynamics of Conflict, Violence, and Development.* Oxford, UK: Oxford University Press, 2013.

Kahler, Miles, and Barbara Walter, eds. *Globalization, Territoriality, and Conflict.* Cambridge, UK: Cambridge University Press, 2006.

Kahsay Berhe. *Ethiopia: Democratization and Unity—the Role of the Tigray People's Liberation Front.* Munich: Verlagshaus Monsenstein and Vannerdat, 2005.

Kalyvas, Stathis. *The Logic of Violence in Civil War.* Cambridge, UK: Cambridge University Press, 2007.

Kamski, Benedikt. "The Kuraz Sugar Development Project (KSDP) in Ethiopia: Between 'Sweet Visions' and Mounting Challenges." *Journal of Eastern African Studies* 10, no. 3 (2016): 568–580.

Kassa Belay. "Constraints to Agricultural Extension Work in Ethiopia: The Insider's View." *South African Journal of Agricultural Extension* 31 (2002): 63–79.

Kassahun Berhanu. "Ethiopia Elects a Constituent Assembly." *Review of African Political Economy* 22, no. 63 (March 1995): 129–135.

Katz, Richard S., and Peter Mair. "The Evolution of Party Organizations in Europe: The Three Faces of Party Organization." *American Review of Politics* 14 (Winter 1993).

Katz, Richard S., and Peter Mair, eds. *How Parties Organize: Adaption and Change in Party Organizations in Western Democracies.* London: Sage, 1994.

Keen, David. "Incentives and Disincentives for Violence." In *Greed and Grievance: Economic Agendas in Civil Wars,* edited by Mats Berdal and David Malone. Boulder, CO: Lynne Rienner, 2000.

Keller, Edmond J. "The Ethnogenesis of the Oromo Nation and Its Implications for Politics in Ethiopia." *Journal of Modern Africa Studies* 33, no. 4 (1995): 621–634.

Kifle Wansamo. "Towards Building Stability in a Multinational/Ethnic Society: Conflicts in Sidamaland, Ethiopia." PhD diss., Lancaster University, 2007.

Kiflu Tadesse. *The Generation.* Trenton, NJ: Red Sea, 1993.

Koslowski, Rey, ed. *International Migration and the Globalization of Domestic Politics.* London: Routledge, 2005.

Krishnan, Pramila, Tesfaye Gebre Selassie, and Stefan Dercon. "The Urban Labour Market During Structural Adjustment: Ethiopia 1990–1997." WPS/98-1. Oxford, UK: Centre for the Study of African Economics, 1998.

Lautze, Sue, Angela Raven-Roberts, and Teshome Erkineh. *Humanitarian Governance in the New Millennium: An Ethiopian Case Study.* London: Humanitarian Policy Group, February 2009.

Lavers, Tom. "Food Security and Social Protection in Highland Ethiopia: Linking the Productive Safety Net to the Land Question." *Journal of Modern Africa Studies* 51, no. 3 (2013): 459–485.

———. "Patterns of Agrarian Transformation in Ethiopia: State-mediated Commercialisation and the 'Land Grab.'" *Journal of Peasant Studies* 39, nos. 3–4 (2012).

Lefort, René. *Ethiopia: A Heretical Revolution.* London: Zed, 1983.

———. "Free Market Economy, 'Developmental State' and Party-State Hegemony in Ethiopia: The Case of the 'Model Farmers.'" *Journal of Modern African Studies* 50, no. 4 (2012): 681–706.

———. "Powers—Mengist—and Peasants in Rural Ethiopia: The May 2005 Elections." *Journal of Modern African Studies* 45, no. 2 (2007): 253–276.

———. "Powers—Mengist—and Peasants in Rural Ethiopia: The Post 2005 Interlude." *Journal of Modern African Studies* 48, no. 3 (2010): 435–460.

Lenin, Vladimir. *Revolution, Democracy, Socialism: Selected Writings of Lenin,* edited by Paul Le Blanc. London: Pluto, 2008.

Levine, Donald. *Greater Ethiopia: The Evolution of a Multiethnic Society.* Chicago: University of Chicago Press, 1974.

———. *Wax and Gold: Tradition and Innovation in Ethiopian Culture.* Chicago: University of Chicago Press, 1965.

Levitsky, Steven, and Kenneth M. Roberts. "Latin America's 'Left Turn': A Framework for Analysis." In *The Resurgence of the Latin American Left,* edited by Steven Levitsky and Kenneth M. Roberts. Baltimore: Johns Hopkins University Press, 2011.

Levitsky, Steven R., and Lucan A. Way. "Beyond Patronage: Violent Struggle, Ruling Party Cohesion, and Authoritarian Durability." *Perspectives on Politics* 10, no. 4 (December 2012).

———. *Competitive Authoritarianism: Hybrid Regimes After the Cold War.* Cambridge, UK: Cambridge University Press, 2010.

———. "The Durability of Revolutionary Regimes." *Journal of Democracy* 24, no. 3 (2013): 5–17.

Lewis, Herbert S. *Jimma Abba Jifar: An Oromo Monarchy—Ethiopia, 1830–1932.* Lawrenceville, NJ: Red Sea, 2001.

Lindberg, Staffan I. *Democracy and Elections in Africa.* Baltimore: Johns Hopkins University Press, 2008.

Luckham, Robin. "Radical Soldiers, New Model Armies, and the Nation State in Ethiopia and Eritrea." In *Political Armies: The Military and Nation Building in the Age of Democracy,* edited by Kees Koonings and Dirk Krujt. London: Zed Books, 2002.

Lyons, Terrence. *Avoiding Conflict in the Horn of Africa: U.S. Policy Toward Ethiopia and Eritrea.* Special Report no. 21. New York: Council on Foreign Relations, December 2006.

———. "The Ethiopia-Eritrea Conflict and the Search for Peace in the Horn of Africa." *Review of African Political Economy* 36, no. 120 (2009): 167–180.

———. "Ethiopia in 2005: The Beginning of a Transition?" *Africa Notes* No. 25. Washington, DC: Center for Strategic and International Studies, January 2006, 1–8. http://csis.org/files/media/csis/pubs/anotes_0601.pdf.

———. "Great Powers and Conflict Reduction in the Horn of Africa." In *Cooperative Security: Reducing Third World Wars,* edited by I. William Zartman and Victor A. Kremenyuk. Syracuse, NY: Syracuse University Press, 1995.

———. "The Importance of Winning: Victorious Insurgent Groups and Authoritarian Politics." *Comparative Politics* 48, no. 2 (January 2016): 167–184.

———. "The Transition in Ethiopia." *Africa Notes* No. 127. Washington, DC: Center for Strategic and International Studies, August 1991. https://www.csis.org/analysis/africa-notes-transition-ethiopia-august-1991.

———. "Transnational Politics in Ethiopia: Diaspora Mobilization and Contentious Politics." In *Politics from Afar: Transnational Diasporas and Networks,* edited by Terrence Lyons and Peter Mandaville. Oxford, UK: Oxford University Press, 2012.

Lyons, Terrence, and Peter Mandaville, eds. *Politics from Afar: Transnational Diasporas and Networks.* Oxford, UK: Oxford University Press, 2012.

Lyons, Terrence, Christopher Mitchell, Tamra Pearson d'Estrée, and Lulsegged Abebe. *The Ethiopian Extended Dialogue: An Analytical Report, 2000–2003.* Report No. 4. Fairfax, VA: Institute for Conflict Analysis and Resolution, 2004.

Mackonen Michael. "What Is Amhara?" *African Identities* 6, no. 4 (November 2008): 393–404.

Magaloni, Beatriz. *Voting for Autocracy: Hegemonic Party Survival and Its Demise in Mexico.* Cambridge, UK: Cambridge University Press, 2006.

Magaloni, Beatriz, and Ruth Krischeli. "Political Order and One-party Rule." *Annual Review of Political Science* 3 (2010): 123–143.

Mampilly, Zachariah Cherian. *Rebel Rulers: Insurgent Governance and Civilian Life During War.* Ithaca, NY: Cornell University Press, 2011.

Manning, Carrie. "Assessing African Party Systems After the Third Wave." *Party Politics* 11, no. 6 (2005).

Marcus, Harold G. "Does the Past Have Any Authority in Ethiopia?" *Ethiopian Review,* April 18, 1992.

———. *A History of Ethiopia.* Berkeley: University of California Press, 2002.

———. *Life and Times of Menelik II of Ethiopia, 1844–1913.* Oxford, UK: Oxford University Press, 1975.

Markakis, John. "Anatomy of a Conflict: Afar and Ise Ethiopia." *Review of African Political Economy* 30, no. 97 (2003): 445–453.

———. *Ethiopia: Anatomy of a Traditional Polity.* London: Clarendon, 1974.

———. *Ethiopia: The Last Two Frontiers.* Oxford, UK: James Currey, 2011.

———. "Garrison Socialism: The Case of Ethiopia." *MERIP Reports* 79 (June 1979): 3–17.

Markakis, John, and Nega Ayele. *Class and Revolution in Ethiopia.* Nottingham, UK: Spokesman, 1978.

Matanock, Alia M. *Electing Peace: From Civil Conflict to Political Participation.* Cambridge, UK: Cambridge University Press, 2017.

Matsumoto, Mitsutobo. "Political Democratization and KMT Party-owned Enterprises in Taiwan." *Developing Economies* 40, no. 3 (2002): 359–380.

Matsuoka, Atsuko Karin, and John Sorenson. *Ghosts and Shadows: Construction of Identity and Community in an African Diaspora.* Toronto: University of Toronto Press, 2001.

McWirter, Cameron, and Gur Melamede. "Ethiopia: The Ethnicity Factor." *Africa Report* 3, no. 7 (September–October 1992).

Medhane Tadesse, and John Young. "TPLF: Reform or Decline?" *Review of African Political Economy* 97 (2003): 389–403.

Meheret Ayenew. "A Review of the FDRE's Urban Development Policy." In *Digest of Ethiopia's National Policies, Strategies, and Programs,* edited by Taye Assefa, 451–467. Addis Ababa: Forum for Social Studies, 2008.

Mekuria Bulcha. "Survival and Reconstruction of National Identity." In *Being and Becoming Oromo: Historical and Anthropological Enquiries,* edited by P. T. W. Baxter, Jan Hultin, and Alessandro Triulzi. Lawrenceville, NJ: Red Sea, 1996.

Meles Zenawi. "African Development: Dead Ends and New Beginnings." Paper presented at the Initiative for Policy Dialogue, Africa Task Force Meeting, University of Manchester, August 3–4, 2006.

———. "States and Markets: Neoliberal Limitations and the Case for a Developmental State." In *Good Growth and Governance in Africa: Rethinking Development Strategies,* edited by Akbar Noman, Kwesi Botchwey, Howard Stein, and Joseph E. Stiglitz. Oxford, UK: Oxford University Press, 2012.

Menkhaus, Ken. "Governance Without Government in Somalia: Spoilers, State Building, and the Politics of Coping." *International Security* 31, no. 3 (2006–2007): 74–106.

Messay Kebede. *Ideology and Elite Conflicts: Autopsy of the Ethiopian Revolution.* Lanham, MD: Lexington, 2011.

Milkessa Midega. "Ethiopian Federalism and the Ethnic Politics of Divided Cities: Consociationalism Without Competitive Multiparty Politics in Dire Dawa." *Ethnopolitics* 16, no. 3 (2017): 279–294.

Misganaw Addis Modes. *Practice of Self-government in the Southern Nations, Nationalities and People's Regional State: The Case of the Segen Area People's Zone.* Master's thesis, Addis Ababa University College of Law and Governance, 2014.

Mkandawire, Thandika. "Thinking About Developmental States in Africa." *Cambridge Journal of Economics* 25, no. 3 (2001): 289–314.

Mohammed Hassen. "Conquest, Tyranny, and Ethnocide Against the Oromo: A Historical Assessment of Human Rights Conditions in Ethiopia, ca. 1880s–2002." In *Contested Terrain: Essays on Oromo Studies, Ethiopianist Discourse, and Politically Engaged Scholarship,* edited by Ezekiel Gebissa. Trenton, NJ: Red Sea, 2009.

Morrison, J. Stephen. "Ethiopia Charts a New Course." *Journal of Democracy* 3, no. 3 (Summer 1992).

Mulugeta Gebrehiwot Berhe. "The Ethiopian Post-transition Security Sector Reform Experience: Building a National Army from a Revolutionary Democratic Army." *African Security Review* 26, no. 2 (2017).

———. "Transition from War to Peace: The Ethiopian DDR Experience." World Peace Foundation paper no. 16. *African Politics, African Peace* (June 2016). https://sites.tufts.edu/wpf/files/2017/07/16-Transitions-from-War-to-Peace-DDR.pdf.

Nathan, Andrew J. "Authoritarian Resilience." *Journal of Democracy* 14, no. 1 (January 2003): 6–17.

National Democratic Institute. *An Evaluation of the June 21, 1992, Elections in Ethiopia.* Washington, DC: National Democratic Institute, 1992.

Nilsson, Desirée, and Mimmi Söderberg Kovacs. "Revisiting an Elusive Concept: A Review of the Debate on Spoilers in Peace Processes." *International Studies Review* 13, no. 4 (December 2011): 606–626.

Nishi, Makoro. "Making and Unmaking of the Nation-State and Ethnicity in Modern Ethiopia: A Study on the History of the Silte People." *African Studies Monographs* (March 2005): 157–168.

Østebø, Terje. "Islam and Politics: The EPRDF, the 2005 Elections, and Muslim Institutions in Bale." In *Contested Power in Ethiopia: Traditional Authorities and Multi-party Elections,* edited by Kjetil Tronvoll and Tobias Hagmann. Leiden: Brill, 2011.

———. "Salafism, State Politics, and the Question of 'Extremism' in Ethiopia." *Comparative Islamic Studies* 8, nos. 1–2 (2014): 165–184.

Ottaway, Marina. "Democracy and New Democracy: The Ideological Debate in the Ethiopian Revolution." *African Studies Review* 21, no. 1 (April 1978): 19–31.

———. "Eritrea and Ethiopia: Negotiations in a Transitional Conflict." In *Elusive Peace: Negotiating an End to Civil Wars,* edited by I. William Zartman. Washington, DC: Brookings Institution, 1995.

———. "Social Classes and Corporate Interests in the Ethiopian Revolution." *Journal of Modern African Studies* 14, no. 3 (September 1976): 469–486.

Ottaway, Marina, and David Ottaway. *Ethiopia: Empire in Revolution.* London: Africana, 1978.

Paczynska, Agnieszka, ed. *The New Politics of Aid: Emerging Donors and Conflict Assisted States.* Boulder, CO: Lynne Rienner, 2019.

Pankhurst, Alula. *Resettlement and Famine in Ethiopia: The Villagers' Experience.* Manchester, UK: University of Manchester Press, 1992.

Paulos Chanie. "Clientelism and Ethiopia's Post-1991 Decentralization." *Journal of Modern Ethiopian Studies* 45, no. 3 (September 2007): 355–384.

Paulos Milkias. "Ethiopia, the TPLF, and the Roots of the 2001 Political Tremor." *Northeast African Studies* 10, no. 2 (2003).

Pausewang, Siegfried. "A Population Resisting Local Control and Intimidation? The Elections in Gedeo, Southern Region." In *Ethiopia Since the Derg: A Decade of Democratic Pretension and Performance,* edited by Siegfried Pausewang, Kjetil Tronvoll, and Lovise Aalen. London: Zed, 2002.

Pausewang, Siegfried, and Lovise Aalen. *Withering Democracy: Local Elections in Ethiopia, February/March 2001.* Working Paper 2001:07. Oslo: Nordem, 2001.

Pausewang, Siegfried, and Kjetil Tronvoll, eds. *The Ethiopian 2000 Elections: Democracy Advanced or Restricted?* Oslo: Norwegian Institute of Human Rights, 2000.

Pausewang, Siegfried, Kjetil Tronvoll, and Lovise Aalen, eds. *Ethiopia Since the Derg: A Decade of Democratic Pretension and Performance.* London: Zed, 2002.

Pei, Minxin. "Is CCP Rule Fragile or Resilient?" *Journal of Democracy* 23, no. 1 (January 2012): 27–41.

Perham, Margery. *The Government of Ethiopia.* London: Faber and Faber, 1948.

Piccolino, Giulia. "Peacebuilding and Statebuilding in Post-2011 Côte d'Ivoire: A Victor's Peace?" *African Affairs* 117, no. 468 (July 2018): 485–508.

Planel, Sabine. "A View of a Bureaucratic Developmental State: Local Governance and Agricultural Extension in Rural Ethiopia." *Journal of Eastern African Studies* 8, no. 3 (2014): 420–437.

Plaut, Martin. "The Oromo Liberation Front." *Review of African Political Economy* 33, no. 109 (September 2006): 587–593.

Plummer, Janelle, ed. *Diagnosing Corruption in Ethiopia: Perceptions, Realities, and the Way Forward for Key Sectors.* Washington, DC: World Bank, 2012.

Pool, David. *From Guerrillas to Government: Eritrea People's Liberation Front.* Athens: Ohio University Press, 2001.

Prendergast, John, and Mark Duffield. *Without Troops and Tanks: The Emergency Relief Desk and the Cross Border Operation in Eritrea and Tigray.* Trenton, NJ: Red Sea, 1994.

Quehl, Hartmut, ed. *Living in Wartimes—Living in Post-wartimes.* Proceedings of an international workshop on the Horn of Africa held in Melsungen, Germany, 2002.

Rakner, Lise, and Nicolas van de Walle. "Opposition Weakness in Africa." *Journal of Democracy* 20, no. 3 (July 2009).

Reid, Richard J. *Frontiers of Violence in North-east Africa.* Oxford, UK: Oxford University Press, 2011.

———. "Old Problems in New Conflicts: Some Observations on Eritrea and Its Relations with Tigray, from Liberation Struggle to Inter-state War." *Africa* 73, no. 3 (2003): 369–401.

Reuter, Ora John, and Graeme B. Roberton. "Subnational Appointments in Authoritarian Regimes: Evidence from Russian Gubernatorial Appointments." *Journal of Politics* 74, no. 4 (October 2012).

Richmond, Oliver P., and Roger MacGinty. "Where Now for the Critique of the Liberal Peace?" *Cooperation and Conflict* (2014).

Roeder, Philip G., and Donald Rothchild, eds. *Sustainable Peace: Power and Democracy After Civil Wars.* Ithaca, NY: Cornell University Press, 2005.

Ryle, John. "Letter from Ethiopia: An African Nuremberg." *New Yorker* (October 29, 1995).

Sartori, Giovanni. *Party and Party Systems: A Framework for Analysis.* Cambridge, UK: Cambridge University Press, 1976.

Schaefer, Charles. "Serendipitous Resistance in Fascist-occupied Ethiopia, 1936–1941." *Northeast African Studies* 3, no. 1 (1996): 87–115.

———. "'We Say They Are *Neftenya*; They Say We Are OLF.'" In *Contested Power in Ethiopia: Traditional Authorities and Multi-party Elections,* edited by Kjetil Tronvoll and Tobias Hagmann. Leiden: Brill, 2011.

Schedler, Andreas. "Authoritarianism's Last Line of Defense." *Journal of Democracy* 21, no. 1 (January 2010): 69–80.

———. "Elections Without Democracy: The Menu of Manipulation." *Journal of Democracy* 13, no. 2 (April 2002): 36–50.

———. "The Logic of Electoral Authoritarianism." In *Electoral Authoritarianism: The Dynamics of Unfree Competition,* edited by Andreas Schedler. Boulder, CO: Lynne Rienner, 2006.

Schedler, Andreas, ed. *Electoral Authoritarianism: The Dynamics of Unfree Competition.* Boulder, CO: Lynne Rienner, 2006.

Scheiner, Ethan. *Democracy Without Competition in Japan: Opposition Failure in a One-party Dominant State.* Cambridge, UK: Cambridge University Press, 2006.

Scott, James C. *Seeing Like a State: How Certain Schemes to Improve the Human Condition Have Failed.* New Haven, CT: Yale University Press, 1999.

Seegers, Kaatje, Joost Dessein, Sten Hagberg, Patrick Develtere, Mikiku Haile, and Jozef Deckers. "Be Like the Bees: The Politics of Mobilizing Farmers for Development in Tigray, Ethiopia." *Africa* 109, no. 430 (2009): 91–109.

Simegnish Yekoye Mengensha. "Silencing Dissent." *Journal of Democracy* 27, no. 1 (January 2017): 89–94.

Sindre, Gyda Marås, and Johanna Söderström. "Understanding Armed Groups and Party Politics." *Civil Wars* 18, no. 2 (2016): 109–117.

Smith, Gayle. "Ethiopia and the Politics of Famine Relief," *MERIP Reports* 17, no. 145 (March–April 1987).

Smith, Lahra. *Making Citizens in Africa: Ethnicity, Gender, and National Identity in Ethiopia.* Cambridge, UK: Cambridge University Press, 2013.

———. "The Politics of Contemporary Language Policy in Ethiopia." *Journal of Developing Societies* 24, no. 2 (2008): 207–243.

———. "Voting for an Ethnic Identity: Procedural and Institutional Responses to Ethnic Conflict in Ethiopia." *Journal of Modern African Studies* 45, no. 4 (2007): 565–594.

Solomon Negussie. *Fiscal Federalism in the Ethiopian Ethnic-based Federal System.* Ottawa: Forum of Federations, 2008.

Southall, Roger. *Liberation Movements in Power: Party and State in Southern Africa.* Oxford, UK: James Currey, 2013.

Spielman, David J., Dawit Kelemwork Makonnen, and Dawit Alemu. "Seed, Fertilizer, and Agricultural Extension in Ethiopia." In *Food and Agriculture in Ethiopia: Progress and Policy Challenges,* edited by Paul A. Dorosh and Shahidur Rashid. Philadelphia: University of Pennsylvania Press, 2012.

Staniland, Paul. *Networks of Rebellion: Explaining Insurgent Cohesion and Collapse.* Ithaca, NY: Cornell University Press, 2014.

Stedman, Stephen John. "Spoiler Problems in Peace Processes." *International Security* 22, no. 5 (1997): 5–53.

Stedman, Stephen John, Donald Rothchild, and Elizabeth Cousens, eds. *Ending Civil Wars: The Implementation of Peace Agreements.* Boulder, CO: Lynne Rienner, 2002.

Stevens, Franklin. "Regime Change and War: Domestic Politics and the Escalation of the Ethiopia-Eritrea Conflict." *Cambridge Review of International Affairs* 16, no. 1 (2003).

Stremlau, Nicole. "The Press and Political Restructuring of Ethiopia." *Journal of Eastern African Studies* 5, no. 4 (2011): 716–732.

Svolik, Milan W. *The Politics of Authoritarian Rule.* Cambridge, UK: Cambridge University Press, 2012.

Taddesse Berisso. "Modernist Dreams and Human Suffering: Villagization Among the Guji Oromo." In *Remapping Ethiopia: Socialism and After,* edited by Wendy James, Donald L. Donham, Eisei Kurimoto, and Alessandro Triulzi. Oxford, UK: James Currey, 2002.

Takkele Taddese. "Do the Amhara Exist as a Distinct Ethnic Group?" In *Ethnicity and the State in Eastern Africa,* edited by Mohamed A. Salih and John Markakis. Stockholm: Elanders Gotab, 1992.

Teferi Abate Adem. "The Local Politics of Ethiopia's Green Revolution in South Wollo." *African Studies Review* 55, no. 3 (December 2012): 81–102.

Tegegne Gebre-Egziabher. "Decentralization and Regional and Local Development: Trends and Policy Implications." In *Reflections on Development in Ethiopia: New Trends, Sustainability, and Challenges,* edited by Dessalegn Rahmato and Meheret Ayenew. Addis Ababa: Forum for Social Studies, 2014.

Tewodros Mezmur and Raymond Koen. "The Ethiopian Federal Ethics and Law Anti-corruption Commission: A Critical Assessment." *Law, Democracy, and Development* 15 (2011): 1–29.

Tronvoll, Kjetil. "Ambiguous Elections: The Influence of Non-electoral Politics in Ethiopian Democratisation." *Journal of Modern African Studies* 47 no. 3 (2009): 449–474.

———. "Borders of Violence—Boundaries of Identity: Demarcating the Eritrean Nation-State." *Ethnic and Racial Studies* 22, no. 6 (November 1999).

———. "Human Rights Violations in Federal Ethiopia: When Ethnic Identity Is a Political Stigma." *International Journal on Minority and Group Rights* 15 (2008).

———. "The 'New' Ethiopia: Changing Discourses of Democracy." In *Contested Power in Ethiopia: Traditional Authorities and Multi-party Elections,* edited by Kjetil Tronvoll and Tobias Hagmann. Leiden: Brill, 2012.

———. "Voting, Violence, and Violations: Peasant Voices on the Flawed Elections in Hadiya, Southern Ethiopia." *Journal of Modern African Studies* 39, no. 4 (2001): 697–716.

———. *War and the Politics of Identity in Ethiopia: The Making of Enemies and Allies in the Horn of Africa.* Oxford, UK: James Currey, 2009.

Tronvoll, Kjetil, and Tobias Hagmann. "Traditional Authorities and Multi-party Elections in Ethiopia." In *Contested Power in Ethiopia: Traditional Authorities and Multi-party Elections,* edited by Kjetil Tronvoll and Tobias Hagmann. Leiden: Brill, 2012.

———, eds. *Contested Power in Ethiopia: Traditional Authorities and Multi-party Elections.* Leiden: Brill, 2012.

Tronvoll, Kjetil, Charles Schaefer, and Girmachew Alemu Aneme, eds. *The Ethiopian Red Terror Trials: Transitional Justice Challenged.* Oxford, UK: James Currey, 2009.

Tucker, Stevens. *Ethiopia in Transition, 1991–1998.* Geneva: UNHCR Writenet, 1998.

Turton, David, ed. *Ethnic Federalism: The Ethiopian Experience in Comparative Perspective.* Oxford, UK: James Currey, 2006.

Ufen, Andreas. "The Transformation of Political Party Opposition in Malaysia and Its Implications for the Electoral Authoritarian Regime." *Democratization* 16, no. 3 (June 2009): 604–627.

van Veen, Erwin. *Perpetuating Power: Ethiopia's Political Settlement and the Organization of Security.* The Hauge Clingendael Institute, September 2016.

Vaughan, Sarah. *The Addis Ababa Transitional Conference of July 1991: Its Origins, History, and Significance.* Edinburgh: Edinburgh University, Centre for African Studies, 1994.

———. "Responses to Ethnic Federalism in Ethiopia's Southern Region." In *Ethnic Federalism: The Ethiopian Experience in Comparative Perspective,* edited by David Turton. Oxford, UK: James Currey, 2006.

———. "Revolutionary Democratic State-building: Party, State, and People in the EPRDF's Ethiopia." *Journal of Eastern African Studies* 5, no. 4 (November 2011): 619–640.

Vaughan, Sarah, and Mesfin Gebremichael. *Rethinking Business and Politics in Ethiopia: The Role of EFFORT, the Endowment Fund for the Rehabilitation of Tigray.* Africa Power and Politics Program Research Report No. 2. London: Overseas Development Institute, August 2011.

Vaughan, Sarah, and Kjetil Tronvoll. *The Culture of Power in Contemporary Ethiopian Political Life.* SIDA Studies No. 10. Stockholm: Swedish International Development Cooperation Agency, 2003.

Walle Engedayehu. "Ethiopia Democracy and the Politics of Ethnicity." *Africa Today* 40, no. 2 (1993): 29–52.

Waller, Michael. *Democratic Centralism: An Historical Commentary.* Manchester, UK: Manchester University Press, 1981.

Watson, Elizabeth. "Capturing a Local Elite: The Konso Honeymoon." In *Remapping Ethiopia: Socialism and After,* edited by Wendy James, Donald L. Donham, Eisei Kurimoto, and Alessandro Triulzi. Oxford, UK: James Currey, 2002.

———. "Making a Living in the Postsocialist Periphery: Struggles Between Farmers and Traders in Konso, Ethiopia." *Africa* 76, no. 1 (February 2006): 70–86.

Widner, Jennifer. "Political Parties and Civil Societies in Sub-Saharan Africa." In *Democracy in Africa: The Hard Road Ahead,* edited by Marina Ottaway. Boulder, CO: Lynne Rienner, 1997.

———. *The Rise of the Party State in Kenya: From Harambee! to Nyayo!* Berkeley: University of California Press, 1992.

Winrow, Gareth M. *The Foreign Policy of GDR in Africa.* Cambridge, UK: Cambridge University Press, 2009.

Woldemariam, Michael. *Insurgent Fragmentation in the Horn of Africa: Rebellion and Its Discontents.* Cambridge, UK: Cambridge University Press, 2017.

Wondwosen, Teshome B. "Ethiopian Opposition Political Parties and Rebel Fronts: Past and Present." *International Journal of Human and Social Sciences* 4, no. 1 (2009): 60–68.

Wood, Elisabeth Jean. *Insurgent Collective Action and Civil War in El Salvador.* Cambridge, UK: Cambridge University Press, 2003.

———. "The Social Processes of Civil War: The Wartime Transformation of Social Networks." *Annual Review of Political Science* 11, no. 1 (2008).

World Bank. *Ethiopia: Enhancing Human Development Outcomes Through Decentralized Service Delivery.* Report No. 32675-ET. Washington, DC: World Bank, May 2007.

World Bank. *Toward the Competitive Frontier: Strategies for Improving Ethiopia's Investment Climate.* Washington, DC: World Bank, 2009.

Yilmaz, Serdar, and Varsha Venugopal. "Local Government Discretion and Accountability in Ethiopia." International Studies Program Working Paper 08-38. Atlanta: Georgia State University, December 2008.

Young, John. "Along Ethiopia's Western Frontier: Gambella and Benishangul in Transition." *Journal of Modern Africa Studies* 37, no. 2 (1999): 321–436.

———. "Development and Change in Post-revolutionary Tigray." *Journal of Modern African Studies* 35, no. 1 (March 1997): 81–99.

———. *Peasant Revolution in Ethiopia: The Tigray People's Liberation Front, 1975–1991.* Cambridge, UK: Cambridge University Press, 1997.

———. "Regionalism and Democracy in Ethiopia." *Third World Quarterly* 19, no. 2 (1998): 191–204.

————. "The Tigray and Eritrean People's Liberation Fronts: A History of Tensions and Pragmatism." *Journal of Modern African Studies* 34, no. 1 (March 1996): 105–120.

Zartman, I. William. "Opposition as Support for the State." In *Beyond Coercion: The Durability of the Arab State,* edited by Adeed Dawisha and I. William Zartman. New York: Croom Helm, 1988.

Zemelak Ayitenew Ayele. "The Politics of Sub-national Constitutionalism and Local Government in Ethiopia." *Perspectives on Federalism* 6, no. 2 (2014): 89–115.

Zittlemann, Thomas. "Toward Acquisition of Conflict Knowledge: Fieldwork Among the Oromo Liberation Front and Oromo Refugees During the 1980s." In *Fieldwork: Social Realities in Anthropological Perspectives,* edited by Peter Berger, Jeanne Berrenberg, Berit Fuhrmann, Jochen Seebode, and Christian Strumpell. Berlin: WeiBensee Verlag, 2009.

Zolberg, Aristide. *Creating Political Order: The Party-States of West Africa.* Chicago: Rand McNally, 1967.

Zürcher, Christoph, Carrie Manning, Kristie D. Evenson, Rachel Hayman, Sarah Riese, and Nora Roehner. *Costly Democracy: Peacebuilding and Democratization After War.* Palo Alto, CA: Stanford University Press, 2013.

Index

235

About the Book

How did a group with its origins in a small Marxist-Leninist insurgency in northern Ethiopia transform itself into a party (the EPRDF) with eight million members and a hierarchy that links even the smallest Ethiopian village to the center? How do the legacies of protracted civil war and rebel victory over the brutal Derg regime continue to shape contemporary Ethiopian politics? And can the EPRDF, after widespread protests and a state of emergency, transform itself under new leadership to meet popular demands?

Answering these questions in his comprehensive study of nearly three decades of Ethiopian politics, Terrence Lyons argues that the very structures that enabled the ruling party to overcome the challenges of a war-to-peace transition are the source of the challenges that it faces now. While the new political leadership has promised dramatic reforms, Lyons observes, the powerful authoritarian ruling party remains in place, unreconstructed.

Terrence Lyons is associate professor in the School of Conflict Analysis and Resolution at George Mason University.

Wholesome

Over 100 nourishing sugar-, gluten-
and carb-conscious recipes

SARAH GRAHAM

A HUGE AND HEARTFELT THANK YOU

To Rob, Sophie and Isla, for being there every step of the way. I love everything about being on this journey with you. And to my family and friends, without you this would all be meaningless.

To Linda and your wonderful team at Penguin Random House, for giving me the opportunity to do this again. It's a joy writing books with you.

To Bev, Curtis, Luisa and Strone, for pouring so much beauty into the book during the creative process. It's so special to me that your fingerprints and cleverness are all over this.

Also, Luisa, besides styling this book so ridiculously brilliantly, thank you for generously contributing your recipes for Turmeric and Cinnamon Spiced Oats, Spiced Pork Ramen, and Lamb and Barley Bowls – they are full of goodness and I know that they will be instant favourites. Also, thank you for being such a special friend in food – your styling for all my TV work is amazing, your work ethic unparalleled. You are a treasure.

To Peter and Precious Bhasa, thank you for your generosity, patience, kindness and endless smiles. Pete, thank you for so many hundreds of hours spent in the kitchen testing recipes with me. We couldn't do this without you both.

And to some of my favourite friends who were also recipe testers (again!), you're scattered around the world and precious in so many different ways – your input is invaluable. A sung-from-the-rooftops and very sincere thank you to Debbie Buchner; Lucy Bell; Pamela Berry; Kimbo Brown-Schirato; my dearest and endlessly generous and kind and clever Mum, Wendy Conolly; Tracy Dane; Teneale Holley; Jenna Hutchings; Trudi Naylor; Justine Passaportis (and for so many moments spent brainstorming fun food ideas together); Luciana Popiol; Angela Ridge; Ruth Tanser; Yvonne Turner; Katherine Tyler (my special cuz!); Claire Van Tonder; and Elsie Velacott.

Published in 2016 by Struik Lifestyle
(an imprint of Penguin Random House South Africa (Pty) Ltd)
Company Reg. No. 1953/000441/07
The Estuaries, 4 Oxbow Crescent, Century Avenue,
   Century City, 7441
PO Box 1144, Cape Town 8000, South Africa

Reprinted in 2017, 2018

ISBN 978-1-43230-702-8

Publisher: Linda de Villiers
Managing editor: Cecilia Barfield
Editor and indexer: Joy Clack
Designer: Beverley Dodd
Photographer: Curtis Gallon
Food stylist: Luisa Farelo
Food stylist's assistant: Strone Henry
Proofreader: Bronwen Maynier

Reproduction by Hirt & Carter Cape (Pty) Ltd
Printed and bound in China by C&C Offset Printing Co., Ltd.

CONTENTS

INTRODUCTION

Hello again! I feel ridiculously lucky to be back here, with another book. And that's mostly thanks to you being part of the journey.

And so, **please read this part** – because if you *get it*, this book will change the way you think and the way you eat, and that will change the way you live.

I have poured much love and care into writing what I hope will be a guide to living well and eating mindfully, and to making small, positive changes every day. I want this book to be about goodness, and about food that nourishes our minds and our bodies. Putting goodness back in and getting goodness out.

I fully realise that I am not a qualified nutritionist or health professional, and I am not advocating to be that, but rather offering people ideas and inspiration for eating delicious, close-to-the-earth whole foods that are free of refined carbohydrates and sugars.

I grew up on a farm, where the milk came from down the road and the veggies grew in the back garden. It was no surprise to head off to bed with my mother's cottage cheese-filled muslin cloths hanging from our kitchen cupboards to make overnight cheese. Living simply and cleanly is what I love.

We are starting to see a really exciting and sustainable food revolution, and it begins with educating ourselves, and in our very own kitchens.

MY HEALTHY FOOD STORY

A few years ago, I had a rare stomach issue, which resulted in a fairly dramatic operation. I came out of hospital having lost a lot of weight much too quickly, and with serious blood sugar issues. On some days, several times a day, I would stand up and have to count to at least 10 before the black fog of dizziness would lift and I could see clearly again. This lasted for a good couple of months before I went to see a dietician.

To get me back on track and to regulate my blood sugar, the dietician created a healthy eating programme for me, and along with that and a lot of extra reading I learnt a massive amount about good and bad fats, carbohydrates and sugars. The whole experience drastically changed the way that I cook and eat. Ever since, I've limited sugar, gluten and refined or processed carbohydrates without even thinking about it, but haven't stuck to particularly hard and fast rules.

Over the last couple of years, I've revisited the whole conversation. I think a large part of it has been due to having children and striving to feed them well.

A FEW THINGS WORTH CHATTING ABOUT, LIKE, WHERE DOES OUR FOOD COME FROM?

A proviso: If you believe that we should be eating better food – that is, produced with a conscience, because it's kinder to the planet, to the livestock and produce involved, and ultimately to our own health – but you want to understand WHY, then here is some research that I've put together for you. As I mentioned previously, I am not technically qualified to have an opinion, so I've spent hours researching what the experts say to try to simplify the conversation for you. Also, although I love living and eating whole foods that are unprocessed and unblemished as far as possible, and I love the results I've seen in my own and other's lives, the information in this book is not intended to treat, diagnose, cure or prevent any specific diseases or act as a weight-loss guide. There is no one-size-fits-all when it comes to this kind of thing – our bodies are far too clever and complex for that – so you need to find what works best for you. It is worth consulting with your personal doctor or dietician if you have any specific conditions or concerns.

'Imagine if we had a food system that actually produced wholesome food. Imagine if it produced that food in a way that restored the land. Imagine if we could eat every meal knowing these few simple things: What it is we're eating. Where it came from. How it found its way to our table. And what it really cost. If that was the reality, then every meal would have the potential to be a perfect meal. We would not need to go hunting for our connection to our food and the web of life that produces it. We would no longer need any reminding that we eat by the grace of nature, not industry, and that what we're eating is never anything more or less than the body of the world. I don't want to have to forage every meal. Most people don't want to learn to garden or hunt. But we can change the way we make and get our food so that it becomes food again – something that feeds our bodies and our souls. Imagine it: Every meal would connect us to the joy of living and the wonder of nature. Every meal would be like saying grace.' – Michael Pollan, The Omnivore's Dilemma: A Natural History of Four Meals

Growing up on a farm, the food that reached our plates was almost always perfectly good and whole and locally sourced. Now, we have to go into supermarkets armed and aware. I have wanted to stamp my feet and shout at this machine that consumes us and propels us forward, helter skelter and with little consciousness of what is going into it, and about the state of what it is belching out. Where do we begin?

We have to be in this with our whole hearts, because our health and happiness are very much linked to what we are eating. We need to be educated, selective omnivores. And if we're going to buy really good ingredients, let's make them work hard for us. Let's be mindful of food waste, and let's love our leftovers. I have included tips for this where relevant throughout the book, showing you how to make your food and your budget travel further with you.

SHOULD I PANIC ABOUT ORGANIC?
[Sources: Eating Well; Marissa Lippert, Newcastle University; Health24.com; drweil.com; News24.com; SA Journal of Natural Medicine; Compassion in World Farming SA; Health.com; Michael Pollan; wwfsassi.co.za; Jeffrey M. Smith]

The rules for what classifies a product as organic seem to vary a little from country to country. The thing with South Africa is that, here, they are not laws, they are 'guidelines'. That makes this a fairly tricky topic with a lot of grey areas. I've referred as much as possible to South African information sources in my research, but if your home country is not South Africa, I suggest that you spend some time researching standards for where you live.

Generally, there are three main reasons why it makes sense to choose organic produce. I haven't gone into detail here – although there is so much to be aware of – so I suggest you do some further reading of your own.

1. **Fewer chemicals.** No antibiotics or growth hormones for animals, and they are fed organic feed. No pesticides or synthetic fertilisers for fruit and vegetables. No toxins leeching into the surrounding soils and water tables. The food reaches you in a natural state with its nutrient content intact.

2. **It's kinder to the plants and animals involved.** A lot kinder. Dramatically kinder.

3. **More nutrients.** In fact, organic produce boasts up to 40 per cent higher levels of some nutrients (including vitamin C, zinc and iron) than its commercial counterparts.

Obviously, we don't all have the budget to eat organically, and don't necessarily all have access to organic produce. So let's break it down further to the essentials versus the nice-to-haves.

FRUIT AND VEGETABLES

Dr Andrew Weil is a Harvard-educated and world-renowned leader and pioneer in the field of integrative medicine. He has turned what is a very lengthy conversation into two user-friendly and simple lists.

The Dirty Dozen

If you have the budget to buy these organic, or the time and space to grow your own, they are worth the effort.

Peaches | Apples | Sweet peppers (Sweet chillies/Capsicums) | Celery | Nectarines | Strawberries | Cherries | Lettuce | Grapes | Pears | Spinach | Potatoes

The Clean 15

These are less likely to be badly contaminated or produced and are not necessarily worth buying organic.

Avocados | Sweetcorn | Pineapples | Cabbage | Peas (frozen) | Onions | Asparagus | Mangoes | Papayas/Pawpaw | Kiwi | Aubergine | Grapefruit | Melons | Cauliflower | Sweet potatoes

Because of high exposure to GMOs and pesticides, it's also worth considering investing in carefully produced grains (including grain products such as pasta) and nuts.

LIVESTOCK – ORGANIC VS FREE RANGE

All organic livestock are free range, but not all free-range animals are necessarily organic. 'Free range' means that the animals are given the chance to live natural lives, space to roam, interact with other animals and eat a plant-based diet. But often these free-range animals are treated using conventional veterinary methods and the plant-based food that they eat may contain artificial additives. Free range also does not always mean that the animal has been in an open area its whole life. Organic livestock are fed with only 100 per cent natural feed and treated with approved homeopathic remedies.

THE CHICKENS WE EAT

According to Compassion in World Farming SA, in 1968 broilers (eating chickens) in South Africa were slaughtered at 62 days, weighing 1.2 kg. Today, they are slaughtered at 42 days (sometimes less), weighing about 1.9 kg. How on earth do they grow so fast? They are given growth hormones, which means that their bodies grow faster than their hearts

and lungs can support, often resulting in heart failure and tremendous death losses. In many cases, the chickens become crippled because their legs can't support the weight of their bodies. The list goes on, including cutting off beaks to prevent them from pecking each other to death.

THE CHICKENS THAT LAY OUR EGGS

For commercial egg-laying hens, or so-called 'battery hens' (hens permanently confined in small battery cages), life is no better. Twenty-two million laying hens live trapped in a space that's about 20 cm x 25 cm for life. Currently only three per cent of laying hens are free range in South Africa. Also, besides being treated unkindly, as with the chickens that we eat, these chickens are often pumped full of growth hormones and antibiotics, which can wreak havoc on our health.

OUR MEAT AND DAIRY

Eighty per cent of South African meat comes from animals that are either fed with feed that has been grown with artificial fertilisers and has been sprayed with pesticides, or they are reared in a feedlot system where they are given a cocktail of hormones and antibiotics.

Also, when it comes to pigs, research shows that in South Africa, two million breeding sows live in metal cages without enough room to move forwards or backwards, separated from their piglets. They eventually become our ham and bacon.

GRAIN FED VS GRASS FED

Basically, cattle and sheep that we eat should be eating grass. Grass-fed animals live in pastures of green grass and fresh air, not feedlots. Grass fed also usually means that the animals were raised without the use of genetically modified (GM) feed, antibiotics or growth hormones designed to fatten them up as quickly and as cheaply as possible, or to produce milk faster.

SEAFOOD
[Source: wwfsassi.co.za]

A huge increase in the amount of seafood taken out of the sea in recent decades means that our global fish stocks are dramatically (and in many cases irrevocably) depleted.

Sustainable seafood is also about how seafood is traded – how it's bought and sold and how it ends up on your plate. In South Africa, the Southern African Sustainable Seafood Initiative (SASSI) started in 2004, and has taken a brilliantly simple green (good), orange (tread with caution) and red (avoid altogether) 'traffic light' approach.

WHAT ABOUT GM FOODS?
[Sources: care2.com; thechalkboardmag.com; Gary Hirshberg; I have also referred to Jeffrey M. Smith, one of the world's leading advocates against GM foods]

This is a long, complicated story, and it's different in different corners of the world. It's been called a 'Giant Science Experiment' (Gary Hirshberg) and, if you dig a little deeper (which you really should), you'll find that it's a whole labyrinth of scary conspiracy theories and mutating genetic monsters and it's a toxic legacy to leave our children.

Firstly, what are GMOs?

Gary Hirshberg (JustLabelIt.org): *'This relatively new science allows DNA (genetic material) from one species to be transferred into another species. The mixing of genes from different species that have never shared genes in the past is what makes GMOs … unique. Basically, scientists have figured out how to manipulate plants at the genetic level to do things like resist damage from pesticides. GMOs are made in a lab. They breed one kind of corn with, for example, a pesticide. When the corn grows, it produces a pesticide within itself.'*

And we are EATING this stuff!

There are links to health issues from autism to cancer and lots in between; the seeds self-propagate and are basically indestructible, so we can't get them out of the system once they're in it; and they end up increasing herbicide use because pesticide-resistant 'superweeds' are joining in the fray, with horrific environmental consequences. Politicians and power-houses have too much invested, so government supervision is dangerously lax. As consumers, we have the power to sway what has become a nasty status quo, and to demand change.

Between 70 and 80 per cent of the maize that we eat in South Africa is genetically modified and, as the world's eighth largest producer (theepochtimes.com, 2012) South Africa is one of the only countries in the world whose staple (maize) is primarily GM. Even your simple supermarket loaf of bread is likely to be loaded with GM maize and soy.

DEMYSTIFYING SUGAR

[Sources: *I Quit Sugar* and *Simplicious*, Sarah Wilson; UCLA's Jonsson Comprehensive Cancer Center; Harvard School of Public Health; *Yale Journal of Biology and Medicine*; *British Medical Journal*; *Annals of Internal Medicine*; The Healthy Home Economist; *Fed Up* documentary; thechalkboardmag. com; MindBodyGreen.com; authoritynutrition.com; 'Sugar, The Bitter Truth', Dr Robert Lustig; *That Sugar Film*]

Where do we start with understanding, and ultimately conquering, something that has quietly taken over our lives? It's everywhere, it's addictive and the excess of it is making us sick. And it will make our children sick if we don't turn the tide, which can start in your very own kitchen. It's not so much the sugar we eat today, but the accumulation of it in our systems over time that is the real problem.

Much cleverer and more experienced people explain it far better than I do, and I've referred to them in my research and referenced them above. Here is how I see it in layman's terms.

What sugar does to us

Obviously based on your level of fitness, exercise and overall health, there is quite a lot of individual variation here, but excessive sugar consumption is linked to inflammation (which wreaks havoc on your immune system), hormonal complications, insulin resistance and metabolic complications, increased blood pressure and heart disease. It's addictive (some say almost as much as cocaine, and that it has similar effects on our neurological pathways), it spikes our blood sugar and saps our energy, and it makes us fat.

Also, you should note that I am not advocating no sugar at all; that isn't necessarily realistic. In fact, general health guidelines allow for nine teaspoons a day for men and six teaspoons a day for women. But you'd be surprised how quickly that adds up in a day.

Rather, I am speaking for sugar consciousness: eating healthy, natural sugars, and drastically reducing how much we casually consume on any given day, a lot of which is disguised in processed foods, even supermarket bread. Sweet treats should be just that, treats. But if you're living a life of less sugar, a little goes a long way, and smaller portions taste sweeter and richer.

Breaking down sugar – glucose and fructose

When we talk sugar consciousness, the main culprits that we should be taking into consideration (because they're the kinds that we're consuming the most) are glucose and fructose. Glucose can be absorbed and used by all of the cells in your body, which means that it can be broken down fairly quickly and used up fairly effectively (though, as with everything, too much is not a good thing either).

Fructose, on the other hand, can only be processed, or me-tabolised, by our livers. It's also addictive and twice as sweet as glucose. 'Humans don't produce fructose and throughout evolutionary history have never consumed it except season-ally when fruit were ripe. In the last century, we've gone from eating less than two pounds a year, to eating 132 pounds a year of added sugar,' writes Sarah Wilson in *Simplicious*). A build-up of fructose in our systems means an overload on the liver, which in the long term can have dire consequences – everything from fatty liver disease to type II diabetes and lots of nastiness in between. High-sugar diets are also linked to increased risk of heart disease, cancer, diabetes, obesity and more. Pancreatic cancer is said to use sugar as fuel.

Fructose is also, apparently, unstoppable. It doesn't deliver the message our brain needs that tells us we've had enough.

And you might not even know it yet, but you've almost definitely encountered the biggest and nastiest culprit, the sugar bomb that is high fructose corn syrup. It was introduced as a cheap, highly processed 'industrial sweetener' in the 1970s, and since then it's crept its way into a terrifying number of processed foods. With its rise to fame, we've seen an increase in all of the health issues that I mention earlier. Actually, there are over 60 other names used for sugar in processed foods, so it's worth doing your homework – or go by the rule of 'if you don't know or understand (or can't pronounce) what's in it, don't eat it'.

What about fructose from fruit?

Fruits are generally full of healthy fibre and water, which have a basic balancing effect on the fruit sugars and means that the fructose is released into your system more slowly. Also, they are real, whole foods, high in minerals and antioxidants. It's difficult to overdose on fructose from fruit, so how much you eat is up to you, but in general I prefer to choose low-sugar fruits and combine them with other foods such as protein or good fats. An apple or a handful of blueberries with a slice of my sugar-free Banana Bread with nut butter (see page 45) is a really satisfying snack, and more complex for our digestive system to break down, which in turn means that the sugars are released more slowly into our system.

In fruit juices, all the good fibre is stripped away, which means it enters our system as a sugary shot. And with dried fruit, the sugars are concentrated when the water is removed. Also, they're often full of preservatives.

Notes on alcohol and sugar

Again, this is quite a long and complicated conversation, and it's best to do your own research and chat to a health professional if you have any specific queries or health issues. Research seems to point to drier red wines as the best option.

My favourite sugar alternatives

Stevia – A plant-based sweetener that contains no sugars of any kind. You only need about six drops of the liquid or a tiny pinch of the powder to sweeten a whole cup of tea, so a little goes a long way. The flavour does take some getting used to, but if you can make it work it's a brilliant alternative. Fructose: 0. GI: 0. Win!

Coconut sugar – About 45 per cent fructose (similar quantity to table sugar), but it's one of my favourite natural alternatives if included in moderation in a generally low-sugar diet. The GI is 35, much lower than table sugar. It's also said to be more nutritious than regular table sugar. It has a delicious caramelly flavour.

Rice malt syrup (also known as brown rice syrup) – A fructose-free blend of complex carbohydrates made up of glucose and maltose. It looks like honey and is usually available from health food shops. People following strict high-fat low-carb diets or those with serious blood sugar issues tend to avoid this option because of the high carb levels, but it is a complex carbohydrate, made from fermented brown rice, which your body has to work harder to break down. It substitutes fairly well 1:1 with regular sugar in baking. Fructose: 0. GI: 25.

Honey and maple syrup – Fructose: about 40 per cent for both. GI: also between 45 and 50. On both levels they should be used sparingly. I use them as treats, to drizzle over porridge, or stirred into homemade hot chocolate.

Our ultimate goal? To quit the sweet stuff as much as possible; to get our sugar bliss from natural sources, fruits (in moderation), vegetables and grains; and to treat sweet treats as *treats*.

THREE MORE THINGS
Agave – It's a common alternative in 'healthy eating' circles, but it contains about 90 per cent fructose (more than white processed table sugar!) so it's worth avoiding. The GI is very low, however, at 15, which is why a lot of people opt for it.
Artificial sweeteners – Aspartame, saccharin, etc. are all chemically produced and toxic to our systems, causing havoc with our natural metabolic processes and 'tricking' our systems, leading to confusion and, in some cases, further weight gain.
Xylitol – Derived from xylan, which is found in the fibres of many plants, including berries, oats, sugar cane and birch. But, it can also be extracted from corn, most of which is GM. So unless your packaging stipulates that it's non-GM, it's probably best to avoid it. Also, it's processed via *sugar hydrogenation,* which basically means that it's violently industrialised and a bit scary. Sugar alcohols like xylitol are not broken down in the stomach like other sweeteners. This means that they arrive in your intestines intact and can provide a perfect breeding ground for unhealthy bacteria to thrive. Discuss extensive use with a health professional. Fructose: 0. GI: low, between 7 and 12.

In summary
My preferences are for moderate amounts of stevia, coconut sugar and rice malt syrup. As far as possible I use honey, maple syrup and dates as 'treats' and to add flavour, e.g. a small drizzle of maple syrup in a cosy winter porridge or over homemade granola.

WHAT ABOUT GLUTEN AND WHOLE GRAINS?
[Sources: *I Quit Sugar*; The Natural Nutritionist; Michael Specter, *The New Yorker*; www.health.harvard.edu]

Gluten is a buzzword and has become a bit of a culinary villain. You don't necessarily have to have full-blown and dramatic adverse reactions to have an intolerance that is negatively affecting your health without you knowing about it. Also, it's *everywhere,* from soy sauce to packet sauces and most processed foods in between.

You need to draw your own conclusions based on what is right for you and your digestive system. In my case, I choose to avoid it because of the stomach issues that I've suffered in the past, and because of the 'environment' that the gluten is generally found in – highly processed refined carbohydrates and sugar, and often genetically modified wheat or soy. Also, these products usually translate into our blood streams as high sugar, once the carbohydrates are broken down. So then we're back to sugar, and for that, don't count me in.

If your body tolerates it well, I see nothing wrong with making beautiful homemade bread with carefully produced and sourced stone-ground flour from time to time, and you can try my Spelt Soda Bread (see page 44) and Wholewheat-Rye Bread (see page 47) to see how beautiful a simple loaf of homemade bread can be.

The same goes for whole grains – most have a relatively high carbohydrate content, so I choose to cook and eat grains that are unrefined and as close to their natural state as possible. Some people don't tolerate grains well at all, and find it best to avoid them. Check with your health professional or dietician if you have any concerns.

AND WHAT ABOUT FATS?

Fat has been vilified for so many years, and there's a lot of confusion surrounding good and bad fats. It's worth doing a little reading and learning, but I love incorporating beautiful, healthy, natural fats into my food, and can definitely see and feel the benefits. They are highly nutritious and full of slow-releasing energy, but need to be eaten in moderation. I use a lot of avocado, coconut oil, milk and cream, nuts and nut butters, seeds, quality cold-pressed extra-virgin olive oil, animal fats from healthy, grass-fed animals, carefully sourced fish and seafood, quality cheeses, eggs and full-cream dairy.

OILS

My preferences are natural oils full of good fats – coconut oil, olive oil, avocado oil and good-quality butter. Avoid processed seed and vegetable oils, and canola oil.

SUPER FOODS

These are some of my favourites that you'll find dotted throughout the book. Even though some of them are quite expensive, it's worth building up your arsenal bit by bit.

They are not quick fixes, they are not band-aids. They are health-boosting add-ins. Little miracles created by nature.

Apple cider vinegar – Brilliant alkalising effects on your digestive system. Drink a tablespoon in a glass of lukewarm water to start your day. Preferably buy organic.

Avocado – One of my favourite favourites. It's incredibly densely nutritious and full of good fats (which, among other things, keep you fuller for longer and regulate blood sugar), has more potassium than bananas (great for healthy blood pressure), and contains lots of fibre and antioxidants.

Baobab powder – Baobab is considered a super fruit and I love its gentle tartness. It's extremely high in vitamin C, has more antioxidants than blueberries and goji berries, and has more potassium than bananas. Sprinkle over homemade granola or blend into smoothies.

Raw cacao powder – Good-quality raw cacao powder also has a long list of accolades to its name, including antioxidants, fibre and iron, and blood pressure and sugar levelling properties.

Chia seeds – Chia seeds are South American in origin and said to be among the most nutrient-dense foods on the planet. They're full of fibre, and two tablespoons have more healthy omega-3 than a serving of salmon. They're also really high in protein and are significant contributors to good heart health and blood sugar regulation.

Coconut oil – Full of 'good fats' and ideal for cooking at high temperatures. It also has great health-boosting properties.

Eggs – Good old eggs! They're densely nutritious and high in good cholesterols and good proteins, among other things.

Raw garlic – High in vitamins and minerals, and great for fighting colds and a whole lot of other things, including blood pressure.

Hemp seeds – Rich in good fats and fatty acids, they're nutrient dense and full of healthy plant-based proteins.

Raw honey – Nectar from nature! Raw honey is unprocessed and unpasteurised so it's full of goodness. It has anti-inflammatory and alkalising properties.

Kale – Said to be one of the most nutrient-dense foods on the planet, kale is the king of leafy greens. It's full of antioxidants, vitamin C, vitamin K (supports healthy blood clotting) and a long list of minerals.

Kefir – Kefir is a fermented yoghurt-style drink that's full of good probiotics and helpful bacteria. I've got more to say about it on page 14.

Lemon (and lemon water) – Lemons are obviously full of vitamin C (and a perfect simple salad dressing when paired with a drizzle of good-quality olive oil), but they're also brilliantly alkalising, and drinking a glass of just-warm lemon water in the morning will flush out your digestive system and rehydrate your body.

Moringa powder – You can sum moringa up as a miraculous, energy-boosting, immune-boosting, vitamin-packed, sugar-balancing genius. It's also called 'the miracle tree' because every part of the tree has medicinal uses. It's used to fight malnutrition in desperate parts of the world, is inexpensive and is becoming more widely available. It doesn't taste great, but I add it to my Kefir Breakfast Shots (see page 171). You can also drink it as a herbal tea, adding a teaspoon to a mug of boiled water. **Note:** Not recommended if you are pregnant or breastfeeding.

Nut butter – Nut butters have excellent satiety properties, and are full of good fats and oils, blood sugar stabilisers, protein, fibre and phytochemicals that are said to have cancer-fighting properties. Just take care to buy nut butter that is just that, pure nut butter, without added sugars, stabilisers or preservatives.

Quinoa – Technically, quinoa isn't a grain but a gluten-free grain-like seed, though it's prepared similarly to grains. It's high in protein and fibre, and a long list of added nutrients and amino acids, and originates from South America. It's not necessarily budget friendly though, but a little goes a long way and you can use it as a porridge or salad base, adding in lots of other goodies to make it go further.

Spirulina – This algae powder is full of antioxidant and anti-inflammatory properties. It's been linked with cancer-fighting properties and blood sugar leveling.

Turmeric – It's been a treasured Asian and Indian natural medicine for centuries, thanks mostly to its antioxidant and inflammation-fighting properties. Try the Turmeric and Cinnamon Spiced Oats (see page 28) or my soothing Golden Turmeric Milk (see page 162).

A HAPPY HEALTHY GUT, A HAPPY HEALTHY LIFE

Having had serious stomach and digestive issues in the past, and undergone major emergency stomach surgery, I know first-hand that the stomach is the epicentre of good health for our bodies. It's where our food is processed and where nutrients are extracted and sent out to our bodies, and if that environment is healthy, we're more likely to extract maximum goodness from the food that we eat. One of the best ways to boost gut health is by eating fermented probiotic-rich foods such as sauerkraut and kefir. *WHAT?* Read on, it's fascinating.

A few signs that you might have an unhealthy gut

You could have an unhealthy gut if you have any abnormal bowel function (bloating, gas, cramping, constipation, etc.) or if you have had to take antibiotics in the last few months. They wreak havoc on our digestive systems, killing both good and bad bacteria, and antibiotics found in meat and dairy products that we consume can have similar effects. Blood sugar issues and compromised immune systems can also often be directly linked to gut health.

If you have strong allergic reactions or bad bacterial infections such as candida or H. pylori (both of which I have suffered from), it's worth consulting a health professional and considering thorough tests and possibly a carefully managed elimination diet. I've done it and it works amazingly well – you then build potentially inflammatory foods (e.g. wheat, dairy and sugar) slowly back into your diet and see the effect that they have on your system, and you'll know what agrees with you and what doesn't.

BONE BROTHS AND STOCKS

Broths and stocks are back! They've had a lot of attention lately, and for good reason. The long, slow cooking releases amazing levels of protein, gelatine and essential minerals, all with significant health-boosting benefits.

Also, they require very little effort, just quiet bubbling away on the stove, and they make delicious and nutritious bases for soups, stews, curries and so much more. I make basic bone broth by roasting the bones until golden and almost caramelised, then simmering on the stovetop along with basic stock vegetables, some fresh herbs and water.

Simple stock is easier to make: just add bones and stock vegetables, and herbs if you like, to a large saucepan of water and simmer gently for 1–2 hours. Strain the broth or stock, then store the liquid in the fridge for up to five days or freeze in portions to use as and when needed.

SOAKING AND SPROUTING

Growing up, my mum often had sprouts sprouting in neat stacking containers. I had no idea how good they were for us. Essentially, the original grain, seed or legume that you sprout from has extra nutrients locked inside it in its raw 'sleeping form' – sprouting is like breathing life into it and opening a window to extra goodness. What that actually means is that phytic acid is neutralised and taken out of the equation. Why is that important? Phytic acid can reduce your body's ability to digest and absorb nutrients, so removing it means that the goodness is then more easily absorbable.

Yay! Also, sprouting is alkalising for our bodies and releases extra vitamins and nutrients. The most popular options for sprouting are lentils, beans, pumpkin and sunflower seeds, buckwheat, quinoa and even almonds. See also page 60.

LET'S FERMENT!
[Sources: *Nutrition Stripped,* McKel Hill; TheKitchn.com; Dr Amy Myers, MindBodyGreen.com; AuthorityNutrition.com]

Some of the most fun I had with this book was experimenting with fermenting. And yes, I'm sure that I say sauerkraut and I see some of you involuntarily shudder at the thought of sour, fermented cabbage. But hang in there, we're on to a very good thing. And it's not a new thing. The art of fermenting foods for its many health benefits has been practised around the world for generations. German sauerkraut is possibly most commonly known in the Western world, but Korean kimchi is just as delicious. It's not a global phenomenon for nothing; it's endlessly good for your gut.

Why is it good for you?
Fermented foods are full of probiotics, and probiotics are responsible for boosting immunity and improving digestion. They are wonderfully clever little guys, diligently helping us to extract the goodness from our food. And when it comes to optimal nutrition and holistic health, you'd rather have a strong healthy army on your side, right?

Fermenting involves a process called lacto-fermentation. For example, if you're making fermented cabbage (my Red Cabbage and Caraway Sauerkraut on page 170), it involves good, kind bacteria such as *Lactobacillus* that are present naturally in cabbage (and in products such as yoghurt and kefir) converting sugars in the cabbage to lactic acid, a natural preservative that fights nasty bacteria. Clever, hey? It's also an ancient method of preserving food ... clever again.

What are the options?
These are my favourite sources of probiotic-packed fermented foods.

Sauerkraut – If you buy store-bought sauerkraut, make sure that it's as close to its natural state as possible, and free of preservatives, vinegars or added sugars.

Kimchi – An Eastern-style sauerkraut with zingy additions such as ginger and chilli. I haven't included a recipe here, but you can find it quite easily in health shops.

Kefir – Kind of like a homemade yoghurt, originally from parts of Eastern Europe and Southwest Asia. It tastes a little bit sour, but if you mix in a little honey, nuts and other goodies it's delicious. You can also add it to smoothies for your kids and they won't even know it's there. In a nutshell, kefir is packed full of probiotics and nutrients, is amazing for digestion and good gut health, and has a whole slew of other plusses. I've seen it for sale in health food shops (avoid any with added sugars), but it's also really easy to make at home (see page 171).

Also, because of the fermentation process in kefir, there's very little lactose left in the final product, which means that even lactose-intolerant people can often tolerate it. If you're on a totally dairy-free diet though, there are some dairy-free alternatives, just do a little research.

Kombucha – I love kombucha! It tastes a little like cider and is basically a form of fermented green tea. It can also be found at most health shops. Or you can make your own by getting hold of a kombucha 'starter' called a scobe.

Sourdough – Sourdough bread is beautiful, wise bread made with fermented grains that takes days to coax to glory. Because of the fermentation process, it is also more easily tolerated by some people with milder gluten intolerances.

Alternatively, or additionally, consult your doctor or a dietician and discuss the options of good-quality probiotic supplements.

GETTING STARTED

That's a LOT of information to take on board, and it can be a little overwhelming, so here are a few tips from me on where to start with your own wholesome eating revolution.

1. Plan ahead

Map out a week of recipes – this saves so much time and money, I promise.

2. Stock your pantry

Eating well, sadly, is not always budget friendly, but with planning and preparation it's definitely manageable, and you can build up your stocks slowly. Also, keep a list for family and friends if they'd like to buy you a birthday hamper.

3. Take bite-sized chunks

You don't have to overhaul your entire life and pantry in one go. But every day, or even just every week to start with, make one positive change. A really simple example is to make a batch of Power Bars (see page 37) so that you have something healthy to snack on when you have an energy slump. I don't leave the house without some kind of good snack, even if it's a boiled egg, a handful of nuts or a slice of my favourite Banana Bread (see page 45).

4. Batch cooking and preparation

This is probably the biggest one for me. Take a little time out once a week to stock your fridge and make batch breakfasts and smoothies, storing them in glass jars in the fridge to eat on the go. I really find that if you have a good breakfast, you start your day right and then it's much easier to make healthy food choices after that. I also like to have cooked quinoa and brown rice in the fridge for speedy salads. A cup of quinoa can be used for a trout and avocado salad, a beetroot and feta salad, and then as a base for a simple curry. Cook once, eat two or three times. Also cook double batches of soups and stews and freeze half for next time, or store in the fridge for easy lunches. You can also freeze most of the baked treats in this book.

5. Don't count calories, and don't 'diet' – it's about goodness (and chewing!)

Eat mindfully, eat well and eat moderate portion sizes. Try to combine good fats, protein, unrefined carbohydrates and good green veggies with most meals. You'll feel energised and fuller for longer.

6. Be kind to yourself

RISE AND SHINE

Why drink your smoothie out of a glass when you can spoon it out of a bowl, loaded with toppings? Some of the toppings listed can be expensive and won't be in your everyday supermarket aisles – add them when you feel like your body really needs a boost, and even put them on your birthday list for friends to buy for you if you just can't stretch your budget far enough.

SMOOTHIE BOWLS

THE PRETTY PINK ONE
(Berry and Beetroot)

This is an all-time favourite – it's endlessly prettily pink, and I love the beetroot-berry flavour combination and the little hit of mint that pops through at the end.

Serves 2 | **Preparation time** 10 minutes

WHAT TO DO

Blend the smoothie ingredients together until smooth, add a little extra water to adjust the consistency if you like, pour into a bowl or two, add your toppings and serve. Alternatively, loosen with a little extra water and pour into a jar to enjoy on the go.

Note: Refrigerate any extra for up to 24 hours.

WHAT YOU'LL NEED

Smoothie

1 cup water

1 medium-sized beetroot, peeled and chopped

2 cups frozen mixed berries

2 Tbsp ground almonds (or desiccated coconut)

1 Tbsp baobab powder

1 Tbsp chia seeds

1 Tbsp roughly chopped fresh mint (or basil)

Toppings (all optional)

a few extra frozen or fresh berries

1 Tbsp hemp seeds

1 Tbsp roasted flaked almonds

a few baby basil leaves

small handful Everything Granola
   (see page 32)

THE CHOCOLATE ONE

Serves 2 | **Preparation time** 10 minutes

WHAT YOU'LL NEED

Smoothie

1 cup milk of your choice (I like cow's, coconut or almond milk)

1 large banana, roughly chopped and frozen

2 Tbsp nut butter (I love macadamia, but good old peanut butter is also fine)

2 Tbsp ground almonds

2 Tbsp coconut flour, to thicken (optional)

2 tsp raw cacao powder

½ Tbsp maple syrup (or rice malt syrup or a dash of stevia)

½ tsp ground cinnamon

½ tsp ground ginger

3 Tbsp chia seeds, to stir through after the smoothie has been blended (optional)

Toppings (all optional)

sliced banana

cacao nibs

hemp seeds

fresh raspberries or blueberries

toasted coconut flakes

roughly chopped roasted nuts or a scattering of Everything Granola (see page 32)

WHAT TO DO

Blend the smoothie ingredients together until smooth, stir through the chia seeds, adjust the consistency by adding a little extra water if you like, pour into a bowl or two, add your toppings and serve. Alternatively, loosen with a little extra water and divide between glass jars to enjoy on the go.

This can be eaten as a smoothie bowl with lots of toppings, but I prefer to pour it into a glass jar to drink on the go. These are my favourite greens, but you can use whatever you have available.

Serves 2–3 | **Preparation time** 10 minutes

Green
GOODNESS JARS

WHAT YOU'LL NEED

2–3 cups water or coconut water

2 cups baby spinach or roughly chopped kale

½ avocado or 2 Tbsp coconut oil

¼ medium-sized English cucumber, roughly chopped

1 courgette, roughly chopped

1 stick celery, roughly chopped

1 apple, roughly chopped

squeeze of fresh lemon or lime juice

1 thumb-sized piece of fresh ginger, skin on

2 Tbsp ground almonds

1 Tbsp chopped fresh basil

1 Tbsp spirulina or hemp seed powder (or moringa powder or your favourite green powder)

1 Tbsp chia seeds

1 Tbsp maca powder (optional, it's very expensive)

1 Tbsp baobab powder

WHAT TO DO

Blend the smoothie ingredients together in a high-speed blender until smooth. Loosen with a little extra water if you find it too thick. Divide between glass jars. Refrigerate for up to one day.

Love your leftovers: Save the ends of your courgettes when spiralising by stashing them all in a freezer bag, and add them to your green smoothies as and when needed.

Espresso Cashew
BREAKFAST SHAKES

This is kind of like a breakfast milkshake, but full of goodness – what could be better? I love making these for busy days and breakfast on the go.

Serves 2 | **Preparation time** 15 minutes (plus 2 hours soaking time)

WHAT YOU'LL NEED

½ cup raw cashew nuts, soaked in 1 cup filtered water for 2 hours

2 pitted dates

2 shots hot espresso

2 Tbsp chia seeds

½ tsp vanilla paste or extract

½ tsp ground cinnamon

1 banana, roughly chopped (optional)

1 cup filtered water

WHAT TO DO

1. Soak the dates in the hot espresso for at least 5 minutes to soften.
2. Drain and rinse the soaked cashews and transfer to a deep jug (for less mess when you blend everything together with a stick blender).
3. Add the dates, espresso and all remaining ingredients to the jug, and blend until smooth. Transfer to small glass jars and enjoy.

Note: Add 2 tsp raw cacao powder for a mocha version.

Beautiful Quinoa and Coconut BREAKFAST PUDDINGS

Serves 4 | **Preparation time** 10 minutes | **Cooking time** 15–20 minutes

WHAT TO DO

1. Cook the quinoa with the water, milk and spices in a medium-sized saucepan. Bring to a boil, then simmer for about 15 minutes with the lid askew, or until all the liquid has been absorbed and the quinoa grains are cooked through and creamy. Add a little hot water as it cooks if you find that it becomes too thick, although you are looking for a creamy, porridgy consistency.
2. Lightly toast the coconut shavings and chopped nuts in a dry pan over medium heat.
3. When the quinoa is cooked, layer the breakfast puddings in small glass jars or bowls, dividing and layering the remaining ingredients between them.

WHAT YOU'LL NEED

1 cup quinoa (or millet or oats)

½ cup water

1 x 400 ml can coconut milk (or almond or cow's milk)

½ tsp ground cinnamon

1 vanilla pod, sliced lengthways

To serve

Divide the following between the porridge bowls:

½ cup coconut shavings

¼ cup mixed nuts, roughly chopped

½ cup natural yoghurt or coconut cream

¼ cup mixed seeds (I like sunflower, flax and pumpkin)

maple syrup (or coconut sugar, xylitol or alternative healthy natural sweetener)

fresh pomegranate rubies or berries, for garnishing (if available)

Overnight Rooibos Buckwheat
BIRCHER MUESLI

Serves 4 | **Preparation time** 10 minutes | Refrigerate overnight

WHAT YOU'LL NEED

1 cup buckwheat, rinsed

1 cup whole rolled oats (certified gluten free if necessary)

2 pears (or apples or even carrots or beetroot), grated

½ cup roughly chopped almonds or pecan nuts

½ cup dried cranberries (no added sugar)

2 Tbsp chia seeds

¼ cup mixed seeds (e.g. sunflower, flax and pumpkin)

1 cup fresh orange or clementine juice

1 cup cooled rooibos tea (mixed with 1 tsp honey if you like) or nut milk

1 tsp vanilla extract

1 tsp ground cinnamon

To serve

Greek yoghurt or coconut cream

extra nuts and seeds

fresh or frozen berries

honey or maple syrup

WHAT TO DO

1. Mix everything together in a large glass jar and refrigerate overnight.
2. Divide into portions the following morning, top with Greek yoghurt or coconut cream, a scattering of extra nuts and seeds, berries and a drizzle of honey or maple syrup, and enjoy. You can also add Quick Chia Berry Jam (see opposite) as an extra topping.

I love feasting on little pots of Chia Pudding (see page 31), or adding swirls of this ludicrously pink jam to Everything Granola (see page 32) or a giant bowl of Greek yoghurt. And so much more. I hope you'll move straight on to making some as speedily as you can. If you're in two minds, then maybe if I tell you that this is Sophie and Isla's current sweet snack obsession you might be convinced? Surely a five year old and a two year old are the very best sounding boards for such things? Also, the chia seeds! They're on my Food Superheroes list, and I know they're a little annoyingly *à la mode* at the moment, but that's because their list of accolades is *long*. They're packed full of so-good-for-you proteins, omega-3 fatty acids (two tablespoons has more than a serving of salmon), antioxidants (three times more than blueberries), fibre and calcium, and they have also been linked to blood sugar leveling. Also, you can use them as an alternative to eggs in baking. To replace one egg: add 1 Tbsp chia seeds to 3 Tbsp water, leave the seeds to stand in the water for at least 15 minutes, and then add to your baking mix. Magic!

Makes 2 cups | **Preparation time** 5 minutes | **Cooking time** 20–30 minutes (mostly unattended)

Quick Chia
BERRY JAM

WHAT TO DO

1. Simmer the berries, honey, juice and zest in a heavy-based saucepan over low heat for 20–30 minutes, or until reduced by half and starting to thicken. Remove and set aside to cool.
2. Once the berry mixture has cooled slightly, stir through the chia seeds and then transfer to a sterilised glass jar and store in the fridge. Lasts up to two weeks.

WHAT YOU'LL NEED

2 cups fresh or frozen mixed berries (or even fresh stone fruit, roughly chopped – this is a great way to use up fruit that is really ripe)

2–3 Tbsp honey (or alternative healthy natural sweetener)

juice and zest of 1 orange or clementine (optional)

¼ cup chia seeds

CHOCOLATE BUCK-WHEAT CRÊPES
with Cappuccino Ganache

Serves 4 | **Preparation time** 10 minutes | **Cooking time** 15–20 minutes

WHAT YOU'LL NEED

Cappuccino ganache
1 Tbsp raw cacao powder
¼ cup coconut oil
¼ cup coconut cream
1–2 tsp maple syrup (or rice malt syrup)
½ tsp instant espresso powder

Pancakes
1 cup milk (or coconut milk)
1 cup buckwheat flour
2 eggs
1 tsp vanilla extract
1 Tbsp honey or alternative healthy natural sweetener (try a little coconut blossom sugar or rice malt syrup)

To serve
fresh banana slices or fresh berries
chopped roasted hazelnuts or pecan nuts

WHAT TO DO

1. To make the cappuccino ganache, heat the ingredients together in a heavy-based saucepan over very low heat until melted. Whisk together until smooth and set aside. Reheat just before serving if necessary.
2. To make the pancakes, whisk all of the ingredients together until you have a smooth batter.
3. Heat a little dollop of butter or coconut oil in a nonstick pan and pour in about ¼ cup of the mixture at a time. Swirl the pan to spread the mixture out as thinly as possible and, when bubbles rise on the surface of the pancake and the underside is lightly golden, flip and cook on the reverse side, also until lightly golden. It takes 3–4 minutes per pancake. Set the cooked pancakes aside on a warmed dinner plate and continue until you have used up all the batter.
4. Serve with the warm cappuccino ganache and top with the fruit and roasted nuts.

Notes: To cook these as fluffier American-style pancakes, add ½ tsp baking powder to the batter.
To make your own buckwheat flour at home, blitz 1 cup whole buckwheat in your food processor until fine, then pass through a sieve to remove any lumps.

Here's a budget-friendly, gluten-free, high-protein alternative to your favourite creamy morning oats. And it's just as easy to make. It's also great as a salad base, similar to how you'd use couscous, or you can add a handful to soups and stews to give them a bit of bulk. But my favourite way to enjoy this miracle grain is just like this, spiced gently with a little cinnamon and vanilla, and a drizzle of maple syrup to make merry; finished off with a handful of glossy berries or a good old banana and a scattering of roasted nuts. Use a ratio of about three or even four parts liquid to one part millet for a creamy, porridgy version; use a 2:1 ratio for a fluffier, more couscous-like result. Here I've used half water and half milk so that it's nice and creamy. You could also swap out cow's milk for coconut milk or nut milk and top with roasted pistachios and a small handful of coconut flakes if you like.

Serves 2 | Preparation time 5 minutes | Cooking time 15 minutes

MILLET PORRIDGE
with Lavender and Maple Syrup

WHAT TO DO

1. In a medium-sized saucepan, gently toast the millet for a minute or so over low heat, just until lightly fragrant. Add the water, milk, vanilla, cinnamon and salt, and simmer gently, partially covered, for 10–15 minutes. Add extra water or milk as you go, depending on the desired consistency.
2. Remove from the heat, stir through the lavender flowers, add your toppings and serve.

WHAT YOU'LL NEED

½ cup millet
1 cup water
1 cup milk (and a little more to add along the way if necessary)
1 tsp vanilla paste or extract
½ tsp ground cinnamon
pinch of salt
½ tsp lavender flowers, plus extra, for garnishing

Toppings (all optional)
fresh berries or roughly chopped banana, pear or apple
small handful toasted mixed seeds and nuts
maple syrup

MERIC AND CINNAMON SPICED OATS

with Fresh Raspberries and Maple Syrup

This recipe was kindly shared with us by my friend and food stylist, Luisa Farelo. It's just gently spiced with cinnamon and turmeric, which gives it a warm golden hue that can only leave you smiling.

Serves 2 | **Preparation time** 10–15 minutes | **Cooking time** 15 minutes

WHAT YOU'LL NEED

1½ cups full-cream milk or rice milk, plus extra for serving
¼ tsp ground cinnamon
¼ tsp turmeric
pinch of salt
pinch of grated nutmeg
¾ cup whole rolled oats (certified gluten free if necessary)
handful fresh raspberries
2 Tbsp sunflower seeds, lightly toasted
maple syrup, for drizzling

WHAT TO DO

1. Place the milk into a saucepan together with the cinnamon, turmeric, salt and nutmeg.
2. Add the oats and bring to a gentle simmer.
3. Simmer the oats for 8–10 minutes, stirring occasionally until thickened slightly and creamy.
4. Pour into bowls and scatter with raspberries and toasted sunflower seeds.
5. Drizzle over a little maple syrup and pour in a dash of cold milk.

Teff is a gluten-free whole grain native to northeast African countries, such as Ethiopia. It's as versatile as some of its favourite friends buckwheat and quinoa, and it's mild and nutty and yummy as a creamy porridge. This recipe also works beautifully with another African favourite, sorghum, which is also gluten free and highly nutritious.

Serves 4 | **Preparation time** 5 minutes | **Cooking time** 20 minutes
(mostly unattended)

Comforting TEFF PORRIDGE

WHAT TO DO

1. Add the teff and water (or water and milk if using) to a medium-sized saucepan along with the cinnamon and salt. Bring to a gentle bubble and leave to cook for about 20 minutes until the teff is fluffy and almost creamy (it looks similar to polenta when cooking). Remove from the heat and stir through the nut butter.
2. Serve in warmed bowls topped with banana slices, a drizzle of maple syrup and the chopped nuts and cacao nibs if using.

WHAT YOU'LL NEED

1 cup teff

3 cups water (or 1 cup milk/coconut milk/ nut milk and 2 cups water for a creamier version)

1 tsp ground cinnamon

pinch of salt

2 Tbsp nut butter (I like macadamia nut butter, or simply use peanut butter)

1–3 ripe bananas, thinly sliced

2–3 tsp maple syrup (or honey)

small handful roasted hazelnuts, roughly chopped (or just use mixed seeds)

cacao nibs (optional)

One of our girls' favourite anytime treats is a bowl of berry-ripple Greek yoghurt (our homemade chia jam swirled through the lovely white creaminess of the yoghurt). They are always delighted at how beautiful it is as it all changes colour. What could I do, then, but crank things up a notch and create these pretty little chia puddings just for them. I make them in dinky little glass jars and they think that's delightful too. The gelatinous nature of the chia seeds means that the mixture will set and have the consistency of a panna cotta – and how could that be anything other than wonderful?

SOPHIE AND ISLA'S PRETTIEST PINK CHIA PUDDING POTS
with Basil and Berries

Serves 4 | Preparation time 15 minutes |
Setting time 3 hours or overnight

WHAT TO DO

1. Mix together the chia seeds and Greek yoghurt. Then stir in the jam and mix as much or as little as you like (berry ripple or pink perfection, you choose). Divide between four small glass jars or pretty glasses and refrigerate for at least 3 hours, or preferably overnight.
2. Just before serving, garnish with fresh baby basil leaves (or use mint) and berries.

On the go: Make these in small glass jars with lids for breakfast on the go, adding a generous scattering of Everything Granola (see page 32) or mixed seeds and nuts once they are set.
Make them chocolate! Leave out the berry jam and instead add 2–3 tsp cacao powder, a dash of vanilla extract and 1–2 tsp maple syrup. Mix well and refrigerate until serving. Top with a little Everything Granola or a dollop of berry jam if you like.

WHAT YOU'LL NEED
2–3 Tbsp chia seeds
1 cup double-thick Greek yoghurt (or, my preference, coconut cream)
¼ cup Quick Chia Berry Jam (see page 23)
baby basil leaves (or mint), for garnishing
fresh or frozen berries, for garnishing

EVERYTHING GRANOLA
aka Chocolate Cinnamon Buckwheat Granola

I've probably eaten my weight of this gorgeous, golden, crunchy granola long ago, even for supper, and Sophie would be hot on my heels. (I think I'm at the stage when panic sets in if supplies run low.) Also, you should know that buckwheat has nothing whatsoever to do with wheat. It's a gluten-free, grain-like seed that's high in protein, budget friendly and happy to be toasted, like it is here, or simmered gently on the stove to make a creamy porridge, or stashed in a jar in the fridge overnight with all sorts of other goodies, waiting to transform into delicious Buckwheat Bircher Muesli (see page 22).

Makes about 24 servings | **Preparation time** 15 minutes | **Baking time** 30–45 minutes

WHAT YOU'LL NEED

2 cups whole rolled oats (certified gluten free if necessary)
2 cups buckwheat
1 heaped cup raw mixed nuts (I like pecan nuts, almonds and cashews)
1 cup mixed sunflower and pumpkin seeds
1 heaped cup coconut shavings
1 cup dried cranberries (no added sugar), to add after the granola has cooked and cooled

To bind everything together
⅓ cup coconut oil
¼ cup honey (or rice malt syrup)
¼ cup hot water
1 heaped tsp raw cacao powder (optional)
1 tsp ground cinnamon
1 tsp ground ginger

WHAT TO DO

1. Preheat the oven to 150 °C and ready two large nonstick baking trays.
2. Place the oats, buckwheat, nuts, seeds and coconut shavings in a large mixing bowl.
3. Heat the coconut oil until it's liquid, then add it to a small mixing jug along with the remaining binding ingredients. Stir well and pour over the granola ingredients. Mix well. If everything is not moist and well coated, add another ¼ cup hot water.
4. Spread the mixture onto the baking trays and bake for 30–45 minutes, or until fragrant and golden. Swap the baking trays around halfway through the cooking process if they are not baking evenly, and you can also stir it gently when you do to further help with even baking.
5. Remove from the oven and allow to cool completely before adding the cranberries and transferring to an airtight container. Lasts up to four weeks; or store half in the freezer for use at a later date.

Notes: We layer this into glass jars along with a dollop of full-fat yoghurt or coconut cream, Quick Chia Berry Jam (see page 23) and a few slices of fresh fruit for breakfast on the go, making four to five days' worth at a time. Add a handful to baked fruit for an almost-instant crumble topping.
Don't forget to sprinkle a little over Lovely Lemony Spelt and Granola Breakfast Muffins (see page 43) before baking.

Yes, breakfast crumbles are *a thing*. And, come to think of it, it's hardly surprising, right? I mean, when your morning disposition needs all the kindness it can muster (me!), what better place to start than with (healthy!) dessert for breakfast? This is a treasure. Also, you can mix it up according to what's in season and whatever your favourite fruits are. Make one at the start of the week and divide it up to take a portion to work each day with a dollop of Greek yoghurt or coconut cream on the side.

Serves 4–6 | **Preparation time** 10 minutes | **Baking time** 15–20 minutes

Nectarine and Blueberry BREAKFAST CRUMBLE

WHAT TO DO

1. Preheat the oven to 200 °C.
2. To make the fruit filling, place the fruit and berries in a shallow baking dish. Add the remaining ingredients, tossing gently until everything is well coated in the maple syrup.
3. Mix together the crumble ingredients until it has the consistency of rough breadcrumbs, and spoon the mixture over the fruit. Don't pat the topping down too heavily as it will become dense.
4. Bake for 15–20 minutes, or until the crumble topping is golden and fragrant. Serve immediately with Greek yoghurt or a drizzle of coconut milk or coconut cream (or coconut yoghurt if available).

Note: If you have any leftover crumble, refrigerate in a small container and use for an almost-instant breakfast the next time. Or, be super organised and make a double batch for the same reason, or make two crumbles at the same time and freeze one for later use. Full of good ideas, hey?

WHAT YOU'LL NEED

Fruit filling

4–6 ripe nectarines, halved, stones discarded
1 cup blueberries
1 heaped tsp lemon zest, and a little juice
1 heaped tsp orange zest, and a little juice
½ tsp vanilla extract
1–2 Tbsp maple syrup (or honey)
2–3 sprigs fresh thyme or 1 sprig fresh rosemary (optional, but delicious)

Crumble topping

125 g cold butter, cut into cubes (or ½ cup cold coconut oil)
½ cup almond flour
½ cup desiccated coconut
½ cup whole rolled oats (certified gluten free if necessary)
½ cup chopped pistachio or pecan nuts
1 Tbsp coconut sugar
½ tsp ground cinnamon
½ tsp ground ginger

These are good. They are packed full of all kinds of natural, nutritious, healthy, delicious amazingness; they are no-bake and take about 10 minutes to make; and they are the perfect afternoon pick-me-up. A few caveats before I continue – I make just palm-sized ones, because they're so nutrient dense and quite sweet, that's all you need. Also, they have dates in them, and they are very high in natural sugars (fructose) – in fact, I always explain them to Sophie as 'nature's caramels', so tread lightly, just one at a time will do.

Makes about 20 | **Preparation time** 10–15 minutes | **Setting time** about 1 hour

POWER BARS

WHAT TO DO

1. Place the dates and apricots in a large heatproof bowl or glass jug and cover with hot water. Leave to soak for 5–10 minutes while you add the remaining ingredients to a food processor.
2. Drain the fruit (reserving the liquid) and add to the food processor. Blitz well for about 2 minutes, until everything comes together in a sticky paste, although I prefer it still a little chunky and not absolutely smooth. Add a little of the reserved fruit-soaking water as you blend if you need to. You don't want the mixture to be too wet though as then you won't get nice solid bars.
3. Tip the mixture into a lined baking tin, and spread and smooth out using the back of a tablespoon (dipped in water from time to time so it doesn't stick to the mixture).
4. Place the baking tin in the freezer for up to 1 hour, remove and cut into squares or bars. Wrap the individual bars in baking paper and store in the fridge for up to two weeks, or in the freezer for up to a month.

Espresso Bliss Balls: I love these! Take the same ingredients, along with 1 tsp instant espresso powder, and instead of pressing the mixture into a baking tin and cutting into squares, take the blended mixture and roll it into small truffle-sized balls. Roll gently in a little raw cacao powder or finely chopped nuts if you like, and refrigerate in an airtight container. You can also add a handful of rolled oats to make the mixture go further.

WHAT YOU'LL NEED

1 cup pitted dates
½ cup dried apricots
1 cup dried cranberries (no added sugar)
1 cup ground almonds (or cashews)
½ cup whole almonds
¼ cup chia seeds
¼ cup mixed seeds (I use a mix of pumpkin, sunflower and linseeds)
¼ cup coconut oil
¼ cup nut butter
2 Tbsp baobab powder
2 Tbsp raw cacao powder
1 Tbsp hemp seed powder
1 tsp ground cinnamon
1 tsp ground ginger
pinch of salt

You could also add ½ cup whole rolled oats (certified gluten free if necessary) and/or ½ cup desiccated coconut to make them go further. You might need to add up to ¼ cup extra liquid if you do.

Chèvre, Courgette and Mint FRITTATA

Serves 4 | **Preparation time** 10 minutes | **Cooking time** 15–20 minutes

WHAT YOU'LL NEED

1 Tbsp olive oil

400 g courgettes, thinly sliced

1 Tbsp chopped fresh mint, plus extra for garnishing

½ cup frozen peas, thawed

75 g goat's cheese (chèvre) or feta

4 eggs

½ cup milk

salt and freshly ground black pepper

WHAT TO DO

1. Preheat the oven to 200 °C.
2. Heat the olive oil in a frying pan over medium-high heat. Fry the courgettes gently for 2–3 minutes, or until softened. Remove the pan from the heat, add the mint and transfer to a medium-sized lightly greased tart dish (unless you're using an ovenproof frying pan). Sprinkle over the peas and crumble over the cheese.
3. Lightly beat the eggs in a separate bowl. Add the milk and a pinch each of salt and freshly ground black pepper and pour over the filling. Bake for 15–20 minutes, or until golden. Remove from the oven, allow to cool slightly, and serve immediately garnished with the extra chopped mint.

Cauliflower and Chorizo HASH

Serves 4 | **Preparation time** 10–15 minutes |
Cooking time 10 minutes

WHAT TO DO

1. Heat the oil in a large pan. Add the onion, sausage, cauliflower, thyme, rosemary, spices, chilli and a pinch of salt and fry, over medium heat, for 5 minutes, or until the vegetables have softened.

2. Add the tomatoes, honey and vinegar, turn up the heat, and cook, uncovered, for 3–5 minutes, or until the tomatoes are starting to blister. Season with freshly ground black pepper and more salt if needed.

3. Serve immediately on warmed plates with toast or fresh bread, and top with an egg, a scattering of feta or goat's cheese and fresh basil or parsley, as well as a few slices of avocado.

WHAT YOU'LL NEED

1–2 Tbsp olive oil

1 medium-sized red onion, roughly chopped

150 g chorizo sausage, or similar, sliced

1 medium-sized cauliflower, roughly chopped

2 sprigs fresh thyme

1 sprig fresh rosemary

1 tsp ground cumin

1 tsp ground coriander

1 Tbsp sweet paprika

1 red chilli, deseeded and finely chopped

salt and freshly ground black pepper

2 cups cherry or rosa tomatoes, halved

1 tsp honey (or rice malt syrup or your
      preferred healthy natural sweetener,
      to taste)

1 Tbsp balsamic vinegar

To serve

toast or fresh bread

poached, fried or soft-boiled eggs

200 g feta or soft goat's cheese

handful chopped fresh basil
      and parsley

slices of ripe avocado

CAULIFLOWER RÖSTIS
with Smoked Trout, Avocado and Hollandaise

Serves 4–6 | **Preparation time** 15 minutes | **Cooking time** 15 minutes

WHAT YOU'LL NEED
Röstis

½ head cauliflower, roughly chopped

2 eggs, lightly beaten

1 Tbsp chopped fresh chives

2 Tbsp coconut flour

1 Tbsp psyllium husks

salt and freshly ground black pepper

2 Tbsp coconut oil

Hollandaise sauce

100 g butter

1 egg

2 Tbsp lemon juice

salt and freshly ground black pepper

To serve

slices of ripe avocado

slivers of smoked trout or salmon
(or crispy bacon)

soft-poached eggs

chopped fresh chives

WHAT TO DO

1. Cook the cauliflower for about 15 minutes in a saucepan of salted boiling water until tender. Remove from the heat, drain and set aside to steam for a few minutes (if you have a steamer, cook the cauliflower that way).

2. Add the cauliflower to a bowl and blend using a stick blender – the röstis hold together better when the mixture is left a little chunky. Mix in the eggs, chives, coconut flour and psyllium husks and season to taste.

3. Heat 1 Tbsp coconut oil in a large nonstick pan over medium-high heat and dollop in four tablespoons of the mixture (to make four röstis). Leave to cook until the underside is golden and crispy and the rösti is holding together (4–5 minutes). Turn over, cook on the other side until golden and then remove and set aside to drain on kitchen paper. Wipe the pan out with extra kitchen paper, add the remaining coconut oil and repeat until you have used up all the mixture.

4. While the röstis cook, make the hollandaise. Melt the butter in a saucepan until it is clear liquid, but not boiling. Cool slightly. Then, in a blender, gently blend the egg for a few seconds. Slowly pour in the melted butter, blending all the while, and continue blending for a further 20 seconds. Add the lemon juice and salt and pepper to taste, and then pour into a serving bowl. If the mixture seems too runny, it will thicken slightly as it cools. If it is too thick, loosen slightly by mixing in 1–2 Tbsp hot water.

5. To serve, top each rösti with slices of avocado, trout slivers and a poached egg. Sprinkle over a few chopped chives and serve immediately with the warm hollandaise sauce on the side.

Spelt is a beautiful, ancient whole grain that is sweet, nutty and delicious (try making my Gem Squash and Barley Risotto on page 49 using spelt instead). Ground spelt makes a brilliant all-purpose wholegrain flour that is high in protein and fibre, although it's not gluten free, so if you are highly sensitive to gluten, this is not for you.

LOVELY LEMONY SPELT
and Granola Breakfast Muffins

Makes 10–12 | **Preparation time** 10 minutes | **Baking time** 15 minutes

WHAT TO DO

1. Preheat the oven to 180 °C and lightly grease a nonstick muffin tray.
2. Mix together all the ingredients, except the granola, in a food processor until well combined.
3. Divide the mixture between 10–12 muffin holes. Sprinkle 1 tsp granola or mixed seeds and nuts onto each muffin, if you like.
4. Bake for 15 minutes until lightly golden and a skewer inserted into the centre of each muffin comes out clean. Serve as soon as possible. Extras can be frozen and warmed through when needed. These are delicious served warm with a dollop of natural yoghurt and a spoonful of Quick Chia Berry Jam (see page 23).

Note: You can make a double batch of these and prepare another fully prepared but unbaked muffin tray filled with the mixture. Place in the freezer until needed and bake straight from frozen, just cook for an extra 2–3 minutes.

WHAT YOU'LL NEED

100 g rice malt syrup
100 g unsalted butter
2 Tbsp lemon zest
1 large egg
1 egg yolk
1 cup natural yoghurt or buttermilk
300 g spelt flour
¼ cup roughly chopped pecan nuts
1 tsp baking powder
1 tsp bicarbonate of soda
½ tsp salt
½ cup Everything Granola (see page 32)
  or mixed seeds and nuts, for sprinkling
  over the top of each muffin before baking
  (optional)

Speedy Spelt
SODA BREAD

Makes 1 small loaf | **Preparation time** 10–15 minutes | **Baking time** 30 minutes

WHAT YOU'LL NEED

500 g spelt flour

2 tsp bicarbonate of soda

400 ml buttermilk

1 Tbsp olive oil

2 tsp honey (or alternative healthy natural sweetener)

1 tsp salt

WHAT TO DO

1. Preheat the oven to 200 °C and grease and line a medium-sized loaf tin.
2. Add the spelt flour and bicarbonate of soda to a large mixing bowl and whisk together thoroughly to make sure that the bicarb is evenly distributed. Add the remaining ingredients and mix until just combined. If it seems very dry, add ¼ cup water.
3. Transfer the mixture to the loaf tin.
4. Bake for about 30 minutes, or until golden and fragrant and the bread makes a hollow sound when overturned and knocked gently.

Note: My preference is to shape the dough gently into a small round, criss-cross the top using a sharp knife, place on a baking tray and bake free-form. A useful tip is to leave the loaf to cool to room temperature, slice and then freeze the extra slices, to be toasted directly from frozen when you're in need of a quick snack.

I love banana bread. Partly because it comes in the form of a loaf, and I LOVE bread in all its forms (although, of course, this is not technically a bread, but we are talking form here); and partly because of its dark-specked deliciousness and how ridiculously amazing it smells when it's baking. Oh and then there's the part that you're 'upcycling' food and turning bananas into something glorious, when they might otherwise have been sent packing for the compost heap. See, wins all round. PLEASE make this asap. I almost always have a sliced loaf in the freezer so that I can just pop a slice in the toaster and slather it with nut butter when I need a speedy snack. Also, it's one of Isla's favourites, and she subsists mainly on plain spaghetti ('no sauce Mum!') and bananas, so it must be good, right?

Makes 1 small loaf | **Preparation time** 15 minutes | **Baking time** 30–35 minutes

Beautiful BANANA BREAD

WHAT TO DO

1. Preheat the oven to 180 °C. Grease and line a small loaf tin.
2. For speediest results, add all the ingredients to a food processor and mix for 1–2 minutes until combined. Alternatively, mix with a hand mixer, stand mixer or a wooden spoon and mixing bowl.
3. Pour the mixture into the loaf tin and bake for 30–35 minutes, or until golden (and smelling delicious) and a skewer inserted comes out clean.

WHAT YOU'LL NEED

3 very ripe bananas, broken into chunks
3 eggs
½ cup pecan nuts (or any nuts of your choice; roughly chopped if you are not using a food processor)
¼ cup coconut oil, warmed until liquid (or vegetable oil or even olive oil)
¼ cup honey (or alternative healthy natural sweetener of your choice)
¼ cup natural yoghurt
1 cup almond flour
1 cup coconut flour
1 tsp bicarbonate of soda
1 tsp ground cinnamon
pinch of salt

...-changing
...TH LOAF
(...N FREE)

Makes 1 small loaf | **Preparation time** 15 minutes |
Baking time 30 minutes

WHAT YOU'LL NEED

1 cup almond flour

1 cup coconut flour

1 cup mixed seeds (I have a pre-mix that I buy
with sunflower, pumpkin and linseeds)

½ cup raw almonds

2 cups water (start with 1½ cups and add more
as needed; I find coconut flour very thirsty)

3 Tbsp psyllium husks (not expensive, available from health stores, they help to bind
everything together as there is no gluten)

1 tsp bicarbonate of soda

½ cup coconut oil, warmed until liquid

¼ cup natural yoghurt (or coconut milk or
extra water)

2 tsp honey (or alternative healthy natural
sweetener, to taste)

½ tsp salt

WHAT TO DO

1. Preheat the oven to 180 °C and grease and line a small loaf tin.

2. Mix all the ingredients together (this is easiest using a food processor,
   but a stand mixer also works well). If it seems very dry, add another
   ¼ cup water. It will NOT be like usual bread; it will seem quite crumbly
   and have the texture of damp beach sand – that's fine.

3. Transfer the mixture to the loaf tin, smooth out the surface gently using the back of a spoon and bake for about 30 minutes, or until golden.
   Cool completely before slicing, as it can be quite crumbly when warm.
   (A great tip is to leave the loaf to cool, remove from the loaf tin, slice
   and then freeze in slices and remove a slice at a time to thaw or toast
   just before eating.)

Love your leftovers: A slice of toasted health bread makes a great snack
or light lunch topped with mashed avocado, a squeeze of lime juice and
a dash of salt and pepper. Add a spoonful of Red Cabbage and Caraway
Sauerkraut (see page 170) for extra goodness.

This recipe can easily be doubled, just increase the kneading time by another 5–10 minutes.

Makes 1 small loaf | **Preparation time** 10 minutes |
Kneading time 15 minutes | **Resting and rising time** 13 hours |
Baking time 30–35 minutes

Wholewheat RYE BREAD

WHAT TO DO

1. In a bowl, mix together the water, yeast and olive oil, stir and leave to stand until the yeast is activated (the water will start to foam gently).
2. To a large mixing bowl, add the flours. Add the salt on one side of the bowl (you will add the yeast to the opposite side of the bowl – salt and yeast are not friends, so minimise initial contact).
3. Pour in the yeasted water and mix by hand until everything comes together in a rough ball. Knead by hand for 15 minutes, or in a food processor with a dough hook attachment, until the dough is smooth and elastic. Clean the bowl and grease lightly with olive oil, then return the dough to the bowl, cover with clingfilm or a damp kitchen towel and leave to rise for 8–12 hours (preferably overnight).
4. Transfer the dough to a lightly greased loaf tin and leave to rise again for another hour. Cut three or four diagonal slices into the surface of the bread just before baking to give the bread room to rise in the oven.
5. Bake in a preheated oven at 220 °C for 30–35 minutes, or until the loaf is fragrant, golden and it sounds hollow when knocked gently.

Notes: Wholewheat flour is, of course, heavier than white, so this bread is quite dense. I probably don't need to tell you that it's ridiculously delicious straight out of the oven with cold butter. It's not ideal for sandwiches, but amazing for toast. I cool the loaf, slice and then freeze in slices so that we can take out what we need when we need it. For a lighter loaf, substitute half white flour (unbleached, stone ground, non GM). You can also add mixed seeds and nuts if you like, but I tend to prefer the exquisite simplicity of the plainer version. Also, ask your local bakery (or supermarket bakery) for fresh yeast; they often give it away for free, and you'll notice such a difference. Substitute for dried yeast as explained above.

WHAT YOU'LL NEED
300–325 ml lukewarm water
1 x 7 g sachet yeast (or double weight fresh)
1 Tbsp olive oil or melted butter
250 g good-quality wholewheat flour
250 g good-quality rye flour
1 tsp salt

BOUNTY BOWLS

In our home, this is how we share our meals most nights when it's just Rob and me. There are all sorts of kind-of salads, kind-of soups, sort-of stews and lots of beautiful, simple, wholesome food in between. They're big bowls of goodness and kindness, and they are perfect for speedy, unfussy weeknight feasting.

Gem Squash and Barley RISOTTO

Serves 4 | Preparation time 5–10 minutes | Cooking time 40 minutes
(mostly unattended)

WHAT TO DO

1. Add the gem squash halves to a large saucepan of salted boiling water. Cook for about 15 minutes, or until the flesh is tender. Remove from the heat, drain and set aside to cool before removing the seeds.

2. Meanwhile, add the butter and olive oil to a large heavy-based saucepan over medium-high heat. When the butter starts to foam, add the onion and herbs and cook for 10 minutes, or until the onion has softened and is translucent.

3. Add the garlic and barley and stir until the barley is well coated in any remaining oil and butter. Add the wine and stir for about 5 minutes until the liquid has been absorbed.

4. Add the stock and milk and leave to simmer, uncovered and stirring occasionally, until the liquid has been absorbed and the barley is cooked through and creamy. Add a little extra water along the way if necessary. It should be creamy and not too dry.

5. Scoop out the flesh of the gem squash and add it to the risotto. Stir until everything is well mixed together. Add the Parmesan, check for seasoning and serve immediately in warmed bowls with a little extra grated Parmesan and fresh parsley to garnish.

WHAT YOU'LL NEED

3–4 gem squash, halved
1 Tbsp butter
1 Tbsp olive oil
1 medium onion, chopped
1–2 sprigs fresh rosemary (or thyme or oregano)
1 clove garlic, minced
1 cup barley, rinsed
½ cup white wine (optional, otherwise use extra stock)
2 cups chicken or vegetable stock
1 cup milk
¼ cup grated Parmesan cheese (or hard cheese of your choice), plus extra for garnishing
salt and freshly ground black pepper, to taste
fresh parsley, roughly chopped, for garnishing (or oregano)

Coconut
MUNG DAHL

Serves 2 | **Bean soaking time** 2–4 hours |
Preparation time 15 minutes | **Cooking time** 30 minutes

WHAT YOU'LL NEED

1 cup mung beans, soaked in water for
2–4 hours and then drained
1 Tbsp butter
1 Tbsp olive oil
1 small onion, finely chopped
1 large clove garlic, minced
1 heaped tsp grated fresh ginger
1 tsp each of ground cumin, ground coriander,
turmeric and mustard seeds
2–3 tsp medium curry powder
3–4 green cardamom pods, bruised to open
and release the seeds
½–1 tsp dried chilli flakes
2 curry leaves (if available)
2 Tbsp ground almonds
1 x 400 ml can coconut milk
pinch of salt

To garnish

scattering of lemon zest and a little squeeze
of juice
roughly torn fresh coriander
sprinkling of roasted slivered almonds

WHAT TO DO

1. Soak the beans first.
2. Add the butter and olive oil to a medium-sized heavy-based saucepan over medium heat. When the butter starts to foam, add the onion and cook for 8–10 minutes, until softened but not crisp or golden.
3. Add the garlic, ginger, spices, chilli flakes and curry leaves and cook for another 2–3 minutes.
4. Drain and rinse the mung beans and add them to the saucepan along with the ground almonds, coconut milk and salt. Stir, bring to a bubble and then leave to simmer with the lid on for 20–30 minutes until creamy and the mung beans have cooked through. Add water if necessary as you go along.
5. Remove from the heat and leave to stand while you prepare the garnish, then serve in warmed bowls. Tastes even better the next day when all the flavours have really had a chance to mellow and marry.

Notes: This can also be made with lentils and, of course, you could add a little meat in the form of shredded roast chicken. Or you could fry off a little lamb meat before you add the onion and then continue with the cooking process as explained, returning the lamb to the saucepan when you add the almonds and coconut milk.

Serves 4 | **Preparation time** 15 minutes | **Cooking time** up to 2 hours
(mostly unattended)

WHAT TO DO

1. Preheat the oven to 180 °C.
2. Mix together the ginger, garlic and chilli paste, smoked paprika, cinnamon and olive oil.
3. Rub the mixture onto the pork belly, season with salt and pepper and transfer to a roasting tray.
4. Add the chicken stock and roast for 1½ hours, or until cooked through and tender.
5. To make the broth, add all the broth ingredients to a medium-sized saucepan and allow to simmer for 15 minutes.
6. Season to taste and set aside until the pork is done.
7. To serve, reheat the broth over low-medium heat. Divide the noodles between four warm bowls and place half a head of bok choy into each bowl.
8. Pour over the simmering broth and top each bowl with a few slices of pork belly, sliced radishes, spring onions, chilli and two halves of a soft-boiled egg. Garnish with coriander and serve immediately.

WHAT YOU'LL NEED

1 tsp garlic, ginger and chilli paste
1 tsp smoked paprika
½ tsp ground cinnamon
2 Tbsp olive oil
600 g pork belly
salt and freshly ground black pepper
1 cup chicken stock

Miso broth

1 litre good-quality chicken stock
2 Tbsp light soy sauce
2 Tbsp miso paste
2 tsp garlic, ginger and chilli paste
1 tsp sesame seed oil

Garnish

250 g egg noodles or instant ramen noodles,
  cooked according to packet instructions
2 heads baby bok choy, halved and lightly steamed
4 radishes, thinly sliced
2 small spring onions, thinly sliced
1 chilli, thinly sliced
4 soft-boiled eggs, halved
handful fresh coriander, picked

HONG KONG HOISIN DUCK
with Pak Choi and Soba Noodles

Soba noodles are made from buckwheat, which is gluten free and easier for a lot of us to digest. Alternatively, serve this with my other favourite – simple and speedy courgette noodles.

Serves 2 | **Preparation time** 15 minutes | **Cooking time** 15 minutes

WHAT YOU'LL NEED
1 large duck breast
salt and freshly ground black pepper
200 g soba noodles
3–4 heads pak choi, halved lengthways (or 6–8 tenderstem broccoli)
2 spring onions, sliced diagonally, including tops
1–2 Tbsp chopped fresh coriander
1 red chilli, thinly sliced
lime wedges, for serving

Dressing
2 Tbsp hoisin sauce
1 tsp chopped fresh chilli
1 tsp grated fresh ginger
1 Tbsp honey
1 Tbsp sesame oil
1 Tbsp soy sauce
2–3 Tbsp lime juice

WHAT TO DO
1. Preheat the oven to 200 °C.
2. On the stovetop, heat a nonstick (and preferably ovenproof) pan over medium-high heat.
3. Cook the seasoned duck for 3–4 minutes, skin-side down, or until skin is golden and starting to crisp. Remove the pan from the heat, place the pan in the oven and cook for a further 5–8 minutes (for medium), and then remove and set aside to rest until serving.
4. Meanwhile, in a separate saucepan, cook the noodles according to the packet instructions, or until just al dente, adding the pak choi or broccoli for the last 2–3 minutes of cooking. Drain and set aside.
5. Prepare the dressing by mixing all the ingredients together. Check for seasoning.
6. To serve, divide the noodles and pak choi between warmed bowls, top with thinly sliced duck breast, and sprinkle over the chopped spring onions, coriander and chilli. Drizzle over the dressing and serve immediately with a few lime wedges on the side.

Notes: For a lighter version you can swap in courgette noodles for the soba noodles if you like.
This recipe also works brilliantly with pork medallions that are fried until golden and just cooked through.

BUTTER CHICKEN
with Coconut and Cardamom Cauli Rice

Serves 4 | Preparation time 15 minutes | Cooking time 30 minutes

WHAT TO DO

1. Add the olive oil and butter to a medium-sized saucepan over medium-high heat. When the butter starts to foam, add the chicken and cook for about 5 minutes until golden on all sides. Remove the chicken with a slotted spoon and set aside.

2. Add the spices and fresh ginger to the saucepan and cook for about 1 minute until fragrant. Add the garlic and cook for another minute.

3. Add the remaining ingredients, as well as the chicken pieces, turn the heat down to medium-low, and leave to simmer for about 15 minutes.

4. To make the cauli rice, roughly chop the cauliflower and add to a food processor. Pulse until you have rough, rice-like grains. Add the coconut milk to a saucepan, bring to a simmer and then add the cauliflower and cardamom. Cook for 3–4 minutes, drain off any excess liquid and season to taste.

5. Serve the butter chicken and cauli rice in warmed bowls topped with fresh coriander, slivered almonds and an extra drizzle of coconut milk.

Note: The cauli rice is optional. Add a can of rinsed and drained lentils for a speedier, simpler option if you prefer.

WHAT YOU'LL NEED

1 Tbsp olive oil

1 Tbsp butter

600 g skinless, deboned chicken thighs, cut into 2 cm cubes

1 tsp each of turmeric, ground coriander, ground cumin and dried chilli flakes

2 tsp medium curry powder or garam masala

1 cinnamon stick, snapped in half

2 tsp grated fresh ginger

1 clove garlic, minced

1 x 410 g can peeled, chopped tomatoes

2 Tbsp tomato paste

1 tsp coconut blossom sugar (or alternative)

1 x 400 ml can coconut milk (reserve 2–3 Tbsp)

3 Tbsp ground almonds (not vital)

Coconut and cardamom cauli rice

1 large head cauliflower

½ x 400 ml can coconut milk

4 green cardamom pods, bruised

To serve

1 small bunch fresh coriander

2 Tbsp roasted slivered almonds

2–3 Tbsp reserved coconut milk (see above)

Roast Chicken, Mushroom and Truffle Oil
LINGUINI

Serves 4 | **Preparation time** 10 minutes | **Cooking time** 15 minutes

WHAT YOU'LL NEED

400 g wholewheat linguini (or gluten-free pasta of your choice)

1 Tbsp olive oil

1 Tbsp butter

250 g mixed mushrooms, roughly chopped

1–2 sprigs fresh thyme or rosemary (or ½ tsp dried mixed herbs)

1 heaped cup shredded roast chicken

1–2 tsp truffle oil

½ cup fresh cream (or ¼ cup fresh cream and ¼ cup full-cream milk for a lighter version)

about ½ cup Parmesan cheese shavings, for serving

WHAT TO DO

1. Cook the pasta in a large saucepan of salted boiling water until al dente. Drain, drizzle with a little olive oil and set aside.
2. Meanwhile, heat the olive oil and butter in a large nonstick pan over medium-high heat. When the butter starts to foam, add the mushrooms and herbs. Cook for 4–5 minutes, or until lightly golden.
3. Add the chicken and truffle oil and cook for another minute before adding the cream. Leave to simmer gently for another 2–3 minutes, adding a little boiling water to loosen if necessary.
4. To serve, divide the pasta between warmed serving bowls, and top with the chicken and mushrooms and a generous scattering of Parmesan cheese. Serve immediately.

Note: Add a dash of balsamic vinegar to cut through some of the richness of the cream if you like.

SMOKED TROUT AND CAULIFLOWER COUSCOUS SALAD BOWLS
with Horseradish Dressing

Serves 2 | Preparation time 15 minutes | Cooking time 2–3 minutes

WHAT TO DO

1. Roughly chop the cauliflower and add to a food processor. Blitz for 1–2 minutes, or until the cauliflower has a grain-like consistency, similar to couscous.
2. Prepare the dressing by mixing all the ingredients together. Check for seasoning.
3. Add the cauliflower to a large saucepan of lightly salted boiling water and cook for 2–3 minutes. Drain well and divide between two serving bowls.
4. Top the 'couscous' with flaked smoked trout, sprinkle over the peas, and add the avocado slices and mint leaves. Season to taste with salt and pepper and dress generously with the horseradish dressing. Eat as soon as possible.

Notes: Add a handful of Home-grown Mung Bean Sprouts (see page 60) for a dose of extra goodness.
To make your own trout at home, preheat the oven to 190 °C, place the raw trout fillet in a shallow baking dish, drizzle with olive oil and a sprinkling of whole yellow mustard seeds and a little chopped fresh dill, season, and then bake for about 8 minutes, or until just cooked through.

WHAT YOU'LL NEED

1 small to medium-sized head cauliflower
250 g smoked trout fillet
small handful frozen peas, thawed
1 ripe avocado, roughly sliced
a few fresh mint leaves, for garnishing
salt and freshly ground black pepper

Horseradish dressing
¼ cup olive oil
2 Tbsp lemon juice
1–2 tsp creamed horseradish
pinch of salt
a little healthy natural sweetener

RED QUINOA AND FRESH BEETROOT SALAD

Serves 4 | **Preparation time** 10 minutes |
Cooking time 30 minutes (mostly unattended)

WHAT YOU'LL NEED

1 cup red quinoa, rinsed thoroughly
olive oil and a squeeze of lemon juice
salt and freshly ground black pepper
1 cup frozen peas
2 cups loosely packed grated raw beetroot
100 g feta or goat's cheese
1 ripe avocado, roughly chopped
2 Tbsp sunflower seeds, toasted
2 Tbsp pumpkin seeds, toasted
1 Tbsp each of roughly chopped fresh mint and basil
handful Home-grown Mung Bean Sprouts (see right), for extra goodness

Horseradish and dill dressing

¼ cup olive oil
2–3 Tbsp lemon juice
2 tsp creamed horseradish
1 Tbsp chopped fresh dill
pinch of salt
a little healthy natural sweetener

WHAT TO DO

1. Cook the quinoa in 2 cups of lightly salted and gently simmering water, with the lid off, for approximately 30 minutes, or until fluffy and cooked through. Once the grains are cooked through and the water has been absorbed, fluff it gently with a fork and add a drizzle of olive oil and lemon juice. Season with salt and pepper. Stir through the peas –they will warm through from the residual heat. Set aside.

2. Mix together the dressing ingredients, adjust to taste if necessary, and set aside until serving.

3. Transfer the quinoa to a serving platter and scatter over the beetroot, cheese, avocado, seeds, fresh herbs and sprouts. Serve immediately with an extra drizzle of olive oil and the dressing on the side.

Home-grown Mung Bean Sprouts: Rinse 1 cup mung beans (or your preferred option, such as lentils or chickpeas), then soak in filtered water overnight. Drain and rinse and then transfer to a sterilised glass jar. Cover with a breathable lid, such as muslin, secured in place with a ribbon or elastic band (or just leave in a colander covered with a clean tea towel). Leave to stand, rinsing every 8–12 hours until they start to sprout. This usually takes two to three days, depending on the temperature. When all the beans have sprouted, transfer to a glass jar and store in the fridge for four to six weeks.

AUBERGINE S~~TACKS~~
with Speedy Salsa Verde

WHAT TO DO

1. Preheat the oven to 200 °C.
2. Add a drizzle of olive oil and a generous sprinkling of Parmesan to the top of each aubergine slice and lay them side by side on a nonstick baking tray. Bake for 25 minutes, or until golden and the edges are starting to crisp. Remove and set aside.
3. While the aubergines bake, prepare the tomato sauce by placing a small heavy-based saucepan on the stove over medium heat. Add the olive oil and, when it's hot, cook the garlic for a minute until fragrant. Add the remaining ingredients, stir, bring to a gentle bubble and leave to simmer with the lid off for 20 minutes, or until the colour has deepened and the mixture has thickened.
4. Prepare the salsa verde by finely chopping the basil, garlic and sunflower seeds on a wooden chopping board. Once chopped, add to a small bowl along with the lemon zest. Drizzle in the lemon juice and olive oil, season with salt and a dash of your preferred natural sweetener and adjust to taste.
5. To serve, layer into large bowls or onto plates as follows: aubergine slice, tomato sauce, crumbled feta; repeat until you have used all of the ingredients. Drizzle 1–2 tsp of salsa verde over each serving, add a few fresh baby basil leaves to garnish and serve immediately.

Tip: Place a damp cloth under your chopping board so that it is secure and doesn't move around. This makes you more efficient and also gives you better control over the knife.

WHAT YOU'LL NEED

Aubergines
olive oil
about ⅓ cup finely grated Parmesan cheese
2 medium-sized aubergines, sliced lengthways 1 cm thick
about ⅓ cup crumbled feta cheese
baby basil leaves, for garnishing

Tomato sauce
½ Tbsp olive oil
1 clove garlic, crushed
4 ripe tomatoes, roughly chopped (set over a sieve
   for 5–10 minutes)
1 Tbsp roughly chopped fresh basil, stalks too
1–2 sprigs fresh oregano (if available)
1 level tsp dried chilli flakes
pinch each of salt, freshly ground black pepper and
   preferred healthy natural sweetener

Speedy salsa verde
handful fresh basil
1 small clove garlic
1–2 tsp sunflower seeds
1 tsp lemon zest
1–2 Tbsp lemon juice
1–2 Tbsp olive oil
pinch of salt
healthy natural sweetener, to taste

ROASTED TROUT
with Courgetti and Sesame-Soy Dressing

For this, you will need a spiraliser. If you're like me, and you shun things that are mainstream just because they've become a cliché, do away with that thinking very quickly because it's essential that you buy a spiraliser very urgently. You don't need a fancy pants one, just the pencil-sharpener kind will do fine, or even use a vegetable peeler and make wider 'pappardelle' if left with no other option. You still have all the satisfying fork-twirling that goes with ordinary pasta.

Serves 2 | **Preparation time** 10 minutes | **Cooking time** 15 minutes

WHAT YOU'LL NEED
2 x 200 g trout fillets (or salmon)
salt and freshly ground black pepper
1 cup baby tomatoes, halved
200 g courgette noodles (or buckwheat noodles)

Dressing
3 Tbsp sesame oil
3 Tbsp soy sauce
1–2 tsp fish sauce
3 Tbsp honey
1 clove garlic, minced
1 red chilli, deseeded and finely chopped
1 Tbsp grated fresh ginger
juice of 2 limes

To serve
chopped fresh coriander
1 Tbsp toasted sesame seeds

WHAT TO DO
1. Preheat the oven to 200 °C. Season the trout fillets lightly with salt and pepper and place them on a nonstick baking tray along with the tomatoes.
2. Mix together the dressing ingredients, pour about a third over the fish fillets and tomatoes and bake them for 10–12 minutes.
3. Meanwhile, prepare the courgette noodles. When you take the fish out of the oven, set aside to rest for a few minutes. Cook the noodles in a large saucepan of salted boiling water for 2 minutes, drain and divide into serving bowls.
4. Top the noodles with the fish fillets and roasted tomatoes, sprinkle over the chopped coriander and sesame seeds, drizzle over extra dressing and serve immediately.

Serves 4 | **Preparation time** 15 minutes | **Cooking time** 5–10 minutes

WHAT TO DO

1. First make the pesto. Blitz together all the pesto ingredients and check for seasoning. Loosen with a little extra olive oil and 1–2 Tbsp hot water if necessary and set aside.
2. Rinse the calamari rings, drain in a colander and set aside on a plate lined with kitchen paper or a clean dishcloth to dry off. The drier the squid, the crispier the end result. Season with the chilli flakes and a generous pinch each of salt and pepper.
3. Heat a large frying pan over medium-high heat and add the olive oil. Fry the calamari for 4–6 minutes, or until lightly golden and crispy. Remove from the heat and set aside.
4. Meanwhile, cook the courgette noodles in a large saucepan of salted boiling water for 1–2 minutes, drain and set aside in a large mixing bowl.
5. Add half the pesto to the courgette noodles and mix until they are well coated. Divide between warmed serving bowls, top with the calamari and serve with the extra pesto on the side. Garnish with shavings of Parmesan cheese.

WHAT YOU'LL NEED

500 g fresh calamari rings
½–1 tsp dried chilli flakes
salt and freshly ground black pepper
1 Tbsp olive oil
500 g courgette noodles (or wholewheat or gluten-free linguini)
shavings of Parmesan cheese, for garnishing

Pea and mint pesto

1 cup frozen peas, thawed (soak in 1–2 cups just-boiled water for a few minutes and then drain)
1 Tbsp chopped fresh mint
2 Tbsp raw almonds, roughly chopped
2 Tbsp freshly grated Parmesan cheese
3–4 Tbsp olive oil
zest of ½ lemon
juice of 1 lemon
1 clove garlic, chopped
½ tsp healthy natural sweetener

Speedy
TUNA NIÇOISE SALAD

Serves 2 | **Preparation time** 10 minutes | **Cooking time** 15–20 minutes

WHAT YOU'LL NEED

Vinaigrette
juice of 1 lemon
3 Tbsp olive oil
1 tsp Dijon mustard
healthy natural sweetener, to taste
½ small onion or shallot, finely chopped
(or 2–3 spring onions)
½ clove garlic, minced
salt and freshly ground black pepper, to taste

Salad
½ cup red quinoa
10 fresh asparagus spears
1 Tbsp sesame seeds
pinch each of salt and freshly ground
black pepper
1 small tuna fillet
1 Tbsp olive oil
1 ripe avocado, roughly chopped
½ small red onion, thinly sliced
2 soft-poached eggs
micro greens, for garnishing

WHAT TO DO

1. Whisk all the vinaigrette ingredients together, adjust to taste if necessary and set aside.
2. Cook the quinoa according to the packet instructions. Bring a saucepan of salted water to a simmer on the stove to cook the asparagus just before serving.
3. Add the sesame seeds to a dinner plate along with a pinch each of salt and pepper. Roll the tuna in the seeds until well coated.
4. Heat the olive oil in a large pan over high heat. Sear the tuna for 1–2 minutes on each side, remove and set aside to rest before slicing into 1 cm thick slices.
5. Finally, cook the asparagus for 1 minute and drain, then layer all the salad ingredients prettily onto two dinner plates, drizzle over the vinaigrette, garnish with micro greens and serve immediately.

This is earthy and comforting and wonderfully satisfying. It's generous, whole-hearted food that's hard not to love. For best results and maximum nutritional benefits, it's best to soak the brown rice for 8–12 hours in filtered water and then drain and rinse again before cooking.

Serves 4–6 | **Preparation time** 10–15 minutes | **Cooking time** 15 minutes

BARLEY, LENTIL AND BROWN RICE
Harvest Bowl

WHAT TO DO

1. Prepare the dressing by whisking all the ingredients together. Taste and check for seasoning and set aside in a small glass jar in the fridge until serving.

2. Rinse the barley, rice and lentils and add to a medium-sized saucepan along with 2 cups cold water and a generous pinch of salt. Bring the water to a bubble, turn down to a simmer and leave to cook until the barley and rice are fluffy, adding a little extra water along the way if necessary. Once cooked, drain and set aside.

3. To a large heavy-based pan over medium-high heat, add 1 Tbsp olive oil and the butter. When the butter starts to foam, add the mushrooms and fry for 2–3 minutes, then add the garlic and cook for another minute. Add the now-cooked barley, rice and lentils and allow to toast gently in the pan, then add the remaining 2 Tbsp olive oil and the honey and mix well. Add the balsamic vinegar and simmer gently for a further minute or two before adding the spinach leaves. Remove the pan from the heat and stir gently until the spinach leaves have wilted. Transfer the mixture to a suitable serving platter or bowl.

4. Scatter over the feta and avocado, as well as a sprinkling of salt, pepper and herbs. Serve with the dressing on the side.

Note: Add a handful of Home-grown Mung Bean Sprouts (see page 60) for an extra dose of goodness.

WHAT YOU'LL NEED

Creamy dressing
2 Tbsp sour cream
3 Tbsp olive oil
zest and juice of 1 lemon
1 Tbsp red wine vinegar
2 tsp runny honey
small handful fresh parsley, roughly chopped
salt, to taste

Salad
⅓ cup pearled barley (or white quinoa)
⅓ cup brown rice
⅓ cup brown lentils
3 Tbsp olive oil
1 Tbsp butter
250 g mixed wild mushrooms, chopped or torn
1 clove garlic, minced
2 tsp honey
1 Tbsp balsamic vinegar
100 g baby spinach leaves, rinsed
100 g feta cheese, crumbled
1 ripe avocado, cut into cubes
salt and freshly ground black pepper
1 Tbsp each of chopped mint, basil and parsley

Strawberry and Avocado
SALAD BOWLS

Serves 4 | **Preparation time** 20 minutes | **Cooking time** 10 minutes

WHAT YOU'LL NEED

Honey-balsamic dressing

1 Tbsp honey

1 Tbsp balsamic vinegar

1 Tbsp lemon juice

3 Tbsp olive oil

1–2 Tbsp hot water

salt, to taste

Salad

1 cup quinoa, rinsed (or barley or millet)

2 cups baby spinach, rinsed

2 cups fresh strawberries, roughly sliced at different angles (rustic)

1 ripe avocado, roughly cut into cubes

100 g soft goat's cheese (or feta)

1 Tbsp roughly chopped fresh basil

1 Tbsp roughly chopped fresh mint (or whole leaves)

WHAT TO DO

1. Shake all the dressing ingredients together in an old jam jar until the mixture emulsifies and looks 'creamy'. Set aside.
2. Cook the quinoa according to the packet instructions until light and fluffy.
3. To assemble the salad: scatter the spinach leaves over a platter, add the quinoa, strawberries, avocado, cheese and herbs. Dress just before serving.

Notes: For a speedier salad dressing, simply drizzle with olive oil and a squeeze of lemon juice or balsamic vinegar.

Add a handful of Home-grown Mung Bean Sprouts (see page 60).

Smoky Lentil and Bean
CHILLI

WHAT TO DO

1. In a large saucepan on the stovetop, heat the olive oil over medium heat, then add the red onion and cook for 5 minutes, or until starting to soften. Add the red pepper, garlic, herbs and spices and cook for another 2–3 minutes, taking care not to let the garlic burn.
2. Add the tomato paste, canned tomatoes, rice malt syrup, lentils and soy sauce, stir and reduce the heat to medium-low and simmer with the lid askew for 10 minutes.
3. Add the carrot and beetroot, stir again and add a little water if the sauce is becoming too thick. Simmer for a further 10 minutes.
4. Remove from the heat, stir though the drained beans, sprinkle over the corn kernels and serve in the lettuce cups with fresh coriander and sour cream or yoghurt on the side.

WHAT YOU'LL NEED

1 Tbsp olive oil or coconut oil
1 medium-sized to large red onion, chopped
1 small to medium-sized red pepper, chopped
1 clove garlic, minced
½ tsp dried mixed herbs
1 tsp sweet paprika
1 tsp ground cumin
½–1 tsp dried chilli flakes
½ tsp ground cinnamon
2 Tbsp tomato paste
2 x 410 g can chopped tomatoes
1 Tbsp rice malt syrup (or 6–8 drops stevia liquid or a pinch of stevia powder)
½ cup brown lentils, rinsed
1 Tbsp soy sauce or tamari (gluten-free soy sauce)
½ cup grated carrot
½ cup grated raw beetroot
1 x 400 g can red kidney beans, drained
1 x 400 g can cannellini beans, drained
sweetcorn kernels, shaved off 1 cob of grilled corn (organic)

To serve
large gem or butter lettuce leaves
small handful roughly chopped fresh coriander
sour cream or double-thick Greek yoghurt

SPEEDY BEEF AND RAINBOW SALAD
with Spicy Ginger and Lime Dressing

This is fresh and clean and pretty and punchy and, all things considered, fairly marvellous.

Serves 4 | **Preparation time** 10 minutes | **Cooking time** 8–10 minutes

WHAT YOU'LL NEED

400 g steak (I use well-aged rump)
salt and freshly ground black pepper
1 Tbsp olive oil
2 cups shredded red cabbage
1 cup grated or finely sliced courgettes
1 cup grated carrot
handful Home-grown Mung Bean Sprouts (see page 60)
handful peanuts, roasted and salted (or cashews or toasted sesame seeds)
1 Tbsp each of chopped mint and coriander
2 spring onions, finely sliced

Spicy ginger and lime dressing
3 Tbsp sesame oil
3 Tbsp soy sauce
2–3 tsp fish sauce
1–2 Tbsp honey
1 clove garlic, minced
1 red chilli, deseeded and finely chopped
2 tsp grated fresh ginger
juice of 2 limes
2–3 Tbsp hot water

WHAT TO DO

1. Season the steak with salt and pepper on both sides. Heat a good-quality heavy-based pan on the stove and add the olive oil. Test that it's hot enough by dipping the corner of the steak into the oil – it should sizzle immediately. Cook the steak for 3–4 minutes on each side for medium-rare (for steak that is about 1.5 cm thick). Remove and set aside to rest.
2. While the steak cooks, mix the dressing ingredients together and set aside.
3. While the steak rests, chop the salad ingredients using a food processor (or do it by hand).
4. Divide the salad ingredients between four bowls, top with thin slivers of steak, sprouts, roasted peanuts, fresh herbs and spring onions and then add a generous drizzle of dressing.

Notes: The dressing can be doubled and stored in the fridge for up to one week.
This is a great recipe to double up and take for lunch the next day.

ASPARAGUS, BROCCOLI AND KALE SOUP
with Mixed Seed Croutons

Serves 4 | **Preparation time** 10 minutes | **Cooking time** 25 minutes

WHAT TO DO

1. In a large heavy-based saucepan, heat the olive oil and butter over medium-high heat. When the butter starts to foam, add the onion and cook for 3–4 minutes, or until starting to soften. Add the garlic and thyme and cook for another minute, or until fragrant, then add the asparagus and broccoli.

2. Pour in the stock and a good pinch each of salt and freshly ground black pepper and leave to simmer for 15 minutes. Remove from the heat, stir through the kale and allow to cool.

3. Blend and then check for seasoning, adding lemon juice, salt and pepper to taste.

4. Just before serving, toast the seeds in a dry pan until just golden and fragrant. Serve the soup in warmed bowls, sprinkled with the seeds, roughly chopped herbs and cheese if using.

Note: This soup freezes well for up to two months.

WHAT YOU'LL NEED

1 Tbsp olive oil
1 Tbsp butter
1 onion, roughly chopped
1 clove garlic, chopped
2 sprigs fresh thyme
300 g asparagus, roughly chopped (and roughly 2.5 cm removed from all ends)
300 g broccoli, roughly chopped
2 cups chicken or vegetable stock
salt and freshly ground black pepper
100 g roughly chopped fresh kale (or baby spinach leaves)
1–2 Tbsp lemon juice

Mixed seed croutons and garnish

2 Tbsp sunflower seeds
2 Tbsp pumpkin seeds
1 Tbsp roughly chopped fresh parsley
1 Tbsp roughly chopped fresh basil
100 g feta or goat's cheese, crumbled (optional)

ROASTED TOMATO AND RED ONION SOUP
with Oregano Oil

Serves 4–6 | **Preparation time** 5 minutes | **Cooking time** 1 hour (effortless)

WHAT YOU'LL NEED

Soup

1 kg mixed and very ripe tomatoes, roughly chopped
2 medium-sized red onions, roughly chopped
1 red pepper, deseeded and roughly chopped (optional)
6–8 cloves garlic
3–4 sprigs fresh thyme or 1 tsp dried
1 sprig fresh rosemary
2 Tbsp olive oil
2 Tbsp balsamic vinegar
healthy natural sweetener, to taste (I usually use 6–8 drops stevia liquid)
½ tsp dried chilli flakes
good pinch of salt and freshly ground black pepper
2 cups stock (I like to use lamb)

Oregano oil

1 Tbsp finely chopped fresh oregano
½ clove garlic, minced
3–4 Tbsp olive oil
pinch of salt, or more to taste
a little healthy natural sweetener, if necessary

WHAT TO DO

1. Preheat the oven to 180 °C. Place all the soup ingredients, except the stock, together in a wide, shallow ovenproof dish. Roast for about 45 minutes, or until the tomatoes are roasted and starting to caramelise.

2. Remove the dish from the oven and set aside to cool to room temperature. Remove the thyme and rosemary sprigs if you used fresh. Spoon the mixture into a large blender and blend until you achieve the desired consistency.

3. To make the oregano oil, mix the ingredients together and adjust to taste as necessary.

4. Just before serving, transfer the soup to a large saucepan on the stovetop, bring to a boil, add the stock and simmer gently for 2–3 minutes. Remove from the heat and serve immediately with a drizzle of oregano oil.

Love your leftovers: This soup freezes well for up to two months.
The oregano oil can be used on sandwiches and wraps, or drizzled over avocado toast or salads, so store it in a jar in the fridge for up to two weeks.

SPICY CARROT, GINGER AND LENTIL SOUP
with Coconut Milk

Serves 4 | **Preparation time** 10 minutes | **Cooking time** 20–25 minutes
(mostly unattended)

WHAT TO DO

1. In a large saucepan, heat the olive oil and butter over medium heat until the butter starts to foam. Add the spices, ginger, tamarind (if using) and garlic and cook for about 1 minute until fragrant.

2. Add the stock and bring to a gentle bubble. Add the lentils and carrots and leave to cook for 15–20 minutes, or until the carrots are tender and can be easily pierced with a knife.

3. Add the coconut milk (reserve a tablespoon or two for serving), stir through, remove the saucepan from the heat and allow to cool for about 10 minutes before blending until smooth.

4. Divide the soup between warmed bowls, garnish with a drizzle of coconut milk, and then scatter over a few nuts and/or coconut shavings, and a little roughly chopped fresh coriander before serving immediately. Squeeze over fresh lime juice to taste.

Note: Use leftover soup as a poaching liquid for fish or prawns.

WHAT YOU'LL NEED

½ Tbsp olive oil
½ Tbsp butter
1 tsp ground cumin
1 heaped tsp ground coriander
1 tsp dried chilli flakes (or half for a milder version)
2 tsp grated fresh ginger
1 tsp tamarind paste (if available)
1 large clove garlic, crushed
3 cups good-quality stock
¼ cup red lentils
10 medium carrots, roughly chopped
1 x 400 ml can coconut milk

To serve
1 Tbsp flaked almonds and/or small handful lightly toasted coconut shavings
small handful fresh coriander, roughly chopped
lime wedges

LUISA'S LAMB AND BARLEY BOWLS

Serves 4 | **Preparation time** 15 minutes | **Cooking time** up to 2 hours (mostly unattended)

WHAT YOU'LL NEED

olive oil

1 red onion, finely chopped

3–4 cloves garlic, crushed

4 rashers bacon, chopped

1 carrot, finely chopped

1 stick celery, finely sliced

1 bay leaf

1 fresh chilli, chopped

4 sprigs fresh thyme, picked

1 tsp smoked paprika

4 rounds lamb neck

¼ cup white wine

1 cup tomato purée

2–3 ripe tomatoes, chopped

4 cups lamb stock (I use Nomu Lamb Fond)

salt and freshly ground black pepper

½ cup barley

300 g baby spinach, rinsed

small handful fresh parsley, chopped

WHAT TO DO

1. Heat a saucepan with a little olive oil and gently sauté the onion, garlic, bacon, carrot, celery, bay leaf, chilli and thyme for about 5 minutes, or until the vegetables are beginning to soften and the onion is lightly golden brown.

2. Add the smoked paprika and lamb neck and brown well.

3. Deglaze with the white wine and then add the tomato purée, chopped tomatoes and lamb stock. Season with a little salt and pepper.

4. Cover with a lid, reduce the heat to low and cook slowly for 1½–2 hours.

5. When the lamb is tender, remove from the saucepan and shred the meat. Return the meat to the saucepan and discard the bones.

6. Add the barley and continue to cook for a further 20 minutes or until the barley is tender.

7. Stir through the baby spinach until just wilted.

8. Check seasoning and garnish with chopped parsley.

Prawn
LAKSA BOWLS

Serves 4 | **Preparation time** 15 minutes | **Cooking time** 15–20 minutes

WHAT TO DO

1. To a large saucepan over medium-high heat, add the olive or coconut oil and fry the curry paste until fragrant. Add the ginger and garlic and cook for another minute before adding the coconut milk and stock and bringing it to a gentle simmer.

2. Add the mushrooms and cook for 3–4 minutes (if using chicken, add it in here and cook for about 6 minutes or until just cooked through).

3. Add the remaining ingredients, except the lime juice, nuts and coriander, and cook for a further 5 minutes, then remove the saucepan from the heat.

4. Stir through the lime juice, check for seasoning (add extra fish sauce or a dash of soy sauce if necessary) and then serve immediately in warmed bowls with a sprinkling of toasted cashew nuts and fresh coriander.

Laksa for lunch: This is a fun, delicious and nutritious version to take to work (makes 1 serving): The night before, to a medium-sized glass jar with a lid (the jar should be able to hold about 2 cups liquid), add 1 Tbsp curry paste, ½ tsp grated fresh ginger, 1 tsp fish sauce, handful chopped fresh mushrooms, 1 head pak choi (halved lengthways), 100 g courgetti or rice noodles, and a few slivers fresh red pepper. In the morning, add a handful shredded roast chicken. Take the jar to work, keep it in the fridge and top with boiling water and a squeeze of fresh lime juice just before serving.

WHAT YOU'LL NEED

1 Tbsp olive oil or coconut oil

1–2 Tbsp Thai red curry paste

1 heaped tsp grated fresh ginger

1 tsp minced garlic

1 x 400 ml can coconut milk

800 ml good-quality chicken or
    vegetable stock

250 g mushrooms, thinly sliced

around 20 prawns, deveined (you can
    cook from frozen; or 3 thinly sliced
    chicken breasts)

300 g rice noodles (or courgette noodles for a
    lighter version)

2 heads bok choy, halved lengthways

1 red pepper, deseeded and thinly sliced

2 tsp coconut blossom sugar (or your
    preferred healthy natural sweetener)

2 tsp fish sauce

1 Tbsp lime juice

¼ cup roasted cashew nuts or peanuts,
    for serving

2–3 Tbsp roughly chopped fresh coriander,
    for serving

FEAST

These are intended to be bun-less burgers, and believe me, by the time you add the crispy bacon and avocado, and have the zingy fresh and pretty pink pickle on the side, you won't even spare them a thought. If that's just not realistic for you though, by all means add burger buns. You can even make quick homemade ones by using the dough from my Speedy Spelt Soda Bread (see page 44): shape into rolls and bake for 10–12 minutes until golden and just cooked through. These burgers are also just as lovely served in crispy lettuce cups.

Serves 4 | **Preparation time** 10 minutes | **Chilling time** 30 minutes | **Cooking time** 15 minutes

LEMONY, HERBY CHICKEN BURGERS
with Bacon and Avocado, and Pink Pickle

WHAT TO DO

1. Add all the patty ingredients to your food processor and pulse until the meat is roughly chopped (not too smooth).
2. Roll the mixture into palm-sized balls, flatten gently and refrigerate for at least 30 minutes, or until serving.
3. Just before serving, heat a large pan over medium-high heat and add the olive oil. Fry the burgers for 5 minutes on each side, or until golden and just cooked through. Remove and set aside to rest.
4. To the same pan, add the bacon and cook for about 10 minutes until golden and quite crispy. Assemble the burgers as follows: bun (if using), avocado slices, bacon, burger patty, pickle, fresh herbs and a squeeze of lemon or lime juice.

Note: Make these go further – use the same burger-patty filling to roll into small golf ball-sized dumplings and poach in a Thai curry.

WHAT YOU'LL NEED

Patties

400 g chicken thigh meat, roughly chopped

1 Tbsp chopped fresh mint

1 Tbsp chopped fresh parsley

1 Tbsp chopped fresh basil (or coriander if you prefer)

2 tsp lemon or lime zest

1 Tbsp lemon or lime juice

150 g feta cheese, roughly crumbled

1 egg

salt and freshly ground black pepper, to taste

Pink Pickle

Use the Red Cabbage and Caraway Sauerkraut (see page 170)

To assemble the burgers

1 Tbsp olive oil

4 rashers streaky bacon

1 ripe avocado, thinly sliced

fresh basil leaves or micro greens

lemon or lime wedges

COQ AU CHARDONNAY

It's no secret that the much-adored French dish 'coq au vin' has taken various wine routes all the way through from Cabernet to Riesling (arguably, nothing can compete with Nigel Slater's version), but my preference is for the creaminess of Chardonnay. And where we end up is with a one-pot wonder that can stand up and be counted with the best of them.

Serves 4 | **Preparation time** 15 minutes | **Cooking time** 1 hour

WHAT YOU'LL NEED
1 whole chicken (or 8 chicken thighs)
salt and freshly ground black pepper
½ Tbsp butter (plus 1 Tbsp extra, to rub the chicken)
½ Tbsp olive oil (plus extra, to rub the chicken)
4 rashers streaky bacon, chopped
6 baby leeks, chopped (or 1 large onion)
400 g mixed mushrooms, roughly chopped
2 sprigs fresh rosemary (or 2 tsp dried rosemary or dried mixed herbs or dried tarragon)
1 cup Chardonnay (or white wine of choice)
½ cup chicken stock
½ cup fresh cream (or full-fat natural yoghurt)
1 head garlic, halved down the middle
1 cup frozen peas

To serve
small handful chopped fresh parsley
squeeze of fresh lemon juice
Creamy Cauliflower Mash (see page 108) or
sweet-potato mash

WHAT TO DO
1. Preheat the oven to 180 °C, season the chicken and rub with the extra butter and a drizzle of olive oil.
2. To a large ovenproof pan or shallow casserole on the stovetop, add the butter and olive oil and fry the bacon, leeks, mushrooms and herbs for about 5 minutes, until the leeks and mushrooms have softened.
3. Add the wine, stock and cream and a good pinch of salt and pepper. Bring to a simmer and leave to bubble away for 5 minutes, then remove from the stovetop and place the whole chicken on top of the vegetables and bacon. Add the garlic, cut-side up, and place in the oven, uncovered, for 1 hour, or until the chicken is cooked through and the skin is golden and crispy.
4. When the chicken is cooked, remove from the oven and leave to rest. If you would like to thicken the sauce, remove just the chicken, place the pan back on the stovetop and simmer the sauce for 5–10 minutes until thickened. Then stir through the frozen peas and serve the sauce alongside the chicken. Add a scattering of fresh parsley and a squeeze of lemon juice to taste if you like, and serve with creamy cauliflower or sweet-potato mash.

CHICKEN, BUTTERNUT AND FETA CRUMBLE

This is one of Rob's favourites, so I'll urge you to make it soon and leave it at that.

Serves 4 | **Preparation time** 20 minutes | **Cooking time** 20–25 minutes

WHAT TO DO

1. Cook the butternut in a large saucepan of lightly salted boiling water for 10 minutes, or until cooked through and it can be easily pierced with a knife.
2. Meanwhile, preheat the oven to 190 °C.
3. Heat the butter and olive oil in a large pan over medium heat and cook the onion for 7–8 minutes, or until translucent. Add the garlic and sage, and cook for another 2–3 minutes.
4. Lightly grease a small to medium-sized shallow ovenproof dish and to it add the butternut, onion mixture, cheese and chicken. The filling should fit snugly and be quite deep – this will give you a moister crumble. Season to taste.
5. In a separate bowl, mix the crumble topping ingredients together until it has the consistency of rough breadcrumbs. Scatter this over the filling and place the dish in the oven for 20–25 minutes, or until golden. Garnish with fresh sage.

Cook smarter: Make double the crumble and save half in the freezer for next time.

WHAT YOU'LL NEED

300 g butternut, peeled and cut into
   1 cm cubes
½ Tbsp butter
½ Tbsp olive oil
1 medium-sized onion, chopped
1 clove garlic, minced
1 tsp dried sage (or thyme or rosemary)
150 g feta cheese
300 g chopped cooked chicken breast
   (preferably shredded leftover
   roast chicken)
salt and freshly ground black pepper
fresh sage, for garnishing

Crumble topping
125 g cold butter, cut into cubes
   (or ½ cup cold coconut oil)
½ cup almond flour (or extra oats for a more
   budget-friendly version)
½ cup rolled oats (use gluten-free oats if
   necessary)
½ cup chopped pecan nuts (or almonds)
¼ cup grated Parmesan cheese

ΚAH CHICKEN FLATBREADS
with Lemony Yoghurt

Serves 2–4 | **Preparation time** 15 minutes | **Cooking time** 15 minutes

Note: For a more rustic finish, roll the flatbreads out to about 1 cm thick so that they are fluffier and more bread-like.

WHAT YOU'LL NEED

Flatbreads
½ cup wholewheat flour
½ cup plain flour
1 tsp baking powder
½ cup full-fat natural yoghurt
1 Tbsp olive oil
½ tsp salt
pinch of freshly ground black pepper

Dukkah spice mix
(Makes about ¾ cup)
¼ cup pistachio nuts, finely chopped
¼ cup almonds or hazelnuts, finely chopped
2 Tbsp sesame seeds
2 Tbsp coriander seeds
1 Tbsp cumin seeds
½ tsp salt
freshly ground black pepper, to taste

Yoghurt dressing
½ cup full-fat natural yoghurt
1 heaped tsp lemon zest
1 Tbsp lemon juice
½ tsp minced garlic

Topping
1 heaped cup shredded roast chicken
1 tsp ground cumin
1 tsp ground coriander
½ tsp dried chilli flakes (optional)
1 Tbsp olive oil

100 g feta cheese
¼ red onion, finely sliced
1 cup baby tomatoes, halved
1 ripe avocado, sliced
small handful fresh mint or
    coriander, for garnishing

WHAT TO DO

1. Preheat the oven to 220 °C. Mix all the flatbread ingredients together in a stand mixer with a dough hook attachment. Add extra flour if necessary, but the dough should be quite wet and sticky. When the dough comes together, knead for 2–3 minutes on a lightly floured surface.

2. Take a golf ball-sized piece of dough and roll out as thinly as possible with a floured rolling pin, again on a lightly floured surface. For these flatbreads I like to make them loosely rectangular in shape.

3. Bake on a lightly greased baking tray for 8–10 minutes, or until golden. Alternatively, cook in a hot griddle pan until golden and cooked through.

4. For the dukkah, lightly toast all of the ingredients in a dry pan over a gentle heat. Be careful not to let anything burn. When the nuts and sesame seeds are golden and fragrant, remove the pan from the heat and set aside to cool completely. Store in an airtight container.

5. For the dressing, stir all the ingredients together and adjust to taste.

6. For the topping, fry the chicken and spices in the olive oil until golden and fragrant. Spread some of the yoghurt dressing onto the cooked flatbreads, then top with the chicken, a generous sprinkling of your dukkah spice mix, crumbled feta, red onion slices, baby tomatoes, avocado, and fresh herbs. Serve immediately.

This is a version of a recipe that we cooked on my TV show, *Sarah's Food Safari*, on the banks of the Zambezi River in Zimbabwe, so for that reason it will always be special and have amazing memories attached to it. But you should also know that it's deliciously fresh and healthy, and the salsa is zingy and YUM.

Serves 4 | **Preparation time** 25 minutes | **Cooking time** 30 minutes

FISH FRIKKADELS
with Pineapple Salsa

WHAT TO DO

1. Preheat the oven to 200 °C. Place the fish on the shiny side of a large sheet of tinfoil, sprinkle with a pinch of salt and pepper and add the olive oil. Wrap up tightly and bake for 10–12 minutes, or until just cooked through, then remove and set aside to cool.

2. Meanwhile, halve and boil the sweet potatoes with their skins on for 15 minutes, or until soft, adding the peas for the last 2 minutes of cooking time. Drain the sweet potatoes and peas, allow the sweet potatoes to cool and steam for a few minutes and then remove the skins, season with salt and pepper and mash roughly. (Alternatively, steam or bake the sweet potatoes in their jackets.)

3. Flake the fish into a bowl, then add the mashed sweet potatoes and peas, herbs, lemon juice, lemon zest, spices and the egg. Season with salt and pepper and mix until combined.

4. Shape the mixture into 10–12 golf ball-sized patties, just gently flattened, and arrange them in a lightly greased baking dish or shallow nonstick baking tray. Refrigerate for about 15 minutes to firm up a little or until you are ready to cook.

5. While the frikkadels are in the fridge, mix together all the salsa ingredients in a pretty serving bowl and season to taste.

6. Just before cooking the frikkadels, brush with a little olive oil. Then bake at 200 °C for 8–10 minutes, or until golden. If you'd like a crispier finish, then turn on the grill for the last 2–3 minutes.

7. Serve immediately with the pineapple salsa on the side.

WHAT YOU'LL NEED

400 g firm white sustainable fish fillets
salt and freshly ground black pepper
1 tsp olive oil
3 medium-sized sweet potatoes
1 cup frozen peas
1 Tbsp chopped fresh mint
1 Tbsp chopped fresh coriander
1 Tbsp lemon juice
2 tsp lemon zest
pinch each of ground cumin, ground coriander
    and curry powder
1 egg, lightly beaten

Pineapple salsa
1 small ripe pineapple, peeled and cubed
1 Tbsp chopped fresh mint
1 Tbsp chopped fresh coriander
1 heaped tsp grated fresh ginger
1 small red chilli, deseeded and
    finely chopped
juice and zest of 1 lime
pinch of sugar or drizzle of honey, or to taste

BAKED FISH
with Basil and
Blistered Tomatoes

Serves 4 | **Preparation time** 10 minutes | **Cooking time** 30–35 minutes

WHAT YOU'LL NEED

1 Tbsp olive oil

1 medium-sized red onion, halved lengthways and then thinly sliced

1 clove garlic, minced

½ tsp dried chilli flakes

2 Tbsp chopped fresh basil (or ½ Tbsp chopped fresh oregano)

3 cups roughly chopped fresh tomatoes (regular or baby)

1–2 Tbsp balsamic vinegar

healthy natural sweetener, to taste (I use about 8 drops stevia liquid)

salt and freshly ground black pepper

4 x 200 g white fish fillets

about 12 pitted black olives

1 x 400 g can cannellini beans, drained

crumbled feta cheese and small handful fresh basil leaves, roughly chopped, for serving

WHAT TO DO

1. Heat the olive oil in a medium-sized saucepan over medium heat. Cook the onion for 5 minutes, or until just starting to soften. Add the garlic, chilli, chopped basil, tomatoes and balsamic vinegar, and cook for another 10–15 minutes. Sweeten and season to taste.

2. Meanwhile, preheat the oven to 190 °C, season the fish fillets with salt and pepper and place in a shallow ovenproof dish.

3. When the tomato mixture has cooked for the allocated time, remove from the heat and pour over the fish fillets. Scatter the olives around the fish and bake for 10–12 minutes, or until the fish fillets are just cooked through and the flesh flakes apart easily with a fork.

4. Remove the dish from the oven and stir through the cannellini beans. Crumble over some feta, add an extra sprinkling of basil and serve immediately.

Note: This is perfect with a light green salad or served over Cauliflower Couscous (see page 59).

Socca are thin crêpe-like pancakes made from chickpea flour, so they're gluten free and have the earthy deliciousness of chickpeas thrown in for good measure.

Serves 4 | Preparation time 10 minutes | Cooking time 2–3 minutes

FISH SOCCA
with Strawberry, Basil and Lime Salsa

WHAT TO DO

1. To make the socca, mix the chickpea flour, water and cumin together and leave to stand for at least 5 minutes.
2. Mix together the salsa ingredients, check for seasoning and balance of flavours, and set aside.
3. Add the beaten egg to a shallow plate, and the coconut flour to another. Coat the fish first in the egg and then the coconut flour, season and set aside.
4. Heat 1 Tbsp olive oil or coconut oil in a large nonstick pan over medium-high heat and add 2–3 Tbsp of the socca mixture. Swirl the mixture around the pan so that it makes a thin pancake and cook for 3–4 minutes on each side, until golden and almost crispy. Remove, set aside on a warmed plate and repeat until you've used up all the batter; wipe the pan with kitchen paper in between each one if necessary.
5. Once you have used up all the batter, give the pan a final wipe and fry the fish in a small drizzle of olive oil or coconut oil for 2–3 minutes on each side, or until golden and cooked through. Remove from the pan and slice into 1 cm slivers.
6. Fill each socca with a little sliced avocado and fried fish, top with salsa and serve immediately.

WHAT YOU'LL NEED

Socca
1 cup chickpea flour (or spelt or wholewheat flour)
1 cup water
1 tsp ground cumin

Strawberry, basil and lime salsa
1 cup strawberries, roughly chopped (or mango)
2 Tbsp chopped fresh basil
zest and juice of 1 lime
¼ red onion, finely chopped
1 tsp grated fresh ginger
coconut sugar (or your preferred healthy natural sweetener), to taste
1–2 Tbsp olive oil or coconut oil (warmed until liquid)

Filling
1 egg, lightly beaten
¼ cup coconut flour
400 g fresh white fish
salt and freshly ground black pepper
olive oil or coconut oil, for frying
1 ripe avocado, roughly chopped

PERI-PERI PRAWN, CALAMARI AND CHICKPEA SALAD

Rob travels to Mozambique a lot for work, and he's eaten peri-peri sauce that can stand up and be counted with the best of them. That means I had to work extra hard to get the recipe just right, and where we ended up, I like to think, is somewhere pretty delicious.

Serves 4 | **Preparation time** 15 minutes | **Cooking time** 10 minutes

WHAT YOU'LL NEED

Peri-peri sauce
2 lemons and 2 limes
¼ cup olive oil
¼ cup chopped garlic
5 bird's-eye chillies, deseeded and chopped
1 red pepper, deseeded and chopped
1 Tbsp paprika
1 tsp salt
¼ cup lemon juice
2 Tbsp white wine vinegar

Calamari and chickpea salad
1 tsp each of olive oil and butter
400 g fresh prawns, deveined
400 g fresh calamari, cleaned
100 g chorizo sausage, chopped
salt and freshly ground black pepper
1 x 400 g can chickpeas, drained
1 cup baby tomatoes, halved
½ small red onion, finely sliced
1 ripe avocado, roughly cubed (optional)
small handful each of chopped fresh parsley, basil and mint
1 Tbsp each of lemon juice, red wine vinegar and olive oil, for dressing

WHAT TO DO

1. To make the peri-peri sauce, halve the lemons and limes and place cut-side down in a preheated griddle pan over medium-high heat. Cook for 4–5 minutes, or until blistered and starting to blacken and caramelise.
2. Meanwhile, add the remaining peri-peri ingredients to a food processor, then squeeze in the lemon and lime juice. Blitz well and check for seasoning.
3. For the salad, add the olive oil and butter to a large pan over high heat. When the butter starts to foam, add the prawns, calamari and chorizo and cook for 4–5 minutes until golden. Add half the peri-peri sauce and stir through. Remove from the heat.
4. Mix all of the salad ingredients together on a large serving platter, dress with the lemon juice, red wine vinegar and olive oil and serve immediately with lemon or lime wedges and extra peri-peri sauce on the side.

Note: Make extra sauce, store in a glass jar in the fridge for up to two weeks and use as a basting for chicken.

Yes, there's a version of these in nearly every one of my books. Rice paper rolls are endlessly welcome to so many different textures and flavours, and perfect for summer snacking. Here, with the prettiness of the coral-pink salmon and the pop of colour of the strawberries, they're hard not to love.

Makes 10–12 rolls | **Preparation time** 10 minutes | **Assembly time** 20 minutes

Sweet and Spicy Vietnamese SALMON ROLLS

WHAT TO DO

1. Place all the filling ingredients in a large mixing bowl.
2. Mix all the ingredients for the sauce together (if you don't have coconut milk just use a little warm water to loosen) and pour half the sauce over the filling mixture, then toss gently to coat.
3. Dip one rice paper sheet at a time into a large bowl of lukewarm water. Place on a clean dinner plate and fill down the centre with filling, leaving a 2–3 cm space at the bottom and top. Fold up the bottom, fold in one side and roll until sealed neatly.
4. Repeat with the remaining ingredients and serve with the extra sauce on the side.

Notes: This recipe also works well with pan-fried prawns or leftover shredded roast chicken.
Double the sauce recipe and store in the fridge for up to two weeks, and use as a salad dressing or for your next round of rice paper rolls.

WHAT YOU'LL NEED
10–12 rice paper sheets

Filling
1 Tbsp sesame oil (or olive oil)
100 g smoked salmon or trout ribbons
½ cup strawberries, rinsed, hulled and
    thinly sliced
½ cup grated carrot
½ cup shredded red cabbage
2 Tbsp chopped fresh coriander
2 Tbsp chopped fresh mint
1 red pepper, deseeded and thinly sliced
    lengthways
¼ cup peanuts or cashew nuts, roasted and
    roughly chopped

Sauce
3 Tbsp sesame oil
3 Tbsp soy sauce
2 tsp fish sauce
3–4 Tbsp coconut milk, to loosen (optional)
1 large clove garlic, minced
3–4 Tbsp lime juice
1 red chilli, finely chopped (deseeded if you prefer)

MUSTARD PORK CHOPS
with Broccoli and Fennel Slaw

Serves 4 | **Preparation time** 10 minutes | **Cooking time** 10 minutes

WHAT YOU'LL NEED

4 pork chops (or pork steaks)

generous pinch each of salt and freshly ground black pepper

1 Tbsp olive oil

1 Tbsp Dijon mustard

½ cup fresh cream

Broccoli and fennel slaw

½ small cabbage, finely chopped

1 bulb fennel, finely sliced

2–3 stalks tenderstem broccoli, finely sliced

1 green apple, cored and grated

2 sticks celery, finely chopped

2 Tbsp lemon juice

1 cup Greek yoghurt

1–2 Tbsp chopped fresh dill and/or mint

⅓ cup roasted pecan nuts or walnuts, roughly chopped (or 3 Tbsp toasted sunflower seeds)

WHAT TO DO

1. Make the slaw first (it's easiest using a food processor and just finely slicing everything together) by mixing all the ingredients together. Set aside in the fridge until just before serving.
2. Season the pork with salt and pepper on both sides. Heat the olive oil in a large pan over medium-high heat and brown the meat for 3–4 minutes on each side, or until golden and no longer pink in the middle.
3. Remove the pork chops from the pan and set aside on a warmed plate to rest. Add the mustard and cream to the pan, stir and leave to simmer for a minute, adding a little extra hot water to loosen if necessary. Check for seasoning, adjust if necessary and then remove from the heat.
4. Serve the pork chops with the slaw and the creamy mustard sauce on the side.

Notes: Serve with Creamy Cauliflower Mash (see page 108) for more generous portions.
This recipe also works well with thinly sliced duck breast.

ROAST PORK FILLET
with Figs and Red Onions, and Cider Gravy

Serves 4-6 | Preparation time 5-10 minutes | Cooking time 30 minutes (mostly unattended)

WHAT TO DO

1. Preheat the oven to 200 °C.
2. Parboil the sweet potatoes in a large saucepan of salted boiling water for 10-15 minutes, or until they can be easily pierced with a knife. Drain and set aside.
3. In the meanwhile, season the pork fillet with salt and freshly ground black pepper, and then coat with the mustards, fennel and sage.
4. Heat a large ovenproof frying pan over medium-high heat and add the olive oil. When the oil is hot, sear the pork fillet for 2-3 minutes on each side, or until golden. Remove the pan from the heat, add the onions, figs and garlic, drizzle with a little extra oil and then transfer to the oven (if you don't have an ovenproof pan, just sear the fillet on the stovetop and then transfer to an ovenproof baking dish and add the remaining ingredients).
5. After 25 minutes, remove the pork from the pan and rest for 10-15 minutes. Add the butter to the vegetables along with a drizzle of maple syrup or rice malt syrup and return them to the oven while the meat rests so that they will be nice and caramelised.
6. Remove the vegetables with a slotted spoon and make a quick gravy as follows: add the flour to the pan and place over medium-high heat. Add the cider and stock and leave to simmer, stirring often, for about 5 minutes, or until the gravy is glossy and thick. To make the gravy extra creamy, add the cream or yoghurt. Season to taste and then remove from the heat and set aside.
7. Slice the pork fillet and serve immediately on warmed plates with the vegetables and gravy. Garnish with thyme.

WHAT YOU'LL NEED

2 sweet potatoes, cut into 2 cm cubes
1 x 900 g pork fillet
salt and freshly ground black pepper
1 Tbsp Dijon mustard
1 Tbsp wholegrain mustard
1 tsp dried fennel
1 tsp dried sage
1 Tbsp olive oil, plus extra for drizzling
2 red onions, cut into sixths
4 firm figs, halved (or 2 firm pears, cut into sixths lengthways; or stone fruit of your choice)
2-3 large cloves garlic, skin on but 'smashed'
knob of butter
maple syrup or rice malt syrup, for drizzling
sprigs of fresh thyme, for garnishing

Gravy
1 Tbsp plain flour (or gluten free if necessary)
½ cup cider
½ cup chicken or vegetable stock
¼ cup fresh cream or natural yoghurt (optional)

Eastern
AUBERGINES

I love how this is delicately flavoured with those distinct Eastern spices of cumin and coriander, and then crowned prettily with pomegranate rubies and a burst of freshness from the mint. It's all kinds of wonderful and one of my favourites.

Serves 4 | **Preparation time** 15 minutes | **Cooking time** 40 minutes (mostly unattended)

WHAT YOU'LL NEED

Aubergines
4 medium aubergines, halved lengthways
olive oil

Mince
½ Tbsp olive oil
½ Tbsp butter
250 g beef, lamb or chicken mince
1 small onion, chopped
1 clove garlic, chopped
½ tsp ground cinnamon
1 tsp ground cumin
1 tsp ground coriander
1 tsp dried chilli flakes
1 Tbsp tomato paste
healthy natural sweetener, to taste
salt and freshly ground black pepper, to taste
1 heaped cup roughly chopped tomatoes

To serve
½ cup Greek yoghurt
fresh mint leaves
2 Tbsp slivered almonds or pine nuts, roasted
pomegranate rubies
1 ripe avocado, sliced

WHAT TO DO

1. Preheat the oven to 200 °C.
2. Drizzle the aubergines with a little olive oil and place on a nonstick baking tray. Place in the oven for 30–40 minutes.
3. While the aubergines are in the oven, prepare the mince. Heat the olive oil and butter in a medium-sized saucepan over medium-high heat. When the butter starts to foam, add the mince and cook for 4–5 minutes until golden. Add the remaining ingredients, except the tomatoes, and cook for a further 5 minutes until the onion has softened. Add the tomatoes, bring to a simmer and then leave to cook gently with the lid on for another 25–30 minutes.
4. When the aubergines are cooked, remove from the oven and serve immediately on warmed plates. Spoon over some of the cooked mince, then add yoghurt, mint leaves, nuts and pomegranate rubies to garnish. Serve the avocado slices on the side.

Notes: Add lentils and grated carrot and/or courgette to the minced meat to make this recipe go further.
Make a double batch and freeze the extra for a speedier supper next time around.

BOBOTIE
Pappardelle

WHAT TO DO

1. Heat the oil and butter in a large pan over medium-high heat and fry the mince, stirring often until loose and crumbly. Add the onions and fry until soft and translucent.
2. Add the garlic, apple, ginger, spices, dried herbs and dates and continue cooking for another minute. Season with salt, pepper and lemon juice, then add the raisins and almonds. Add ¼ cup hot water and leave the sauce to continue cooking over a gentle heat for about 20 minutes while you make the pasta and prepare the eggs. Add extra water to the sauce if necessary as it cooks, another ¼ cup at a time.
3. Cook the pasta in a large saucepan of salted boiling water until al dente. Drain, drizzle with a little olive oil and divide between warmed serving bowls. Top with the bobotie mixture and a poached or boiled egg, scatter over fresh herbs and serve immediately.

WHAT YOU'LL NEED

400 g wholewheat pappardelle (or gluten-free pasta of your choice)

4 eggs, soft-boiled or poached, for serving (optional)

chopped fresh parsley or coriander, for serving

Bobotie

1 Tbsp olive oil

1 Tbsp butter

400 g beef or lamb mince

2 medium-sized onions, chopped

1 clove garlic, minced

1 apple, peeled, cored and grated

1 tsp grated fresh ginger

2 tsp medium curry powder

1 tsp ground coriander

1 tsp turmeric

½ tsp ground cinnamon

½ tsp dried chilli flakes

½ tsp dried mixed herbs

3 dates, soaked in hot water for a few minutes and then pitted and finely chopped

½ tsp salt

pinch of freshly ground black pepper

1 Tbsp lemon juice

⅓ cup seedless raisins

2 Tbsp flaked almonds

SLOW, SLOW BEEF SHORT RIB AND ROSEMARY RAGÙ
with Creamy Cauliflower Mash

Serves 4 | **Preparation time** 15 minutes | **Cooking time** 3–4 hours (mostly unattended)

WHAT YOU'LL NEED

1.5 kg beef short rib

1–2 Tbsp olive oil

1 medium-sized red onion, chopped

2 cloves garlic, roughly chopped

2 sprigs fresh rosemary (or 1 tsp dried)

1 x 410 g can peeled, chopped tomatoes

1 Tbsp tomato paste

1 fresh chilli, deseeded and chopped, or ½ tsp dried chilli flakes

1 Tbsp balsamic vinegar

1 Tbsp tamari (or Worcestershire or soy sauce)

1 cup red wine

1 cup good-quality beef or vegetable stock (and another cup to add as you go, if necessary)

¼ cup lentils

generous pinch each of salt and freshly ground black pepper

WHAT TO DO

1. Preheat the oven to 140 °C. On the stovetop, in a heavy-based pan (preferably an ovenproof one with a lid), brown the short rib in the olive oil for 4–5 minutes, or until lightly golden, turning halfway.

2. Remove the meat and set aside. Add the onion to the pan and cook for 5 minutes, then add the garlic and rosemary. Cook for another minute, or until the garlic is fragrant, then add all the remaining ingredients.

3. Bring to a bubble on the stovetop and then transfer to the oven with the lid on for another 3–4 hours, adding a little extra stock every hour or so along the way.

4. Serve with the Creamy Cauliflower Mash (see below).

Creamy Cauliflower Mash: Roughly chop 1 large head cauliflower, then cook in a large saucepan of salted boiling water for 10–15 minutes, or until easily pierced with a knife. Remove, drain and allow to steam-dry for a few minutes. Add 1 Tbsp each of butter and olive oil and blend until smooth using a stick blender. Add salt and freshly ground black pepper to taste.

This dressing is wildly delicious – it's nutty and creamy and just limey enough to be light and fresh. I definitely suggest making double and using it to drizzle over everything from salads to chicken and fish.

Serves 4 | **Preparation time** 20 minutes | **Cooking time** 8 minutes

Asian
TAHINI SKEWERS

WHAT TO DO

1. Thread the meat onto the skewers, season with salt and pepper and set aside.
2. For the dressing, mix together all the ingredients and adjust to taste. Add extra water to loosen if necessary – it should be a fairly runny pouring consistency. The coconut cream or natural yoghurt will dilute the taste of the tahini a little, which some people find quite strong.
3. Just before serving, heat your barbecue or braai grill, or a griddle pan on the stove, and cook the skewers, turning from time to time, for about 8 minutes, or until cooked through and lightly charred.
4. Remove from the heat and serve with the sauce on the side, a scattering of fresh coriander, a sprinkling of sesame seeds, chopped spring onions and lime wedges.

Note: Serve as a snack just as they are, or as a real feast with the Rainbow Salad from page 74. Loosen a little of the sauce with coconut milk or water to dress the salad.

WHAT YOU'LL NEED
Skewers
2 x 250 g rump steaks (or lamb chump chops or chicken thighs), cut into slivers that are roughly 5 mm thick
10–12 bamboo skewers
pinch each of salt and freshly ground black pepper

Tahini dressing
1 Tbsp tahini
1 Tbsp soy sauce
1 Tbsp sesame oil
3 Tbsp lime juice (or lemon juice or rice vinegar)
1 tsp grated fresh ginger
1 clove garlic, crushed
2 tsp honey (or a few drops of stevia liquid or rice malt syrup), or more to taste
2–3 Tbsp coconut cream or natural yoghurt (optional)

To serve
1–2 Tbsp roughly chopped fresh coriander
toasted sesame seeds
2 spring onions, finely chopped
lime wedges

FIERY LAMB KOFTAS
with Hummus

Serves 4 | **Preparation time** 35 minutes | **Cooking time** 10–12 minutes

WHAT YOU'LL NEED
8 bamboo skewers

Lamb koftas
400 g lamb mince
100 g feta cheese, crumbled
1 Tbsp chopped fresh mint
1 tsp lemon zest
2 tsp lemon juice
½ tsp ground cumin
salt and freshly ground black pepper, to taste

Basting
2 tsp harissa paste
1 clove garlic, minced
¼ cup olive oil

Hummus
1 x 400 g can chickpeas, drained
2 tsp tahini
1 clove garlic, minced
½ tsp smoked paprika or ground cumin
1–2 Tbsp lemon juice
1 tsp rice malt syrup (or honey)
salt and freshly ground black pepper, to taste
chopped fresh coriander and lightly toasted
pumpkin, sunflower and sesame seeds,
for garnishing

WHAT TO DO
1. Place all the kofta ingredients in a mixing bowl and mix until well combined. Divide into eight portions and roll into sausage shapes. Thread each portion onto a bamboo skewer.
2. Mix the basting ingredients together and brush each of the koftas until well coated, reserving a little basting sauce to brush the koftas as they cook.
3. Refrigerate until it's time to cook, then remove from the fridge and allow 20 minutes to come to room temperature. Cook in a griddle pan over medium-high heat for 10–12 minutes, turning and basting from time to time, or until cooked through and just starting to char on the outside.
4. To make the hummus, blitz all the ingredients together (except the garnish) using a food processor or stick blender, adjust to taste and refrigerate until needed. Serve in a pretty bowl topped with a sprinkling of fresh coriander and toasted seeds.
5. Once the koftas have cooked, serve immediately with the hummus for dipping and a simple Greek-style salad on the side.

SPICY LAMB CHOPS
with Roasted Cauliflower, Crispy Lentils and Za'atar

Serves 4 | **Preparation time** 15 minutes | **Cooking time** 30 minutes
(mostly unattended)

WHAT TO DO

1. Preheat the oven to 200 °C.
2. First make the za'atar. Mix all the ingredients together and store in a small glass jar.
3. Rub the cauliflower with 1 Tbsp of the olive oil and the za'atar and place in a shallow baking dish. When the oven reaches temperature, place the dish on the middle shelf and leave to bake for 25–30 minutes, or until golden and fragrant.
4. When the cauliflower has been in the oven for 15 minutes, season the lamb chops with salt and pepper, cumin and dried thyme. Fry in a non-stick pan with the remaining olive oil for 4 minutes on each side (for medium). Remove and set aside on a warmed plate to rest.
5. Add the lentils to the same pan and cook for 2–3 minutes, or until warmed through and just starting to crisp on the outside. Remove from the heat and transfer to a warmed serving platter.
6. Remove the cauliflower from the oven, chop roughly and place the florets on top of the bed of lentils. Sprinkle over a little extra za'atar. Scatter over the fresh herbs and cheese, drizzle with the lemon juice and serve immediately with the lamb chops.

WHAT YOU'LL NEED

Za'atar
1 Tbsp sumac
1 Tbsp sesame seeds
1 tsp ground cumin
1 tsp dried mixed herbs (or just thyme)
pinch each of salt and freshly ground
    black pepper

Vegetables
½ head cauliflower
2 Tbsp olive oil
1 Tbsp za'atar, plus 1 tsp extra
1 x 400 g can lentils, drained and rinsed (or
    ¼ cup dried lentils, cooked according to
    packet instructions)
handful fresh mint and/or coriander, chopped
100 g feta or creamy goat's cheese, crumbled
1 Tbsp lemon juice

Lamb chops
4 lamb chops
salt and freshly ground black pepper
½ tsp ground cumin
½ tsp dried thyme
1 Tbsp olive oil or coconut oil, for frying

LAMB STEAKS
with Chopping Board Chimichurri

Serves 4 | **Preparation time** 10 minutes | **Cooking time** 10 minutes

WHAT YOU'LL NEED
4 x 200 g lamb steaks or shoulder chops
salt and freshly ground black pepper
1 Tbsp olive oil

Chimichurri
¼ cup fresh flat-leaf parsley, quite
tightly packed
¼ cup fresh mint, quite tightly packed
½ tsp minced garlic
1 tsp lemon zest
pinch of dried chilli flakes
2 Tbsp lemon juice
¼ cup olive oil
1–2 Tbsp warm water
salt and healthy natural sweetener, to taste

WHAT TO DO
1. Make the chimichurri first. On a large chopping board (secured by placing a damp kitchen cloth underneath it), finely chop the parsley and mint. Transfer to a jar and add the remaining ingredients. Check for seasoning and balance of flavours and adjust if necessary. Leave to stand until needed.
2. Meanwhile, season the lamb steaks and cook for 3–4 minutes on each side in a large pan over medium-high heat with the olive oil. Remove and set aside to rest for about 5 minutes before serving immediately with the chimichurri.

Note: Serve with a simple side salad or baked sweet potatoes.

Serve with a fresh green salad on the side if you like.

Serves 4 | **Preparation time** 10–15 minutes | **Cooking time** 1 hour (mostly unattended)

Auberg PARM

WHAT TO DO

1. Add a little of the olive oil to a medium-sized saucepan over medium heat and fry the garlic and dried herbs for 1–2 minutes until fragrant. Add the tomatoes, balsamic vinegar, rice malt syrup and fresh oregano and basil and leave to simmer for 20–30 minutes until reduced by about one-third. Taste and season accordingly with salt and pepper. (Add about ¼ cup dried lentils along with the tomatoes if you'd like. If you'd prefer using canned, they can be added later.)

2. Meanwhile, slice the aubergines lengthways into 1 cm thick slices (or just slightly thinner).

3. Add the remaining olive oil to a nonstick frying pan over medium-high heat and cook the aubergines in batches until golden and almost slightly charred, adding more oil if you need to. Set aside to drain on kitchen paper and season lightly.

4. Preheat the oven to 180 °C. Add a thin layer of tomato sauce to a medium-sized baking dish, followed by a layer of aubergines and then a scattering of grated mozzarella and Parmesan. Repeat the layers, and then finish off with a final layer of tomato sauce and a final layer of cheese.

5. Bake for about 30 minutes, or until bubbling and golden. Remove from the oven and allow to cool slightly. Sprinkle with basil leaves before serving as soon as possible with slices of avocado and a scattering of feta.

WHAT YOU'LL NEED

2 Tbsp olive oil
2 cloves garlic, minced
½ tsp dried mixed herbs
2 x 400 g cans chopped tomatoes
1 Tbsp balsamic vinegar
2 tsp rice malt syrup (or 8–10 drops stevia liquid)
1–2 sprigs fresh oregano, picked
small handful chopped fresh basil, plus extra, for garnishing
salt and freshly ground black pepper
1 x 400 g can lentils, drained
3 medium-sized aubergines
2 cups grated mozzarella cheese (or Cheddar)
½ cup grated Parmesan cheese (or hard cheese of your preference)

To serve
1 avocado, sliced
100 g feta cheese, crumbled

RED ONION, FETA AND BEETROOT TART

It took me ages to create a gluten-free pastry that wasn't so crumbly it just fell apart, and I'm so glad I ended up where I did with this one. It's now my much-loved and foolproof go-to. It's also really versatile – you can use it with your favourite quiche filling, or add a dash of coconut sugar and you have a sweet pastry to fill (see Millionaire's Shortbread Tart on page 149).

Serves 4 | **Makes** 1 x 20 cm tart | **Preparation time** 15 minutes | **Cooking time** 45 minutes (mostly unattended)

Gluten-free tart pastry
150 g almond flour
75 g coconut flour
150 g cold butter or coconut oil
1 egg
1–2 Tbsp cold water, to bind, if needed
pinch of salt

Filling
½ Tbsp olive oil
½ Tbsp butter
2 medium-sized red onions, chopped
1 tsp chopped fresh rosemary
1 Tbsp balsamic vinegar
½ Tbsp honey (or coconut sugar or rice malt syrup)
salt and freshly ground black pepper, to taste
3 medium-sized beetroot
100 g feta cheese, crumbled (or Gorgonzola or goat's cheese)
3 eggs, lightly beaten
½ cup milk

WHAT TO DO

1. Preheat the oven to 180 °C.
2. For the pastry, blitz the ingredients together in a food processor until the mixture forms a dough, then press into a lightly greased 20 cm tart tin using the back of a tablespoon to smooth out the dough if necessary. Prick the base a few times with a fork and blind bake for 15 minutes, or until lightly golden. Remove from the oven and allow to cool slightly before adding the filling.
3. For the filling, heat the olive oil and butter in a large heavy-based saucepan over medium heat. When the butter starts to foam, add the onions, rosemary, balsamic vinegar and honey and cook gently for 15 minutes, or until sticky and starting to caramelise. Remove, check for seasoning and set aside to cool slightly.
4. Meanwhile, cook the beetroot in a saucepan of boiling water until tender, also about 15 minutes. Remove, allow to cool, peel and cut into 1 cm cubes (alternatively, use precooked store-bought beetroot, but not the kind stored in vinegar).
5. Once the tart shell has cooled slightly, add the onions, beetroot and feta. Mix together the eggs and milk, season and pour over the tart filling.
6. Return the filled tart to the oven and bake for 20–25 minutes, or until the egg mixture is fluffy and golden. Remove and serve immediately with a light green salad.

Note: For foolproof regular pastry, use 150 g plain flour, 75 g cold butter, 1 egg and a pinch of salt, and follow the same method as above.

Very Cheesy, Very Easy Fig Jam, Rosemary and Brie PIZZAS

Serves 4 | **Preparation time** 35 minutes | **Cooking time** 10 minutes

WHAT TO DO

1. Add the butter and olive oil to a medium-sized saucepan over medium heat. When the butter starts to foam, add the onion and cook for 10 minutes, or until softened and starting to caramelise. Add the rice malt syrup, rosemary and four of the figs and simmer gently for a further 10 minutes, or until golden and sticky.

2. Preheat the oven to 200 °C and prepare your 'pizza' bases. Divide the grated mozzarella between the tortillas, spoon over some of the fig and onion jam and then top with slivers of Brie and the two remaining figs, thinly sliced.

3. Place the tortillas onto nonstick baking trays and bake for 8–10 minutes, or until the Brie is golden and bubbling. Remove from the oven, top with fresh rocket and serve immediately.

Note: Make your own speedy pizza bases using the flatbread dough on page 90.

WHAT YOU'LL NEED

1 Tbsp butter
1 Tbsp olive oil
1 medium-sized red onion, chopped
2 Tbsp rice malt syrup (or honey or coconut sugar)
1 sprig fresh rosemary, picked (or ½ tsp dried)
6 fresh figs, halved
4 wholewheat tortillas (or make your own pizza bases, see note)
200 g mozzarella cheese, grated
200 g Brie cheese, thinly sliced
fresh rocket, for garnishing

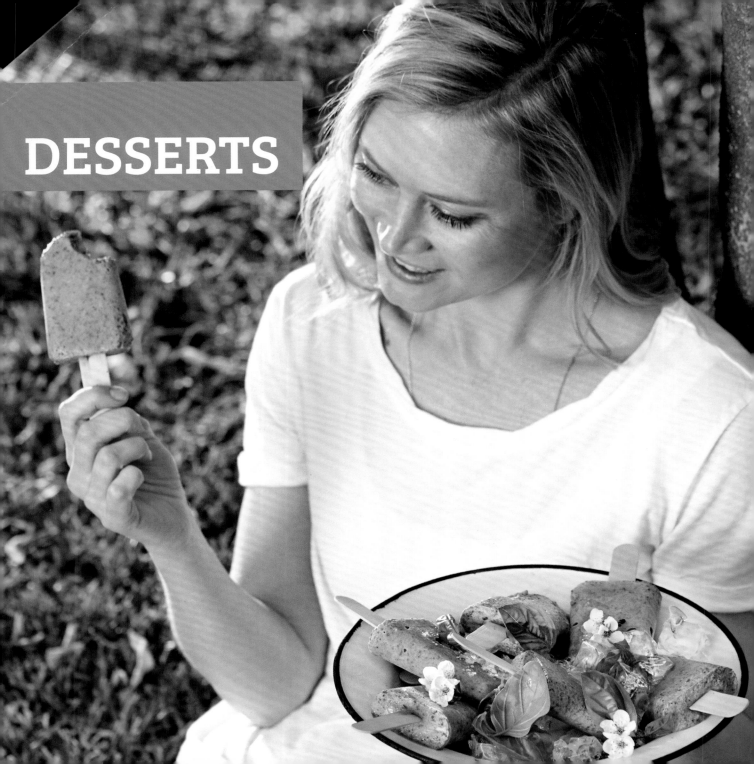

DESSERTS

These are pretty pretty, endlessly cheering and such a favourite in our house.

Makes 6-8 lollies | **Preparation time** 10 minutes | **Setting time** 3-4 hours

Basil and Raspberry
CHIA PUDDING LOLLIES

WHAT TO DO

Purée the raspberries using a stick blender, then mix all of the ingredients together, adjust for sweetness if necessary, divide between ice-lolly moulds and freeze until set.

WHAT YOU'LL NEED

1 cup fresh or frozen raspberries
(or mixed berries)
2-3 Tbsp chia seeds
1 x 400 ml can coconut milk
1 Tbsp honey (or rice malt syrup or a few
drops of stevia liquid), or more to taste
1 Tbsp chopped fresh basil (or mint)

...nd Passion Fruit CHEESECAKES

These were a unanimous favourite when we were doing the book shoot. Make them soon so that you can gobble them greedily too.

Serves 4 | **Preparation time** 10 minutes | **Setting time** at least 1 hour

WHAT YOU'LL NEED

Biscuit base

¼ cup ground almonds

¼ cup desiccated coconut

2 Tbsp butter

1 tsp ground ginger

1–2 tsp coconut sugar (or a pinch of stevia powder)

Filling

1 cup full-fat cream cheese or mascarpone, at room temperature (or 1 cup coconut cream)

1 Tbsp lemon juice

1 tsp vanilla paste

1–2 Tbsp honey (or rice malt syrup or a few drops of stevia liquid), or more to taste

¼ cup passion fruit pulp, plus extra for garnishing

½ cup puréed fresh mango

fresh baby mint leaves, for garnishing (optional)

WHAT TO DO

1. Add all of the biscuit base ingredients to a nonstick pan over medium heat. Allow the butter to melt and then continue cooking, stirring from time to time, until the almonds and coconut are golden and toasted. Remove from the heat and divide between four pretty glasses.
2. To make the filling, whisk together the cream cheese, lemon juice, vanilla and honey until light and fluffy. Add the passion fruit and mango and mix just a few times so that it is incorporated in 'swirls'. Divide between the serving glasses and refrigerate for at least 1 hour, or until serving.
3. Just before serving, add a drizzle of passion fruit pulp to each dessert and a little fresh mint if you like.

There's a version of these in a couple of my books, partly because I love the delicate prettiness of figs, and partly because when they're gently spiced and roasted, and you add a halo of sweet crumble, they are one of the most delicious things I can imagine eating.

Serves 4–6 | **Preparation time** 10 minutes | **Baking time** 10–15 minutes

MAPLE AND ROSEMARY ROASTED FIGS
with Almond Crumble

WHAT TO DO

1. Preheat the oven to 200 °C.
2. Place the figs, cut-side up and packed close together, into a shallow oven-proof dish.
3. Mix together the crumble ingredients in a food processor or by hand in a mixing bowl, then add about 1 heaped teaspoon to the top of each fig half.
4. In a small saucepan on the stovetop, heat the maple syrup, juice and rosemary until just before it simmers, then remove from the heat and allow to steep for a few minutes. Drizzle half the syrup over the figs and set aside the rest to drizzle over just before serving.
5. Roast the figs in the oven for 10–15 minutes, or until the crumble topping is golden and the figs are cooked through and just starting to caramelise.
6. Serve with a drizzle of the rosemary syrup, a dollop of mascarpone or yoghurt and a sprinkling of chopped fresh mint.

WHAT YOU'LL NEED

Figs

8 fresh figs, halved

2 Tbsp maple syrup (or honey or coconut sugar)

¼ cup clementine or orange juice

2 sprigs fresh rosemary

either mascarpone or full-fat natural yoghurt and chopped fresh mint, for serving

Almond crumble

80 g cold butter, cut into cubes

¼ cup almond flour

¼ cup rolled oats (gluten free if necessary)

¼ cup chopped pecan nuts or almonds

2 Tbsp coconut sugar

½ tsp ground cinnamon

½ tsp ground ginger

BASIL, CLEMENTINE AND LIME JELLIES
with Smashed Berries

These are really cute and quirky, and like a little party in a glass.

Serves 4 (in very small glasses) | **Preparation time** 15 minutes | **Setting time** 3 hours

WHAT YOU'LL NEED

Jellies

1 Tbsp chopped fresh basil
1 heaped tsp lime zest
¼ cup lime juice
1 heaped tsp clementine (or orange) zest
½ cup clementine (or orange) juice
¼ cup water
1–2 Tbsp honey (or rice malt syrup or 6–10 drops stevia liquid), or more to taste
2 gelatine leaves

Topping

½ cup mixed fresh or frozen berries
1 Tbsp rice malt syrup (or honey, or a few drops of stevia, to taste)
fresh baby basil leaves, for garnishing

WHAT TO DO

1. Add the basil, zests and juices, water and honey to a small saucepan over medium heat. Bring to a gentle simmer and then remove from the heat. Remove the basil leaves and set aside.

2. Meanwhile, soak the gelatine leaves in a bowl of cold water for 2–3 minutes until they have collapsed and are soft and pliable. Remove, squeeze out any excess water and add to the saucepan of fruit juices. Whisk together until the gelatine has dissolved – this should take less than a minute.

3. Divide the mixture between four small pretty serving glasses and refrigerate for at least 3 hours. These can be made a day in advance.

4. For the topping, add the berries to the same small saucepan that you used for the fruit juices, add the rice malt syrup and a dash of water and bring to a quick bubble. Remove from the heat, mash roughly with a fork and set aside in a small jar in the fridge until serving.

5. Just before serving, add a small spoonful of the smashed berries to each jelly, and a baby basil leaf or two.

Note: Add a tot or two of gin or Pimm's for a grown-up, party-ready version.

Serves 4 | **Preparation time** 10 minutes | **Setting time** 3 hours

WHAT TO DO

1. Grind the chia seeds roughly in a pestle and mortar.
2. Add the chia seeds and all of the remaining ingredients to a mixing bowl, whisk until smooth and then divide between four small serving glasses or pretty cups.
3. Leave to set in the fridge for at least 3 hours, or until serving.
4. Garnish with roasted hazelnuts and fresh raspberries.

WHAT YOU'LL NEED

1 heaped Tbsp chia seeds

1 x 400 ml can coconut milk

2 Tbsp coconut oil

2 Tbsp raw cacao powder

3 Tbsp maple syrup (or honey or rice malt syrup)

½ tsp instant espresso powder dissolved in 1 tsp warm water (optional)

½ tsp ground cinnamon (optional)

To garnish

¼ cup finely chopped roasted hazelnuts

fresh raspberries (optional)

Dreamy
DARK CHOCOLATE AND PECAN NUT ICE CREAM

This is pretty much everything you'd hope it would be. Creamy, richly dark and beautifully smooth.

Serves 8–10 | **Preparation time** 30 minutes (including cooling time) | **Freezing time** at least 3 hours

WHAT YOU'LL NEED

1 x 400 ml can coconut milk
1 x 400 ml can coconut cream
¼ cup honey (or rice malt syrup or a few drops of stevia liquid)
¼ cup coconut oil
⅓ cup raw cacao powder
1 tsp instant espresso powder (optional)
1 tsp vanilla paste or extract
2 bananas, roughly chopped
½ cup roasted pecan nuts, roughly chopped (optional)

WHAT TO DO

1. While you prepare the chocolate base, place the coconut milk and coconut cream into the freezer to chill – this will help to speed up the overall process.
2. Heat the honey, coconut oil, cacao powder and espresso powder together in a heavy-based saucepan over medium-low heat until smooth and silky. Remove from the heat and allow to cool to room temperature.
3. Blend together the cooled chocolate mixture and all of the remaining ingredients in a blender until well incorporated. Pour into a large zip-seal bag and seal, then lay the bag flat on a shallow baking tray and place in the freezer for 1 hour, or until set.
4. Remove the baking tray, break up the chocolate 'slab' inside the zip-seal bag and place the chunks into a food processor. (This extra step might seem fussy, but it will give you beautifully smooth ice cream as it breaks up all the ice crystals.) Blitz the ice-cream chunks until smooth, pour into a suitable freezerproof container or lolly moulds and return to the freezer for at least another 2 hours before serving.

Serves 6 | **Preparation time** 10 minutes | **Baking time** 10–12 minutes

WHAT TO DO

1. Preheat the oven to 180 °C. Lightly grease six ramekins.
2. Mix all of the ingredients, except the salt, together in a food processor until smooth.
3. Divide the mixture between the ramekins and then sprinkle a pinch of sea-salt flakes over the top of each pudding.
4. Place the ramekins onto a baking tray, place in the oven and bake for 10–12 minutes, or until just cooked but still a little gooey in the centre.
5. Remove from the oven and serve with double-thick cream or Dreamy Dark Chocolate and Pecan Nut Ice Cream (see page 134).

WHAT YOU'LL NEED

¼ cup honey (or coconut sugar or maple syrup or rice malt syrup)

¼ cup raw cacao powder

¼ cup coconut oil, warmed until liquid

¼ cup nut butter (I like macadamia)

1 heaped tsp clementine zest

¼ cup water

½ cup buckwheat or coconut flour

1 tsp vanilla extract

½ tsp baking powder

3 eggs, lightly beaten

1 tsp sea-salt flakes

and Lavender
TARTE TATIN

I think that tarte Tatins are utterly lovely. Here, I've adjusted the pastry so that it's gluten free, and very merrily light and flaky. It's a great go-to gluten-free flaky pastry if you are ever in need, and it works just as well to crown a chicken pie.

Serves 4–6 | **Preparation time** 25 minutes | **Baking time** 25–30 minutes

WHAT YOU'LL NEED

3 Tbsp coconut sugar, honey or rice malt syrup

75 g butter, cut into cubes

2 Tbsp water

6 pink apples, peeled, cored and quartered (enough to cover the base of the pan)

1 Tbsp lemon juice

1 tsp lavender flowers (picked from the head)

1 tsp vanilla extract

1 vanilla pod, halved lengthways

double-thick cream or mascarpone, for serving

Gluten-free flaky shortcrust pastry

¼ cup ice-cold water

100 g cold butter (or coconut oil), cut into cubes

100 g full-fat cream cheese

150 g almond flour (about 1½ cups)

25 g coconut flour (about ¼ cup)

1 Tbsp ground chia seeds (use a coffee grinder)

1 Tbsp psyllium husks

1 Tbsp coconut sugar (or a pinch of stevia powder)

1 tsp baking powder

pinch of salt

WHAT TO DO

1. Make the pastry first. Pulse all of the ingredients together in a food processor until combined, but still rough and flaky and 'marbled' with butter. Remove, bring together gently into a rough ball, wrap in clingfilm (or a large zip-seal bag) and place in the freezer for 10 minutes to chill and firm up. Remove the pastry, roll out into a rectangle, fold into thirds, wrap again and refrigerate again until just before using.

2. Preheat the oven to 180 °C.

3. While the pastry chills for the second time, place the sugar, butter and water into a heavy-based pan (preferably ovenproof) over medium-high heat. Stir two or three times and then leave until the sugar has melted.

4. Add the apples to the caramel mixture, as well as the lemon juice, lavender and vanilla extract and pod. Stir gently until the apples are well coated and arrange them so that they are lying as flat and close together as possible. Remove from the heat and set aside. Remove vanilla pod.

5. Roll out the chilled pastry until about 5 mm thick, dusting the work surface with a little extra coconut flour to prevent sticking if necessary. Cut out a circle that is just wider than the width of the pan, lay it over the apples and tuck the sides down so that everything is well covered. (If you don't have an ovenproof pan, just transfer the apple mixture to a shallow, greased ovenproof dish at this stage.) **Note:** It's easier to handle the pastry using a palette knife to slide underneath and lift it off the surface if you find that the pastry is sticking.

6. Pierce the pastry a few times to allow steam to escape during cooking. Bake for 25–30 minutes, or until the pastry is puffy and golden.

7. Leave the tart to cool to room temperature, then turn out onto a plate using a dish cloth to hold the plate over the pan while you turn it out – be very careful as the caramel can spill out and will be extremely hot. Serve with cream or mascarpone.

These need very little introduction. The combination of a syrupy spiced red wine, tender poached pears and a rich chocolate sauce is utterly wonderful.

Serves 4 | **Preparation time** 5 minutes | **Cooking time** 1 hour (mostly unattended)

CABERNET POACHED PEARS
with Espresso Ganache

WHAT TO DO

1. In a medium-sized saucepan over medium-high heat, add the wine, thyme, star anise, vanilla and honey. Bring to a simmer and reduce the heat to low-medium.
2. Add the pears to the wine syrup and leave to simmer for a further 15–20 minutes, or until cooked through and they can be easily pierced with a knife. Remove the pears and allow the sauce to reduce further until syrupy, up to 30 minutes if you have the time. Strain the syrup and return the pears to heat through.
3. Heat all the ganache ingredients together in a heavy-based saucepan over low-medium heat, whisking until it makes a silky sauce.
4. Serve the pears with a drizzle of the reduced syrup and the espresso ganache.

Note: For a speedier version, omit the ganache and serve with a dollop of full-fat natural yoghurt or mascarpone and a drizzle of maple syrup.

WHAT YOU'LL NEED

1 cup red wine
3–4 sprigs fresh thyme
2 star anise
1 tsp vanilla extract
2–3 Tbsp honey (or rice malt syrup or coconut sugar)
4 medium-sized ripe but firm pears, peeled and cored

Espresso ganache
⅓ cup raw cacao powder
⅓ cup coconut oil, warmed until liquid
⅓ cup coconut cream
1–2 Tbsp maple syrup (or honey or rice malt syrup)
1 tsp instant espresso powder
½ tsp sea-salt flakes

d Pistachio Nut
CHOCOLATE BARK

Sometimes after a meal, you just need that little something. Well, this is that. I like to store ours in a glass jar in the fridge, or add a ribbon and gift them to a friend.

Makes about 18 pieces | **Preparation time** 10 minutes | **Freezing time** 20–30 minutes

WHAT YOU'LL NEED

100 g cacao chunks, roughly chopped
1 Tbsp coconut oil
1 Tbsp honey (or rice malt syrup or a few drops of stevia liquid)
⅓ cup roasted pistachio nuts, roughly chopped
½ tsp sea-salt flakes

WHAT TO DO

1. Line a shallow baking tray with nonstick baking paper.
2. Heat the cacao, coconut oil and honey in a heavy-based saucepan over low-medium heat, whisking from time to time until the oil has melted and the mixture is silky smooth. Remove from the heat and pour the mixture onto the baking paper in a thin layer, about 5 mm thick.
3. Scatter over the pistachios and sea-salt flakes and place in the freezer for 20–30 minutes, or until set. Remove, break the bark into rough pieces and place in an airtight jar in the fridge. Lasts up to one month.

When I started living a more sugar-free lifestyle, one of the things I felt terribly sad to part with were my much-loved Salted Caramel Banoffee Pudding Pots. Here, I've managed to take out all refined sugars and make a beautiful raw caramel using dates. Be warned, dates are still very high in fructose, so this absolutely needs to be a 'sometimes' pudding rather than a regular feature at your dinner table.

Serves 4 | **Preparation time** 10 minutes |
Cooking time 5 minutes (for the biscuit base)

Raw Caramel Banoffee
PUDDING POTS

WHAT TO DO

1. Add all of the biscuit crumble ingredients to a nonstick pan over medium heat. Allow the butter to melt and then continue cooking, stirring from time to time, until the almonds, coconut and oats are golden and toasted. Remove from the heat and divide between four pretty glasses.

2. Slice the bananas and add the equivalent of half a banana to each glass.

3. Prepare the caramel by adding all of the ingredients to a blender and mixing until smooth. Add a little extra coconut cream or hot water to loosen if desired. Divide between the glasses, pouring over the bananas and biscuit crumble.

4. Spoon 1–2 Tbsp whipped cream into each glass, top with a sprinkling of roasted nuts and serve immediately.

WHAT YOU'LL NEED

Biscuit crumble
¼ cup ground almonds
¼ cup desiccated coconut
2 Tbsp rolled oats (use gluten free if necessary)
½ tsp ground cinnamon
2–3 Tbsp butter or coconut oil

Caramel
½ cup pitted dates, soaked in 1 cup hot water for about 10 minutes
¼ cup nut butter (I use macadamia or cashew)
¼ cup coconut cream (or fresh cream)
1 Tbsp maple syrup (or coconut sugar or a few drops of stevia liquid)
pinch of sea-salt flakes

To serve
2 ripe bananas
½ cup whipped cream or coconut cream (coconut cream should be whisked to loosen beforehand)
2 Tbsp roasted pistachio nuts or almonds, roughly chopped

Maple PECAN PIE

Serves 4-6 | **Preparation time** 15 minutes | **Baking time** 45 minutes

WHAT YOU'LL NEED

Pastry
100 g almond flour

50 g coconut flour

100 g cold butter or chilled coconut oil

1 egg

1 Tbsp coconut sugar

pinch of salt

Filling
½ cup pitted dates, soaked in 1 cup hot water for about 10 minutes

¼ cup nut butter (I use macadamia or cashew)

¼ cup coconut flour

¼ cup maple syrup (or rice malt syrup)

¼ cup ground almonds

1 tsp vanilla paste

1 tsp ground cinnamon

2 eggs

1 cup pecan nuts, roughly chopped

WHAT TO DO

1. Preheat the oven to 180 °C. Lightly grease a 15 cm tart tin.
2. To make the pastry, blitz the ingredients together in a food processor until the mixture forms a dough. Press into the prepared tart tin, using the back of a tablespoon to smooth out the dough if necessary. Prick the base a few times with a fork and blind bake for 15 minutes, or until lightly golden. Remove and allow to cool for about 10 minutes before adding the filling.
3. To make the filling, drain the dates (reserve the liquid), then add all of the ingredients, except the pecan nuts, to a food processor. Add 2 Tbsp date liquid and blitz for about 2 minutes until fairly smooth.
4. Add the pecans and mix gently using a spoon until all of the nuts are well coated. Pour the mixture into the slightly cooled tart shell and bake at 180 °C for 30 minutes, or until the pastry is golden and the filling is fragrant and cooked through.

While I've mixed things up a little here, with the cream filling as panna cotta-style instead of a heavier set custard, I like to think that this little pudding still has all the charm and sentimentality of our beloved South African milk tart.

Serves 4–6 | **Preparation time** 20 minutes | **Setting time** 3 hours

Milk Tart
PANNA COTTAS

WHAT TO DO

1. To make the pastry, add all of the ingredients to a nonstick pan over medium heat. Allow the butter to melt and then continue cooking, stirring from time to time, until the almonds, coconut and oats are golden and toasted. Remove from the heat and, once cooled, set aside in an airtight container until just before serving.
2. To make the filling, heat the milk in a saucepan, along with the cinnamon, vanilla, star anise and cloves, until it just starts to boil, then remove from the heat.
3. Meanwhile, soak the gelatine leaves in cold water until soft.
4. Remove the cinnamon stick, vanilla pod, star anise and cloves from the milk. Squeeze any excess water out of the soaked gelatine leaves and add them to the milk. Whisk gently until the gelatine has dissolved.
5. Pour the mixture into pretty little glasses/ramekins. Leave to set in the fridge for at least 3 hours, or cover with clingfilm and leave overnight.
6. Sprinkle each panna cotta with a little crunchy pastry topping just before serving.

Notes: Instead of using gelatine, you could use 1 Tbsp finely ground chia seeds to set the panna cottas.
For a more traditional version, as shown in the picture, add the pastry crumble to the base of your serving glasses and then pour the filling over the top before leaving to set.

WHAT YOU'LL NEED
Pastry
¼ cup ground almonds
¼ cup desiccated coconut
2 Tbsp rolled oats (use gluten free if necessary)
½ tsp ground cinnamon
2–3 Tbsp butter or coconut oil

Filling
2 x 400 ml cans coconut milk (or full-cream milk)
1 cinnamon stick (or 1 tsp ground cinnamon)
1 vanilla pod, split lengthways
2 star anise
3 cloves
3 gelatine leaves
⅓ cup honey (or rice malt syrup)
pinch of salt

This dramatic, decadent tart is one of my very favourites in this book, and it also makes a great dessert.

Serves 4–6 (Makes 1 x 20–22 cm tart) | **Preparation time** 20 minutes | **Baking time** 20 minutes | **Setting time** 2–3 hours

WHAT TO DO

1. Preheat the oven to 180 °C. Lightly grease a 20 cm loose-bottomed tart tin, or just a fluted tart dish.
2. Prepare the pastry by blitzing the ingredients together in a food processor (or mixing by hand) until it comes together in a rough ball.
3. Press the pastry into the prepared tart tin, prick a few times with a fork and bake for 15–20 minutes or until golden and cooked through. Remove and set aside to cool.
4. While the pastry bakes, prepare the other layers. For the caramel layer, soak the dates in 1 cup hot water for about 10 minutes. Drain the soaked dates, reserving ¼ cup of the liquid. Add the dates and the remaining ingredients to a food processor and blitz until smooth (add a little of the reserved liquid to loosen further if needed – it needs to be quite thick though, otherwise it won't set).
5. To make the chocolate layer, warm all of the ingredients, except the salt, together on the stovetop until the cacao powder and coconut oil have just melted and the mixture is silky smooth. Be careful not to overheat or the mixture will split. Remove and set aside to cool.
6. Add the caramel filling to the cooked tart shell and place in the freezer for about 15 minutes, or until just set.
7. Remove the tart from the freezer, pour over the chocolate filling, sprinkle over the sea-salt flakes and refrigerate for 2–3 hours until set, or until just before serving. Garnish with the pistachios and raspberries just before serving.

WHAT YOU'LL NEED

Pastry
100 g almond flour
50 g coconut flour
100 g cold butter
1 egg
1 Tbsp coconut sugar (or alternative healthy natural sweetener, to taste)
pinch of salt

Caramel layer
½ cup pitted dates
¼ cup coconut cream
¼ cup coconut oil, warmed until liquid
¼ cup nut butter (I use macadamia or cashew)
3 Tbsp maple syrup (or honey or rice malt syrup)
1 tsp vanilla extract

Salted dark chocolate layer
¼ cup raw cacao powder
¼ cup coconut oil, warmed until liquid
¼ cup coconut cream
2 Tbsp maple syrup (or honey or rice malt syrup)
½ tsp sea-salt flakes

To serve
¼ cup roughly chopped roasted pistachio nuts
1 cup fresh raspberries

ORANGE AND ROSEMARY CAKE

Serves 6–8 (Makes 1 x 20 cm cake) | **Preparation time** 10 minutes | **Baking time** 35–40 minutes

WHAT YOU'LL NEED

1 cup almond flour
½ cup coconut or spelt flour
1 tsp bicarbonate of soda
125 g unsalted butter (or coconut oil), at room temperature
2 heaped tsp orange zest
1 tsp dried rosemary
½ cup coconut sugar (or honey or rice malt syrup)
3 eggs, lightly beaten
½ cup natural yoghurt or buttermilk

Orange and rosemary syrup

2 tsp orange zest
⅓ cup orange juice
1–2 Tbsp fresh lemon or lime juice (or more to taste)
2–3 Tbsp honey (or coconut sugar or stevia, to taste)
1 sprig fresh rosemary (or 1 tsp dried), plus extra for decorating
lavender flowers, for decorating (optional)

WHAT TO DO

1. Preheat the oven to 170 °C. Lightly grease and line a loaf tin or 20 x 20 cm baking tray and dust lightly with flour to make absolutely sure the cake won't stick.
2. Mix together the flours and bicarbonate of soda for the cake batter with a whisk until well mixed, then add the remaining cake ingredients and whisk again until smooth.
3. Pour the batter into the prepared tin and bake for 35–40 minutes, or until golden and a skewer inserted into the centre comes out clean. Remove from the oven, prick holes in the top and allow to cool for a few minutes while you make the syrup.
4. To make the syrup, simmer all the ingredients, except the extra rosemary and lavender flowers, in a small saucepan for 3–5 minutes, then remove the sprig of rosemary if using. Allow to cool slightly then pour over the now partially cooled cake. Decorate with a little fresh rosemary and fresh lavender flowers, if available.

Note: This also makes a delicious sponge pudding, baked whole or in small ramekins (reduce baking time with ramekins to about 20 minutes).

CARROT CAKE

WHAT TO DO

1. Preheat the oven to 180 °C. Grease and line a 22 cm round spring-form cake tin.
2. Soak the dates in hot water for about 10 minutes, then drain.
3. For speediest results, use a food processor: grate the carrots, apple and ginger. Then change to the chopping adapter and add the remaining ingredients. Blitz for 2–3 minutes until the ingredients are well combined. If the mixture seems too dry, add about ¼ cup warm water.
4. Pour the batter into the cake tin and bake for 25–30 minutes or until a skewer inserted into the centre comes out clean.
5. Make the icing by mixing all the ingredients, except the nuts, together until smooth.
6. Ice the cake and garnish with roasted pecan nuts.

Note: For a dairy-free version, replace the natural yoghurt in the cake with coconut milk, and replace the cream cheese in the frosting with coconut cream.
Omit the icing and serve as slices spread with nut butter.

WHAT YOU'LL NEED

10 pitted dates
300 g carrots, peeled and grated (about 2 cups)
1 apple, grated
1 thumb-sized piece fresh ginger, grated
    (or 1 tsp ground ginger)
3 eggs
¼ cup coconut oil, warmed until liquid
¼ cup maple syrup or coconut blossom sugar
¼ cup natural yoghurt
2 Tbsp psyllium husks (to bind)
½ cup pecan or any nuts, roughly chopped
1 cup coconut flour
1 cup buckwheat flour
1 tsp bicarbonate of soda
1 tsp baking powder
1 tsp ground cinnamon
1 tsp ground ginger
1 tsp vanilla extract
pinch of salt
juice and zest of 1 orange (optional)

Maple cream cheese icing (optional)
250 g cream cheese, at room temperature
2–3 Tbsp maple syrup
1 tsp vanilla paste
1 tsp orange zest (optional)
chopped, roasted pecans, for garnishing

THE ULTIMATE CHOCOLATE CAKE
with Coffee Ganache

Serves 6 (Makes 1 x 22 cm cake) | **Preparation time** 10 minutes | **Baking time** 30–40 minutes

WHAT YOU'LL NEED

¼ cup coconut sugar (or maple syrup or rice malt syrup)

¼ cup raw cacao powder

¼ cup coconut oil, warmed until liquid

¼ cup nut butter (I like macadamia)

1 tsp vanilla paste

1 tsp instant espresso powder

1 cup just-boiled water

½ cup coconut flour (or buckwheat flour)

½ cup almond flour

1 tsp baking powder

pinch of salt

3 eggs, lightly beaten

raspberries and/or roasted nuts of your choice, for decorating

Coffee ganache

⅓ cup raw cacao powder

½ cup coconut oil, warmed until liquid

½ cup coconut cream

2 Tbsp maple syrup (or rice malt syrup)

½ tsp instant espresso powder, dissolved in 1 tsp hot water (optional)

pinch of sea-salt flakes

2–3 Tbsp peanut butter or nut butter (optional)

WHAT TO DO

1. Preheat the oven to 170 °C and lightly grease a 22 cm round cake tin.
2. Mix together all of the cake ingredients, except the eggs. When you have a smooth batter, add the eggs and mix again until combined.
3. Pour the batter into the cake tin and bake for 30–40 minutes, or until the cake is just cooked through and a skewer inserted into its centre comes out clean.
4. To make the ganache, mix all the ingredients until smooth, altering the quantities to suit your preferred consistency.
5. Once the cake has cooled completely, pour over the ganache and decorate with fresh raspberries and/or roughly chopped roasted nuts, and serve as soon as possible.

Oats are inherently gluten free, but are sometimes processed in factories that contain traces of gluten from other products, so if you are highly gluten intolerant then I suggest you purchase specifically gluten-free oats from your nearest health shop.

Makes about 24 | **Preparation time** 15 minutes | **Baking time** at least 3 hours, plus drying overnight (mostly unattended)

RUSKS

WHAT TO DO

1. Preheat the oven to 160 °C. Lightly grease and line a large, deep baking tray, roughly 22 cm x 30 cm.
2. Place the flours, oats, coconut, psyllium husks, bicarbonate of soda and baking power in a large mixing bowl and whisk together until well combined. Add the remaining ingredients and mix again – I find it's best to mix by hand, or use a stand mixer with a dough hook attachment. If you find that the mixture is too dry to mix, add a little more milk or lukewarm water.
3. Transfer the mixture to the baking tray, patting it down gently to level it off slightly and neaten it. Bake for 45–50 minutes, or until golden.
4. Remove the baking tray from the oven and allow to cool to room temperature before cutting into rusks (roughly 2.5 cm x 5 cm). Place the rusks onto a cooling rack set in the oven over a large baking tray (so that they dry evenly). Turn the temperature down to 100 °C and bake for another 2–3 hours, or until the rusks are golden and fairly crunchy. Switch the oven off and leave the rusks to dry out completely, at least 5 hours, or preferably overnight – this gives the crunchiest end result, very important!

Note: Instead of the nuts and seeds, add 2 cups Everything Granola (see page 32).

WHAT YOU'LL NEED

½ cup almond flour
1 cup coconut flour
1 cup rolled oats
½ cup desiccated coconut (or digestive bran)
3 Tbsp psyllium husks
½ Tbsp bicarbonate of soda
½ Tbsp baking powder
½ cup roughly chopped pecan nuts or almonds
½ cup dried cranberries
½ cup sunflower seeds
½ cup pumpkin seeds
¼ cup linseeds
1 tsp ground cinnamon
1 tsp ground ginger
1 tsp ground allspice
½ cup coconut sugar (or rice malt syrup)
2 eggs, lightly beaten
1 cup buttermilk or coconut milk (or ¾ cup full-fat natural yoghurt mixed with ¼ cup milk)
½ cup melted coconut oil or melted butter
1 cup water
1 tsp salt
1 tsp vanilla extract

and Cranberry
GRANOLA BARS

This is adapted from a brilliant health food blog that my mum and I follow, called 'Clean Eats'. There is quite a long list of ingredients, but the recipe can easily be doubled and the extra granola bars frozen until needed.

Makes about 20 | **Preparation time** 10 minutes |
Baking time 30–40 minutes

WHAT YOU'LL NEED
1 Tbsp chia seeds
½ cup dried cranberries (preferably without added sugar)
¼ cup coconut oil, warmed until liquid
¼ cup preferred nut butter or peanut butter
½ cup coconut sugar (or honey or rice malt syrup)
1 tsp vanilla extract
2 tsp ground cinnamon
1 tsp ground ginger
½ tsp ground allspice
1 cup buckwheat flour
½ cup oats (certified gluten free if necessary)
½ cup almond flour
¼ cup coconut flour
¼ cup mixed seeds

WHAT TO DO

1. Preheat the oven to 180 °C. Grease and line a 20 cm x 20 cm shallow baking tray.
2. Grind the chia seeds in a coffee grinder or pestle and mortar and soak in 3 Tbsp water until it forms a thick, sticky paste (this will bind the granola bars together and add extra nutrients and fibre). Set aside.
3. Soak the cranberries in a little hot water for a few minutes and then drain and set aside.
4. Place the remaining ingredients in a food processor and pulse until combined. Add the chia seed paste and cranberries, and about ¼ cup water to help bring the mixture together, and mix again until everything is well incorporated.
5. Press the mixture into the baking tray, smooth out with the back of a tablespoon and bake for 30–40 minutes, or until golden and fragrant. Remove, allow to cool for a few minutes, cut into squares and then transfer to a cooling rack. Once cool, store in an airtight container for up to two weeks. Extras can be frozen for up to two months.

DRINKS

Spiced HOT CHOCOLATE

Serves 2 | **Preparation time** 10 minutes

WHAT TO DO

Bring the milk to a simmer in a saucepan, then add all the remaining ingredients, whisk well and reduce the heat to low. Leave to simmer for 5 minutes, then strain, divide between two small mugs or glasses and serve immediately.

WHAT YOU'LL NEED

400 ml full-cream milk (or alternative)

2 Tbsp raw cacao powder

2 tsp maple syrup (or honey)

2–3 cardamom pods, bruised

1 cinnamon stick

1 star anise

1 vanilla pod, split lengthways

pinch of salt

Frosted CHAI LATTÉ

Serves 2 | **Preparation time** 10 minutes

WHAT TO DO

Bring the milk to a simmer in a saucepan, add all the remaining ingredients, except the ice, whisk well and reduce the heat to low. Leave to simmer for 5 minutes, then strain and allow to cool. Blend in a high-powered blender with 1 cup ice cubes for a frosted version, or allow to cool completely and serve over lots of ice.

Note: This is also delicious served warm on a chilly night.

WHAT YOU'LL NEED

400 ml full-cream milk (or almond milk)

2 tsp maple syrup (or honey)

1 cinnamon stick (or ½ tsp ground cinnamon)

½ tsp ground ginger

½ tsp ground allspice

1 vanilla pod, split lengthways

pinch of salt

1 cup ice cubes

Golden
TURMERIC MILK

Warming, soothing and as pretty as liquid sunshine.

Serves 2 | **Preparation time** 5–10 minutes

WHAT YOU'LL NEED

1½ cups full-cream milk (or alternative)

1 tsp turmeric

1 tsp ground cinnamon

½ tsp ground ginger

1 tsp maple syrup (or honey) (optional)

WHAT TO DO

Heat all of the ingredients together in a small saucepan over medium heat. Whisk well, taste and adjust for sweetness if necessary. Serve immediately in pretty mugs.

Pomegranate, Rosewater and Raspberry
COOLERS

Serves 4 | **Preparation time** 5–10 minutes

WHAT YOU'LL NEED

1 cup water

1 cup pomegranate juice

¼ cup pomegranate rubies, if available

1 cup raspberries (fresh or frozen), blended until smooth

2 Tbsp honey, dissolved in 2 Tbsp hot water

1–2 tsp rosewater

handful fresh mint, for serving

1–2 cups ice

WHAT TO DO

Mix the water, pomegranate juice and rubies, raspberries, honey and rosewater together. Adjust sweetness to taste. Serve in pretty glasses with mint and ice.

Rooibos, Straw... and Ginger ICED TEA

Serves 4 | **Preparation time** 15 minutes

WHAT TO DO

1. Place the tea bags, honey, juices, ginger and mint in a jug and pour over the boiling water. Let the tea brew for about 5 minutes before removing the tea bags and the mint.
2. Leave to cool, adjust to taste by adding extra sweetener or lemon or lime juice, and serve with ice, mint leaves, cucumber and fresh strawberries.

Note: Make pretty ice blocks by freezing extra strawberries and mint leaves in individual ice blocks the night before.

WHAT YOU'LL NEED

4 rooibos tea bags
¼ cup honey (or rice malt syrup)
¼ cup apple juice (or any fruit juice of your choice)
2–3 Tbsp lemon or lime juice
1 thumb-sized piece fresh ginger, peeled and thinly sliced
small handful fresh mint leaves
1.5 litres boiling water

To serve
lots of ice
extra fresh mint leaves
thinly sliced cucumber
fresh strawberries, halved and with stalks intact (or stone fruit slices)

BITS AND BOBS AND FERMENTING

Homemade KETCHUP

Makes 2 cups | Preparation time 10 minutes | Cooking time 45 minutes

WHAT TO DO

1. Heat the olive oil in a medium-sized saucepan over medium heat and add all the remaining ingredients. Stir well.
2. Simmer gently with the lid off for 45 minutes, or until the mixture has thickened and reduced by at least half. Remove from the heat, allow to cool and then blend until smooth. Season to taste and then transfer half to a sterilised glass jar to store in the fridge – use within two weeks. The other half can be stored in the freezer until needed.

WHAT YOU'LL NEED

1 Tbsp olive oil

1 kg ripe tomatoes, roughly chopped

¼ cup tomato paste

1 Tbsp red wine vinegar or lemon juice

1 Tbsp soy sauce or tamari

8–10 drops stevia liquid (or 2 Tbsp rice malt syrup), or more to taste

pinch of salt, or more to taste

Easy Avocado MAYONNAISE

Makes 1 cup | Preparation time 5 minutes

WHAT TO DO

Add all the ingredients, except the oil, to a jug blender, turn on and then slowly drizzle in the oil. It should emulsify and thicken to the usual consistency of mayonnaise within 1 minute.

WHAT YOU'LL NEED

1 egg

½ clove garlic (optional)

½ avocado, chopped

juice of 1 lemon or lime

small handful fresh basil leaves (optional)

salt and freshly ground black pepper, to taste

¾ cup avocado oil (or half avocado oil and half good-quality olive oil)

Homemade
NUT MILK

If you're dairy intolerant, nut milks are a great alternative. They're deliciously creamy and actually really easy to make at home. Try this in Spiced Hot Chocolate (see page 161). If you use cashews, soaking time only needs to be about 2 hours.

Makes 2 cups | **Preparation time** 15 minutes | **Soaking time** up to 8 hours

WHAT YOU'LL NEED

1 cup raw almonds (or cashews)

2 cups filtered water

½ tsp vanilla paste (optional)

You will also need a muslin cloth and a sieve, for straining the milk

WHAT TO DO

1. Soak the nuts in filtered water overnight, or for at least 8 hours.
2. Drain, rinse thoroughly and add to a high-powered blender. Add the 2 cups filtered water and the vanilla if using, and blend for 2–3 minutes until smooth.
3. Pour the milk through a muslin-lined sieve that is resting over a bowl or large glass jug.
4. Gather the corners of the muslin and squeeze out any excess liquid, then pour the newly made almond milk into a sterilised glass jar with a lid and store in the fridge for up to four days.

Note: Reserve the nut 'pulp' – this can be kept in the freezer for up to two months. Use as a coarse almond flour in baking.

Homemade
NUT BUTTER

You need a fairly powerful food processor to make this with the least amount of fuss. But the end result is luxuriously creamy roasted nut butter with a hint of vanilla. I love to spread a dollop on a slice of my Beautiful Banana Bread (see page 45) for a mid-afternoon snack.

Makes about 1 cup | **Preparation time** 20 minutes

WHAT YOU'LL NEED

2 cups whole almonds or cashews

¼ cup coconut oil, at room temperature

2 tsp honey (helps to emulsify the nut butter)

½ tsp vanilla paste or extract

pinch of salt

WHAT TO DO

Roast the nuts lightly in a dry pan until just golden and fragrant, and then blend in your food processor with the remaining ingredients for up to 15 minutes or until the nuts start to release their natural oils and you have a smooth, creamy mixture.

EASY HERB LABNEH *(Cream Cheese)*

Makes 1 cup | Make 2 days ahead

WHAT TO DO

1. Line a sieve with a large piece of muslin. Pour in the yoghurt. Tie the muslin into a 'parcel' so that the yoghurt is contained. Squeeze out excess moisture. Place the sieve over a bowl and drain in the fridge for up to two days.
2. You will be left with a soft cheese. Mix through the zest and herbs. Roll into thumb-sized balls. Store in a glass jar in the fridge with the garlic, and cover with olive oil. It will keep for 7–10 days.

WHAT YOU'LL NEED

2 cups Greek yoghurt

zest of ½ lemon

1 Tbsp chopped fresh mixed herbs, such as mint and coriander

2 cloves garlic

olive oil, to cover

Homemade RICOTTA

Mix through lemon zest and/or chopped herbs of your choice for delicious herbed ricotta that you can spread on toasted ciabatta or rye bread, or serve over pasta.

Makes 1½–2 cups | **Preparation time** 30 minutes

WHAT TO DO

1. Place the milk and salt in a saucepan over medium-high heat until the mixture reaches a consistent simmer (but not boiling). Remove from the heat and stir through the lemon juice. Gently stir three or four times and then return to a low heat for another 1 minute before removing again. The mixture will immediately start to separate into curds (the ricotta) and whey, and will continue to do so over a period of about 15 minutes.
2. After 15 minutes, pour the mixture into a sieve lined with cheesecloth and place it over a bowl to drain. Pull the corners of the cloth together, squeeze out excess whey, add any optional ingredients you prefer, and then either use the ricotta immediately or spoon into an airtight container and refrigerate for up to four days.

WHAT YOU'LL NEED

2 litres full-cream milk

1 tsp salt

5 Tbsp lemon juice

Optional extras

1 tsp lemon zest

1–2 Tbsp chopped fresh mint and/or basil or parsley, to mix through the ricotta before chilling

Red Cabbage and Caraway
SAUERKRAUT

Makes about 2 cups | **Preparation time** 20 minutes

WHAT YOU'LL NEED

2 small red cabbages, thinly shredded
(discard outer layer of leaves)
1 heaped Tbsp sea salt
1 Tbsp caraway or fennel seeds

WHAT TO DO

1. Sterilise a large glass jar with a screw-top metal lid (either by submerging in just-boiled water or placing in a 200 °C oven for 10 minutes), and wash your hands well.

2. Add the cabbage, salt and spice to a mixing bowl, mix well and 'massage' with your hands or using a pestle for up to 10 minutes, or until the cabbage is quite limp and watery.

3. Transfer the wilted cabbage and any juices to the jar, packing it in tightly. A good idea is to place one of the outer leaves of the cabbage over the top to help keep the shredded cabbage submerged in the pickling juices. It's important that the cabbage stays submerged as any contact with air can ruin the fermentation process. To aid this, I suggest using a jam jar or a small zip-seal bag filled with small stones to weigh it down.

4. Place the jar on a shelf in the pantry or in a dark cupboard with the lid ajar so that the mixture can 'breathe', and press down on the weight every day or so to help the cabbage release more pickling liquid. If, after a day or so, you find that there is not enough liquid available to cover the cabbage, dissolve 1 tsp salt in 1 cup lukewarm water and add that to the jar.

5. After three to eight days, or when it tastes delicious and 'pickled', the sauerkraut should be ready to store in the fridge, where it will last for up to two months.

Refer to page 14 for more info on this wonderful probiotic.

Makes about 1 cup | **Preparation time** 10 minutes | **Fermenting time** 2 days

KEFIR

WHAT TO DO

1. Add the kefir grains to a large, sterilised glass jar. Add the milk.
2. Cover with a breathable lid such as a muslin cloth, secured in place with a ribbon or elastic band, and place in a dark cupboard for 24–48 hours (the longer you leave it the stronger it is, and for obvious reasons it takes longer to ferment in winter than in summer).
3. When you see the grains have 'separated' and there is a watery liquid at the bottom of the jar, you know fermentation has taken place and the kefir is ready.
4. Strain the kefir through a sieve over a clean glass bowl or large glass measuring jug. Stir it gently to make sure all the 'yoghurt' passes through.
5. Wash and dry the glass jar, add the kefir grains back, top up with fresh milk and start the cycle again.
6. Keep the 'harvested' kefir in a clean glass jar in the fridge for up to five days.

Note: Preferably use plastic utensils (sieves, spoons, etc.) as this is less damaging to the kefir grains.

Kefir Breakfast Shots: Great to drink first thing in the morning. To 100–150 ml kefir, add ½ tsp turmeric and ½ tsp ground cinnamon for added flavour, as well as a small drizzle of vanilla extract and maple syrup. On days when I'm feeling really brave, I'll mix in 1 tsp moringa powder (it has quite a bitter taste, but amazing health benefits).

WHAT YOU'LL NEED
3 Tbsp kefir grains
about 1 cup full-cream milk (preferably organic; you can use cow's, sheep's or goat's milk)

KIDDIE-FRIENDLY GUIDE

Here are some of the recipes that get the biggest thumbs up from Sophie and Isla.

Rise and Shine

- Chocolate Smoothie Bowls (page 18)
- Beautiful Quinoa and Coconut Breakfast Puddings (page 21)
- Overnight Rooibos Buckwheat Bircher Muesli (Isla's favourite!) (page 22)
- Quick Chia Berry Jam (page 23)
- Chocolate Buckwheat Crêpes with Cappuccino Ganache (page 24)
- Millet Porridge with Lavender and Maple Syrup (page 27)
- Sophie and Isla's Prettiest Pink Chia Pudding Pots with Basil and Berries (page 31)
- Everything Granola aka Chocolate Cinnamon Buckwheat Granola (page 32)
- Nectarine and Blueberry Breakfast Crumble (page 35)
- Power Bars (page 37)
- Lovely Lemony Spelt and Granola Breakfast Muffins (page 43)
- Speedy Spelt Soda Bread (page 44)
- Beautiful Banana Bread (page 45)
- Wholewheat-Rye Bread (with ricotta and chia jam) (page 47)

Bounty Bowls

- Gem Squash and Barley Risotto (page 49)
- Roast Chicken, Mushroom and Truffle Oil Linguini (page 56)
- Aubergine Stacks with Speedy Salsa Verde (Sophie loves this, preferably with lots of feta sprinkles) (page 63)
- Barley, Lentil and Brown Rice Harvest Bowls (page 71)
- Smoky Lentil and Bean Chilli (I go low on the chilli for the girls) (page 73)
- Asparagus, Broccoli and Kale Soup with Mixed Seed Croutons (page 77)
- Roasted Tomato and Red Onion Soup with Oregano Oil (page 78)
- Spicy Carrot, Ginger and Lentil Soup with Coconut Milk (page 79)
- Luisa's Lamb and Barley Bowls (page 80)

Feast

- Lemony, Herby Chicken Burgers with Bacon and Avocado, and Pink Pickle (page 85)
- Chicken, Butternut and Feta Crumble (page 89)
- Fish Frikkadels with Pineapple Salsa (page 93)
- Baked Fish with Basil and Blistered Tomatoes (page 94)
- Eastern Aubergines (page 104)
- Aubergine Parmigiana (page 119)
- Very Cheesy, Very Easy Fig Jam, Rosemary and Brie Pizzas (page 123)

Desserts

- Basil and Raspberry Chia Pudding Lollies (page 125)
- Mango and Passion Fruit Cheesecakes (page 126)
- Basil, Clementine and Lime Jellies with Smashed Berries (page 130)
- Dreamy Dark Chocolate and Pecan Nut Ice Cream (page 134)
- Gooey Baked Clementine Chocolate Pots (page 137)
- Maple Pecan Pie (page 144)
- Milk Tart Panna Cottas (page 147)

Tea Time Treats

- Gluten-free Orange and Rosemary Cake (page 150)
- Carrot Cake (page 153)
- Our Ultimate Chocolate Cake with Coffee Ganache (page 154)
- Rusks (page 157)

Drinks

- Spiced Hot Chocolate (page 161)
- Frosted Chai Latté (page 161)
- Rooibos, Strawberry and Ginger Iced Tea (page 165)

Bits and bobs

- Homemade Ketchup (page 167)
- Homemade Nut Butter (page 168)

INDEX

CONVERSION TABLE

Metric	US cups	Imperial
5 ml	1 tsp	1 tsp
15 ml	1 Tbsp	1 Tbsp
60 ml	4 Tbsp (¼ cup)	2 fl oz
80 ml	⅓ cup	2¾ fl oz
125 ml	½ cup	4½ fl oz
160 ml	⅔ cup	5½ fl oz
200 ml	¾ cup	7 fl oz
250 ml	1 cup	9 fl oz